With love from
Paul & Margaret.
(sorry we were late for your
birthday!)

JONATHAN CAPE
PAPERBACK
JCP 10

THE MEN WHO RULED INDIA
THE GUARDIANS

Michael Marple
2004

by the same author

PHILIP WOODRUFF

The Men Who Ruled India
* *
# THE GUARDIANS

JONATHAN CAPE
THIRTY BEDFORD SQUARE LONDON

VOL. II   THE GUARDIANS: FIRST PUBLISHED 1954
THIS PAPERBACK EDITION FIRST PUBLISHED 1963
REPRINTED 1965, 1971

Jonathan Cape Ltd, 30 Bedford Square
London WC1

ISBN 0 224 60575 5

Condition of Sale

*Reprinted by lithography in Great Britain
by Jarrold & Sons Ltd, Norwich*

CONTENTS

CONTENTS

PART II

The Demission of Power

CONTENTS

MAPS

To the Peoples of India and Pakistan
whose tranquillity was our care
whose division is our failure
and whose continuance
in the family of nations to which we belong
is our Memorial

INTRODUCTION

THE three hundred and fifty years the English spent in India make one story, but a story which unfolds itself like a stage play in a series of acts. The curtain falls for the interval after the third act; the fourth and fifth remain to be played. The third act has shown the hero — who is not one man but a thousand — at the height of his glory, but the contradiction in his own character and the conflict in the whole situation are already apparent; he has triumphed for the moment but the conflict is unresolved. The fourth act will show a hardening of the elements of strife, both in the general situation and in the hero's character. And the last act shows the result, which has in it triumph as well as tragedy.

The hero is a thousand men, not a service nor a system, but a thousand individuals, each different from the next. Go to stay a night with a certain kind of English family and a portrait or a book will come out from the lumber-room, a sword or a writing-desk or a bundle of letters; he served in India, they will tell you, and gazing at the fading sepia of the photograph or the long sloping characters of his hand, you try to picture the man and what he did, what he felt about his part in life and his fantastic exile in an empire seven thousand miles across the sea. It is easy to simplify, to pick out one quality or another in these men, and ascribe it to them all. But no one acts always in character; even one man feels differently at different times and how much more a thousand!

In the long crowded period from the Mutiny to the end of the century it would be wrong then to suppose that one tendency or another reveals the essence of what is happening or of what these men were like. To understand the truth you must pick out strands of interwoven thought, feeling, and action, which are like the scores for the different instruments in a piece of music. It is easy to stress one and forget the others, but to hear the music as a whole you must dwell on each in turn without forgetting the others and so hear them all distinctly yet at the same time.

There is the will of England, political control from Westminster and Whitehall, alternating in the fourth act between the kind of views represented by Gladstone and Morley and those of Disraeli and Joseph Chamberlain. Liberals and Conservatives had much in common, but the emphasis was different and one party had more faith than the other in the ability of Indians to govern themselves eventually. Both believed that the English were trustees, but in a different sense. To one it seemed inevitable that the wards should come of age and right that the trustee should train them for responsibility by giving it them in small but increasing doses; the other was less sure that for a long time to come there would be much lightening of the White Man's Burden, which was, all the same, believed to be:

> To seek another's profit
> And work another's gain.

This party conflict in England was the sign of an inner conflict between profound but simple ideas. A man who believes in individual liberty for himself can deny it consciously and explicitly to other people only if he can persuade himself that the other people are really quite different, another order of being altogether. The English did believe in personal liberty for themselves, and in their own country were steadily moving in the direction of a wider distribution of political power. But there was real confusion about other people; to a nation who wished to be Christian it seemed sometimes that the people of their Empire were their brothers, while in another and more frequent mood they were not of the same clay. In this prevailing mood they would bring care, protection, guidance, but not yet liberty.

English ideas then were at root confused, but there was no doubt that those which prevailed for the moment were asserted on behalf of Parliament with less and less attention to views which came from India. This of course was bound to happen; steam, the electric telegraph, the canal, brought England nearer; the Press and the vote spread interest in India and brought responsibility home to Parliament. As London tried to tighten control on India, so Simla tried to tighten on the provinces and the provinces on the district officer. And at the same time, individual officers were far more certain of England's imperial destiny, far more conscious of the lead given her by industry and sea power, conscious too of a moral rectitude that no one else seemed to possess in quite the same degree as themselves. One might expect to find, then, right through the system, a growing rigidity, a hardening of the arteries, an increasing uniformity, a sense of superiority and a lack of human sympathy, more red tape, more office work, less of the old direct human rule of one man which India had always understood.

And of course this was one strain in the music. But it must be heard against another and contradictory strain, something proceeding from English character and from the understanding between individual Englishmen and individual Indians that was always there. The men of the service were chosen and trained on Plato's principles as Guardians who would rule in the light of their own vision of the Good and the Beautiful — or, at least, on an English compromise with Plato. Such a system aims at producing confidence and certainty, virtues in a ruler which may degenerate into arrogance towards the ruled. But among the English in India this confidence turned at least as often to an easy and humorous defiance of authority. As the system grew stiffer, character became more and more what saved it, the character of individual district officers, choleric, eccentric, warm-hearted men, who did not always pay attention to Government orders.

James Bryce in 1888 wrote to his mother that he was disappointed in the Indian Civil Service. 'There is a high average of ability among the service men in the upper posts — 'tis these chiefly I have seen — but a good deal of uniformity and a want of striking, even marked, individualities. They are intelligent, very hard-working, with apparently a high sense of public duty and a desire to promote the welfare of the people of India. But they seem rather wanting in imagination and sympathy, less inspired by the extraordinary and unprecedented phenomena of the country than might have been expected . . . too conventionally English . . .' It was not really surprising that that judgment should have been passed and no doubt it was true at the time and of the men 'in the upper posts'. The man Bryce dined with had, perhaps, been chosen for an Under Secretary's post in Simla fifteen years before, mainly on his examination record, which might mean no more than that he was precocious and hard-working. A good Under Secretary is patient and industrious; he makes suggestions but is submissive if they are treated with scorn; fire and imagination, burning zeal, anything at all un-English, are qualities that it may well be politic to suppress if the Under Secretary is to have a career. And by the time he is a Member of Council, the fires may have been banked down for ever.

But it is not so in a district. The young District Magistrate in a lonely district is monarch of all he surveys and can be as un-English as he likes, provided he has sense enough to keep most of his ebullience out of his fortnightly reports. And in fact the system did produce plenty of men whose fads provided just that warmth the centre lacked, men with hobbies they enjoyed which happened very often also to be something the district needed.

There are contradictory elements in England, then, at least two main alternating strains, and it is the same in the system; the man on the spot is never so stiff-necked and so wooden-hearted as the centre would have him be. The men themselves are always at odds with the system. Nor is there any single phrase that will convey the relations between this curiously English caste of Guardians and their wards. The only generalization that can be ventured is that on the whole the nearer men were to each other, English or Indian, the kindlier — as a rule — they felt. It was in Calcutta or Simla, or in the long vacuum of the Northern hot weather, that thoughts turned sour and stale and men spoke of 'the natives' with dislike, contempt, or even a touch of unconscious fear. Impossible, once the smell of canvas and smoky fires was in your nostrils, a horse between your knees on a dewy morning, or walking home in the darkness through the wafts of rich scent that eddy slowly round the village — impossible then to think of Sohan Singh or Mohammad Khan in such terms as that! No, he was a man — a man to be circumvented in some nefarious plot, to be encouraged by promotion or reward, or simply helped because you liked him — but in every case much more real than that shadowy and usually hostile abstraction the Government.

But so far as there was a general attitude, it was changing all through the century. To Thomason in the 'thirties and 'forties, as to Elphinstone in the 'twenties, education had seemed the answer to India's social problems; as more and more Indians came to look with rational inquiring eyes at the rigid crust that had come to overlay their own society, more and more — so Thomason believed — would be ready to abjure their own institutions and their religion and accept everything the English brought. There seemed no doubt at all that once men had seen what for him was so blinding a light, they could not turn back to darkness. To him, it seemed that the few Indians who had crossed the sea and come to look at the world with a wider knowledge were pioneers, wholly to be praised. But by the 'eighties it was much more difficult to feel like that; a generous few, Hume, Wedderburn, Cotton, Beveridge and others, could still welcome with outstretched hand the ward who seemed about to come of age, but many more were irritated by the airs of adult independence he already gave himself.

And far from coming to accept all that Macaulay and Thomason had believed, Hinduism had turned back to its own traditions and for a time was inclined to hang out its banners even over positions quite untenable, even over institutions such as child marriage and caste, just because the attack on them came from the West. Instead of turning Christian or utilitarian, nationalism turned defiantly Hindu. And more and more educated Indians were in varying degrees nationalist at heart. They were rivals for power and knowledge, sharp critics too of all that Western world in which they claimed a share, and it was easy to be jealous and resentful of them, to fall into the habit of glorifying instead the villager, the soldier, the servant, all who had not yet been 'spoilt by education', who were still ready to use the old obsequious expressions of respect.

It would be wrong to suggest that there was anything insincere about those old terms of respect and all that went with them, the tolerant and bantering but none the less real affection of master or officer on one side, the soldier's or villager's trust, the confidence he mingled with a shrewd perception of character like that with which small boys nickname a schoolmaster. Those feelings were real; servant and master, officer and soldier, risked and sometimes laid down their lives for each other. The bitterness of 1857 was for a time tucked firmly away among memories that no one looked at very often. But until the last few years the relationship was not one of equality; there could be no familiarity and no unguarded speech.

By the end of the century, contrast was at its clearest between on the one hand the ideal of a liberal empire, an India held in trust, and on the other the reality of despotic power wielded by Platonic Guardians in the interest of order and tranquillity. It was an odd kind of despotism, for which there is no parallel anywhere else, because its distinguishing principle was the delegation of power. Almost from the day he arrived in India, a member of the Guardian caste was given authority which anywhere else he could hardly have attained with less than twenty years' experience; he felt confident that he would be supported and that what he did would be understood. And he too must learn to delegate if he was to get through the day's work. The result was a great economy in the number of despots needed and, on the whole, much less rigidity than might have been expected. It was a despotism tempered by the despot's liberal upbringing and by the knowledge of Parliament's usually liberal attitude. But despotism it was all the same, as any system must be in which people are given what is good for them instead of what they want.

This is a book about men, not about systems or philosophies. As in the first volume, I have tried as far as possible to illustrate a point by displaying a human being. No generalization is true about all these men. And yet one is bound to notice in most of them a change, as the centuries progress, of profound importance, a change which can only be touched on here and yet of which a whole book might be made. Hawkins and the Elizabethans believed that the hand of God was active about them in all they did; they made no more question of His lively presence in the world than did the Muslims or Hindus around them. The Victorians of the fourth act in this long play lived in a world of doubt; it was the age of Darwin, Tennyson and Matthew Arnold. An assertive note creeps into the voice with which most men speak of the Almighty. They protest perhaps rather loudly that they are doing the Lord's work. And they are inclined, on the conscious level, to stress that masculine austerity in the God of the Old Testament that seemed to them to distinguish Him most sharply from the many-armed divinities of the Hindu.

In the fifth act, the period of reform, this tendency changes and merges into something about which it would be rash indeed to speak with certainty. Religion in this period is seldom mentioned. But the moral framework within which each man proceeds is distinctively Christian; it insists on the value of the individual. As to dogma, this is not a word that has a pleasing ring to men who have spent their lives trying to prevent the bloodshed that is likely to follow the clash of hostile creeds, who have known men of other faiths who are transparently good. It would be wrong however to suppose that most men in the twentieth century had deliberately and consciously put aside their faith, that they followed its moral code from an arid lack of anything better to put in its place. A handful of professed agnostics, a handful of the orthodox, you would find; most, if questioned, would admit to an acceptance of the fundamentals of Christianity, to a scepticism as to the detail of dogma formulated in periods when thought was shaped by conceptions no longer accepted, to a profound belief that man is here to do what he can in this world rather than prepare for the next. With that change in religious outlook came, on the whole, less sense of a mission but also less sense of strain in dealing with people of other creeds.

Early in the new century came the beginning of change, political as well as religious and social, and with increasing speed steps were taken that would hand over power to Indian parties responsible to an electorate in India. But though to many of the Guardians the pace might seem too swift, to many politically minded Indians it seemed too slow, while among the wards there was bitter and rapidly increasing dissension as to who was to be the controlling partner. The last years are years of tension and shifting emphasis. In theory, the wards were learning how to manage their own affairs in readiness for complete control one day; in practice they were fighting hard to get control at once. To the Deputy Commissioner, engaged in a battle to keep a hold on his district and prevent people killing each other, utterances from London or Delhi seemed often enough fantastically unreal; this contrast between tactical and strategic aims is one reason why the man on the spot sometimes appeared hostile to the declared policy of his country. But though there were many different views about the right pace, almost everyone by the end was agreed that trustees cannot go on for ever, particularly when the ward has come of age and no longer wants advice.

The last part of the story is one, then, in which against a background of political change and of growing complexity in the business of government, a caste of Guardians who had been amateur despots — expert in nothing or everything, answerable in practice mainly to themselves, foreign to the country they ruled — transform themselves into a modern civil service, indigenous and answerable to a legislature. While they did this, they had to carry on a surreptitious, intermittent and undeclared civil war with the people to whom they were handing over power and whom they were supposed to be training for responsibility. At the same time they could never lose sight of their first main task, which was to preserve order, to keep chaos at bay.

It is not the aim of this book to analyse the growing bitterness between Hindu and Muslim that is one feature of the last act. But it must be stressed. The two religions are alike in one respect only, that for their devotees they affect every aspect of life — clothes, food, attitude to the family, sacred books, language, mythology. At best they can be oil and water, but historically Islam had been the faith of conquerors, last made manifest in the active persecution of Aurangzebe, breaker of idols and temples. For a hundred years now the two creeds had lain down unwillingly together beneath a yoke alien to either. The suggestion that the yoke might soon be removed was itself enough to bring both to their feet in wary but hostile surmise. Thus the main stream of nationalism became militantly Hindu and Islam at the same time remembered the valour of past generations and realized with a shock that her sons were unfitted for the new warfare of ballot-box and competitive examination. As the end grew nearer, strife increased between these two and the chance became almost daily less that unity would remain as England's one indubitable gift to India.

But the district officer did not think in such terms as this. He tried to keep his people from cutting each other's throats. That in itself was task enough, even if he had not also to train his own successors and the sometimes bored and frequently hostile members of district and municipal boards and committees. At the same time a revolution was taking place in ideas of what a government ought to do. As little as possible — that had been the classical answer in the nineteenth century, though Simla had been socialist compared with Westminster. Now that was changed and a government was expected to develop, to stimulate, to encourage, to originate. And for this kind of government, the despotism of a foreign caste, however benevolent, is not really suitable, even if the caste had not been trained in the old ways and had not had its hands quite full enough with transforming itself and advising people who did not want advice. If Simla had been ahead of Westminster in the last century, in this it fell behind in that function of government which initiates and develops. It was unfortunate that the departments handed over to Indian ministers in 1919 were those concerned with this new aspect of administration. They came to be regarded by the Guardians as secondary to the old main business of seeing that chaos did not come again. To the Guardians they were frills. To the nationalist therefore they became immensely important and he by contrast came to take for granted or even to forget finance, police and defence, the essential pillars of the state.

The whole tale cannot yet be told finally. There is much that cannot yet be said and much that will look different in fifty years. There is much to regret in the way the end came. But that the end could not have been longer delayed, that it was the fulfilment of the best part of what the English had stood for — of all but unity — hardly one of the Guardians would have denied. In a final assessment — made perhaps a hundred years from now — the awakening of India's spirit which took place in the nineteenth century will have to be assessed carefully and a balance struck. In the one scale will be weighed all the best that India acquired from contact with England — a liberal and rational approach to human institutions, a sense of the individual's value and yet of his duty to the state; in the other scale must come the lack of self-confidence bred by alien rule, the lack of realism encouraged by an alien educational system, the instinct to resist even a reasonable suggestion because it came from the patronizing, superior West. China too has awakened from millennia of slumber, later than India and without foreign rule, but whether to a more or less fruitful and vigorous life it is too soon to say.

Here then are the last two acts in the story of the Guardians. Here are the Guardians, selected and trained now on more Platonic lines than before, being, as Plato says, 'brought up from their childhood to imitate whatever is proper to their profession and to model themselves on brave, sober, religious and honourable men'. The words are Plato's, but they might be Dr. Arnold's: 'if he'll only turn out a brave, helpful truth-telling Englishman and a gentleman and a Christian, that's all I want', was the meditation of Squire Brown, as he said goodbye to Tom on the morning he left for Rugby. But the Guardians' task became more complex. They had been, as Plato dreamt, 'released from every other craft that they may acquire consummate skill in the art of creating their country's freedom' — but Plato had not really meant freedom so much as a more perfect servitude. And it was with some surprise that in the fifth act the Guardians suddenly perceived that freedom was in fact what they had been creating, that all they had been doing wrote their own death-warrant. Yet from beginning to end they seem the same men. Hawkins and Peter Mundy, Verelst and Pattle, Roberdeau, Beames, Edye, Lane and Lambrick — with all their differences there is something in common to them all. They think their own thoughts and do their duty in their own way — and it is a way of which no people need be ashamed.

In the early part of this story, interest shifts from one part of India to another. In this second half, it is hard to keep away from the northern plains. My own writing, too, is coloured by experience of the North; that cannot be helped because that is the India I knew. And since no one can know intimately Munro's Madras, Cornwallis's Bengal and the Maratha country, it is perhaps most useful to know the country whose administration developed from Bengal's and provided the basis for the Punjab's and the Central Provinces'. It must also be added that not only are there far more published books but that more unpublished material has been sent me from the United Provinces and the Punjab than from the rest of India put together.

I have tried to acknowledge in the notes the help I have received from many people, both in conversation and in the form of letters and unpublished memoirs. I thank those helpers again, and also the committee of the former members of the Indian Civil Service who made it possible for me to write this book. I also thank Sir Richard

Tottenham who conceived the idea and who has been constant in advice to keep this 'a book about men'. I wish I felt the result was at all adequate to the subject — but if a dozen more books were written each could show a different angle and still all would not be said.

P. W.

THE GUARDIANS

I

THE SYSTEM AT WORK

1858-1909

CHAPTER I

BARTLE FRERE AND THE YEARS AFTER THE MUTINY

1. AFTER THE MUTINY

IT would be absurd to pretend that the Mutiny was not of immense importance to the way Englishmen and Indians came to look at each other. On the other hand, it is easy to make too much of it. The Mutiny happened, after all, in Hindustan, the country between Patna and Delhi, and hardly anywhere else. For the Punjab, Bengal and Sind, it was a time of great anxiety, but for those in the South it was something in the newspapers and to picture what was happening required imagination. Even in the North, after a very few months things on the surface were almost as they had been. In the districts round Delhi, the instalment of land revenue that fell due in the summer of 1857 was paid in part that autumn and the winter instalment was paid as usual. And writing to the government of the North-West from Mr. Traill's hill country of Kumaon, a district officer mentioned that he had had no answer to a letter sent in May, the reason no doubt being, he added mildly, the 'late disturbance in the plains'.

Bitterness of course remained. The civilian seems on the whole to have recovered more quickly than the soldier, both much more quickly than the trader or planter. Alfred Lyall, two years out of Haileybury, had been in the thick of the fighting, had killed a man in battle, had hanged sepoys afterwards. But he could feel no animosity against villagers who 'thought we were all gone and reverted to the fashion of their forefathers', killing, he adds, far more of each other than they of us or we of them. 'In spite of all that has happened,' he wrote in November 1858, 'I take immense interest in the natives of India and like to be constantly among them.'

And Lord Roberts, writing years later, remembered that racial hatred very soon began to go as Englishmen remembered the fidelity of servants and villagers, of the Hindustani sepoys who fought with Henry Lawrence in defence of the Residency at Lucknow, of the Punjabis with whose help Delhi was taken, as they heard too of the anger shown even in the worst days of the summer of 1857 by many Indians at the behaviour of the sepoys.

On the English side, the sharpest rancour remained among the traders and planters and in England. *The Times* and *The Spectator* were impressed by the civilian's inordinate bias in favour of 'the native', the fact being that the civilian saw Indian villagers every day and could not go on hating them for ever. He really had no time for bitter memories — not at least when he was in camp, riding every day among the young green wheat and tall sugar-cane, listening to grave long-winded rustic debates, sympathizing over a crop damaged by locusts or a well that had been maliciously spoiled. But in Calcutta no doubt it took longer to forget.

Read such a book as *Curry and Rice* and you would find it hard to say whether it was written before or after the Mutiny; there is estrangement certainly, arrogance no doubt, a light-hearted disregard for the whole Indian world except in so far as Indians minister to English needs, but there is no suggestion of a desire for vengeance. As a matter of fact, the second edition appeared in 1859, while the first must have been published in India and one may guess that the drawings were made before the Mutiny; there is one reference to 'scenes of horror' in the Introduction to the second edition, but nothing else. Outwardly at least the official world had resumed its aloof and disregardful way.

The Indian view of the English, however, is much more a matter of speculation. There are no letters home on the Indian side and very few memoirs; what the villager thinks in his heart is something few know, even today, when his rulers are of his own race. All one can say with confidence is that the Indian reaction must have been different from the English and that it must surely be wrong to attribute to anyone in 1860 the emotions and arguments of 1920. Asia is careless of human life, used to stern measures, respectful of power. It is my guess that in the villages there was, on the surface, some anxiety to display repentance; in the heart, not much hatred and no sense of injustice but an awed and rather chilled fear of the English in general, a gloomy acquiescence in the inevitable. But the fear did often lift like morning mist for the cultivator who met his district officer strolling near his tent with a gun under his arm.

Bitterness on the Indian side was to be found not among the villagers but among some of the princes and nobles and the more educated; it was, I believe, not so much on account of the ruthless suppression of the revolt as at subsequent slights, exclusion, and rudeness. G. O. Trevelyan has a story, almost inconceivable to anyone who knew India only in the next century, of a planter lashing out indiscriminately with a hunting-crop at a group of Indians; having paid to come on to a race-course, they had had the effrontery to stand in a good place for the finish. That kind of thing would cause more bitterness than hangings; memories of such incidents lived on one side and the attitude that inspired them would flare up again on the other.

There were also many decisions that appeared inevitable to everyone in the 'sixties but which had become a grievance to Indians by the 'twenties; in the army, for instance, all gunners were in future to be British. That must have seemed natural enough to Indians at the time; it was a sign of distrust about which there was no lack of candour. It came to be an indication of insincerity only when we professed to be making the Indian Army into the weapon of a new dominion.

Nor did the change from the Honourable East India Company to the Crown make so much difference as might have been supposed. The Company's servants had long regarded themselves as servants also of the Queen; for long the Court of Directors had been as much a convenience to Parliament as an independent body. The Directors had been useful to Parliament because they exercised a patronage that would have made the Ministry too formidable, because they supplied some continuity when the Ministry changed, and because they provided an opinion on Indian affairs that was seasoned with more experience of India than Parliament could muster. Their place was now to be taken by the Council of India, who were to be 'neither the masters nor the puppets but the valuable advisers to the new Minister'. The majority of the Council were to be former servants of the Company or the Crown, so that the seasoning of experience would be stronger than before, but to the men in India it did not seem that there was much difference between the Court and the Council.

As a matter of fact, English views about India as expressed in Parliament had been remarkably consistent and there was no new principle expressed in 1858. As long ago as 1813, Lord Grenville had said:

'The British Crown is *de facto* sovereign in India. How it became so it is needless to enquire . . .' But 'the sovereignty which we hesitate to assert, necessity compels us to exercise', and it ought to be exercised, first, to provide for the welfare of the Indian people, next, but ranking far below the first, to promote the interests of Great Britain. Lord Grenville's views had been accepted by almost everyone and three steps had been taken to give them effect, in the Acts of 1813, 1833 and 1853. In each, the sovereignty of the Crown had been asserted with less hesitation, the influence of the Company subjected to limits narrower and more precise. The last step, taken in 1858, was no longer or bolder than those that went before.

To the men still serving in India, the most disturbing change was the introduction of competitive examinations in 1853. Not that there was anything new about the idea; it had been suggested by Lord Grenville in 1813 and for a very short time given partial effect in 1833. But when it actually came, it seemed to the older Haileybury men that the 'competition-wallah' belonged to a new race. They were bookish hobbledehoys who fell off their horses, misunderstood Hindustani and made silly mistakes about the ways of the country. But, seen from a distance, even here there does not seem so great a change; the old hand had always made fun of the 'griffin' — the new arrival — for just these mistakes and many of the first competition-wallahs had fathers or brothers in the service.

There is no sharp line across the page then, no new beginning. But of course there is a change. Looking at the men most typical of the 'sixties, one is aware at once of a different mental atmosphere. They have lost the certainty of Lawrence, Edwardes and Nicholson that they are angelic heralds of a new order. There is doubt, detachment of outlook, mental independence again, as there was in the time of Elphinstone. It is perhaps significant that the most outstanding figure of the ten years after the Mutiny looked back always to Elphinstone as the hero of a golden age.

'From the first day I went to Court,' wrote Bartle Frere, 'and had as my first charge to pay pensions to old men who had fought and laboured, some under him, some against him, but who all loved and venerated him, . . . I never heard his name mentioned but in terms which made me feel proud that I was a countryman of his. Since then, many an idol of my earlier days has been shattered . . . but I never found him wrong. . . .'

Frere was lucky in his first superiors. He came to India in 1835 and there is a pleasant picture of him learning his work: 'Young Frere was always seen sitting on the carpet by the side of old Narso-pant Tatia, for whom he entertained the highest respect, and whom he used to call by the respectful name of Kakaji (elder uncle).' He was soon assistant settlement officer under Goldsmid, of whom he wrote: 'Ask the old and middle-aged how they fared . . . before Gold-smid and Wingate Sahib's time, before the assessment was fixed, and how they fare now. And should newcomers chance to hear, as I have heard, ten years after the Sahibs had left, the same names introduced into the doggerel lay which the Maratha housewife chants to lighten her daily task of grinding grain, they would confess that . . . Goldsmid had gained the highest honours . . . a simple race . . . could pay.'

Frere succeeded Goldsmid and came directly under the Revenue Commissioner. 'Since I have been working with Williamson, working himself, and making me work, as hard as we well could, he never once said or wrote a word to let me know he was master . . . It is true that this is the best way of getting work out of people, but it is not one man in five hundred who does so . . .' It was, as a matter of fact, to be a tradition of the service, one that Frere learnt from a good master and himself helped to fix.

From settlement and revenue work he went in Lord Dalhousie's time to be Resident at Satara, the Maratha state which Elphinstone had raised from the degradation of mere ritual kingship to something of its former glory. The last Raja of Satara had no son; he asked Frere to obtain leave for him to adopt as heir a relative who, according to Hindu rites, had already become his son. The Raja died before the answer came; he had been loved in his State and his subjects were anxious that the throne should go to Sivaji's descendants. Frere fought hard for the adopted heir, though so complete was his loyalty that no one in the state knew what his recommendation had been. But Dalhousie was adamant and the State was annexed.

Frere had to administer the territory which he thought had been unjustly acquired. He refused the offer of troops; he could manage without them. And he did. On paper, the most noteworthy development of his reign in Satara was the introduction of municipalities, the first in India, committees who collected funds and kept the towns clean; but it is perhaps not less important that when he left 'the grief of both Europeans and natives was evident . . . I saw men of both nationalities in tears. . . .'

2. SIND AND THE FRONTIER

In 1850, Frere succeeded Sir Charles Napier as Commissioner in Sind. Here, too, there were municipalities, and great battles with Bombay on behalf of the port of Karachi. All Indian governments were conservative in finance; outlay on the port of Karachi, if unsuccessful, would be wasted, and if successful would set up a rival to Bombay. It was only by incredible persistence that Frere was able to obtain a hundred pounds to spend on a survey of the harbour bar. But he did persist; year in and year out he battled on and by 1859, when he left Sind, although much remained to be done, he had convinced the Secretary of State that 'Kurrachee and not Calcutta is the natural port for the Punjab'.

He had done a great deal more than that. Roads, railways, post-offices, travellers' bungalows, above all canals — it was desolate desert country and in Sind itself, if only he could get money and sanction from Bombay, there were no vested interests to oppose him. The country was his own, a sheet of blank paper to cover with the creations of his own mind and will. In the older parts of India the use of postage-stamps was opposed on the grounds that the country was not yet sufficiently advanced for such an innovation. In the newest and least developed province, Frere printed his own stamps and devised without sanction a means of forwarding stamped letters.

But canals and roads came before anything else. The simplest means were used. On a still day a fire would be lighted at the point to be reached, and the road or canal would be aimed directly at the smoke. A network was gradually spread over the country; a sample was the work carried out in the frontier districts, where Jacob 'cleared and laid out 2589 miles of road . . . furnished with 786 masonry bridges, 88 of which, across navigable canals, were passable by boats of the largest size'.

John Jacob had begun his work under Napier, but most of it was done in Frere's time and the bond between them was one of trust, friendship, and admiration on both sides. The Sind frontier is the southern end of the chain of mountains and desert that make the North-West Frontier. But while in the Punjab section the barrier is mountains and nothing else, the Sind section is composed of mountains interspersed with desert. Jacob's work lay at the junction of these two sections, where the people of Sind confront tribesmen, Baluch and Afghan, wild moss-troopers who until now had lived by loot, men among whom the blood-feud was the only justice known, who in theory might pay some shadowy allegiance to the Khan of Kalat or the Amir of Kabul but in practice followed no rule but their own will. From their stony and icy heights, it had long been their custom to raid the plains of Sind, carrying off not a miserable dozen or so, but camels, cattle and goats by the ten thousand.

Here Jacob made his headquarters, in a sandy country below the mountains, where the heat in summer is as intense as any man has to

AFGHANISTAN

Khyber Pass

Kabul

DURAND LINE

Tribal Territory

HAZARA

NORTH-WEST
Peshawar

FRONTIER
Kohat
PROVINCE

Bannu

WAZIRISTAN

Wana

DERA
ISMAIL
KHAN

Ft.Sandeman

PUNJAB

Kandahar

ZHOB

Chaman

DERA
GHAZI
KHAN

Quetta

Marris

Bolan Pass

Sibi

Bahawalpur

Bugtis

PUNJAB
STATES

Kalat

Jacobabad

BALUCHISTAN

Indus

SIND

Karachi

Mouths of
the Indus

NORTH-WEST
FRONTIER PROVINCE
Tribal Territory
Administered
Territory

E.G.M.

endure on the earth's surface. He built houses, planted trees, covered the country with a network of roads and canals, while with two regiments of irregular horse — the Sind Horse — he so chastised the raiding tribesmen that he brought peace to the border.

Frere gave him a free hand and saw that he was disturbed as little as possible. 'Jacob is not an ordinary man,' he wrote to Lord Falkland, the Governor of Bombay . . . 'he is a very first-rate engineer and never fails to succeed in all he undertakes. I hope therefore you will not think me inconsistent in exempting his plans from that criticism and supervision to which everything else in the canal department in the province is subject.' And, indeed, he was not an ordinary man. A gunner originally, he became cavalry leader, engineer and civil administrator, all superlatively. Everyone at Jacobabad, clockmaker, instrument maker, gunsmith, brought the technical problems of his own craft to Jacob as a master who knew more than he did and could advise him. 'When English soldiers in the Crimea were making tardy acquaintance with . . . Minié rifles, with which eight hundred and nine hundred yards were unattainable ranges, Jacob and his officers were hitting the target at three thousand yards with a rifle of his own invention or igniting combustibles a mile off with explosive bullets. . . .'

'I must have no courts-martial or articles of war,' Jacob wrote to Frere. 'I want no lawyers among my men, neither do I wish to govern them by force or fear. I will have "sober God-fearing men in my troops" as said old Cromwell, and will govern them by appealing to their higher, not to their basest, attributes . . .' In fact the punishment on which he relied was to turn a man out of the regiment; it was felt so bitter a disgrace and deprivation that no other was needed. Though most of his men were from Hindustan, their fidelity in the Mutiny was never doubted. Every man was inspired with his commander's spirit. Instant readiness for action, unshakable tenacity in pursuit of law-breakers — these were the watchwords. Once, when information reached an outpost of the Sind Horse that raiders from the Baluch tribes had carried off some camels, Durga Singh, the officer in charge of the outpost, rode after them at a gallop with fifteen troopers. When at last he came up with them he had covered thirty miles and killed two horses; thirteen of his men had been left by the way with foundered beasts. He and two troopers and a Baluch guide faced an enemy, perhaps forty strong, who had come to realize how few were their pursuers. The guide begged him to go back, but Durga Singh replied that 'he should be ashamed to show his face to

Major Jacob if after coming in sight of the robbers he should retire without killing some of them'.

He thereupon attacked the enemy who, being in overwhelming numbers, cut him and his two troopers in pieces — but not before they had killed or disabled fifteen tribesmen. The remnant of the raiding party tied round Durga Singh's wrist the scarlet thread, the highest honour the border tribesman can bestow on the valiant dead.

That was the spirit of Jacob's men, English or Indian alike. The English officers were not expected to take leave; both their private fortune and their pay were spent on the regiment or on the new town. They scorned fans, thermantidotes and ice; they endured the heat without mitigation. The few huts with which Jacob began grew in seven years to a town of seven thousand inhabitants, with a laboratory, engineers' and carpenters' workshops, a large and valuable library. 'I have just returned', wrote Frere in 1855, 'from that wonderful place Jacobabad. Yesterday morning I went with Jacob nine miles into what four years ago was real desert . . . without a tree, a drop of water, or a blade of grass . . . All is now . . . stubble and from the top of a surveying tower, as far as the eye could reach . . . we could see the fields extended, the cultivators and cattle not appearing to dream of the possibility of plunderers attacking them. . . .'

With Frere's backing, Jacob made a lasting peace on the Sind border, 'converting the murderer and robber into a harmless and industrious peasant', and Frere always believed that if the principles used on that frontier had been accepted further North, if Jacob or half a dozen of his men — Merewether, Pelly, Macaulay, Malcolm, the Green brothers — had been moved North, the Punjab border too could have been settled. No Frontier officer will today assent to that belief, but it was not only Frere who held it. 'Can anyone believe', asked Frere, 'that human nature changes where the Sind frontier meets the Punjab?' 'No one can say', wrote Sir George Clerk, himself a Punjab man but by 1861 Governor of Bombay, 'that Afridis, Yusufzais and such up there are a bit worse or more wild than Marris, Brahuis, and Baluchis down here. But here, on the frontier under the mountains, not a mouse stirs without Merewether's permission — and aloft in the fastnesses of the wild tribes there is now no fighting without Green's sanction.'

The first difference was that in Sind Jacob was Deputy Commissioner of the frontier districts as well as commandant of the Sind Horse, whereas in the Punjab the Political Officer did not command the troops. This was in accordance with Frere's lifelong belief that in

India there should be one head only to whom power is delegated. Bombay, for example, should delegate all the power it was prepared to relinquish in respect of Sind to the Commissioner only and should have no direct dealings with judges, canal officers or educationalists in that area. The Commissioner in Sind should deal in the same way with his district officers; no specialized department should make any arrangements in the district that were not subject to the district officer's comment and control. The best system for India, Frere thought, was 'a good vigorous despotism, in which the risks of tyranny and arbitrary oppression are minimised, one in which the despot is accessible, when every man sees, knows, and can appeal to his own despot'.

The second great difference in frontier policy between Sind and the Punjab was even more far-reaching. The Punjab made the tribe responsible for any breach of the peace. If a raid took place and the tribe did not make immediate amends, the crops and villages of the tribe were burnt. This, argued Frere, was not only unjust in itself but put the tribe in an economic position from which the only escape was another raid. In Sind, the actual raiders must be followed up and either killed in fight or captured; at the worst, the tribe must be given their names and ordered to hand them over. In September 1847, some seven hundred Bugtis from the hills entered the Sind plains to plunder; Merewether followed them with one hundred and thirty-three troopers, brought them to bay and repeatedly charged them, killing or disabling five hundred and sixty, before the rest would accept the offers of quarter which they had several times previously refused.

Again, Frere and Jacob strengthened the hand of the Khan of Kalat in every possible way. Their troopers did not hesitate to pursue a criminal into the Khan's territory, but when he was captured they would hand him over for justice, while they behaved across the border as civilized troops should in the territory of an ally. The Khan counted them his chief supporters. Again, the Sind authorities would not permit internecine tribal warfare and forbade anyone on British territory to carry arms without a licence; most rigorously they forbade any form of private vengeance. Justice was in the hands of the Khan on one side of the frontier, of Jacob on the other. To plead a blood-feud was so far from extenuating murder that it was taken as proof that the crime was premeditated.

In the Punjab frontier districts, on the other hand, the customs were almost exactly opposite. Every man bore arms by right, the tribes were encouraged — Frere believed — to avenge offences committed against them by other tribes, the authority of the Amir was denied and troops never crossed the frontier except to inflict punishment, which was directed not against individuals but against the tribe and was therefore indiscriminate.

To all this, the Punjab frontier man would reply that Sind methods could not be applied to different people in different country, but Frere was never convinced. He particularly disliked indiscriminate punitive raids and the covenanting Old Testament language about them that was fashionable in the Punjab. 'I confess to a feeling which I am not anxious to define very accurately when I read of such proceedings being successful "under the guidance of Providence",' he wrote. And again, in a private letter to Henry Green: 'If you two and Merewether were moved North and left to your own devices, we should in three years have every tribe from the Indus to Ghazni and Kabul, and probably the Amir himself, wanting us to call them our subjects. . . .'

3. A LIBERAL CONSERVATIVE

During the Mutiny, Frere's part was not unlike that of John Lawrence. The people of Sind remembered the misrule of the Amirs and did not want a change; here, as in the Punjab, there was no general disaffection. But there were units of the mutinous Bengal Army in Sind and no one could feel unshakably certain about the Bombay regiments. Frere held the province; he organized a supply line into the Punjab and postal lines both into the Punjab and across the desert to Agra and Calcutta; he dealt with the mutinies that did occur, he checked others before they reached a head. In July, he had only one hundred and thirty-nine effective British bayonets at his disposal for the whole of Sind — 'a weak wing of a sickly regiment'. For four months he never passed a night without being disturbed by dispatches, 'often three or four times in a night', yet he was always able to lie down at once and go peacefully to sleep. He was able to spare troops for the Deccan and would have sent some to the Punjab if they had been accepted. His letters are always calm, cheerful and confident at a time when there was much hysteria. His belief in God sustained him, as it sustained the Lawrences, but it was a quieter belief and less exacting for other people.

It was not a time for hesitation and Frere did not shrink from executing the ringleaders of the risings that occurred in the 16th and

21st Native Infantry. But even here there was something character-istic. Finding on one occasion that a gallows had been put up before a trial began, he gently but firmly insisted that it should be taken down and the issue not prejudged. And before long he succeeded in per-suading the General that courts-martial should consist of native officers. They were 'even more prompt and as severe as the European court', while the troops were made much more clearly aware of what was happening and convinced of its justice. From Frere's letters at this time come many wafts of fresh air. 'Some of the more designing', he wrote of one regiment, 'thought the whole body was more ripe for mischief than the event proved them to be, . . . but a *plot*, such as Mazzini and his friends would call a plot, we have no evidence of and I think it is a waste of time to seek for one. . . .'

Frere was a Tory by family tradition, his conservatism being of the liberal school of his uncle, Hookham Frere, the translator of Aris-tophanes, and of Hookham's friend Canning, the great Foreign Secretary. The heart of his political creed is expressed in a letter he wrote immediately after the Mutiny, before he went to the Council in Calcutta, at a time when there was much controversy among Indian officials about the attitude the Government ought to take towards Christianity. Herbert Edwardes — once of Bannu — had come to believe that the Mutiny was a divine chastisement for the sin we had committed as a nation by accepting a compromise with false religions. He wished to observe no Hindu or Muslim holidays, to refuse all recognition to caste, to teach from the Bible in all schools. Many other evangelicals were half inclined to agree with him because their principles logically pointed the same way. Others saw the dangers and rather uneasily disagreed, half suspecting themselves of a too worldly compromise.

Frere felt no contradiction and no need for compromise. 'There can be no safe rule of guidance for a Christian Government different from that of a Christian individual — to do as we would be done by. And what Colonel Edwardes and Sir J. Lawrence would do is just what we would ourselves resist to the death if attempted on us, — not by Hindoos or Moslems but by a Roman Catholic or Greek autocrat.' This, by the way, is not fair to Lawrence, whose conclusion, after pondering deeply, was not far from Frere's. And again, 'Let the Government of this world keep the peace and do justice and mercy to the best of its power, and rule the people so that peace and plenty prevail throughout the land, but let not Government presume to dictate to the meanest of its subjects what he shall believe or, however indirectly, to bribe or coerce him into any particular form of belief. . . .'

This was true tolerance, for he had always 'felt convinced that the conversion of the natives to Christianity was the greatest blessing our rule could confer on them, and, as far as human reason could see, one of the great objects for which our rule was permitted'. It was tolerance in the true line of descent from Warren Hastings, Elphinstone and Metcalfe, and when Frere became Member of the Viceroy's Council all his utterances bear the stamp of that majestic dynasty, a liberal recognition that it is wise to be conservative about Indian society, to support Indian institutions, to admit Indian nobles and professional men to a share of power, to foster an upper class of Indians with an interest in the continuance of the régime. He disliked 'a policy which puts all real power into the hands of European officials and European colonists and treats the natives as at best *in statu pupillari*, to be ruled, taught and perhaps petted, but to be excluded from all real power or influence . . . and to be governed . . . according to our latest English notions of what is best for them.'

These 'Colonial' principles, he feared, were common 'among the present race of officials, but there is, no doubt, a large and, I trust, an increasing school . . . who hold with Warren Hastings and Cornwallis, Wellesley, Malcolm and Mountstuart Elphinstone rather than with Lord Dalhousie and Mr. Thomason and the later school of levelling, resumption and annexation. . . .'

There is so much common sense, so wise and so conservative a liberalism in Frere, that one could go on quoting him for ever. He became the close friend and constant adviser of Lord Canning, as his uncle had been to the Viceroy's father, and he was entirely at one with him over the well-known 'adoption dispatch'. He had no doubt that Dalhousie's policy of refusing to recognize adoption and of annexing a State to which there was no direct male heir was regarded as an interference with Indian custom and most unjust. He believed it had been a main cause of the Mutiny and was still a source of uneasiness to all chiefs and princes. 'It is impossible to exaggerate the evil of this state of uncertainty,' he wrote, and again, 'Nothing could be more blighting to every good and loyal feeling than such a state of doubt as to our intentions.' The views of the dispatch were accepted; they were embodied in Queen Victoria's proclamation, the Princes were assured of the right to adoption, and the States were petrified for ninety years. At the time, hardly any Indian could have been found who did not think this just. That the settlement proved an obstacle to progress sixty years later, when it became desirable to group the smaller States into larger units, was a development which no one then foresaw or could have foreseen.

There is another controversy belonging to the years after the Mutiny in which Canning and Frere were in agreement. In 1833, the Governor-General's Council had been enlarged by a Law Member, who was, as it happened, Macaulay. He had no vote on executive matters; he was there to advise on Legislative proposals and to shape them, a glorified Parliamentary Draftsman. In 1853, the Law Member became a full member and, for legislative purposes only, the Council was further enlarged. Two judges were added in the interests of technical competence and two civilians, one from Madras and one from Bombay, to give a wider knowledge of conditions outside Bengal.

But something in the English character — whether a love of political freedom or a pig-headed refusal to be driven — led this unpromising quartet to re-enact on a small scale the struggle of Crown and Parliament in Stuart times. These four officials set themselves up as a check on the Executive; they claimed to represent English business, the planters, the readers of *The Times* in England; they called for papers, they demanded inquiries. All this was in the teeth of Sir Charles Wood's intentions either when, as President of the Board of Control in 1853, he had brought these Calcutta Hampdens into existence, or when he observed the result as Secretary of State in 1861. 'Nobody ever dreamed of a debating body with open doors and even quasi-independence,' he wrote. It must be added that the views of their leader, Sir Barnes Peacock, the Chief Justice of Bengal, were almost always illiberal and narrow, while those of Canning and Frere — the executive — were broad, tolerant, and reasonably far-sighted.

Neither Frere nor Canning however were prepared to play Charles I. Whatever the intentions may have been eight years before, Frere believed the time had now come to recognize what had happened and go further. 'You can have little idea', he wrote to Sir Charles Wood from Calcutta, 'how much India is altered ... We have changed from an aggressive and advancing power to a stationary one ... the sympathy which Englishmen ... felt for the natives has changed to a general feeling of repugnance ... instead of a general feeling of content with their Indian lot ... the English here are almost generally openly discontented, disinclined to remain here or to care for India, and disposed to look at things in anything but an Indian

light . . . all this feeling is inevitably reciprocated by the natives . . .'
He is speaking, it must be remembered, of non-officials in Calcutta,
not of all India; he argues that they will never accept purely official
legislation; 'unless you have some barometer and safety-valve in the
shape of a deliberative Council I believe you will always be liable to
unlooked-for and dangerous explosions . . . then, if you admit non-
official Europeans, you must also admit, in at least equal proportions,
natives, who in intelligence and education are their equals and who
have a far greater stake in the country.'

Frere forecast a widened legislative council, representative but not
elected, its proceedings being public and the members being nom-
inated by the Government from non-officials, European and Indian,
with legislative bodies framed on similar lines for the provinces. An
Act to this effect was passed by Parliament; three Indians became
Members of the Viceroy's Legislative Council; in Bombay, Sir
George Clerk, an intimate friend of Frere's, appointed four Indians.
It was an important first step—'the germ of much good', wrote
Frere, 'accompanied by much dross'.

From Calcutta he went back as Governor to Bombay where he
gave first place in his interests to public works. 'You ask why I am
always thinking and talking of irrigation,' he wrote to one of his
children. 'If you had seen men's bones, as I have, lying unburied by
the roadside, and on entering a village had found it untenanted by a
living person, you would understand why.' And one of the shrewdest
of judges — Miss Nightingale — wrote to him in 1860 after he had
left Bombay: 'Bombay has a lower death-rate on the last two years
than London, the healthiest city in Europe. This is entirely your
doing. If we do not take care, Bombay will outstrip us in the sanitary
race. People will be ordered for the benefit of their health to Bombay. . . .'

Lord Canning was succeeded as Viceroy by Lord Elgin and he by
John Lawrence. Frere welcomed Lawrence with an offer of loyal
co-operation in which he never failed, but there were bound to be
differences between them. John Lawrence was the first of the level-
lers, those protectors of the poor who had little respect for Indian
institutions and the old order, who believed that hereditary chiefs
were usually encumbrances who kept the light of the sun from the
poor peasant. Frere on the other hand belonged to the school of
Elphinstone and Henry Lawrence, men whose reforms would never
be radical, who thought rather of individuals than of systems and
wished no one to be the worse for British rule. There were too the

clearly expressed differences on frontier problems. Both however were men of size enough to respect each other and there would not have been much controversy if John Lawrence had ruled India as well as he had ruled the Punjab.

Unfortunately, he came to his last spell of Indian service without the elasticity to learn new ways. He had been to the Punjab exactly the 'good vigorous despot' of Frere's ideal; he had been prompt, laconic, accessible; generous in delegating power to his chosen subordinates, he more than any man had been responsible for the Punjab creed of always backing them up. But he had known what was happening in every district, he had kept his finger on everything that stirred.

No one could have the same detailed knowledge of everything in India. No political aristocrat from Whitehall would have dreamt that such knowledge could exist, and simply because of his ignorance almost any lord but another Auckland would have made a better Viceroy than John Lawrence. He tried to govern India as though it were the Punjab and to control everything from the centre. And finding the old informal flexible Punjab system would not work — how could it, between men who were too far apart to make a family party on the Punjab model? — he fell back on rigidity, on hard and fast rules and no exceptions, that debilitating disease that sooner or later invades the bureaucratic system. It is sad that to him of all men Frere should have had to write:

'There is always in India some need for public servants acting without orders, on the assurance that, when their superiors hear their reasons, their acts will be approved and confirmed; and I hold that when you have extinguished that feeling of mutual confidence between superior and subordinate authorities and made public men as timid as they are in England, you will have removed one great safeguard of our Indian Empire. It does not take long so to bridle a body of public servants as to paralyse their power of acting without orders.'

There were differences too over foreign policy, with which Frere was directly concerned only in respect of Aden and the Persian Gulf. In the Gulf, 'for the last forty-five years', wrote Frere, 'our policy has been one of active interference and avowed assumption of the duty and responsibility of protecting general commerce. Trade has greatly increased, not less, I believe, than fourfold in forty years. It has been generally under the British flag and carried on by men who claimed protection as British subjects, and received it from the

Resident . . .' Lawrence, however, wanted 'to confine our labours, as a rule, to the suppression of piracy on the high seas. This seems to me quite as much as we can undertake with any advantage. . . .'

This was part of his general foreign policy of 'masterly inactivity', of 'keeping within our shell', that to Frere seemed 'a tempting sort of policy that looks safe and cheap, but it is not easy to carry out where we have treaties, and other obligations as strong as treaties, incurred by men of old time, who knew what honour and empire meant; and one of these days we shall reap bitter fruit from our present selfish and timid way of dealing with all our independent neighbours'.

Frere, it will be seen, was deeply conscious of the destiny of Victorian England to police the seven seas and in a hundred ways to use her influence for peace and for the suppression of evils. In 1867 he left Bombay, after thirty-two years without furlough, but he does not entirely leave the Indian stage. He was a more than usually active and valuable member of the Council of India and there are glimpses of him working out a health plan for the whole of India — 'It is a noble paper — and what a present to make to a Government! . . . God bless you for it!' wrote Miss Nightingale — reforming the administration of the British Army, working always at articles, speeches, minutes. And his Indian training, surely, was responsible for the action he took on two occasions when he was dispatched on missions for the British Government.

He was sent to Zanzibar with the object of inducing the Sultan to end the slave trade. In the past few years, Zanzibar had supplied more than thirty thousand African slaves to Arabia, while for every slave who reached Zanzibar alive ten had died by the spears of the slavers, from hunger or neglect, or under the whip during the journey from the interior. The Sultan, an independent Prince, drew a considerable part of his revenue from an import duty on each slave. Frere's instructions were not very precise; when at last his negotiations ended in polite refusal he did not apply to England for more. He informed the Sultan that in future British naval vessels would stop the transport of slaves to or from his island, while his customs authorities would be supervised by the British consul. These orders, he added, were subject to confirmation by the Queen's Government but would be acted upon at once.

The news seems to have come as a greater shock to the British Cabinet than to the Sultan, who did as he was told; the Cabinet after some hesitation accepted what had been peacefully accomplished and indeed completed Frere's work by a Treaty which they forced on the Sultan. The trade was ended. It can hardly be doubted that a politician or a diplomat, trained in Whitehall or the embassies of Europe, would have waited for further instructions; it may well be that the Cabinet would have shrunk from taking such forthright action as Frere's. Perhaps another thirty thousand slaves would have reached Arabia if Frere had not done what he thought would best effect the purpose of his instructions, if, in short, he had not behaved as he had been taught in India.

Governor of the Cape Colony and High Commissioner for South Africa, he was instructed to effect a Federation of the four South African states, a task he accepted with some reluctance. Once again he acted in perfect simplicity, as he would have done had he been a district officer, confident that his Commissioner would back him up. That he was dealing with politicians who had not been trained in the same way, that he was in the end recalled, that his life ended in misunderstanding and gross misrepresentation, is another story and a sad one.

Sir Bartle Frere is a man for whom one's admiration grows steadily and yet it is difficult to seize on the man's character and understand it. His biographer wrote despairingly that he could find no shadows in his nature, that the evidence of all who had known him, of the thousands of letters he wrote, all seemed too good to be true. There was no sign of conflict in his life; it was 'as though the battle had been fought and won in some previous existence'. That too is the impression made by the calm brow, the steady jaw, the forthright gaze. But there is no smack of priggishness about his quiet faith in God, his complete lack of selfishness. He was deeply loved. 'I have never known his like—' 'I loved him as a father — ' 'I never spoke to him without being the better for it — ' those were the phrases used of him by all who knew him.

As a public servant, the clarity with which he could express subtle arguments on complex subjects, his wide sympathies, his chivalrous courtesy, his courage, his calm, his common sense, his obedience to duty — all are impressive. But the quality which gave worth to everything else was moral stamina. He judged every question by his own standards, which were absolute and admitted of no compromise. He did not consider whether his views would please his superiors or magnify his own importance but whether they were right. There cannot have been many periods in the world's history when it has been possible to rise to the highest posts in a public service by the unfaltering practice of such a principle as this. Nor could any other service in the world have given the opportunity for so prolonged and independent an exercise of such high responsibility as had been Frere's. Yet in all those years of power it did not occur to him to let power corrupt his simplicity.

CHAPTER II

CLODHOPPING COLLECTOR

I. A YOUNG MAN IN THE PUNJAB

T HE Mutiny was over; things settled down. In the letters and biographies of the 'sixties and 'seventies, English administrators do not often betray a feeling of insecurity. Indeed, in the whole of human history, there can hardly have been another class of men so sure of themselves and of their wives, of reasonable prosperity on earth and a merciful heaven after death. They belonged to a service which gave them an assured position and the right to be themselves. They were the leaders of the official world, the rulers of India. They were doing work they knew was good.

In his district, the district officer was supreme; if he had a normal allowance of tact and intelligence, tenacity of purpose allotted perhaps on a more generous scale, and above all the good luck not to be transferred too often, he could get his way sooner or later in most things that he undertook. His work was extremely varied; there was plenty of it but most of it was interesting. He had the respect and indeed the adulation of the people among whom he lived. His pay never seemed quite enough for the education of eight or nine children in England, but he had no serious complaints on that score and he had the prospect of an annuity on retirement or a pension for his wife if he died. He could afford to think for himself and say what he thought.

Even if he distinguished himself in no way at all, if he never became any more than a 'clodhopping Collector', or by natural processes a Commissioner, his life would not have been a bad one. He could probably count to his credit roads, bridges, a school or two, a hospital or canal, perhaps the field maps of a district. These were capital gains, solid achievement, something beyond the bread of his day to day business of settling disputes, preserving the peace, keeping the wheels smoothly running. If, on the other hand, he had emerged from the ruck, there was hardly a limit to what he might do; he might find himself a statesman, advising on war and peace, framing a country's budget, making plans that would affect the happiness of millions; he might govern a province the size of Great Britain.

Entry was by competition but the new entrants were some of them the sons of civilians and of course for these two decades the service was still led by Haileybury men. In Madras and Bombay, a man went out to a district on arrival, but a Bengal man still had to pass language examinations in Calcutta. John Beames, the same who had been disturbed by revellers when he sat late over his books at Haileybury,[1] has left a detailed account of those first months in Calcutta in 1858 and 1859.

He lived in a boarding-house, where he shared a sitting-room with a friend; they rose early, at five or soon after, drank tea on a balcony in their pyjamas, and about six went to ride on the *maidan* — that is, an open plain. 'At seven we came in and got into pyjamas again. Many of our old Haileybury friends would drop in and our cool shady veranda was full of men drinking tea, smoking, reading the papers or letters, talking, laughing and enjoying themselves.' At nine, this party broke up and breakfast followed. 'This was rather an elaborate meal, consisting of fish, mutton chops, cutlets or other dishes of meat curry and rice, bread and jam and lots of fruit . . . Some drank tea but most of us had iced claret and water.' Two hours work on languages was supposed to follow, then calls on ladies, then lunch — which was 'also an elaborate meal of soup, hot meat, curry and rice, cheese and dessert with claret or beer. After this we felt naturally lazy and drowsy and lay about idly dozing . . .' They rode again at five and dinner was at half past seven; they were soon afterwards in bed unless they were dining out, as was often the case, the young civilian, a Lieutenant-Governor in embryo, being much sought after by mammas.

Beames writes with some irritation of this idle life. He had a real interest in languages but felt frustrated by what remained of the College of Fort William and thought he knew no more Persian at the end of it all than when he first came up the Hooghly. Certainly, keenness on his duty as an officer was the last thing such a course was likely to instil in a young man. If Calcutta had been a healthier spot, there might have been something to be said for a few slack months in which to become acclimatized. But it is perhaps as enervating and unhealthy a place as any in India, and in this pointless year there were other dangers besides the physical.

Many men fell hopelessly into debt and were crippled for the rest of their service. The competition-wallahs were on the whole more sensible about this than their predecessors, but in Beames's day there

[1] See *The Founders*, part III, chapter VIII, p. 282.

were still young men who remarked complacently that they had 'turned their lakh' — that is, accumulated a debt of £10,000. Others, lonely no doubt in a strange land and confused by a way of life to which their old standards did not seem to apply, fell into arms which were stretched wide to catch them and made unhappy marriages. John Beames was engaged to a girl in England, which was unusual; in his innocence he did not even know that he was being pursued in Calcutta. Friends told him later how amused they had been at his unconsciousness of the dark Lulu's charming wiles. 'I told her I was engaged . . . she told me she was also engaged . . . We agreed there was no reason why we should not be good friends . . . we talked a great deal about religion and certainly had no conversation about love.' He may stand for many young men before and after who knew more of Horace and Ovid than of Lalage or Amaryllis, but not all were so fortunate or so steadfast as he. 'I suppose I was a very green conceited young prig,' he writes.

When at last Beames escaped from the College of Fort William, he travelled up the country for some days. For the first short stage, a hundred and twenty miles only, he went by railway, thereafter by a *dak-gari*, an oblong box on four wheels, drawn by a variety of ill-trained ponies. He was posted to the Punjab and at Lahore had an interview with Sir Robert Montgomery, now Lieutenant-Governor. This was Thomason's brother-in-law; he was generally known as Pickwick because of his spectacles, his roundness and his air of benevolence, but he had been a fierce man after mutineers and had thought John Lawrence an old woman for not showing who was master by pulling down the Great Mosque at Delhi. Beames was appointed to the district of Gujrat and ordered to go there at once.

He soon found that Gujrat was seventy miles away on the road to Peshawar; he managed to get a seat on the mail-cart, 'a small box on two wheels painted red', which was the only vehicle that so far could travel beyond Lahore. Perched on this, with an iron bar in the small of his back, he drove the seventy miles, over unmade roads, jolting, lurching and bumping, as fast as a wild driver could urge relays of half-broken ponies. It was bitterly cold — and there is a particularly penetrating bite about the night air of Northern India. Beames had been used to Calcutta for a year and had only Calcutta clothes. He must indeed have been, as he says, 'almost frozen through' when at last, after hours of 'the agonizing bumping and the piercing cold', the driver put him down in the small hours, 'bewildered and aching in every limb', at 'a little lonely post-house'. 'The night was so dark and the fog so thick that nothing could be seen, but we seemed to be standing on the edge of a broad flat plain, with no houses or trees.' But there was a policeman at the post-house and after exasperating wanderings — and once losing the way completely — he led Beames at last to a traveller's bungalow, where there was a bed on which 'I incontinently flung myself, dressed as I was, and fell asleep immediately'.

It was a temporary building, already beginning to tumble down. Everything in those first days in the Punjab was improvised; a district officer lived in tents while he built himself a house at his own expense, which he must sell to his successor. On this chilly morning, Beames woke to find himself 'greasy, dust-begrimed, aching all over, with a parched mouth and a swimming head'. He managed to get a cup of tea. It is easy to imagine that cup of tea, weak and greyish, reeking of wood-smoke, made with buffalo-milk and speckled with spots of butter-fat. It is a cup of tea that hangs on the palate; it is heavily sugared with that coarse sugar in which still lingers the fragrance of the boiling-pans in the corner of the field; it is a cup of tea that has been stirred outside the door with a grimy forefinger. But Beames drank it and felt better; he next got the attendant to persuade 'one even greasier than himself' to bring several jars of cold water. It must have been nearly freezing, but he poured it over his shoulders and 'scrubbed and deluged himself' till the aching left his limbs. Neither his grandfather nor his grandson would have done that.

The next step was to find the Deputy Commissioner, who was living in a kind of summerhouse with twelve doors that had belonged to some forgotten chief. He was Major Herbert Adams of the Guides; this was his first district and his first question to Beames was: 'What powers have you got?' He had hoped for an experienced assistant, with power to try important cases, and was naturally disappointed at getting a young man who hardly knew what powers were and did not understand Punjabi. However, he gave his Assistant breakfast, and then 'ignoring in true Punjab style the possibility of anyone being tired or wishing to do anything but work', strapped on his pistol, made Beames do the same, and led the way to court — 'a large, long, and not very hideous building in the middle of a plain'. ' "This is your Court," he said, ' "and these are your clerks; now go to work," and before I could open my mouth to ask him a single question, he had left the room.

' "These are the cases on your Honour's file — what are your orders?" asked a young Musulman in beautiful Delhi Hindustani with many courteous periphrases. I said, as by instinct, "Call up the first case," though what I was to do with it I knew as little as the man in the moon . . . He mentioned some names to a six-foot-high Sikh with a turban as big as a band-box, armed with sword and shield, who went out into the veranda and bawled loudly for some minutes. Then entered a dirty greasy shopkeeper who was the plaintiff . . . The defendant was a big powerful peasant with a black beard . . . Both these people spoke Punjabi, of which I could not understand one word . . .' but the clerk translated into Hindustani as they spoke and Beames wrote in English a summary of what they said, 'so I got on wonderfully well . . . I went to bed intensely tired but very much interested in and pleased with my day's experience'.

Beames, who was an unusually good linguist, soon learnt to speak Punjabi fluently; he passed simultaneously the first and second parts of the prescribed examinations in language, law and procedure; he acquired the powers Adams had hoped he would have. And by degrees 'all the native nobility and gentry of the district came to call on me and finding I liked their society, used to drop in of an evening and sit talking for hours. With their swords across their knees they would tell me long stories of their adventures in war and foray under Ranjit Singh, their beloved old Maharaja. Barring their love of brandy, which was excessive, these old lions with their long beards were very good company and I learnt a great deal about the people, their ideas and feelings from them. They are a fine manly race and in those days at least were very friendly to their European conquerors. The majority of the population could still remember the tyranny and oppression of native rule and contrasted it with the justice and security of our rule.'

Adams was succeeded by Hardinge, whom Beames liked better and of whom he always speaks with affection. Hardinge kept six horses, Beames two, and 'we were in the saddle by five in the morning and worked on horseback for two or three hours, riding about inspecting police-stations, roads and bridges and public buildings under construction, tree-planting, ferry-boats, settling disputes about land and property between villagers, and such-like business. Or we would walk, with our horses led behind us, through the narrow lanes of the ancient town accompanied by a crowd of police officers, overseers and others, giving orders for sanitary improvements, repairing roadways and drains, opening out new streets, deciding disputes . . .' As Beames was generally in court from ten to six, this made a stiff day, but the administration was simple. 'There was no law in the Punjab in those days. Our instructions were to decide all cases by the light of common-sense and our own sense of what was just and right.'

Two years after he had left England, his fiancée followed Beames. They met at Bulandshahr, near Delhi, in a friend's house and were married there; the bridegroom says nothing of any trepidation on either part though — after two years apart and a journey half way round the world, after crossing Egypt and sailing down the Red Sea, after three weeks' weary travelling from Calcutta, after *dak-garis* and *dak*-bungalows, meeting now among strangers and in so strange a world the young man to whom so much had happened since she saw him last — she, surely, must have passed some anxious hours. Whatever she thought or felt, they were married and she was induced, reluctantly and with some misgivings as to the modesty of it, to put aside her crinoline for a skirt and so make room for her husband in the dak-gari. They spent two days' honeymoon at a travellers' bungalow in Ambala — to which the English equivalent would be perhaps the waiting-room at Basingstoke — and then he must hurry back to his district.

It was a very happy marriage, though of course it included disappointments. The District Magistrate being summoned out of the district at short notice, his assistant had to ride in twenty miles from camp to headquarters; his wife rode with him and there was a miscarriage. 'The ignorance of matters relating to their health when married in which many young Englishwomen are brought up often leads in India . . . to disastrous consequences. My wife did not know that in her condition she ought not to ride and a long and tedious illness was the consequence. We had only the Bengali doctor at our station and she shrank from consulting him . . .' The same tale, in almost the same words, could be heard from one young wife after another till the end. Later, Mrs. Beames lost her first live child ten days after its birth, owing to injury to the head, caused, Beames believed, by the carelessness of a military surgeon whom he describes as idle and drunken.

Here pause to think for a moment of the Victorian girl, ignorant of her own body and often ashamed of her instincts, alone with the young husband she hardly knows and who is usually as ignorant as herself, thousands of miles from home, surrounded by people utterly alien in upbringing. The gossiping of servants, the wondering eyes of villagers, the publicity that in tent life is inescapable for every act of daily routine — all this must have been repugnant to her, even when things were at their smoothest.

And things were seldom smooth for long. Civilians were always moving and seem to have taken no account of the seasons. In his unpublished memoirs, Colonel Henry Urmston, soldier Deputy Commissioner in the Punjab, speaks of a journey made with his young wife from Mainpuri near Cawnpore to Peshawar, some five hundred miles. It took three weeks, in the burning heat of June, and was nearly all accomplished in a litter carried by men in relays; they did thirty or forty miles a night and were supposed to rest by day, but often at dawn there were still twelve miles to go before the resting-place — twelve miles of jolting, over tracks that in the latter part were rocky and precipitous, under the searing sun. Their first child was born less than two months after that journey. And some years afterwards, at Bannu, Urmston writes: 'My wife was out with me in camp at the time. We had been enjoying the open fertile country and were encamped for the day and night at a large village called Abba Khail (see my sketch) near some fine *Bair* trees and here the little stranger appeared . . .' taking them, apparently, quite by surprise, although this was the seventh. But the doctor was only fourteen miles away and he seems to have arrived soon after the event. A few days later they moved into headquarters, 'by easy stages' one is glad to learn.

Beames and his wife were not to spend all their life in the Punjab. He was a man of forthright opinions, which he did not hesitate to express; witness his views already quoted on John Lawrence.[1] He implies that his view of Lawrence was taken by everyone in the Punjab, and no doubt there were some who to some extent agreed, but there can be still less doubt that Beames expressed his sentiments both more openly and more strongly than most. Perhaps he was also felt to have married too soon, while his dislike of soldier civilians was open and strongly expressed. He says that the military men in civil employ were 'harsh and stuck-up and overbearing and introduced military ideas of subordination instead of the genial brotherly relations which subsisted between members of our own service'. He adds himself that no one felt this so strongly as he did; others seem to have worked together without jealousy, indeed without much thought of whether they had begun at Haileybury or Addiscombe. But Beames thought the soldiers had had to intrigue and fawn for civil employ; he told his own superior that he felt like St. Paul before the chief captain who 'with a great sum obtained this freedom'. 'But I', said Beames, 'was free born.' It is not really surprising that he was transferred from the Punjab.

[1] See *The Founders*, part III, chap. x, p. 338.

2 . PLANTERS AND POLICE

Beames was at once aware of differences when he arrived in Behar, still part of the Presidency of Bengal. Society was more formal; 'people were friendly but a little stiff and punctilious about calling and invitations. At Gujrat, Hardinge would say, "Come and dine to-night and bring your dinner with you . . ." Here they sent us written invitations and requested the pleasure . . .' In work the contrast was even greater. Here the permanent settlement had been made in Cornwallis's day with the *zamindar*, and only gradually was the idea spreading that the Government need be concerned with anyone else. The protection of the cultivator against the zamindar kept pace fairly well with factory legislation and the control of child labour in England. 'When I spoke to my new Collector, Bayley, about the welfare of the peasant class . . . he laughed at me and said it was no business of ours; the zamindar had a right to do what he liked with his ryots.'

This was a change from the Punjab, and again, 'in Bengal, before you could issue an order, you had to find a section of an Act or Regulation empowering you to do so. In the Punjab you did so because you thought it was the proper thing to do . . .' Poor Beames was constantly in trouble for his Punjabi zeal, for his habit of going and looking at things and for 'taking the law into his own hands'. But he came into his own when the Indian Penal Code and the Criminal Procedure Code were introduced into Bengal in 1862. They had been first drafted by Macaulay's Committee thirty years before and now at last replaced what Beames found an 'inefficient intricate chaos'. The Bengal civilians, and still more no doubt the pleaders, liked the old system because they had learnt their way about it; they disliked the new codes. But Beames knew them and preferred them; his seniors came to his court to see the new procedure.

It was an interesting time because a new service, too, was coming into existence, the Police. There was a new Act, the Police Act of 1861, which introduced a uniform system that was gradually to be extended to the whole of British India. The old system had varied from district to district, but usually it had been based on the *darogha* or station officer, a man who was answerable for about fifteen or twenty square miles of country to the District Magistrate. It was the darogha's own business to enlist and discipline his force of a dozen or half a dozen *barkandazes* — literally lightning-throwers, gunmen, the forerunners of constables. Except when the district officer was actually in his area, the darogha was very much his own master.

All this was now to be changed. The police force was to be a provincial army, subject to the civil government of the province of course, but recruited and trained much as soldiers. To each district there was to be a Superintendent of Police, with a hierarchy of deputy superintendents and inspectors. The station officer, the darogha, did not disappear, but he became a sub-inspector subject to regular training and frequent inspection. It was obviously an improvement, for the Magistrate had never had the time to look after the police properly and the people must have suffered much more from their rapacity before there was a Superintendent.

The Superintendent was required to be a man of parts. He had first to recruit, train and discipline his men, build up their physical strength, their self-confidence and their integrity — much the work of a regimental soldier in peace. He must also be a shrewd judge of his officers. He would not see them very often; he had to leave them to act on their own responsibility, he must not stifle their initiative but must encourage them by constant praise, yet they must live in dread of his censure, must know that they would be detected if they lied to him or tried to conceal a tyranny.

Half the crimes reported to the police in India are fabrications; they are meant to get someone else into trouble or to provide an alibi or a defence for some anticipated counter-charge. There is in common use a Hindustani word defined in the dictionary as 'timely preparation' — but it is used only in connexion with crimes or domestic misdemeanours. Before he acts, a man will prepare his defence and make his witnesses word-perfect; the moment he has finished battering his enemy on the head he will hurry his witnesses to the police-station and lodge his complaint against that same enemy for a premeditated assault. The police officer must weigh this report and decide what to do.

If the case is genuine, or there seems no way of proving it is not, he has to make up his mind who is to be the criminal and to find — or at least produce — proof that will satisfy a judge. It is an exceptional police sub-inspector who is much concerned as to whether his proof is true in itself; for an ordinary conscience it is enough if the proof points to the right man and does not fall to pieces in court. The judge or magistrate has then to decide in the first place whether a crime took place at all. If it did, he has next to make up his mind whether he is confronted by the true criminal and true evidence, by the true criminal and bogus evidence, or by a criminal and evidence alike irrelevant to what happened.

The Superintendent of Police has to sift that evidence before it goes to court and to reckon what the judge's or magistrate's reaction will be. He needs to some extent the judicial mind. He needs the quick detective's mind. He must be a trainer. His men must fear him without being frightened. And last, he must be something of a diplomat to live beside the District Magistrate.

In 1861, the District Magistrate handed over to the Superintendent of Police some of his old functions. But he remained responsible for everything that happened in his district and yet acquired a colleague not a subordinate. The Superintendent was responsible for the discipline of his force; the district officer was his director in matters of wide policy, not his superior. The one could not order the other to move a constable. There were bound to be occasions when the Magistrate disbelieved a case the Superintendent thought genuine. And in every district there were plenty of people anxious to play off Superintendent against Magistrate. They would make skilful insinuations to one against the subordinates of the other. They would watch anxiously for the least sign of a rift. Altogether, it was an arrangement peculiarly English which worked on the whole very well. When there was pettiness or spite on one side, things were difficult, but usually there was enough generosity on the other to make up for it.

This new arrangement began while Beames was in Behar and he has a good deal to say about the ludicrous attempts of the old-fashioned darogha to conform to the new pattern of a smart young officer of the Royal Irish Constabulary. It was as though Dogberry had been suddenly posted to Scotland Yard. The daroghas of the old type, says Beames, 'ruled as little kings in their own jurisdiction and reaped a rich harvest of bribes from all classes'. He describes 'a good specimen of the class, . . . a tall portly Mohammedan, grey-bearded, with a smooth sleek look, crafty as a fox, extremely polished in manner, deferential to his superiors, but haughty and tyrannical to his inferiors. With his huge scarlet turban laced with gold, his sword hung from a gold embroidered baldric, spotless white clothes and long riding boots, he bestrode a gaunt roan horse with grey eyes, a pink nose, and a long flowing tail . . .' 'The old daroghas', he goes on, 'were often splendid detectives and they certainly knew all the criminals and suspicious characters.'

And his first Superintendent is just as clear a picture. 'The higher officers of the new service . . . were all English and mostly gentlemen. They had not the faintest or most rudimentary idea of their duties . . . the Indian Government in those days acted on the assumption that military men were fit for any duties and were apparently not required with their regiments . . .' Beames was expected to introduce the new system, 'aided, or rather hindered, by the new Superintendent, Major Francis Crossman, . . . about the most absolutely unfitted man for such a post that one could imagine . . . a tall handsome soldierly man, a perfect *beau sabreur*, extravagant, witty and wild.' Beames tired of urging Crossman to enlist recruits and set about it himself. When he had collected a batch, he would go to find Crossman 'playing cards with his friends, drinking brandy and soda and singing French songs to his guitar. If I did succeed in getting him to ride to the parade-ground he would glance scornfully at my recruits, make one or two very witty and very indecent jokes in excellent Hindustani which set them all laughing, and ride away without rejecting or approving any of them. . . .'

Beames was District Officer at Champaran, the home of indigo-planters, made famous by Gandhi sixty years later; the planters expected the District Magistrate to dance to their tune. Beames was not a man to shrink from a fight but 'it was not', he says, 'from mere lust for power that I insisted on being master in my own district . . . but because the district was a sacred trust delivered to me by Government, and I was bound to be faithful to that charge. I should have been very base had I from love of ease or wish for popularity sat idly by and let others usurp my place and my duties. Ruling men is not a task that can be performed by *le premier venu* and though I was young at it, still I had five years' training and experience prefaced by a liberal education, while these ex-mates of merchant ships and *ci-devant* clerks in counting-houses had had neither.'

The indigo-planter's hold on his *ryots* carries one back to the days of Bolts. The planter let land to peasants on condition that they agreed not only to pay rent but to grow indigo on a quarter of their land. This they must sell to him. He gave them an advance which he was careful they should never repay in full. Thus they were his debtors as well as his tenants.

Soon after Beames came to Champaran one of these villagers refused to sow indigo. The planter sent men who ploughed up the land round the peasant's hut, sowed it, fenced it with a hedge of thorns, and told him that if he set foot on it he would be sent to gaol for trespass. They set watchers. The man and his family could not even go to the well for water. After two days, when no food was left in the house, he escaped by night, eluding the watchers; he lay hidden till daylight, then made his way to Beames and told his story. Beames decided that this was wrongful confinement under the Indian Penal Code and issued a summons against the planter. The planter 'who was as great a coward as he was a bully' paid compensation and ceased to molest the peasant.

This is one story typical of the years after the Mutiny. G. O. Trevelyan found 'not a single non-official person in India . . . who would not consider the sentiment that we hold India for the benefit of the inhabitants of India a loathsome un-English piece of cant'. But the majority of civilians did hold that sentiment and there was sharper feeling between planters and magistrates now than at any other time. There was the Rudd case, when the English overseer of a planter brutally, and with no provocation worth the name, beat and finally shot dead the man who kept sheep and goats in the compound. The Calcutta press had been clamorous a few years earlier against anyone who spoke of clemency, although the offence might be no more than giving shelter to a brother who had belonged to a mutinous regiment. They now clamoured no less loudly, demanding mercy for Rudd in terms of nauseating hypocrisy, but really on the sole ground that he was English and his victim Indian. He was hanged, the Viceroy and the official world refusing to tamper with justice on racial grounds.

There was too the case of the *Nil Durpan*, the Mirror of Indigo. This was a vernacular play which was translated into English by one Long, a missionary. The play stated the point of view of the peasant forced to grow indigo at a price that did not pay him. In the course of the play, the wife of a peasant says to another village woman:

'Moreover, the wife of the planter, in order to make her husband's case strong, has sent a letter to the magistrate since it is said that the magistrate hears her words most attentively.'

'I saw the lady,' replies the other, 'She has no shame at all. When the magistrate goes riding about the villages, the lady also rides on horseback with him. Riding a horse! . . .'

The planter's Association brought proceedings against Mr. Long on this score and others. This particular passage was described by his Lordship the Judge as filthy; he approached the whole subject with sorrow and disgust and asked the jury to consider whether it was not intended as a reproach on the whole middle class of the women of England. Mr. Long was imprisoned and fined, and the case was one more cause for estrangement between planters and civilians. In this, as in other matters, the Lord Chief Justice of Bengal, fresh from England, was uncompromisingly for the planters, while the civilian magistrates and judges, the Haileybury men, like Beames, were on the side of the cultivator.

Beames indeed may well stand for his generation. Pugnacious, arrogant if you like, outspoken, swift to condemn, he was warm-hearted, steadfast in friendship and love, honest and courageous, hot in defence of the oppressed. Later, in Orissa, where he spent the greater part of his service, he found the orders of the Government of Bengal harsh and oppressive. There was a tax on salt and orders against illicit salt-making and smuggling. But in one part of the district an old woman had little more to do than step out of her hut to pick up the salt for her morning rice. She of course would be dragged fifty miles to court and fined; the smuggler on a large scale could never be caught. The police would spread virtuous hands; no, they had not rounded up the gang but they had to their credit the conviction of ten old women last month. Beames disobeyed the orders of Government; he would not have such offences punished and he would not reward the police for bringing them in. He was called sharply to order, took the chance and said what he thought. After long correspondence, the rules were changed; such people were exempted.

3. THOSE ON HIGH

Beames shows no interest in shooting or pigsticking, spending his leisure instead on his *Comparative Grammar of the Modern Aryan Languages of India*. This was unusual and, although outspokenness and independence were general in the service, Beames did carry them further than most; he was moved from Champaran, which borders Nepal, because he offended the Viceroy — John Lawrence — by the freedom of his comment on Nepal police administration. But, with these two exceptions, Beames comes very near being that strange abstraction, the average district officer.

'I was in fact called upon to act and not to act at the same time,' he says on one occasion, 'a false position in which Government is fond of placing officers by way of shuffling off its own responsibility, a regular Secretariat trick.' The average district officer says something like that very often and inveighs with equal vigour against instructions which leave no discretion to the man on the spot. On his lonely peak of responsibility, he is impatient of control; no one else understands his district; 'the Government' wastes his time by interfering and it is an intolerable bore having to explain how inapplicable their ink-fed, paper-nourished schemes are bound to be.

Beames is contemptuous, for instance, of tours by Lieutenant-Governors, which are expensive, encourage the great man to think he knows something when he is utterly ignorant, and leave the district officer with heavy arrears of more important work. Perhaps he was biased, for it was during such a tour that he committed his worst escapade as an *enfant terrible*, making a speech — late at night — in unmistakable parody of the Lieutenant-Governor, Sir Richard Temple. Sir Richard himself had gone to bed, but it reached his ears.

Temple was always Beames's *bête noire* but then he does not really care for Lieutenant-Governors as a class; his modified praise goes only to George Campbell, a vigorous innovator, who instead of: 'His Honour is constrained to express his dissatisfaction . . .' would write: 'The Lieutenant-Governor abhors this kind of muddle and will punish severely anyone who behaves in this absurd way in future.' It is amusing to recognize Beames's Lieutenant-Governors in the verses of 'poor witty Frank Bignold, my predecessor at Balasore, a brilliantly clever man but so unpunctual and unmethodical as to be the ruin of any district that might be in his charge'.

> When Halliday held merry sway,
>   And fiddling was in fashion,
> My Stradivarius I would play
>   For music was my passion;
> Nor hushed my string till Grant was king
>   And indigo unquiet
> Then boldly rushed into the ring
>   The champion of the ryot!

> *For this is law that I'll maintain,*
>   *As ably as I can, Sir,*
> *That whatsoever king shall reign,*
>   *I'll be the rising man, Sir.*

The mere swing of Bignold's verse takes one so fast that it is easy to miss the fact that he has thrown in from sheer exuberance an internal rhyme not to be found in *The Vicar of Bray*. But he does need footnotes. F. J. Halliday had been the first Lieutenant-Governor of Bengal, taking office after the 1853 Act was passed to relieve the Governor-General of local administration. John Peter

Grant was Canning's right-hand man in the Mutiny, and was always champion of the under-dog; he had been reviled as a 'humanity-pretender' or 'white Pandy' perhaps even more bitterly than Clemency Canning by the planters and merchants; like Metcalfe he went on to be Governor of Jamaica, where he reformed the whole administration of the island. Both Halliday and Grant had been Haileybury men in the 'twenties; their interests and Cecil Beadon's are clear enough from the verses.

> When Beadon on the däis sat,
>   I shifted my position,
> Collecting sheep and oxen fat
>   To grace his exhibition,
> And when he broke the court clerk's yoke
>   I felt the inspiration,
> And learned the brogue of every rogue
>   Who filed an application.

Nor is any explanation needed for William Grey, who became Lieutenant-Governor in 1867, and who also went on to govern Jamaica. But Sir George Campbell, the fierce innovator, does need a footnote; he had made Bengal ring with his castigation of an unfortunate young man whom he caught taking two 'puppy-dogs' for a walk before breakfast instead of riding to inspect the scene of a dispute. The ingenuous youth made things worse by saying he thought he might spend his time as he liked 'out of office hours'. But Campbell was a Punjabi and, of course, there were no office hours for a keen officer. He was always on duty.

> When Beadon's day had passed away
>   And Grey assumed his station
> With pen in hand I took my stand
>   On the Higher Education.
> But now that lotteries are put down
>   I cut my friends who gamble
> And rush my puppy-dogs to drown
>   And win a smile from Campbell.

> In framing rules for primary schools,
>   In rural exploration,
> My active mind shall seek and find
>   Congenial occupation.

Then George shall be my king till he
   Shall seek St. Stephen's lobby
When I shall feel an equal zeal
   For his successor's hobby.

For this is law . . . etc

Bignold dealt more fully with Campbell's reforming zeal in admirable heroic couplets:

He found us slow, self-satisfied, serene
The tape-tied captives of a set routine —

and at once he set about introducing into Bengal some of the spirit which Thomason in the North-West had passed on to the Punjab. Campbell told the Bengal civilians they should:

Mount, seek the curdling gore, the stiffening corse,
Press the pale culprit in his first remorse;
Pounce on the quarry ere the scent be cold!
Strangle the lie before the lie be told!
Then, swift remounting, to your law courts scour —
To smile on suitors at the usual hour.

All this energy made Bignold sigh for the day:

When 'neath the punkah-frill the Court reclined
When Court clerks wrote and Judges only signed;
Or, lordlier still, beneath a virgin space
Inscribed their names and hied them to the chase.

He mourns, too, for that well-known figure, the Magistrate of yore,

Prompt with the rifle, niggard of the pen,
By manly deeds he won the hearts of men;
His watchful eye each rival chieftain viewed
And oftener calmed than curbed the rising feud . . .
Nor sought to substitute with ruthless hand
The alien systems of a distant land. . . .

That honoured figure, when

Law was the means and justice was the end

had dispensed justice beneath a tree

And guided less by training than by tact
Could pounce unerring on a trail of fact.

But now circulars from Calcutta inform the Magistrate that the right proportion of convictions to cases tried is just half.

> I must take up some cases; mine the care
> To mend the general average yet be fair;
> For those on High will hardly deign to know
> The harmless arts which flourish here below.
> Ho! Minions, bring me fifty chaukidars
> Whose beats deserted to the midnights stars
> Cry out for vengeance — and a trifling fine
> Shall meet the justice of their case — and mine.

All this is good-tempered enough, but Bignold becomes bitter, as Beames does, on Richard Temple. Beames had first met Sir Richard in the Punjab when the great man had taken the credit — according to Beames — for a bridge of boats built by his newly arrived junior. He had come in more recently for a good deal of criticism in the service over a scare of famine which proved very expensive in 1874. The famine, it is true, was averted, but to the rank and file of the service in Bengal, trained in a strict economy, Temple's prodigality was shocking. An outside observer, Lord Roberts, the Deputy Quartermaster General, speaks of his unbounded resource and energy, but he too shakes his head over the cost. 'He set aside', wrote Beames, 'the opinions of Sir George Campbell and the Collectors of the afflicted districts and followed his own unaided judgment. In his usual theatrical way, he rode at the rate of 50 or 60 miles a day through the districts, forming as he said an opinion on the condition of the people and the state of the crops . . . He would sit down at night after one of these wild scampers and write a vainglorious minute in which he stated that he had that day fully examined such and such tracts and come to the conclusion that so much grain, usually three to four times as much as was really wanted, would be required to feed the people . . .' And Bignold wrote:

> My facile eye can best descry
>   That famine's still impending
> And none but Dick, through thin and thick,
>   Can steer us to its ending.
> Transactions nice in Burmah rice,
>   Colossal cash advances,
> Must needs demand the subtle hand
>   That guided our finances.

'In disgust at this proceeding,' says Beames — but it was genuinely on account of ill-health — 'Campbell resigned and Temple was made Lieutenant-Governor . . . and the reign of trumpet-blowing (his own) began.' 'And nimble Dick? . . .' asked Bignold:

> A portent he in hero-worship's line
> Himself adorer, prophet, priest and shrine;
> And who can better an ovation claim
> Than he whose proper hands prepare the same?

And when Temple leaves Bengal to be Governor of Bombay, he continues:

> Lament, O Muse, the inexorable day
> That dawned on Temple's transit to Bombay!
> The poet loses what the public gain
> And Satire starves when such as Eden reign.

Bignold may have been right in thinking Ashley Eden a better Lieutenant-Governor; but though Temple was not liked by district officers in Bengal, he had consistently won the praise of his seniors. His mother was a Rivett-Carnac, daughter of Sir James, Governor of Bombay, and as everyone knows, 'if there were a single loaf of bread in all India, it would be divided between the Plowdens, the Trevors, the Beadons and the Rivett-Carnacs'. He was at Rugby under Arnold before passing out first from Haileybury; he went to the North-West in 1847 and did some settlement work at Muttra and Allahabad; he caught the eye of Thomason, and was among the picked men sent on to the Punjab. He wrote later that Thomason's farewell letter 'still shines like the evening star in my recollection'. He caught John Lawrence's eye too and was secretary to the Punjab Board and later to John himself, drafting the great reports on the Punjab administration; with less than ten years' service he was Commissioner of Lahore.

He caught the eye of Dalhousie and of Canning, and went to the Government of India as assistant to Wilson, the Finance Member who came from England to settle India's finances. Next he went on special missions to Burma and Hyderabad and in 1862, only fifteen years in India, was the first Chief Commissioner of the Central Provinces. Municipalities, dispensaries, primary schools, district boards, dripped from his pen; he created, built, endowed, set up and vivified. His energy was awe-inspiring. He went everywhere and saw everything.

For Dick can ride in one revolving moon
On horse, cart, camel, railway and balloon. . . .

'The country', wrote Alfred Lyall, 'is very backward and he is determined to shove it forward; the country resists inertly as long as it can, tumbles back as often as Temple props it up, and when forcibly driven forward runs the wrong way, like a pig going to Cork market . . .' Five years he was in the Central Provinces, brilliantly served by Bernard and Elliott, men of immense industry and ability, who came near Lawrence's ideal of governing machines, and served, too, though less whole-heartedly, by Alfred Lyall, who at a saunter, one hand in his pocket, wondering if it was all worth while, could still keep abreast of the cavalcade.

After the Viceroy and the Commander-in-Chief, the two most important posts in the Government of India were Finance Member and Foreign Secretary. Temple held both. The first post in the Political Department was Resident at Hyderabad. Temple held that. He held charge in succession of three Indian provinces, the Central Provinces, Bengal and Bombay. It was characteristic, though, that he left Bombay before the arrival of his successor. He wanted to be home in time to stand for Parliament in his native Worcester:

And fearing lest his candidature fail
Could hurry Worcester-ward and beat the Mail — .

His candidature did fail on that occasion, but later he was member for Evesham for seven years and subsequently for Kingston. The House of Commons, a stern tribunal, 'heard him with impatience', but his books were successful. He edited Peter Mundy with loving and scholarly care. He wrote with piety and affection of the famous men who had preceded him, notably of Thomason. He became a Privy Councillor and a Fellow of the Royal Society.

Yet the judgment of his juniors on this brilliant man was harsh. There is an intimate verdict, not necessarily that of history, often short-sighted, often far from the public's, pronounced by the men of his own profession on every member of a service who reaches high rank. It may not always be just but it does as a rule enshrine a truth. Among Englishmen, that verdict sometimes forgives stupidity, is suspicious alike of brilliance and of unremitting industry, often admires idleness if backed by wit. But it is merciless towards self-seek-ing, hypocrisy and insincerity. A dash of those qualities must have been mixed with much in Temple that was admirable; Beames, the clodhopping collector, his nose to the ground, his vision limited but honest as the day — he and fifty like him were aware of it and their verdict is one that cannot be ignored.

CHAPTER III

MAN OF LETTERS

ALFRED LYALL was an almost exact contemporary of John Beames, but two men similarly educated could hardly be less alike. Lyall wrote many letters and never read them through, so that they stand as they flowed from his pen and show the man he was. But except to close friends and the people he loved he did not reveal himself easily. To some, indeed, he might seem a singularly unsatisfactory character, distrustful of his own powers and judgment, indecisive because he saw both sides of almost every question, too much a poet to be an administrator, too much a scholar to be a statesman, too diffident of himself, his interests too diffuse, to win complete success in any field.

It would not be an entirely valid judgment, because he kept most of his doubts for his letters and his poems; his work was usually decisive enough. He seems, all the same, strangely out of place in Victorian India, a man remote from the fervour of the Lawrences, the self-assertive energy of Temple, the matter-of-fact simplicity of such a soldier as Roberts, the pugnacious common sense of Beames. He did not win the love of all who served under him as Thomason or Henry Lawrence did; indeed, till they knew him well, his juniors seem to have been awed and ill-at-ease with him. But those who did know him felt an affection which was quite free from false hero-worship. What they admired was the man himself; it was because of his ability to see both sides of every question and to smile ruefully at himself that they loved him. When he retired, the same qualities made him much sought after by people in London who would not have cared for the society of John Lawrence or Richard Temple.

Alfred Lyall was seven years at Eton, going on at eighteen to Haileybury, where he did not particularly distinguish himself. He was posted to the North-Western Provinces and arrived in 1856, the year before the Mutiny. He seems to have enjoyed those first months before the storm broke. 'Everybody is so much more cordial and easy of access here', he writes, 'and when I look back upon my experience of English society I think that at home you are horribly frigid and formal . . .' And he enjoyed the vagrant life which at first seems such a release from the ordered ways of England, from the drawing-room on Sunday afternoon, set times for meals and muddy boots that must be taken off in the back porch. 'I have only one chair of my own and but three teacups', he writes, 'but I have two horses and four guns . . .' He rejoiced too in the leisure the first year often gives for reading. Shakespeare, Herodotus, Cervantes, Gibbon, came first in his list.

All this was swept away by the Mutiny. After some stirring days in Bulandshahr, Lyall made his way to Meerut and joined the Khaki Risala, the Dusty Squadron, with whom he saw a good deal of mixed fighting and much mounted outpost work. He had a horse shot under him, killed a man in battle; he seems to have lost himself in the moment to an extent that for him was never again possible. There could be no two sides to this question; it was life or death. He need think no more but must ride, fight, eat, sleep, take cover and shoot before the other man.

He looked back afterwards to those four months in the summer of 1857 as the best in his life. They were months of burning heat, desperate news and daily peril, but when it was all over he found things very flat. 'I look forward with dismay to ten years of peaceful office life', he wrote, but added that he was ready to pay the price, for 'the Mutiny was worth ten years of a young man's life'. His was the kind of nature that in repose must look inwards and does not particularly like what it sees. Years afterwards, sniffing the battle again in the Second Afghan War, he said: 'I should like to go myself and go I will soon, again to see the faces of men hard-set with excitement and danger, instead of sitting here opening telegrams. . . .'

He married a wife who excelled 'in every muscular sport'. She could drive her arrow into the gold right up to the notch; at croquet, at riding, indeed, 'at everything a woman can do as well as a man', she was, he said, better than he was. One pictures her not always understanding him with her intellect but perhaps for that very reason giving him the support he needed, simply by her comely unquestioning presence. There is an incident, described as typical of both, years later when Lyall was about to start from Calcutta for Peshawar, a journey of a thousand miles. As the time of departure came nearer, he grew more and more depressed and uneasy. She asked if he would like her to come with him as far as Allahabad, five hundred miles perhaps. 'I wish you would,' he replied, brightening at once. She disappeared and came back in a few minutes, ready to start. His melancholy vanished and he left for the station cheerful and contented.

In 1864 they were at Agra, then capital of the North-Western Provinces. They were enjoying a round of dinner-parties and Cora's triumphs at archery and croquet, when the news came that Lyall was chosen to go to Temple's new Chief Commissionership in the Central Provinces. It meant promotion and there could be no refusal. The young wife with her baby must pack and be off at ten days' notice on a journey which took three hot and dusty weeks, for there was still no help from the railway between Agra and Hoshangabad in Berar.

In their new loneliness, he missed the society of Agra as much as she did; there was nothing of the Puritan in Lyall's make-up. 'Plain John Lawrence' was far from his ideal; 'I do not like marching because it disarranges my book and papers', he wrote. And — strangest heresy of all — he believed that too much work was a mistake. At Agra, 'I could ride across country after a jackal with the station pack in the morning, work all day and go to a party in the evening; here I can only get excitement out of my work . . .' And he did not think this a good thing; he was unashamedly civilized.

'I cling like a pagan,' he wrote about this time, 'to youth and strength and the flying years.' And in another mood he spoke of 'the dreary desert of scepticism into which I am wandering . . . it seems to me that we overrate altogether the importance of the human race'. It was the attitude of a man not likely to join uncritically in the scramble to return the greatest number of primary schools and municipalities. 'My real sympathies are not with a pushing go-ahead administration like Mr. Temple's.' 'I wish I could feel like so many people that I had a mission to do this or that, that ordinary business was a high and holy work — in short, that I could whip up more of the enthusiasm which others seem to feel. . . .'

Perhaps one reason for his doubts was an understanding of the Indian at once realistic and poetic. 'I have been much refreshed lately by talking with Raja Dinkar Rao', he writes. Gwalior's Premier had assured him 'that the natives prefer a bad native government to our best patent institutions, and I know he is right'. Again, he finds himself in disagreement with most of the ideas about British rule in India which he hears expressed. 'And the wildest as well as the shallowest notion of all seems to me that universally prevalent belief that education, civilization and increased material prosperity will reconcile the people of India to our rule.' He quotes de Tocqueville on *L'Ancien Régime* in refutation; it was when the burden became a little lighter that revolution came.

That is realism; his understanding of what an Indian might feel was intuitive and poetic. It is there in his poems again and again. His old Pindari, remembering the coloured days of his youth, dreams

> . . . Of a long dark march to the Jumna, of splashing across
> the stream,
> Of the waning moon on the water and the spears in the dim
> star-light, . . .
> Then the streak of the pearly dawn — the flash of a sentinel's
> gun,
> The gallop and glint of horsemen who wheeled in the level sun,
> The shots in the clear still morning, the white smoke's
> eddying wreath;
> Is this the same land that I live in, the dull dank air that I
> breathe?

So too Lyall's Rajput rebel knows what is in store for him:

> When the army has slain its fill,
> When they bid the hangman cease,
> They will beckon us down from the desert hill
> To go to ourhomes in peace.

> To plough with a heavy heart
> And, of half our fields bereft,
> 'Gainst the usurer's oath and the lawyer's art
> To battle that some be left.

He would rather die than face that.

It might be supposed that holding such views Lyall would inevitably lose the confidence of such a chief as Temple. But he was too profound an agnostic to express disagreement; Temple might after all be right. Lyall did his work and did it excellently. At thirty-three he was a permanent Commissioner, with four of his seniors under his orders and a salary of three thousand pounds a year. But he was uneasy, for with all his doubts he was ambitious, less for power than for intellectual pleasure. He was no stoic. Very early in his career he had written how much he regretted 'the society of clever and accomplished men'. 'I appreciate intensely all intellectual pleasures', he had written about the same time. He did his work, he wrote his articles and they were accepted, but he felt he was slipping back. 'I was contracting a superstitious notion that I had got jammed into that corner for ever', he writes when in 1873, at thirty-eight, he was appointed Home Secretary to the Government of India.

This uneasiness was something of which he never rid himself. 'I do not make a first-class Secretary'; he wrote, 'the real habit and strength of my mind is reflection and when I have not the time to reflect and work out ideas I become bothered and dispirited . . .' He left the Government of India for a spell as Agent to the Governor-General in Rajputana; it was the post ranking next to Hyderabad in the hierarchy of the Political Department, and at forty-one would have seemed a prize indeed to most men. Lyall looked back wistfully to Simla and had moments when he felt as much on the shelf as Henry Lawrence had in the same post when sent there after the Punjab.

Yet Rajputana stirred him, as it was bound to. 'The whole feeling of the country is mediaeval,' he writes, 'the Rajput noblesse caracoles along with sword and shield, the small people crowd round with rags and rusty arms . . . I am afraid we do not altogether improve the nobles by keeping them from fighting . . .' He knew something of what the Rajput chief felt about the land he lived in and especially the nights:

> . . . after the long scorching days,
> When the hot wind hushes, and falling stays
> The clouds of dust, and stars are bright . . .

And at Mount Abu, the little hill-station where Honoria Lawrence had died, he was deeply aware of the isolated life of the English round him and the contrast with Indian life at the foot of the hill. 'The people who live here regularly can think very little of the deserts about Jodhpur whence I have come, where the cattle are dying from want of forage and they are praying to all their gods for a little rain, where you may see gaunt hard-looking men come riding in across the sands on camels with their matchlocks and water-skins slung beside them.'

He was four years in Rajputana, going back to the Government of India as Foreign Secretary in Lord Lytton's administration. He suited Lytton well, being admirably adapted by temperament to put every point of view to an impulsive masterful man who was naturally too quick to take decisions; perhaps because of a fundamental difference in character, they became not only colleagues but friends.

As Foreign Secretary, Lyall's main preoccupation was the North-West Frontier. Few men at this time realized that when they discussed the Frontier they were arguing about two distinct problems. It took Lyall's clear analytical gaze to perceive that the Frontier 'can be considered as a question of border management, affecting merely the peace of our frontier districts and their security from frontier raids . . .' And 'secondly, in a larger aspect, with regard to the defence of India against attack by a foreign European power . . .' Whichever aspect they were considering, men were inclined to fall into two rigid schools. 'Some consider the Indus valley our proper line of defence . . .' and would let the enemy experience all the hazard and tribulations of the difficult hill country, while 'Others think we ought to hold the mountain passes and meet by a vigorous offensive defence . . . any enemy who may venture to approach us.' Those who held the forward or mountain pass view on foreign defence also believed 'that we should encourage our officers to enter into close personal relations with the tribesmen and to enter their country and should endeavour in the course of time to establish permanent control over the tribes'. But the Indus, or close frontier school, on the other hand thought we should avoid all unnecessary interference.

The concern with Russia was natural. In 1846, two thousand miles had lain between the English frontier and the Russian; by the 'seventies this gap had come down to less than five hundred, in which the only power — and that a shaky one — was the Amir of Kabul. All parties shared the concern and probably all would have agreed with John Lawrence that St. Petersburg, not Kabul, was the place to talk to Russia. Lyall always believed that the first step was a firm understanding with the Russians, and lived to see in 1907 the kind of agreement he had hoped for. He never had any doubts, however, that the Second Afghan War was inevitable. The main object of Lord Lytton's Government was the security of the frontier, and that, in Lyall's view, was 'incompatible with the intrusion of any foreign influence into the great border state of Afghanistan'. Subsidies of money and arms having failed to prevent that intrusion, force alone remained. It may be imagined however what unhappiness it was to a man of Lyall's temperament to 'sit opening telegrams', to hear of disaster and loss of life which he tortured himself by thinking he might have prevented. And the use of force was in this case all the more to be regretted because the war could hardly have a satisfactory outcome. 'If we set up an Amir and leave him', he wrote, 'the people will roll him over in a month; if we leave without setting up anyone, there will be fierce and prolonged faction fighting throughout the land. . . .'

Lyall went on to be Lieutenant-Governor of the North-Western

Provinces, characteristically looking back over his shoulder and half-regretting that he had not instead accepted the portfolio of Finance with the Government of India. He felt out of things as a provincial governor, lonely in his grandeur and condemned to deal with domestic policies which he found on the whole boring. 'The wheels are revolving too fast', he said, and 'The more I get down again to the bottom of things, the nearer, as it were, to the tail of the actual plough, the more I see that the big Government people can only guess faintly and vaguely what will be the effect of their measures. One thing is sure; the natives all discuss our rule as a transitory state. . . .'

Lyall soon became accustomed and even reconciled to his exalted shelf. 'I like the old familiar up-country life of rising early, taking long rides, and seeing all sorts and conditions of natives', he writes from Lucknow. 'It suits me far better than toiling at the Secretarial oar.' And returning from a conference in Simla to Naini Tal, the summer capital of his provinces, he wrote: 'Simla itself has, after Naini Tal, a suburban and shoppy aspect; the woods and crags and lake of my petty capital are more to my mind. . . .'

He had always believed in the diversity of India, which he, like Bartle Frere, pictured as a congeries of states and provinces, differing from each other in their needs and in the stages of development they had reached. It followed that he thought the provinces should be left alone as much as possible within their own limited spheres, and he cultivated something of the district officer's jealous irritation at the ignorant interference of a central authority. But he conducted his warfare with an armament few district officers could command.

> Men who spar with Government need to back their blows
> Something more than ordinary journalistic prose,

as Kipling's Boanerges Blitzen discovered. Boanerges tried to follow Lyall's example,

> Only he did not possess, when he made the trial,
> Wicked wit of C — lv — n, irony of L — l.

It was that irony that taught the Simla secretariat to address the North-Western Provinces in the mood of an experienced terrier approaching a hedgehog already on the defensive.

It fell to Lyall to introduce to the Provinces Lord Ripon's proposals for Local Self-Government. There were already, over almost the whole of British India, committees for each district who were supposed to advise the District Magistrate about roads, education and bridges. They had started in most places without authority, because it had seemed sensible, before spending money, to take the advice of someone who might know where the shoe pinched. Later, legal authority was provided and some uniformity. Members were nominated by the Government on the advice of the District Magistrate; in most areas, they were landowners who had everything to gain by being in his good books. Such men were not likely to oppose him and few had the energy or ambition to give him much help. It was usually sufficient for him to explain his proposals swiftly in the vernacular to a silent but attentive committee. There was seldom enough for the proper provision of roads, and in his view roads and bridges usually came first; schools must make shift with what could be spared. The members of the committee would bow their heads. 'As the Presence orders', they would say. And that would usually be the extent of their advice.

Lord Ripon in 1882 suggested that there should everywhere be smaller committees, each dealing with one of the four, five or six sub-divisions which usually make up a district. The members would be elected and one of them would be chairman and carry out what was decided. Lord Ripon explained that he intended 'a measure of popular and political education' and he did not conceal his fear that the new boards would be less efficient than the old. He suggested; he left it to local governments to work out for themselves the application of the new principles.

Lyall, who considered himself a Radical in English politics, made on these proposals the characteristic comment that 'the general idea, if moderately developed, is good enough'. It was true that the existing district boards dealt with areas much too big. A small landowner could hardly be expected to weigh carefully the merits of a bridge forty miles away. But the more fundamental trouble was apathy and lack of education. If the young brother had been educated, he was away from home earning his living. The landowner himself seldom knew a word of any language but his own, and to him voting, public service and grants-in-aid were words that conveyed no meaning. The appointment of a pound-keeper — ah, that was something he could understand, and indeed there was the son of one of his tenants . . . To start a really live and active sub-divisional board with such material as this would have been a difficult task enough if there had been available for each sub-division an official with the spirit of a missionary who was determined to stand outside the board and yet to see that it did its work. But there were as yet no Indian officials with this kind of outlook, and, as for the English, there was barely one experienced man for every district, let alone for every sub-division, while it was of course by no means every man who could be expected to work in such a way.

Lyall devoted a good deal of time to a long resolution of his Government on this subject; his views were similar to those taken by the Punjab and both were accepted by Lord Ripon. The district board remained, with the district officer as chairman, but the other members were elected instead of nominated; the sub-divisional boards were introduced, but they were to be subordinate committees of the main board.

In the towns, too, almost from the beginning of British rule there had been some kind of semi-official committee to advise the district officer and later a nominated committee with legal powers. Now, from 1882 onwards, the members were most of them to be elected and were usually to elect their chairman. These municipal committees were far ahead of the district committees and often had several members prepared to give some constructive help; all the same, they usually elected the district officer as their chairman under the new dispensation.

Next in importance to the development of local self-government was the Oudh Rent Act, one step of many that were taken to protect the tenant against an unscrupulous landowner. In Oudh, the *taluqdars*, chiefs descended from Mogul officials, had been confirmed after the Mutiny in their vast estates, but it was a slow and laborious business to discover and register the rights of the sub-proprietors and tenants below them who, as in Bengal, formed a pyramid of intermediaries between the soil and the treasury. Gradually they were discovered and gradually the position of the tenant was strengthened. Lyall's Rent Act in Oudh was parallel to similar measures in the Punjab and Bengal.

One other incident of his six years as Lieutenant-Governor must be mentioned. An Englishman in India could until 1883 claim to be tried only by another Englishman, but by the 'eighties at least one Indian covenanted civilian was a District Judge and another was a District Magistrate. Lord Ripon proposed to sweep away the racial distinction by what was known as the Ilbert Bill. Provincial Governments were consulted; Lyall acquiesced in the justice of what to him must have seemed an almost academic problem, for in the North-West there were very few Englishmen who were not officials. But the proposal did not look academic in Behar or Bengal, where there were planters, some of them perhaps with uneasy consciences, all well aware that a false accusation by a disgruntled tenant can easily be made to sound true. There was an uproar in the Calcutta press, a sharp reversion to the language of 1858. Even Bignold, an educated man and an official, in one of his longest poems, could write:

> Woe to the blinded statesman
> Who truckles to the base
> And sets above the nobler,
> The feebler falser race,

with much more to the same effect. There was talk about rights won at Magna Carta but the truth was that the measure inflamed sharp racial feelings, at a time when the emergence of a Westernized upper class of Indians made the situation very delicate. In the end a compromise was framed by which a European could only be tried by a jury, of whom at least half must be his fellow-countrymen. Lyall changed his view on deeper reflection, believing that it had been inopportune to introduce the bill at that juncture; there was for a short time a coolness between himself and Ripon, who felt that he had been abandoned in adversity.

Lyall's time ended; he felt he had been able to help in some 'important steps towards a kind of provincial autonomy which I hold to be one of the cardinal points of our constitutional policy in India'. He did not believe that voting or Parliamentary institutions were likely to help Indians in any foreseeable future. He did believe — as how many had before — that Indians ought to hold more responsible positions. He had appointed the first Indian to the Allahabad High Court, writing privately at the same time: 'I want to push on the native wherever I can, our only chance of placing Government here upon a broad and permanent basis.' And again he had written, right at the beginning of his term of office: 'I intend to push forward the native, quietly and judgmatically, all through my time . . . what I want is time to acquire wide influence among the natives of the North-Western Provinces, so as to carry them with me in anything I may attempt.'

He left India and for fifteen years served in London on the Council of India, where he stood always for the devolution of power to provincial governments and for a progressive foreign policy based on an understanding with Russia. At first he found the Council: 'rather depressing . . . we have all rather the look of old hulks laid up in dock and are men who have said goodbye to active service . . . the distance and difference between London and India makes one feel as if looking at things as through a glass darkly and not face to face'. He became somewhat reconciled but always felt that 'one can prevent some mischief but do little good'. He refused 'he Governorship of the Cape, feeling perhaps that he had been long enough exiled from the pleasures that appealed to him. He liked talking to intelligent and well-informed men; he liked writing scholarly articles on Natural Religion for the *Quarterly*, and biographies of men so different as Tennyson and Warren Hastings. He frequented the Athenaeum and was constant at The Club, The Literary Society, Grant Duff's Breakfast Club and such gatherings; his life in retirement in fact was very like Macaulay's. His radicalism had almost vanished and he was now a Liberal Unionist, a strong free-trader but separated from Gladstone's Liberals by his views on imperial and foreign policy.

The last words on Lyall must be those of his pupil and biographer Durand, who is speaking of 'his quick warm sympathy for the chiefs and peoples of India'. 'His consistent teaching to us younger men was not to be hasty or hard, above all never to be contemptuous, but to recognize and admire all that was admirable even in those who opposed us . . .' To recognize and admire, yes, and also to smile; 'he always saw the amusing side of it, even if a man had got under his guard'. If all Englishmen had been like Lyall, we should perhaps never have been in India at all; empires are not made by men who see both sides of a question. But our presence would have been less of an irritant; there would have been fewer who wanted us to go.

CHAPTER IV

THE GUARDIANS

I. SELECTION

THE fifty years that follow the Mutiny make a period of which it is possible to generalize because there was very little change. On the map, the only addition was Upper Burma; there was the Second Afghan War, there was an unprovoked and unnecessary expedition to Tibet, but it cannot be said that these made much difference to history. Ruling Princes came a little closer under the Viceroy's control but there was no change of principle. The only hint that India was one day to be governed by Indians lay in Lord Ripon's Local Self-Government Acts and the slight enlargements of the Legislative Councils in 1893 — and these, to anyone used to the rapid changes of the twentieth century, do not seem revolutionary.

Most Englishmen still felt that the best government was that which interfered least with its subjects. To prevent foreign war and domestic strife, to keep famine and pestilence at bay, to let wealth grow naturally in the hands of the people, that was the ideal. In our own day there have been critics who have blamed the Victorians for not moving faster, but to themselves it seemed that they were living in a whirl of change and that the pace was too hot. And indeed the Government was doing much more than in England. That this must be so in India was explicitly recognized, even by J. S. Mill, but Viceroys and their Councillors were sometimes a trifle aghast when they contemplated how far they had gone on the road to socialism. They came gradually to own railways, to sell salt, to provide schools, to make rum and carpets.

It was ruled from above by a selected aristocracy, who believed they were acting disinterestedly for the general good. For their ideal of light but benevolent administration, the machinery now forged was admirably adapted. It was indeed in many ways curiously un-English; it had a premeditated logical air, as though worked out by a political philosopher in the study. Indeed, in many details it was very like the most celebrated of all such systems. Plato had entrusted his ideal state to a class of guardians specially trained and chosen. They were to be persuaded that the god who created them had mixed gold in their composition to distinguish them from the common people; the older men among them were to rule over the younger, those being chosen for promotion who 'through their whole life have done what they thought advantageous to the state'; they were not to become householders and cultivators instead of guardians and were therefore to own no property; they were to be the repositories of the wisdom and courage of the state. And Socrates asks, in Plato's book:

'Will you assign to the guardians of the state the adjudication of law-suits?'

'Certainly.'

'Will not their judgments be guided, above everything, by the desire that no one may appropriate what belongs to others, nor be deprived of what is his own?'

That was the Platonic ideal, a state in which property does not change hands, in which anything new, even in music or poetry, is prohibited, in which a rigid caste system keeps each man to his own function. In India, the caste system was there ready-made and it is odd that the four original castes of the Hindus, sages, warriors, traders and menials, correspond with Plato's. The Indian Brahmans of the nineteenth century however were not at all like Plato's guardians; a new caste was needed to complete the state, and the English supplied it. The English Guardians certainly believed there was something in their composition that distinguished them from the people they ruled; they were forbidden to own land in India or to take part in trade; they were governed by their elders on exactly Plato's principles. Plato had called the warriors who defended the state auxiliaries and from their number some were chosen to become guardians. In India, too, the military power was made subordinate to the civil, but military officers were chosen for the Political Department and thus joined the ranks of the Guardians.

A safeguard was provided against too rigid and self-contained a system. This new aristocracy was headed by a Viceroy who did not belong to the caste, chosen from outside its ranks by the English cabinet. It might have been supposed that English statesmen would vie eagerly among themselves for the throne of Akbar and Aurangzebe. But it was not so. It was not easy to find a suitable Viceroy. One man had his eye on the Foreign Office, another did not like to leave his hunters and partridges. Between Dalhousie and Curzon there was no Viceroy who might have held the Foreign Office or the Exchequer in England. Those two masterful, arrogant, and able men could dominate their surroundings and sway the course of events —

not always to the advantage of India. Those who came between found themselves caught up in the strong current of the system and the movements of their limbs were dictated as much by the current as by their own will.

'I never tire of looking at a Viceroy', wrote Aberigh Mackay in 1880, describing The Great Ornamental. 'He is a being so heterogeneous from us! He is the centre of a world with which he has no affinity . . . He, who is the axis of India, . . . is necessarily screened from all knowledge of India. He lisps no syllable of any Indian tongue; no race or caste or mode of Indian life is known to him. . . .'

He would not have called Dalhousie or Curzon The Great Ornamental and the taunt was not entirely fair to those who came between. But in a sense it was true. The Viceroy had a great deal to contend with if he was to assert himself. He was advised by a Council of five or six members, of whom three or four belonged to the caste of Guardians. He was also advised by a Foreign Secretary, while from the provinces came the opinions of the Lieutenant-Governors and Chief Commissioners, all of whom must belong to the caste. The Viceroy himself, perhaps the Commander-in-Chief, probably the Governors of Madras and Bombay — who were increasingly often politicians for whom it was not convenient to make provision elsewhere — possibly the Finance Member of Council, a High Court Judge or so in the Presidency towns — these were the exceptions. The rest of the administration was in the hands of the caste.

Plato's guardians were to be born in the purple, because he believed the best could only be obtained by careful breeding. Logically, then, he ruled out chance mating and haphazard upbringing in the family. The English, being always ready to make concessions to the unforeseen, were prepared to find their Guardians in any class of society and they recruited them by open competitive examination. But Aberigh Mackay in 1880 could still write of 'the thorough-bred Anglo-Indian, whose blood has distilled through Haileybury for three generations and whose cousins to the fourth degree are Collectors and Indian Army Colonels. . . .'

The competition had been devised in 1853 by Macaulay's committee. Jowett, remembering no doubt the words of Plato: '. . . the man whose natural gifts promise to make him a perfect guardian of the state will be philosophical, high-spirited, swift-footed and strong . . .', had recommended that the Commissioners should include a *viva voce*, in which no doubt attention would have been paid to swiftness of foot. This however was not put into effect for many years. What was agreed on from the beginning was that 'no candidate who might fail should ... have any reason to regret the time and labour which he had spent in preparing himself to be examined ...' This greatly widened the field of choice; any young man of ability might sit on the off-chance of success without committing himself to a two-years course in Sanskrit. It was also accepted that 'the civil servant of the East India Company should have received the best, the most liberal, the most finished education that his country affords'.

On this there was general agreement, though there was some fear that the young men who entered by examination would not be so 'high-spirited' as Plato and Jowett would have wished. This fear was also strongly expressed when the idea of a competitive examination for the home civil service was discussed. And, as more than one person has pointed out, 'it was one thing to have required the Directors of the East India Company to abandon patronage in India; it was quite another thing to expect Ministers to surrender it in their own offices at home'. India, thanks to the Company, was many years ahead of England in the matter of a civil service.

The competition took place in a large number of subjects —English, Greek and Latin, French, German and Italian, Mathematics, Science and others. A candidate might offer as many as he liked, a premium thus being set on the ability to get up a subject at short notice and remember enough of it to give the impression of knowing more. This, surely, is a useful accomplishment for a public servant, but it is not admired by scholars; in 1906 the number of subjects was limited and cramming became less valuable. But in Victorian times a good crammer could undertake by six weeks' tuition to add five hundred marks to a young man's total.

If everyone was agreed in condemning specialized education, there was nothing like unanimity about the stage at which a man should sit for the competition. One argument was that the net should be spread wide and the boy caught fresh from school. Neither Warren Hastings nor Charles Metcalfe, each in his day the prize scholar of his school, would have set sail, so the argument ran, once he had realized his ability. Perhaps for this reason, the competition was at one time held at eighteen or nineteen and was followed by two years at a University.

It was Jowett's interest which secured for Oxford more than her fair share of these probationers, of whom at one time as many as half were at Balliol. His methods were not always such as his fellow Heads of Houses would have approved. Monier-Williams, for instance, the 'solemn moneo' who edited the book on old Haileybury,[1] began his undergraduate life at another college; he met Jowett, who suggested that he was wrong to hide his light under this particular bushel and secured his transfer to a more appropriate candlestick. Walter Lawrence passed in at the top of the list and his father received a letter suggesting that there was only one college suitable for so successful a young man. But whatever one thinks of these methods, the young men did find themselves in stimulating company.

There was another view, that it was easier at twenty-two than at nineteen to guess what a man would be like at forty. It was strongly reinforced by Indian opinion; Indians believed that their prize scholars had a much better chance at twenty-two of competing with Englishmen in English. And this view eventually prevailed. But the change in one sense did not make a great deal of difference to the young man himself. When he came out to India, he was in either case a University man and usually a classical scholar. This may have helped him to endure loneliness; it often increased his loneliness in his first months. Unless he was the son of a civilian, he found himself in a strange land, severed by many barriers from the people of the country, while among his own compatriots he usually saw few of his own age who had had the same kind of upbringing. Subalterns were inclined to find him conceited, lively young ladies to tease him for his solemnity.

2. THE FIRST YEAR

'The model young man who has been two years at Oxford or Cambridge as a scholar of his college and is now in a position of authority,' wrote Alban Way, a young man who reached India in 1890, to his mother, 'is often inclined to have a rather too good opinion of himself . . . He is asked to dine at a mess and begins to assert himself and give his opinion . . . in an authoritative manner . . . This the gay young lieutenants, who are being continually snubbed by their superiors and are never allowed to have any opinions at all . . . cannot stand . . .' — and in the end 'the unfortunate victim is seized and tossed in a table-cloth . . .' 'Careful young civilians . . .' he adds, 'usually keep an old suit of dress clothes to wear when they dine at messes . . .' And Way recalled how, when he paid his first visit to the judge's family, he had sat on the edge of his chair and talked in

[1] See *The Founders*, part I, chap. III, p. 285.

'a very mild and perspiring manner'. A year later, when he knew her better, the judge's daughter told him that most young civilians gave her 'the general impression of being youths who were stuffed full of knowledge . . . who had spent their whole time working for exams and had never had time for anything else. . . .'

There was no longer a period of dissipated boredom at the College of Fort William. A young man for a northern Province landed at Bombay, went straight to his district and within three weeks or a month was usually told to try a case. 'Thursday was for me a momentous and eventful day', wrote Way on January 21st, 1891. 'On that day, I tried . . . my first case. The prisoner was accused of stealing twenty-nine stalks of sugar-cane, value one anna [rather more than a penny], from a field in the middle of the night.' Way allowed a remand for six days to give the accused time to summon his defence, but the defence witnesses contradicted each other and the wretch was found guilty and sentenced to twenty-one days rigorous imprisonment — which one may guess was remitted in appeal. 'It took me about six times as long to understand what the witnesses said as it would take anyone who knew the language . . . the lingo of the country peasants I find almost completely unintelligible.'

Every young man spent a good deal of his first year on cases of this kind and by the autumn he usually felt himself an expert. He had become familiar with the man who gets up in the night to answer a call of nature and happens to see what is going forward; he greeted with a sigh defence counsel's questions about the state of the moon and the direction towards which the accused was facing when first seen. He knew by now the vernacular terms for a father-in-law's house, a female buffalo and a field of sugar-cane. He had also spent a dull month in charge of the treasury and another in charge of the copying office. Already he had swallowed his first qualms and certified hundreds of documents which he could not read to be true copies of hundreds he had not seen. He had probably carried out a number of other tasks, such as inspecting a liquor-shop or viewing the bodies of dead wolves, repelling a horde of locusts or welcoming a Viceroy. Now, towards the end of his first year, came the next milestone, his first tour by himself in camp.

'I am going out by myself on a tour of inspection', wrote Way in November 1891. 'I have to inspect everything, schools, roads, hospitals, dispensaries, ferries, police-stations and most important of all, the records of fields and cultivators kept by the village accountants, commonly called *patwaris* . . .' A few days later, he writes: 'I

CROP RECORD

This is a four-year *Khasra* for a village in Delhi district. Reading from the right the columns show: 1. The number of the field. 2 The proprietor. 3. The cultivator. 4. The area. 5. The soil classification. 6. The crop sown in the Hindu year 1996: Autumn 1939. 7. The Spring crop, Hindu year 1996: 1940 A.D. 8. Alterations. The other columns repeat 6, 7 and 8 for the following years.

am out all by myself and on my own resources . . . I inspected the liquor shop and the school. These appear to be the only inspectable institutions in the place . . . During the day I examined some patwaris' registers. . . .'

He was quite right in thinking the patwaris' papers important. They were the mainstay of the whole system, the means by which Thomason's work was carried on and an accurate record provided from one settlement to the next. An Indian field was usually not much larger than an English allotment, half an acre being a good field, and the problem was to keep a record of every crop and every payment for every plot in an allotment area covering hundreds of miles in every direction. The tenure of each fragment of land was unbelievably complicated and shared in varying proportions by a bewildering number of relations.

The business of checking the record did not change much in a hundred years. The young man with a liberal education takes his stand in the middle of the allotment area with a map. It is drawn in Indian ink on cotton cloth and falls over his hand in limp folds like a cheap pocket-handkerchief. There is perhaps a road, a well or a temple to give him a starting-point and this triangular field on the map must surely be the one where he stands. 'This is number 1178,' he says, grateful for the first time for the month in the treasury which has made him so fluent with his numerals. The group of villagers look blank; most of them have never heard the number, but one or two know it because it has been the subject of a lawsuit and these seem ill at ease.

'Gracious and lofty Presence, it is eighty-seven', says the patwari and the youth resolves that this time he really will remember that in Arabic numerals V as in seven means seven and the other way up means eight. 'This is number 1187', he repeats firmly and this time everyone seems pleased.

'Whose field is this?' he continues and there is at once a chorus: 'Munnoo's field.' 'Does he plough it himself?' Yes, Munnoo ploughs it. It does not belong to Munnoo. It belongs to the Strawberry-coloured Combine, of whom the senior partner is Gulab Khan. There are seventy-four members of the Strawberry-coloured Combine.

The graduate in philosophy looks at the field book in the patwari's hand. There is something like a newly-hatched tadpole in the column for cultivators and in the Arabic script, written from right to left, that tadpole must stand for Munnoo. He looks at his feet; it is an

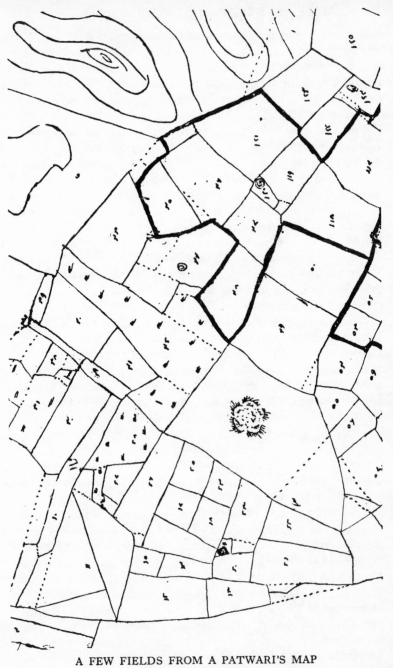

A FEW FIELDS FROM A PATWARI'S MAP
The scale in the original is 64 in. to 1 mile

easy crop to recognize, gram, a small chick pea, that is just pushing its way up through the rough sharp little clods of sun-baked earth. It is a crop which does not like a fine tilth. And easy to recognize in the book too, for the final *alif* is unmistakable. There is another chick-pea very like gram, but the vernacular word for that ends in a *ye*. This entry is correct.

The next field is a square lying snug against the hypotenuse of 1187; this must be 1193. Yes, everyone agrees to that. It is cultivated by Rahim — for this is a mixed village with Muslim cultivators as well as Hindus — and belongs to the Orange Combine, of which the senior member is a Hindu, Gopal Das, who bought the thirty-three shares out of a hundred and eighty-eight which once belonged to Zalim Khan. And this at his feet is barley — no, wheat — no, barley. 'Barley', he says. 'Wheat', everyone else says, and they show him how the blade of wheat fits round the stalk as it unfolds and they fetch some barley to show the difference. And it is clearly wheat in the book; the initial *gaf* with its great double stroke like the arm of a steam crane is the most unequivocal letter in the alphabet.

When he feels satisfied that the field book and the map agree, at least for a score or so of fields, the youth will perhaps go into the village. A bed will be dragged out for him to sit on; there are no chairs in all the village. It is a wooden frame, with four legs, laced across with hairy string like binder-twine. A tall thick glass of greyish tea, generously sugared, generously stirred, is brought him, and there are oranges and perhaps hard-boiled eggs, peeled already and marked with grimy finger-prints. The villagers, in their coarse white cotton, sit closely on the floor and the young man proceeds to verify the shares of everyone who belongs to the Strawberry-coloured Combine. Gulab Khan's grandfather was one of six brothers who had equal shares and whose names were. . .

That was the kind of thing Way — and every young man in the service — had to do. Way had written that he would be entirely on his own, but what was his delight to find himself after a week at the same place as the Deputy Commissioner, by whose tents he pitched his own for four days — 'and they were the pleasantest days I have had this year. Mulock is an awful good chap and Mrs. Mulock is that nice I haven't the langwidge to describe her nohow . . .' It was very refreshing to meet an English lady, particularly one 'so *very* charming as Mrs. Mulock. She is the sort of lady who, one would imagine, would like to stay in the station and shine in society, but she prefers to accompany her husband into the wilds . . .' Way had a lame pony and 'immediately on seeing it, her heart went out to it as it always does to anything in pain or trouble and she immediately took it in hand and prescribed a poultice . . .' He found, too, that Mrs. Mulock 'knows all about her husband's administrative schemes . . . is well up in all the political and social problems of modern India. . .' and 'her husband declares that she would make a first-rate district magistrate, which is quite true'. Altogether, this letter was one over which Way's mother no doubt shook her head with a smile and wished he would meet some nice girl.

3. THE S.D.O.

By November 1891, Way had enough knowledge of the country-side to benefit by something more theoretical and he went to a training-camp at Roorkee, thirty miles from Hardwar, where the Ganges breaks out of the hills. Here with the other men of his year he spent two or three months in study and passed his examinations in languages, law and procedure. Then he was posted to a district and soon became a sub-divisional officer.

Methods of training were not the same in every province nor did every province understand the same thing by a sub-divisional officer. But in every province the young man was first given time to look round and learn the feel of the country, and then he would be given charge of an area with between a quarter of a million and a million inhabitants. It was his duty to see that the land records were kept up to date and in good order, that all disputes were settled without disturbance of the public peace, that the ferries were run with a minimum of inconvenience and extortion, that the pounds, schools and liquor-shops really were in existence and were properly main-tained.

The young man probably took over charge of his sub-division in March or April and for the first six months far too much of his time would be spent in court, deciding formal suits, with witnesses and perhaps counsel. He would also have the opportunity of settling quite a few cases by suggesting a solution and advising the parties to compromise. There were various methods, but almost everyone at some time or another brought some moral pressure to bear on the parties. After all, they alone knew all the facts and they could reach a better solution than a court if they would only try. If they did compromise, they saved themselves much expense and the terms of the compromise were recorded by the court so that they could not be evaded.

The summer would of course be chequered by emergencies, by a murder perhaps that caused intense feeling between two communities, by a threat of famine or locusts, by the depredations of a man-eater or a dispute about the route of a procession. Any of these things might take the S.D.O. into camp for a little, but except for an emergency the months from April to September were regarded in the North — but not in Madras — as too hot for life in tents. Once the rains were over and the dry cool weather had begun, the S.D.O., if he was ever going to make an officer, was eager to get into camp.

The sub-division might be twenty miles long and ten miles across, or it might be as big again. It was possible to choose a score or so of camping sites not more than ten or twelve miles apart and to stay as a rule three nights in each. A cup of tea at dawn and then you would be on a horse and off at a brisk canter. Horse and man would both be keen to keep moving because the cold was still sharp; you had to choose between too few clothes at starting and too many when the sun was up. The fields were grey with dew and villagers were not at all anxious to be stirring so early; their wits seemed numbed with cold these mornings. Perhaps the sanitation of a village six miles away might be the first appointment and then the site of some dispute which had come up in court a month ago, then a school, a ferry or a liquor-shop, perhaps a patwari's papers and so back to the tents by ten or eleven in the morning. A bath in a tin tub in the dark little bathroom behind the tent; it smelt of smoke and damp straw but the towels by now would be crisp and warm from hanging over a tent-rope in the sun. A large confused meal, combining breakfast and lunch, and then again the disputes of villagers.

Custom varied at this point. Some men heard formal suits in camp and even permitted counsel; to others it was anathema. It was, they felt, a sad waste of camping-time to do in the mango-grove outside the tents what could be done at headquarters and in any case there was no shortage of work in camp. Even if no formal cases were heard, petitions would take a long time. 'Petitions!' a court messenger would shout in each corner of the grove, and the patient figures squatting together in a group by the servants' tents would come to life and advance. There would be two or three disputes about fields, about where a field boundary should run, perhaps, or whether Ramu had really said he would let Tulsi plough field number 1239 — the field with the *babul* tree in the corner — if Tulsi would agree to take water from the well every third day instead of every other day. There would perhaps be a woman who had been enticed away from her husband and sometimes the husband would be quite content to let her go if he could have back his savings, the ornaments of silver she was wearing. All these differences could, if a man chose, be dealt with formally and perfunctorily. But with a little trouble it was often possible to settle them without any more waste of money and this was the object of the man who did his camping properly. The patwari could be summoned with his maps and papers and the whole affair ended that evening, or an appointment could be made to see the site of the trouble next morning.

Petitions, and sometimes reports on things seen on the morning ride, would fill the middle part of the day. In the evening, with luck, it might be possible to stroll out with a gun, hoping for a partridge or two, a peacock, a hare, or a few quail, something at any rate to keep the pot from going empty. The stroll always produced at least as many peasants as partridges. A man would appear and walk timidly behind for a little, or perhaps ostentatiously beat the bushes for game; it was not quite seemly to introduce the subject at once, but after a little companionship of this kind, out it would come, the field entered in the wrong name, the path for taking the buffaloes to the water blocked by Loharu's malice, the cruel beating administered only yesterday by Rahim Khan's men — simply because a poor man ventured to ask them to keep their cattle out of his sugar-cane.

'Look at my *mauqa*!' in pleading accents was the cry heard over and over again in camp. A mauqa is the place where something happened, the spot marked with a cross. It may be the scene of a crime or the site of a dispute; to the petitioner it seems crystal clear that once the ruler has seen the mauqa, truth will prevail.

He was a lucky young man who could stay in one sub-division for two or three years. He would learn in the second year what mistakes he had made in the first; he would realize that he never ought to have let the Hindus depart from precedent by holding that apparently innocuous procession at the festival of Ram Lila to which the Muslims had produced such obviously factious objections. He would have learnt the groundwork of his profession and whatever else might happen later he had something firm to build on. But far too often he would be tempted by some meretricious offer to forfeit experience that could never be replaced, and then he would have to make each mistake at least once more.

4. THE SPECIALISTS

Famine, pestilence or some other emergency might lead the young man away from his sub-division and to that of course there could be no answer; he must go. But the offer of a short spell in the secretariat as acting Under Secretary would probably first be made tentatively and he might well be wise to say he would prefer not to accept. Things of that sort were arranged among friends; within the service, and until they were made public, orders were more a basis for argument than what a soldier would understand by a command.

The dilemma might, then, be presented very early, perhaps in some minor form before he had finished a year in his sub-division. If not then, it would come at the end of the third year or the fourth, or perhaps much later, depending on a man's province and temperament. To most men, sooner or later, the choice would come between the executive line — the department 'of land revenue and general administration' — and the various alternatives, political, judicial, secretariat and a dozen odd branches, opium, customs, salt or excise.

At the beginning of the period, in the 'sixties, there was nothing very hard and fast about these different departments. A man might hold a political appointment for a year or two and come back to his province without stigma or reproach. But this grew steadily rarer and going to the political became more and more a question that a man had to decide once and for all, one way or the other. It was not an easy choice, because while by this stage in his career he knew fairly well what life in his own province was like, the alternative involved very different possibilities. It was one thing to administer Aden or to deal with the desert tribes in the country behind Kowait or Oman, to be a consul in Persia or the Gulf, to follow John Jacob on the Sind Frontier or Herbert Edwardes further North; it was quite another to spend one's youth in the steamy idleness of a small State, where there was nothing to do between ceremonial visits but wonder when the Raja really would exceed all reasonable limits and force the paramount power to intervene. There was much to be done in some States, very little in others.

As to the judicial, that choice, in the early part of the period at least, did not arise in the non-regulation provinces, such as Oudh and the Punjab, which had been administered, since they were first annexed, in the spirit of Malcolm and Metcalfe, by the light of a clear conscience and a clear head. In these provinces, the Deputy Commissioner was still all in all. As late as 1877, Mrs. Moss King wrote:

'Robert . . . is to take up the post of Collector at Meerut; it is much the same as a Deputy Commissioner in Oudh, save that the work is less and the pay more . . . All civil and all heavy criminal cases, both of which came before him in Oudh, are here tried by an independent judge. . . .'

This was the wife's point of view; the public's interest was not very different. The rule of one man had been ideal when districts were first annexed, but a change had to be made. No one who went about the country as much as a district officer ought could have time for complicated civil suits. And again, as a judge in criminal cases, the district officer, though he usually knew what had happened, could hardly help inclining a little to the side of the police who had taken such trouble to catch and prosecute the accused. Inevitably, the non-regulation provinces came into line with the others and a judge came to be a judge and nothing else. Moss King — or at any rate his wife — seems to have regarded it as an ideal arrangement to officiate as judge in the hot weather, which gave him higher pay and a month's vacation in the hills, and to revert to an executive post in the winter for the camping. In 1878, however, he was told that the administrative and judicial branches were to be separated. He chose the judicial. Bulman, a Punjab civilian who was asked the same question in 1884, replied that however much faster promotion in the judicial might be, he would prefer the administrative. 'Sitting day after day in a stuffy court trying civil suits seemed to me a dull prospect. . . .'

The decision was a matter of temperament. There were some to whom a judge's life appealed because it satisfied the intellect. It was possible for a judge to feel when he went to bed that he had done all he could do; he had sat in court and heard the witnesses with attention, he had used the full powers of his mind to reach conclusions. He could feel there was no more to do. A district officer, conscious of a score of needs for which there had not been time, could never feel that. Quicker promotion and the prospect of the High Court were held out as inducements to the judge-to-be; at some periods there was a flat £10 a month extra, but all this weighed less as a rule than temperament.

If a man did decide on the judicial side, the 'judgey' as the Indian called it, he would deal with both county court and sessions work, turning from civil to criminal work and back and also hearing a great many appeals from magistrates. There were things about his work that would have surprised an English judge. An English trial, after an Indian, seems a gladiatorial contest between opposing counsel; they pay deference to the judge, who is hedged about with pomp, but he, being himself trained at the bar, leaves them to conduct the case and interferes only when he must. A judge trained as a magistrate in India has often had to try cases without counsel, or with counsel who are neither well-educated nor painstaking. He has been used to asking questions himself. He will not let questions be asked which lead the unsuspecting witness away from his own clear intention. He will spring counsel's carefully laid trap and warn the witness of what a question means. In short, he will himself diligently seek for the truth.

The responsibility of a judge in India was heavier than an English judge's, because he did not have a jury. He had, as a rule, but not always, assessors, four or five men of substance, carefully selected, who were asked their opinion — to which the judge need pay no attention whatever. This curious arrangement of course encouraged an irresponsibility in the assessors to which they were in any case only too prone. The judge had therefore to decide whether a man was guilty before he sentenced him; he had also a wider discretion than an English judge in respect, for instance, of murder, for which death was not the sole and obligatory punishment.

To be a judge, then, was an ambition far from ignoble, but it remained true that the majority of men preferred to keep the habits to which they had been brought up in the administrative branch. Periodically someone whose cast of mind was believed to be judicial had to be deputed to the 'judgey' to make up the number of volunteers and this might happen at various stages in seniority. It was to the sub-divisional officer however that the free choice would first be offered.

The political, the 'judgey', and the Lord Sahib's Office — that is the secretariat — these were the three main alternatives to the life of the district. The secretariat needs little explanation;[1] the work was essentially that done by the civil servant in Whitehall, with the difference that there was far more delegation of power, that a junior could do much more without referring to his seniors, and that his seniors were people trained in the same way as himself. Every district officer despised and hated the secretariat, who would not make up their minds, who hedged and compromised and wrapped up their meaning in provisos; that was inevitable. There was of course some truth in it; the secretariat man had more to bear in mind than a

---

[1] But see also chap. VIII, sec. 4: Hume and the Congress, and chap. X, sec. 1: The War against Paper.

district officer and if he stayed at headquarters too long he did sometimes tend to think of so many possibilities that he could not decide between them. But he was always liable to go back to a district and there were always to be found in the secretariat one or two who remained obstinately district officers at heart. Perhaps because of this umbilical cord to the soil and the plough, there did grow up a loyalty to India, expressed sometimes even in defiance of the authority of Parliament.

The cotton import duties are, of course, the classical example of this. They were abolished in 1879, under Lord Lytton, in the interests of Free Trade and of Lancashire; members of Parliament were no doubt convinced that in filling Manchester's pockets they were following the laws of political economy and increasing the world's wealth. The measure was regarded by Lord Lytton's Council as contrary to India's interests and they protested. The Council protested still more strongly in 1894, when the import duty on manufactured cotton was re-imposed but, to rob it of any protective value, a corresponding excise duty was clapped on Indian cotton. The Council were overruled but expressed their views so strongly that the Secretary of State found it necessary to tell them that 'once a certain line of policy has been adopted under the direction of the Cabinet, it becomes a clear duty of every member of the Government of India to consider . . . how effect may best be given to that policy. . . .'

But a man who had refused the political and the judgey and perhaps never been offered the secretariat might still become a specialist late in life. All through this period the Guardians found the heads for the specialized services; as late as 1930, it was still a man from the Indian Civil Service who was head of the departments of Opium and Salt. The Postmaster-General in a province became a specialist in the 'twenties, but in 1939 the head of all the postal services for all India still belonged to the service, while the same was true in the long administrative period even of the Inspectors-General of Police and of Forests. There was hardly an important post in the whole range of government to which a man might not be asked to turn his hand.

5. THE DISTRICT OFFICER

The young man who resisted the temptation to specialize would come through his years in a sub-division and get a chance to officiate for part of the hot weather in a small and unpopular district. 'Don't try to do your S.D.O.s' work; see that they do it themselves but give them a chance and don't weigh yourself down with detail', a wise Commissioner would tell him. In the winter he would revert, probably becoming City Magistrate in a large and troublesome city, under a senior District Officer. Here his work would be all police, crime and sanitation, with no idyllic camping and no disputes about land. The next hot weather he would officiate for the whole season, and then in a year or two would come the district from which he was not going to revert.

G. O. Trevelyan, the son, it will be remembered, of Macaulay's brother-in-law Charles, was not himself a civilian. But his description of a district officer's day in the 'sixties did not need much modification seventy or eighty years later.

'He rises at daybreak and goes straight from his bed to the saddle. Then he gallops off across fields bright with dew to visit the scene of the late dacoit robbery; or to see with his own eyes whether the crops of the zamindar who is so unpunctual with his assessment have really failed; or to watch with fond parental care the progress of his pet embankment . . . Perhaps he has a run with the bobbery pack of the station, consisting of a superannuated foxhound, four beagles, a greyhound, the doctor's retriever, and a Skye terrier belonging to the assistant-magistrate, who unites in his own person the offices of M.F.H., huntsman and whipper-in. They probably start a jackal, who gives them a sharp run of ten minutes and takes refuge in a patch of sugar-cane; whence he steals away in safety while the pack are occupied in mobbing a fresh fox and a brace of wolf-cubs . . . The full field of five sportsmen . . . adjourn to the subscription swimming-bath, where they find their servants ready with clothes, razors and brushes. After a few headers . . . and tea and toast . . . the collector returns to his bungalow and settles down to the hard business of the day . . . He works through the contents of one dispatch-box after another; signing orders and passing them on; dashing through drafts, to be filled up by his subordinate; writing reports, minutes, digests, letters of explanation, of remonstrance, or warning, of commendation. Noon finds him quite ready for a *déjeuner à la fourchette*, the favourite meal in the districts, when the tea-tray is lost amid a crowd of dishes — fried fish, curried fowl, roast kid and mint-sauce, and mango-fool. Then he sets off in his buggy to the courts, where he spends the afternoon in hearing and deciding questions connected with land and revenue. If the cases are few and easy to be disposed of, he may get away in time for three or four games at rackets in the new court . . . By ten o'clock he is in bed, with his little ones asleep in cribs enclosed within the same mosquito-nets as their parents. . . .'

Trevelyan leaves no time in this day for seeing visitors. He was a lucky man who was able to give all the morning to 'the dawk' — the dispatch-boxes with the day's work from the office. As a rule, the morning from ten to twelve was spent listening to long complimentary speeches in which every now and then there might, or might not, be a point of importance. That day's 'dawk' would have to be done before dinner in the evening, or if the worst came to the worst, next morning's ride might have to be foregone. Dinner might wait till ten o'clock, but in a district nobody worked after dinner.

'To the people of India,' wrote Aberigh Mackay, 'the Collector is the Imperial Government. He watches over their welfare . . . he establishes schools, dispensaries, gaols and courts of justice. He levies the rent of their fields, he fixes the tariff, and he nominates to every appointment, from that of road-sweeper or constable to the great blood-sucking offices round the Courts and the Treasury.

'The Collector', he continues, 'lives in a long rambling bungalow furnished with folding chairs and tables and in every way marked by the provisional arrangements of camp life. He seems to have just arrived from out of the firmament of green fields and mango-groves that encircles the little station where he lives; or he seems just about to pass away into it again. The shooting-howdahs are lying in the veranda, the elephant of a neighbouring landholder is swinging his hind foot to and fro under a tree or switching up straw and leaves on to his back, a dozen camels are lying down in a circle making bubbling noises. . . .

'The veranda is full of fat men in clean linen waiting for interviews. They are bankers, shopkeepers and landholders, who have only come to "pay their respects", with ever so little a petition as a corollary . . . Brass dishes filled with pistachio nuts and candied sugar are ostentatiously displayed here and there; they are the oblations of the would-be visitors . . . They represent in the profuse East the visiting cards of the meagre West.'

Aberigh Mackay, writing twenty years later, strikes a note that after Trevelyan's enthusiasm sounds a trifle cynical. But he was a Simla man and it would be misleading to generalize from this and suppose that the feeling of men in the districts changed much about their work. Edward Thompson sees in the 'sixties the era of paternalism and is able to discern its decay in the 'seventies and 'eighties. I cannot see any ground for such a generalization, nor — up the country — detect any lessening of enthusiasm. One man after another writes in glowing terms of the life he has chosen.

In Simla, it was perhaps another matter; in the Government of India the affectation of being very English, of knowing nothing at all about India, of eschewing Indian words and customs, spread downwards from the Viceroy's staff and was endemic. It carried with it, often enough, the cynicism and conceit of clever young men. But in the districts and the provinces things were still much as Trevelyan had described them.

'I know of no better company in the world,' he wrote, 'than a rising young civilian. There is an entire absence of the carping pining spirit of discontent which is so painfully apparent in able men at home who . . . want interest or money . . . It is impossible for the civilian to have any misgiving concerning the dignity and importance of his work. His power for good and evil is almost unlimited . . . He is the member of an official aristocracy owning no social superior; bound to no man; fearing no man . . . He is well aware that his advancement does not hang upon the will and pleasure of this or that other great man but is regulated by the opinions entertained of his ability and character by the service in general . . . A civilian . . . makes it his aim to turn off his work in good style, trusting for his reward to the sense and public spirit of his chief . . . He never speaks of his duties save in a spirit of enthusiasm or of his profession without a tone of profound satisfaction. . . .'

'But, besides the blessings of absorbing work,' Trevelyan continues, 'a civilian enjoys the inestimable comfort of freedom from pecuniary troubles . . . Tom's assistant-magistrate keeps four horses and lives well within as many hundred rupees a month. If a man puts off his marriage to within a year or two of the age at which he may take a wife in England without being disinherited, he may always have a good house and plenty of servants, his champagne and his refrigerator, his carriage and buggy, an Arab for the Mem Sahib and for himself a hundred guinea horse that will face a pig without flinching. He will be able to portion his daughters and send his son to Harrow and Oxford; he may retire to a villa at Esher or a farm in his native county with a pension of a thousand a year and as much more from the interests of his savings. . . .'

Tom's successors, their pension still a thousand a year, with the pound a quarter of its value and an income-tax that would have made Tom stare, may smile a little wryly at this, but it is pleasant to know that their predecessors had such freedom from anxiety and to read that: 'The public spirit among the servants of the Government at home is faint compared with the fire of zeal which glows in every vein of an Indian official.' And in the spirit of Socrates Trevelyan wonders why this should be. 'Whence comes this high standard of efficiency and public virtue among men taken at random and then exposed to the temptations of unbounded power . . . ?' His answers to the question are the right ones. 'The real education of a civil servant,' he said, 'consists in the responsibility that devolves on him at an early age, which brings out whatever good there is in a man; the obligation to do nothing that can reflect dishonour on the service; the varied and attractive character of his duties; and the example and precept of his superiors, who regard him rather as a younger brother than as a subordinate official.'

All this is very like Plato, although these guardians have been made independent of money in quite a different way from his and it is doubtful whether he would have approved of pigsticking. But he would certainly have felt pleasure at Trevelyan's picture of the progress of English society in India. 'It has generally been found that a manly valiant race, which has imposed its yoke upon an effeminate and unwarlike people, in course of time degenerates and becomes slothful and luxurious . . .' And he gives examples from ancient history. 'But with the English in the East precisely the opposite result has taken place . . . Each generation . . . is more simple, more hardy, more Christian than the last.'

There is of course another side to this. It must have struck many schoolboys that Plato's state would be remarkably dull to live in. It would be worse if the guardians were foreigners, for Plato himself had said: 'Does it not seem to you a scandalous thing . . . to be obliged to import justice from others, in the character of lords and judges, in consequence of the scanty supply at home?' This was already a source of pain to educated Indians and there is more to be said of it later. But the impact on Indians not educated in Western ways, on villagers and on those 'fat clean men' who came to call on the Collector, was less distasteful as a rule than might have been expected. Their own society was static; few born into it were afflicted with the restless ambition common in a modern competitive society. And the system was one that did provide peace and a minimum of interference; with certain exceptions it worked in the interest of the existing order. Nor were the English Guardians the dignified and forbidding creatures pictured by Plato. 'Our guardians', he had written, 'ought not to be given to laughter . . .' but the English on the whole were cheerful men, warm-hearted and human when their strange desires were known. They were given to pigsticking, racing and shooting, and, though they could not be bribed, could be induced to smile by news of a tiger or by a subscription to a pet charity. And once he had smiled, the Englishman often entered into the kind of cheerful bantering relationship which a schoolmaster or an uncle sometimes uses to a mischievous small boy. This paternal banter would be resented by the educated but by villagers was recognized as a form of good humour.

As they grew older, the men of the service did not grow more sedate and more like each other, as Plato would have had them; on the contrary, their diversity, their humanity, and their oddness, increased. Every man had his *shauq*, his pet enthusiasm, and very often two, of which one was pure recreation and the other philanthropy. There was Brown, whose hobbies were tigers and embankments to store water in the rains; Smith who would go miles for a snipe and planted all the roads in every district he was ever in with double avenues of trees; and Jones, who was building hospitals when he wasn't pigsticking.

> 'Why is my district death-rate low?'
>   Said Binks of Hezabad,
> 'Wells, drains, and sewage-outfalls are
>   My own peculiar fad.'

And because of their fads, their humour, and their tolerance, many district officers were not merely much less intolerable than might have been expected but were looked on with real affection by the people of their districts.

All the same, the fabric could only be temporary. It was too rigid and it embodied a fundamental contradiction. England herself was progressing steadily towards giving everyone a say in public affairs; India too was some day to move in that direction. But at present the system by which she was governed did not give Indians much say in her affairs. The similarities to Plato's state were unconscious but they were based on a deep admiration for Plato, not only in Jowett and Macaulay, but throughout the English upper classes, and it was in Plato that the contradiction lay. Plato's state was one which Englishmen would never have tolerated for themselves. They had indeed spent a great deal of blood to make it clear that they would not be ruled by anyone, priest, king or baron, who drew his authority from what he himself knew to be right and would not account for it to his people. Yet just such a rule they did themselves impose on India.

CHAPTER V

FAMINE

I. THE PROBLEM

FLY eastward from the Mediterranean and for thousands of miles the impression is one of drought, of vast sandy plains, of naked rock scorched and split by the sun, of man here and there painfully winning a few tiny squares of green or chocolate-brown from the lion-coloured waste. When you come to India and fly over Sind, man seems for a little to be gaining; over Rajputana, the desert is in the ascendant; it is only as you come nearer to the Bay of Bengal that the impression fades entirely.

India, as everyone knows, is a triangle projecting into the Indian Ocean; more than nine tenths of the rainfall, in most of its vast area, comes in the months of July, August and September, when two sides of the triangle are assailed, one by the South-West and one by the South-East monsoon. In a good year, the two monsoons meet in the middle, everyone has rain, and two crops are taken off the land. In a bad year, the monsoons do not meet, and the centre and the northern part of the triangle seem like a continuation of the Arabian deserts. The devil, the Muslims say, holds an umbrella over Delhi, but there are other parts of the country over which he holds it no less diligently.

In all the central and northern area, the ground for nine months grows harder and harder till it is like dusty concrete, unsympathetic to the foot and impervious to the hoe. Then come the anxious weeks, when, if God so pleases, the rain will come. Sometimes He pleases; sometimes He withholds. If there is no rain, there is no harvest of rice and millet in September and the ground is too hard to sow the wheat and barley that ought to be cut in March. The peasant seldom has grain enough in hand to carry him more than a month or two beyond harvest-time. The grain-dealer of course has stocks, but prices rise and the peasant cannot buy without running into debt. There is scarcity, debt, hunger, and something near starvation. Then perhaps next year there is a poor crop and a partial recovery, then another failure; the dealer's stocks are exhausted and there is no food in the area. This is famine.

Famines, we know, there had always been. In the days of Peter

Mundy, the bodies were dragged stark naked from the towns to lie by the roadside; women sold their children and men ate each other.[1] The Moguls and their predecessors looked on famine as the act of God, something beyond the power of human rulers to mitigate. They had some justification.

If there was no grain for men, there was no fodder for cattle either and grain could hardly be moved into the starving areas. Bullocks in India are fed mainly on the chopped stalks of millet, a bulky food with not much feeding value; a pair of bullocks moving ten or twelve miles a day would eat in a week all they could carry of this kind of fodder. If they are to deliver a load of three hundredweight and get back alive, their range is barely fifty miles. Elephants and mules are no better and though camels can live on desert scrub, they are not always to be found where there is grain. Even as late as 1877, grain lay rotting at the railway stations in Madras, in the very districts where men were starving, because there were no bullocks with strength to drag it away. So long, then, as transport was by means of animals, there was no cure that could be improvised once deaths had begun. The grim course of starvation, flight, and cholera must be faced.

Cure then in Mogul days was out of the question. Prevention or preparation there might have been, but in the eighteenth century it would have been a remarkable government which undertook them. In the early days in Bengal, men saw the ghastly sights of 1770 and some, like John Shore, did what they could privately, buying children from starving parents to feed and rear. But cure the situation they could not. Nor was it yet in their power to devise preventive measures. Only a part of the country was theirs and in that their administrative control was slight. Nor was there much improvement in the handling of that famine during which Lord Auckland had been so wretchedly bored in 1834.[2] No preparation had been made and when there had been no preparation beforehand there was very little that could be done.

In the first half of the century, there were fewer famines than in the second. This was due simply to the vagaries of the monsoon or, as the peasant would say, to the will of God. It would not be true to say that the growth of population was the main reason. Of course, if the land was overstocked with people and holdings subdivided too minutely, each family would have a smaller reserve to carry forward

[1] See *The Founders*, part I, chap. III, p. 46.
[2] See *The Founders*, part III, chap. VII, p. 277.

from a good year. But however big a peasant's holding, he will not store much grain; he will turn it into silver bangles which he cannot eat in a bad year. In the nineteenth century, India exported grain in a good year and buried bullion; there was enough, somewhere in India, to feed everyone, even in a bad year. Famine was a problem of distribution. It happened that there were more bad years in the second half of the century, and that was no one's fault.

In the first half, there was no repetition in Bengal of the famine of 1770; the North-Western Provinces had only Lord Auckland's boring famine in 1832-34; Gujerat had a famine in 1833; Rajputana, Delhi and Central India, the part most diligently sheltered by the devil, shared Lord Auckland's famine and had famines of their own in 1812 and 1824. But there was not much British territory in this area until Dalhousie's day — the 'fifties — and hardly any at all until 1823. It is justifiable to say that between 1801 and the Orissa famine of 1866 the only major famine in British territory was Lord Auckland's, which was a long slow famine, a succession of poor years, and when that was over, the Government turned to war and diplomacy, the settlement of land revenue and the like, instead of preparing for the next. They had some reason for supposing that famine was something that did not happen very often.

But from the Orissa famine of 1866 onwards no one could say that famine was not taken seriously. The startling thing about the Orissa famine was that it was so sudden, so swift and so complete. George Campbell — he who scolded the young man with the puppy-dogs — was later appointed to report on what had happened. 'In April, 1866, he wrote, 'the magistrate of Cuttack still reported that there was no ground for apprehension. A few days later, in May, he and his followers were almost starved.'

The magistrate was not entirely to be blamed. He knew of course that there had been a poor monsoon the previous autumn and that stocks were low. But in only five more months the next harvest would be cut, and the grain-dealers must have believed they had enough; if they had realized how bad things were, prices would have risen. And till May prices did not rise. Then suddenly confidence collapsed. It was like a run on a bank. Everyone strove for what he could get and concealed what he had; prices soared.

The Lieutenant-Governor, Sir Cecil Beadon, had accepted the views of the Magistrate of Cuttack and disbelieved others more pessimistic. He had himself toured in the area that winter. He was not, says Campbell, a man of pronounced doctrinaire views, but he was of a sanguine temperament and slow to believe evil, while his advisers of the Board of Revenue 'held by the most rigid rules of the direst political economy'. They rejected 'almost with horror' the idea of importing grain. They would not even allow the authorities in Orissa to take the grain from a ship which ran ashore on their coast in March. It was bound for Calcutta and to Calcutta the grain must go. In fact, it rotted in the holds while plans were made to move it.

At Haileybury, everyone had learnt that political economy was a matter of laws, that money and goods would move by themselves in ways beneficial to mankind. The less any government interfered with natural movements, the better. If there was real scarcity in Orissa, prices would rise, grain-dealers from elsewhere would be attracted and would hurry grain to where it was needed. If the government tried to anticipate this process, they would cause waste and incur loss.

It is a theory that no doubt would work well in France or the Lombard plain, where people eat other things as well as grain, where distances are much less than in India and where it is possible to move goods across country the whole year round. Even there, the theory does not take enough account of public confidence and possible panic. The people of Orissa depended entirely on grain and they were sealed from the outer world for four months. There were no harbours that could be worked in the monsoon. There were no railways. The country is 'a strip between pathless jungle and impracticable sea'; it is cut by many rivers which become torrents in July, August and September. Orissa was indeed, as Campbell said, like a ship where the stores are suddenly found to have run out. By the time relief came, a quarter of the population was dead.

The rulers of Victorian India were reluctant to interfere with the free flow of trade, and most of them had seen scares caused by hasty action, seen awkward times weathered by patience. They were also afraid of pauperizing and demoralizing the people; it was hardly to be expected that they should be far ahead of England and in England it was believed that some discouragement ought to go with poor relief. To accept it should be felt a disgrace, so that the labouring poor might make every effort to earn their living. And in India although relief must be given when there was famine, it must not continue longer than necessary and as far as possible some work must be done in return. 'There is the constant dilemma', wrote Campbell, 'that if we are too liberal there are sure to be great abuses, if we are too hard the people may starve.'

It is against this background that the famines of the second half of the century must be seen. There was Orissa in 1866 and George Campbell's recommendations; there was Temple's famine in Behar in 1874. There was famine in the North-West in 1868, in 1896 and in 1907. The dangerous central area shared the North-West's three famines and added two more of their own in 1876-78 and in 1899. Indeed, except for the fifteen years from 1880 to 1895 there were hardly five consecutive years free from famine somewhere.

It would be tedious to go through the successive reports and inquiries of Campbell, Temple, the Commission of 1880 and the Commission of 1900. But, though there was a steady development of doctrine and a steady improvement in the means of handling famine, the principles were set out once for all in Campbell's Report.

John Lawrence had blamed himself bitterly for having accepted Beadon's advice over Orissa and he announced in 1868 that the object must be to save every life; every district officer would be held personally responsible for the loss of a single life that might have been saved. It is not easy to know exactly what this would mean in practice but it was repeated by Lord Northbrook in 1873 and applied to Temple's famine. By the end of the century, organization had gone so far that direct deaths from starvation were almost unknown.

The first principle of famine doctrine, which from 1868 on was accepted by everyone, was that work must be provided for every able-bodied man. And there must be grain at the relief works which he could buy with the money he earned. As to those too old or ill to work, there was at first no absolutely agreed doctrine. The Central Government and the Provincial Governments were not yet at one. Some 'gratuitous' relief there must be, that all agreed, but the fear of pauperization was strong with one government, a tender heart stronger with another. One felt there must be no interruption of the normal course of trade, another that famine was like war and everything else must go by the board.

Thus there was some difference of opinion in Temple's famine of 1874 in Behar. George Campbell, now Lieutenant-Governor himself, wanted to prohibit the normal export of grain from Calcutta. This, he thought, would bring down prices in Calcutta and the grain would automatically flow to the high prices in Behar. He would 'dam up the grain and force it back'. Lord Northbrook, however, was 'as much shocked as a bishop might be with a clergyman who denied all the thirty-nine articles'. The Central Government over-ruled Campbell in the sacred name of free trade and imported rice from Burma — 'transactions nice, in Burmah rice' -- in quantities which almost equalled the exports. 'The strange spectacle was seen of fleets of ships, taking rice out from the Hooghly and passing other ships bringing rice in.'

The liberality of 1873-74 was due to the mistaken optimism of 1866 and led in its turn to greater austerity in 1878. In this year's widespread famine, the Government of Madras began by importing grain to keep down prices but they were informed by the centre that they must not interfere with trade. The Viceroy, Lord Lytton, visiting Madras relief camps, found them 'like picnics . . . and the people on them, who do no work of any kind, are bursting with fat . . .' But other people were dying—how many it is not easy to be sure.

The next step was the famous Commission of 1880, under the chairmanship of Richard Strachey. The views of this commission were almost the same as George Campbell's but they received more attention and were formulated in the Famine Code. This meant that when the Famine began all points of principle had already been argued and there in the Code was the answer.

Plans were to be made at once for the works that would be undertaken in a famine. There would be major engineering works in each district and minor village works as well; both were to be as far as possible designed to prevent famine in future, a pond to store water in the rains, a great embankment that would turn the overflow of a river to useful purposes, perhaps a canal, even wells. There were to be two stages, scarcity and famine. Work on the major works would begin in scarcity; the village works would come into operation when there was famine. Wages at the relief works would be fixed according to need and grain would be sold at grainshops at the legal price; there would be an extra allowance for dependants. There would be huts, hospitals and markets at the relief works.

Those who could not work must be helped by the Government; private charity was sure to break down. In normal times, the district must be organized into circles, with an officer already appointed for each circle who would do his best, when famine came, to see that relief went where it was needed and that there was as little waste as possible. To a generation inured in peace to air raid precautions and civil defence, there is a familiar ring to all this; in 1880, it was something unknown in the rest of the world.

There was of course much more than this in the report of 1880; there was provision for remitting land revenue and rent, for giving advances for seed, and above all there was emphasis on 'moral strategy' — creating a feeling of confidence. But the plan made in advance was to be the essence of the cure. As to prevention, railways, irrigation and roads were the answer to famine; from now on a sum of fifteen million rupees, rather more than a million pounds, was set aside every year as Famine Insurance. It might be saved up against a bad year, or used on canals and railways that were intended to prevent famine.

But whatever Commission reported, whatever codes were written, the district officer had as usual to do the work. His main task, once the famine had begun, was to supervise some twenty or more circle officers. What a circle officer actually did in a famine is told well by Herman Kisch, the son of a London surgeon, who arrived in India in 1873 and six months later, in March 1874, was posted to famine duty in Temple's Behar famine. When these letters were written, he was twenty-three years old.

2. ON FAMINE DUTY

... 'All along our ride ... 53 miles or thereabouts,' he writes on March 17th, 1874, 'we saw an almost unbroken stream of bullock carts carrying grain to ... the famine-stricken districts of Tirhut ... The road has been cut up in a horrible way by these carts and is now about eight inches thick in dust ... For the last four days or so I have had to groom my own horse on arrival as my grass-cutter has never arrived till hours after I do and my syce is ill ...' On the 18th, he finds the signs of famine more marked though very few deaths have actually taken place yet. Six days later he has reached his circle and taken up quarters in an indigo factory and he now writes describing his duties in detail:

'I have under my management ... an area of 198 square miles ... I have full liberty to adopt whatever measures I think necessary, subject only to very general instructions ... I have also to give weekly reports to the sub-divisional officer ... When my establishment is complete, I shall have under me at my own office three clerks, 12 sub-superintendents and 24 messengers, while I shall have in the centre of every group of ten villages a store-house, with a storekeeper, a salesman and two messengers, besides watchmen. I am supposed to make myself personally acquainted with the condition of every village ... and I have never had such hard work. Every day I have been from seven to eight hours a day in the saddle, riding about from village to village and searching out those who are able to work ... and those who from weakness or disease can now do no work at all.

Of the latter I have as yet fortunately not come on many . . . In one of the villages that I visited the condition of the villagers was such that I thought it necessary to have them fed on the spot with cooked food, rather than trust to their reaching alive the nearest store . . . It is impossible to describe to you the condition of some of the children in this village; after what I saw there I can readily conceive a skeleton from an anatomical museum being able to walk; unless I had seen it myself I could not have believed that anyone could live with so thin a covering to the bones. The very colour of the bone was visible through the thin black film that surrounded it . . . In some of the villages, the people are quite comfortably off, while within a couple of thousand yards there is the last stage of distress. . . .'

'You can have but the very slightest idea', he goes on, 'of the immense difficulties of dealing with a famine in a country like India. You go into a village where most of the people are Brahmins, the highest caste, and you find among them great distress . . . if you ask one of these men what work he is able and willing to do, he answers that he can pray. There is a great temptation to get in a rage with this answer, which is given perhaps twenty times in one day . . . but the Brahmin . . . would die without a murmur sooner than work on a tank or road with common coolies.'

'You must not think that the seven or eight hours riding a day which I now have to do — at the imminent risk of knocking up my horses — constitutes all my work. I have to organize relief works, arrange for the erection of store-houses, and give directions as to the distribution of gratuitous relief; besides I have to superintend and control the various registers and accounts . . . and give endless minute instructions. I have only one clerk who is supposed to know English and he does not know enough to make his knowledge of any use . . . Today from 6 a.m. till 12.30 p.m., with the exception of breakfast time, I was doing my office work and from 12.30 p.m. till 8 p.m. I was out on my horse. . . .'

Kisch was at this time always worried about his horses; he had two of his own but the work was too much for them; 'another day I was on a horse from 8 a.m. till 9 p.m.', he wrote. 'The result is that the horses are getting rather weak but I hope to get a government horse soon . . .' He had to have two from the Government in the end, which with his own two gave him enough. 'Since I came here I have erected 15 Government grain store-houses and opened about 22 Relief works', he writes by April 8th, only a fortnight after he came. 'I give employment to about 15,000 men and women per day and am feeding gratuitously about 3000 more. I have full authority to do what I choose and I do it . . .' 'If only I could fix an iron fence round my circle, I think I might save everyone in it alive; but . . . men are journeying down from Nepal to join my relief works. . . .'

He speaks often of the rascality that goes on. There is neither the time nor the staff to weigh the grain every time it changes hands and so it is almost impossible to check abuses; storekeepers say they have distributed more free grain than in fact they have, grain-dealers who are allowed grain on condition they sell at a fixed price sell at a higher price. Hearing of a case of this, Kisch 'at once rode off to his shop and found him selling at this rate to hundreds of people who were buying from him in ignorance of the rate fixed. There was of course nothing to be done but to inflict chastisement on the spot . . .' Several other men he tried for misappropriating wages and the like. 'In all these cases, I give the maximum sentence in my power', but with all he did: 'You can form no idea of the amount of swindling and robbery that goes on . . . All the subordinate officers are men who are picked up at a moment's notice, without characters, without money . . . so that I don't know that the state of things shows that the people generally are much worse than those of their education are in other countries.'

Kisch had an Indian doctor to help him but would not at first establish a hospital, because he wanted 'the people to keep to their own villages and homes and not crowd together'. He gave out raw cotton to women of high caste to be spun, had the yarn woven and made into garments for the poorest. By May 13th, Kisch had over forty reservoirs under his own management; some of these were about 'a thousand feet long and nearly as wide; in the rains there will be 20 or 30 feet of water in them and they will have water all the year round'. He had four large grain stores to supply the smaller local stores. 'Each of these four contains from 1,600,000 to 4,800,000 lbs. of grain, of which the intrinsic value must be much over a million rupees, while its value in this crisis is beyond calculation. There is, at each store, a man on fifteen rupees a month [about one pound sterling or half-a-crown more] with a staff of messengers and guards on four rupees a month.' He thought the storekeepers ought to receive at least three hundred rupees a month — a proposal horrifying to anyone who knew the pay and responsibilities of police officers and *tahsildars*.

By the end of May he was watching the sky for rain, and anxious about the next crop and the chance of his stores holding out till the crop was cut. But rain came early in June and by the 15th he could write: 'All day long rice is being poured into my circle by the various military officers engaged in this transport. Every day two or three Lieutenants, Captains and Majors come into Bhikwa with thousands of carts, bullocks and horses and mules . . . Even the officers who bring up these stores of grain say that the whole thing is like the march of an army . . . Each officer brings perhaps 300 or 500 carts with 3 to 5 bullocks each, and they have to move along with mud up to their axles . . .' 'I have to run about like mad to see it stored, to the lasting injury of my own and Government horses. . . .'

It should here be explained that Kisch's area was not more than a hundred miles from the railway at Patna and that two temporary light railways had been constructed to bring railhead nearer the famine. To feed Tirhut by bullocks was not the problem it would have been in Mogul days.

Kisch tells of one day which involved a stage on a horse, one on an elephant, two more on second and third horses, a fifth stage on an elephant and a last stage home on a fourth horse which was not there to meet him. He had not been able to start till 11.30 in the morning because of office work; he walked home the last five miles and was in by two o'clock in the morning.

Already there were criticisms. It was true that for the first time in Indian history there had been a famine with hardly any direct loss of life from starvation; the people too had left the relief works and gone on to their fields as soon as the rain fell. But had it all been necessary? Had not expenditure been too lavish? Kisch's answer was definite. Even in July he wrote: 'If I stopped the sale of Government grain for two weeks, and the same measure was adopted for only fifty miles around me, in my circle alone the air would be so foul with the dead that it would be impossible to move outside the house.'

By August, anxiety was growing again as the rains had abated, and Kisch was planning to dam all the rivers in his circle. 'I cannot conceive so rapid a system of education as an Indian famine . . . When I came up to Tirhut, I knew no more how to dig a good tank or build a grainstore or to store grain so as to avoid injury from damp or heat or to do a hundred other things that I have to do, than I have of how to build an English house or play the piano. Now I can do very well the things I have mentioned . . .' A week later, 'there is fearful anxiety about the crops in Tirhut, for the rains have almost completely been withheld since July . . . By the cessation of the rains, those who have been censuring the measures adopted by the Government have met with the sternest rebuke conceivable, for it was surely the duty of the Government to provide for the support of the people up to such time as the new crop was secured. . . .'

However, on September 3rd, 'we had a tremendous fall of rain during the night and there is now no fear of another famine'. Of Kisch's five dams, three stood the shock of the torrents from the hills and one of the others 'would have stood if it had not been dammed further up and the dam broke and the water came down like a wall ten feet high . . .' For some time, he could only get about his circle on 'a large elephant; a small one is no use at all'. Even when things were dryer, he still had work for four horses and a pony. But the famine was really over now and Kisch became sub-divisional officer, after a first year in India which, one may agree, had been as educative as could well be imagined.

3. THE CONTEST WITH FAMINE

One may guess that his district officer saw from the start that Kisch was a conscientious and sensible young man and left him to himself. He would have plenty to do without fussing over a man who could be relied on. Kisch says himself that he was 'the only C.S.' by which he meant the only officer of the I.C.S. or covenanted service. There were some men from other provinces in Behar for the famine, particularly from the North-West, but they would be divided up between the districts, with not more than one to each; there were also subalterns from Indian Army regiments. But the framework of the famine organization was the normal framework of the district.

The unit was, as a rule, the circle of an inspector of village accountants, a *qanungo*, the descendant in name of the Mogul official who had once been so powerful in Bengal. The circle might include a hundred square miles, and as a rule a group of four or five such circles would go to the sub-division, of which again there would be four or five in a district. In the North-West and the Punjab a district officer would usually have an English assistant of the covenanted service in one of his sub-divisions, the others being in charge of Deputy Collectors, Indians of the provincial service. He would start his famine with this normal district staff; if he was lucky, some help would come when the famine had really begun.

Kisch's famine — it was really Sir Richard Temple's — was the first in which a large-scale attempt had been made to deal with the emergency but neither the work nor the organization changed much in later famines. The district officer had to make sure that his circle officers were doing the kind of things Kisch did — that is, that they in their turn were making sure that their subordinates were really distributing food, work, and money where they were needed. That was his main function; his special cares were legion. He must watch the children of the men on famine works, he must see that some cattle survived the famine, he must take care that all the seed was not eaten, he must do all he could to keep cholera local.

It is no use pretending that complete success was ever achieved, but by 1908 it seemed in sight. The half century from 1858 to 1909 can indeed be looked on as a contest between two evenly matched teams in which one side gains a little, only to find the other stubbornly creeping up again. The team on one side had many members. It included the administration and the doctors, who were introducing vaccination and inoculation for small-pox and cholera. And there were the engineers, who were building roads, railways and irrigation canals; in the later stages, there were agriculturalists, with improved seed.

But on the other side were the goddess Kali, with her chaplet of men's skulls, and Siva, who is the god not only of destruction but of the phallus. The forces of destruction might seem everywhere to be slowly losing ground but because of his twofold nature Siva cannot be defeated. As the canals made fertile land from desert, his millions rolled in and one generation ate up the gains. For every child saved from small-pox he begat two more, so that three mouths gaped for food where fifty years ago there had been one. 'We may compete and struggle with Nature,' wrote Lord Curzon, 'and . . . some day perhaps, we shall obtain the mastery. But that will not be yet.'

The record of the contest is there in the reports of the Famine Commissions that followed each other like Banquo's line of kings, each pointing a moral. Each Commission concludes that preventive measures are on the right lines — though perhaps more elasticity is needed here or there — recommends the development of this road or canal, and records the belief that the people themselves are better able to meet an emergency than they were. '. . . There has been a considerable increase in the incomes of the landholding and cultivating classes and their standard of comfort has also risen . . . Their credit has also expanded . . . During recent famines, they have shown greater powers of resistance', wrote the Commission of 1908. And while the failures of harvest had been at least as great as in 1899-1900, Sir John Hewett could ask, in the midst of the famine of 1907: 'Why are we not brought into contact with people in a state of emaciation? Why do we not see bodies of persons in search of work?' His answer was that since the last emergency the organization was more complete and that railway and canal mileage had each increased in the province by 35 per cent.

It was believed by now that never again need people die from starvation because the rains had failed. Shortage there might be and high prices, which shift distress from the country to the town and in particular to the clerks and artisans, but deaths from starvation, no. During the two years of this famine of 1907, the provincial death-rate had, it is true, risen; it rose from a normal figure of 32.59 per thousand to 36.47. This means that additional deaths, above the average, had been in this famine-stricken province rather less than 200,000 out of more than 47 million; most of these extra deaths were from small-pox or cholera. Against this, consider the estimates for the Bengal famine in 1770 and that lamentable famine of 1866 in Orissa. In both of these, district officers thought that about a third to a quarter of the whole population had died; if they were right and if deaths in the United Provinces in 1908 had been on that scale, the additional deaths would have been not 200,000 but 10 million. There is, obviously, a great deal of conjecture in any such figures, but at least it is clear there had been an improvement.

The network of railways was by now fairly close for a large continent, and it was agreed that there was no more need for railways designed purely as a protection against famine. Indeed, Indian critics of the administration said too much had been spent on railways, more than the country could afford. In 1909, there were 31,500 miles of railway and throughout the great band of flat country that runs from Calcutta to Peshawar it would have been hard to find a village that was fifty miles from a railway, and there were not many that were twenty-five.

It was not a close network compared with England's nor does the total sound impressive compared with the United States. But in both these countries there were men eager to build railways and to find money for them. Indians were more interested in other things; they did not want railways enough to build them or pay for them. Every mile of line in India was built with Government guarantees, nearly all with British capital, nearly all on the initiative of the Government. The true comparison is with China, whose civilization is as ancient as India's and whose territory and population are even vaster. Here whole provinces, four hundred miles across, are without railways and the total length open to traffic in 1910 was 3000 miles, with another 1500 under construction — just a tenth of India's.

Canals cannot be dealt with so shortly as railways. George Campbell's Committee, in their report after the Orissa famine, had recommended irrigation but with some warnings. Not all forms of canal were equally successful, they pointed out, and they were not quite convinced that irrigation did not do as much harm as good, because there seemed little doubt that it brought with it fever — that is, malaria.

In spite of these hesitations, there was steady progress in building up a canal system which by 1909 was the most extensive in the world. Length does not tell everything about canals; an irrigation canal like the majestic stream that leads the Ganges from Hardwar, twice as broad as the Thames, will waste away through secondary canals and distributaries till it comes down to channels a horse can cross with hardly a lengthening of stride. It was this dissipation that to orthodox Hindus seemed impious and which caused much opposition to the Ganges canal. It means more to speak of acres irrigated; by 1909 the 13,000 miles of primary and secondary canals with 42,000 miles of distributaries irrigated 23 million acres of land. That is half the total acreage of Great Britain.

Some of this was in Madras, where most of the irrigation works were in the coastal strip and were made by building near the mouth of a river a dam, locally called an *anicut*; some again was in Sind, a province which like Egypt is the gift of the river and where works planned for the future were greater than any yet attempted by man. Most were in the North-Western Provinces and in the Punjab.

Some of these canals were in themselves feats of engineering by which a people might be content to be judged; there was, for instance, already the tunnel under the Western Ghats, which brings the waters of the Periyar river from the sea coast on the West under the mountains to the Eastern side. And the Upper Ganges Canal, one of the earliest of all, begun in Thomason's day under the Company, takes the waters of the Ganges along the foot of the hills, across the warp of the country, threading its way beneath one Himalayan torrent-bed and over the next. These torrent-beds are in the winter a half-mile of bare shingle with a trickle three feet wide in the middle; in spate they will sweep away walls of concrete as though they were wet cardboard. But the great canal strides over them.

These and many more are technical achievements outside the scope of this book; we are concerned with the administrative effort behind. And it is worth noting that finance was in those days so conservative that only after much debate and with a high sense of daring did John Lawrence and his council, advised by the two Stracheys, John and Richard, decide that it was permissible to borrow for expenditure on canals.

Canals in the North-West or United Provinces secured an area that had previously been uncertain, but men had lived and ploughed there for thousands of years. In the Punjab, irrigation between the rivers meant that a desert suddenly blossomed, that where a few nomad tribes had grazed their goats and camels towns and villages sprang up and good wheat was grown.

The five rivers of the Punjab enclose four areas which once were desert, not absolute desert, but untilled waste land that for nine months of the year was no use except to camels. The water level was eighty feet below the surface, so that irrigation from wells was out of the question, but for canal irrigation the country was ideal. There was a slight fall from North-East to South-West and between every pair of rivers ran a water-shed, invisible to the eye, which dictated the alignment of the main canal.

It is an idea to stir the dullest — a desert ready to be peopled, a Utopia waiting for its architect. And there is something staggering about its success. Before the water flowed, a plan was made, a whole countryside was designed, roads, railways, railway-stations, market towns, villages, the mosque, the temple, the village school, the pound, the side-road, the little bridge, the grove of trees for shade, firewood and timber, the meeting-place, the magistrate's court, the police-station. Everyone has seen the model village in an exhibition, with men an inch high, little cows and hens and horses, shop, church and cinema. But this was real. And it was not a village, but a district with millions of acres of fertile land — made fertile by canal water.

You must picture a 'Through the Looking-Glass' landscape divided into squares, each twenty-seven and a half acres, a peasant's holding. Men had to be picked for these holdings who were sturdy and hardy and ready to work; they had to be moved, and before they came things had to be made ready for them. 'A railway a hundred miles long had to be aligned, running through the centre of the tract, and later another to the East parallel to it at 20 or 25 miles distance', wrote Sir Geoffrey de Montmorency, describing the Lower Chenab Colony of some 2½ million irrigated acres, which was colonized between 1892 and 1896. 'At suitable intervals, sites had to be selected for stations and at every twenty miles or so a site for a country town and market. The general aim was that no colony village should be more than twelve miles from a railway station or market. Main roads had to be planned, to connect stations and town with the villages and to link up with towns, railway junctions and river crossings . . . Minor roads connecting village with village and feeding the main arteries had to be arranged for in the same way. Hard on the heels of the arriving colonists, police-stations and dispensaries had to be built and head-quarters for sub-collectorates chosen. Town plans had to be drawn out for grain-markets, general shops, cotton-ginning factories, urban residences and so forth . . . Water supplies, drainage, sewage-disposal had to be devised. . . .'

That was one side of the colonization officer's work. But it was not all a matter of maps and blue prints. The nomad tribes who had grazed their camels on the scrub were not pleased to see a garden city with mosques and temples, orange groves and cotton fields. They brought their beasts at night to feed on the colonists' crops; they stole the colonists' cattle. The Sikh colonists organized a home guard to patrol the fields and if a nomad was found near the village after dark he was beaten insensible. The colonization officer had to civilize the nomads, to set them to plough and teach them to sow. He must also be judge in a dozen disputes a day; Gulab Singh said the water would not reach his square, but that was because he wanted the vacant square next door, which was meant to be a drinking-place for cattle and a village fuel reserve. Darwan Singh was not fulfilling the conditions of his grant; he had not planted two trees for every acre, he had not set up boundary-marks, he had not yet built his house or subscribed to the village well.

Each man had his square, all the same size, the perfect peasant com-munity; it sounds a little dull. And it was hard to see who would be the leaders in such a community. Here and there, then, larger grants were made, to yeomen of four squares, or to capitalists of more than four. The last were not a success; no Coke of Norfolk, no Turnip Townshend, appeared in Lyallpur.

A time came when the colonies on the Lower Chenab Canal seemed so complete and so successful that they might suitably be combined into the one administrative district of Lyallpur. By 1941 this district, made from the desert, had a population of more than one and a quarter million and a cultivated area over one and a half million acres, its crops being worth six and a half million pounds a year. If the English were to choose one monument by which their years in India were to be remembered, it might well be the canals, the cotton, and the prosperous villages of Lyallpur.

That was one of the Punjab Colonies; there were others. Irrigation, again, was only one part of the contest with famine. Indeed, in the known history of mankind, this antagonist had not before been assailed on so considerable a scale. It may be that different measures should have been taken; that finance should have been less conservative, that the balance between the peasant, who likes high prices, and the clerks and artisans, who do not, should have been altered more radically than it was. It may be that more efforts should have gone to canals and less to railways. All these are controversial points, but in all this period even the critics of the régime agreed in believing that, as one of them said, 'no class of men is more anxious to remedy the evils than British administrators who have devoted themselves to the great task of improving the material condition of the people of India'.

It was a devotion that did not escape without loss. At Jubbalpore in the Central Provinces, there is a cross on which is written:

'To the memory of the officers of the Central Provinces who laid down their lives during the great famine of 1896-1897.'

There are nine names; five civilians, one engineer, one policeman, two subalterns of the Indian Army. It is one example of the losses of one province in one famine year. There were at that time twenty-two officers in the Central Provinces Commission; five of them were lost.

CHAPTER VI

BURMA

I. MADRAS, ASSAM AND BURMA

AFTER the Maratha wars, the centre of interest in India shifts to the Northern plains. There were the Sikh Wars and the Mutiny; when these were over, the only problem of foreign policy that could be called important lay to the North-West. The centre of power was for seven months in Simla and for five in Calcutta, so that twice a year at least the Gangetic plain was brought to the Viceroy's notice. And there was perhaps some feeling that the people who had made the Mutiny and the people who had ended it required more attention than the rest of the empire.

It has been the fashion in books by Englishmen to emphasize the differences between the people of different parts of India. The tendency was natural, because from England the whole country was inclined to look like one pink wedge-shaped mass, while it probably was true to say, as all the books do say, that the differences of language, physique and habit were greater than any to be found in Europe. Sometimes these differences have been made the text for a political sermon which ignored the underlying feeling of unity. But it is not necessary to suppose there was always a political motive in the emphasis; differences were bound to loom large to Englishmen who knew one part of India well. 'They came,' wrote Kipling of his heroine William and two officers sent South from the Punjab on famine duty, 'to an India more strange to them than to the untravelled Englishman — the flat red India of the palm tree, palmyra-palm and rice, the India of the picture-books . . .' 'What can you expect', asked William, 'of a country where they call a *bhisty* a *tunny-cutch*?' And when they came back to the North, she 'looked out with moist eyes and nostrils that dilated joyously. The South of pagodas and palm trees, the over-populated Hindu South, was done with. . . .'

The differences in country and people were real enough but it would be tedious to try to describe them all. And in a sense, within India proper the externals of an Englishman's life in a district were not really very different. To a man from the Punjab, where temperature rigidly defines the camping season, it would be a shock to find that, in Madras, men went into camp when it suited them and made no difference between the seasons. There would be new languages in the South and a strange system of land tenures; more perplexing perhaps would be shades of difference in marriage customs, feasts and the like, which looked at first sight familiar. But the bungalow and the court-room were much the same as in the North; the visitor would still have his morning ride and his evening game of racquets, would still give his orders with confidence, though here perhaps he was the only man of his own nation among a million people of the country and in the North he had been one among a thousand. Whether the tea-party was at Trichinopoly or at Lahore, the odes in his honour and the scent of the wet marigolds round his neck would be much the same.

Districts were larger in Madras and it took longer to reach the seniority needed for charge of a district. In fact, a district was more like the group of four, five or six districts, which in the North were grouped under a Commissioner. A Madras district was divided into divisions, not sub-divisions, and the divisional officer lived in his division and was perhaps a little more independent than the northern S.D.O., a little less so than a northern district officer. But his work and responsibilities were not very different; he too settled disputes and supervised the work of village accountants, though he did call them by names strange to northern ears.

Communications were worse in the South and the pace of life a little slower, the district officer a little more patriarchal. It was widely held in the South that it was no use casting eyes on Simla or Calcutta; the Government of India, you were told, was for the Bengal, Punjab and North-Western men and in Madras you must be a district officer or at the most aspire to the Board of Revenue or the provincial secretariat. To the last, the Government of Madras preserved a separatism of their own and were inclined to regard the Government of India as a rather vulgar late eighteenth-century innovation. The Madras district officer was perhaps one degree deeper in the jungle than his counterpart in the North, who more often saw English soldiers and English women. But he was as likely in the South as in the North to be brought up by someone like W. O. Horne of Madras who wrote: 'Paddison used to say that I trained my Assistants on the lines of the ancient Persians, who, according to Herodotus, taught their boys to ride, to shoot and to speak the truth.'

But if Madras, in spite of differences, was still part of the Indian continent, Burma to an Indian was almost as foreign as England. Burma and Assam are countries of thick steamy forest, of heavy rainfall and rapid rivers; India is dry, baked and dusty. There are no wide plains in Burma and except in the delta it would be hard to go in a straight line for fifty miles without coming to mountains.

The people are no less different. There are many races and languages, Burmans, Talaings, Arakanese, Shans, Karens, Nagas and others, but all, even the primitives from the hills, seem to resemble each other in gaiety, in a love of bright colours, in a dislike — at least on the part of the males — for hard work, in an inconsequent emotional recklessness. And among the civilized people of Burma, that is, the Buddhists, there goes with this, paradoxically enough, an air of being reconciled to the world we live in, a readiness to take life as it comes — and death too for that matter — without making too much fuss.

All this is very unlike India. Whatever critics may say, there are qualities common to all the people of the continent and Indians are serious and introspective people, perhaps the most serious in the world. Their seriousness has led them into religious extremes and some customs hardly defensible by reason. They are hedged about with rules and ritual. But in Burma the people are gay and their religion enjoins nothing at which reason jibs. Their ideals of conduct and their ways of behaviour are much less different than India's from those of the Christian West, or at least the secularized Protestant West. There is none of the hard puritanism of the desert which flowed into Northern India with Islam, no trace of the dark worship of blood and destruction which in parts of India disfigured Saivite Hinduism. Purdah, suttee, caste, child-marriage, all these are unknown. And Indians who have been to Burma shake their heads in horror at people who can lawfully eat anything and who do in fact gladly eat dogs, rats and lizards.

Burma is a poor country but the comforts of life and the civilized decencies are valued; men and women wear silk when they can, cultivate gardens round their houses, put flowers in their hair. In the villages there is often a *pwe*, which means a play, a feast, or a puppet-show, something to which everyone looks forward and which is conducted with a good deal of artistry. Something of the kind, sport, art, excitement, variety, the Burman seems to find essential. There was more robbery by gangs than anywhere else in the world but even the official Burma *Gazetteer* put it down mainly to the desire for sport and excitement.

A gay and violent people, careless of life, hating monotony and discipline, witty, idle and often beautiful, neat and attractive in their dress — that is the impression left by the Burmese of the valleys and cultivated lands. An untamed, an unspoilt, people, and yet their civilization was very far from primitive. Burma for centuries had been Buddhist; there were monasteries everywhere and a monastic brotherhood of some learning and highly organized. In every monastery, there was a school at which every Burmese boy learned to read and write. Many of the girls could read too and women had rights not yet enjoyed in Victorian England. They owned their own property; they managed their own affairs.

In the hills, among the Karens, the Kachins, and the Nagas, there was another world. Nearly all these tribes took heads and until a man had shown himself a man by bringing home the head of an enemy he did not easily find a wife. In every Karen house of certain tribes a stone was kept to which offerings of blood were made, because if the people did not give it blood to eat, it would eat them. War was made on another village with elaborate ritual; the bones of chickens and the gall of pigs were examined for omens; parties were sent to make sure that surprise could be achieved. At a sign of resistance or of preparation for defence the plan would be abandoned, but if the enemy could be surprised they would be mercilessly slaughtered. There were tribes that went entirely naked and tribes among whom money was unknown. It was a primitive half-savage world, remote alike from the monasteries of Buddhist Burma and from India's highly developed Aryan civilization.

Yet Burma, so radically different from India, by the force of circumstance became an appanage of the Indian Empire. This is a book about the English in India and any account of Burma must be inadequate. But some mention there must be, because for fifty years Burma was an Indian province and a young man who went into the I.C.S. might find himself in Burma. The country became a part of India because of three wars, little wars to Victorian England but important to the Burmans. They were separated from each other in each case by a quarter of a century. The first happened mainly, and the others partly, because of the isolation and ignorance of the King of Burma's court at Ava.

BURMA

2. THE THREE BURMESE WARS

The king's house at Ava was called the Centre of the Universe and the kings really believed that the universe contained very little except the sea in the South, Bengal to the West, China to the East, and northward the mountains of Tibet. They had conquered the old kingdom of Pegu; they had brought the hill tribes, the Shans, the Karens, the Nagas, and the rest, to acknowledge a vague suzerainty; they had overrun Assam and the old kingdom of Arakan. They had some excuse for arrogance.

It was an excuse they needed. In 1818, the King of Burma summoned Lord Hastings to surrender three of the richest provinces of Bengal; they were, he said ancient fiefs of the crown of Arakan. He had frequently ordered the Governor-General to do obeisance and would tolerate disobedience no longer. And, in 1823 his leisurely patience being exhausted, the king ordered his troops to advance and take Calcutta. They did advance, bringing a set of golden fetters for the Governor-General, and at first met with some success.

There can hardly have been a war in history in which the provocation was more clearly on one side. But however justifiable, it was conducted on the English side with very little administrative ability. Forty thousand soldiers were at one time or another involved; fifteen thousand of them died. For every man who died of wounds received in battle, twenty-four died of scurvy, dysentery or malaria. Rangoon however was taken from the sea in 1824 and in 1826 a treaty was signed at Yandabu, near Mandalay. By this treaty, the Lord of the Seas and the Earth agreed to pay an indemnity and ceded Assam, Arakan and Tenasserim. The treaty was recorded in the official chronicles:

'White strangers from the West . . . landed at Rangoon . . . and were permitted to advance as far as Yandabu. By the time they reached this place their resources were exhausted and they were in great distress. They then petitioned the King, who in his clemency and generosity sent them large sums of money to pay their expenses back and ordered them out of the country. . . .'

Pegu, that is the delta and the lower reaches of the Irrawaddy, was restored to the King of Burma. This was something new in Burmese experience and not expected by the inhabitants. Most of them were Talaings, not Burmese; most of them had helped the English. Some were crucified, others were exiled. They were not the last friends of England to suffer for English liberalism.

The first Resident at the court of Ava was Major Burney, the brother of Fanny. He was liked and trusted, but it was a principle of Burmese etiquette that one head man could deal only with another head man and in no circumstances with his deputy. The King of Burma could deal only with the King of England and could not recognize a mere governor-general, a view which made many difficulties for the governor-general's representative. Again, when King Bagyidaw became insane, his successor regarded all undertakings of his brother as lapsed and the Treaty of Yandabu with them. This made the Resident's task impossible and he was withdrawn in 1840.

There followed a period during which British subjects were warned that they went to Rangoon at their own risk. After ten years of this, all reasonable limits were exceeded by a governor who committed no less than thirty-six acts of extortion against British subjects, culminating in two of the grossest kind upon the masters of two British ships.

Lord Dalhousie sent a frigate of the Royal Navy to remonstrate. The court of Ava seems to have wished to meet his requests but the whole business was complicated by each party's utter ignorance of what the other thought good manners. Commodore Lambert and the Burmese each erroneously believed that the other had been deliberately insulting; Lord Dalhousie did not want war but he thought it was inevitable in any case, and, as he said, 'We can't afford to be shown to the door anywhere in the East.' He reluctantly sent an ultimatum to which no reply was received and the Second Burmese War began.

It was conducted much more efficiently than the first and within eight months, in December 1852, Dalhousie ended it by a proclamation annexing Pegu. 'Conquest in Burma would be a calamity second only to the calamity of war', he had said at the beginning. Events had frog-marched him along a road that was distasteful. Yet it would have been alien to his nature to restore the conditions that had produced war and he was determined not to waste time on negotiating with a king who did not understand what a treaty was; the simplest thing seemed to be to take what was in his hand and go no further.

Pegu was added to Arakan and Tenasserim; these three made the province of British Burma under a Chief Commissioner. The province lasted until 1885, when it became merged in the larger province of Burma. King Tharrawaddy, like his brother, had become insane and had been succeeded by King Pagan, the fourth in succession to be both bad and mad. But Mindon, who deposed Pagan in 1852, was

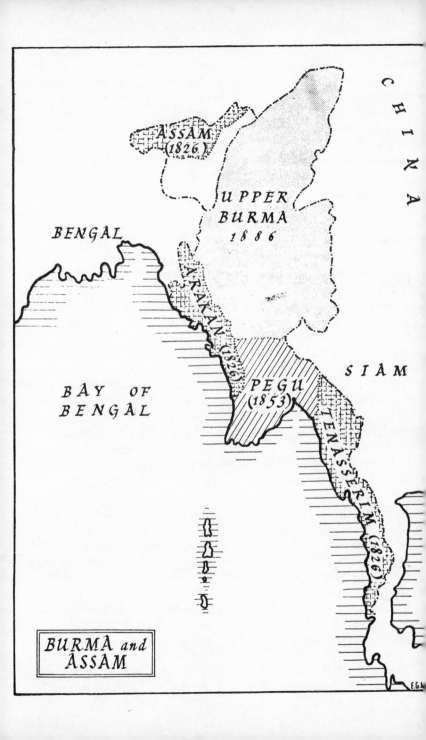

CHINA

ASSAM
(1826)

BENGAL

UPPER
BURMA
1886

ARAKAN (1826)

BAY OF
BENGAL

PEGU
(1853)

SIAM

TENASSERIM (1826)

BURMA and
ASSAM

E.G.M.

a sensible man, tolerant and merciful, reported by European visitors to be 'every inch a king', in spite of his custom of gazing at them through field-glasses when they came in audience. It was remarkable that anyone so normal should have come to be King of Burma, because, to keep the royal blood pure, the first queen had to be the king's half-sister.

The province of British Burma continued for thirty years. Burmans in the narrower sense were in a minority in the British province; they looked to the King in Mandalay with respect and indeed reverence; they were proud that he still ruled but they showed no great anxiety to count among his subjects. The Talaings, the Arakanese, the Karens and the rest had at first been glad to see the English; as the memories of anarchy and extortion faded, they, no doubt, like people in India, began to be less sure. But hardly any native of Burma was pleased by the outcome of the Third Burmese War.

King Mindon encouraged English trade with his own country and through his borders with Yunnan. He agreed to negotiate with a mere Viceroy, though even he could not receive a Resident who would not kneel barefooted in the royal presence. But King Mindon passed away; there followed an intrigue and a *coup d'état* from which emerged the dominant figures of a queen-mother and her daughter Supayalat, a young woman who as a child enjoyed tearing live birds to pieces and who happened to be married to Thibaw, a nonentity among Mindon's forty-eight sons. This couple and the palace staff gave orders for the massacre of the survivors of King Mindon's blood; the victims numbered between seventy and eighty. It was an affair for which there was ample Burmese precedent but it shocked the rest of the world.

There followed a short period during which almost all English, Chinese and other foreign opinion in the British province clamoured for annexation. The mere existence of the kingdom seemed to them an outrage to humanity. There was a good deal of support for their view in London, and no one felt that teak, rubies, silver or oil were adequate reasons for disobeying the dictates of conscience. The Chief Commissioner, however, Sir Charles Bernard, a wise and far-sighted man, believed that to annex Upper Burma would deprive the Burmese of all hope and pride and at the same time would alarm the princes of India. The Government of India accepted his view and continued to do nothing, but without much conviction.

Their hands however were forced. The clique who surrounded

Supayalat and her mother embarked on an intrigue with Paris which aimed at bringing a French railway through Indo-China and Siam to Mandalay, at establishing a French bank and selling French arms in Upper Burma. This was disturbing to the English but did not immediately provoke a breach. Nor did it immediately bring the court the money they needed; in 1885 they borrowed £100,000 from a British firm, found it was not enough, asked for another loan of twice as much and when that was refused brought a false case against the firm and fined them the amount that had been refused.

This did bring the Government of India to the point. Mandalay was instructed to accept suzerainty and a mild degree of control. Thibaw replied by ordering his troops to drive the English into the sea. Within nineteen days, before the end of November 1885, he was a prisoner in his own palace and soon afterwards Upper Burma was annexed. It is not really part of the purpose of this book to pronounce a verdict on every act of Her Majesty's Government and this sequence of events is related merely as a background to the lives of certain men. But it is surely somewhat simple-minded to ascribe to a single cause all that took place. Greed for undeveloped natural resources no doubt was there, but it was hardly possible for any civilized government in Rangoon to condone the behaviour of Supayalat's clique. The magnanimous act of course would have been to impose after the war the terms offered before it.

3. THE THREE NEW PROVINCES

Three new provinces, Assam, Arakan and Tenasserim, were acquired after the First Burmese War. They were administered to begin with chiefly by military officers, for whom life, particularly if they were married, was seldom blessed by that settled comfort which the Victorian English enjoyed at home. Captain John Butler, appointed in 1841 to the civil branch of the service, found himself Assistant to the Political Agent of Upper Assam and in charge of the Hill Tribes. He set out with his wife and child and, after six weeks' journey, reached his headquarters, where 'we were fortunate in meeting with a small bungalow made of bamboos, grass and reed walls; but it was void of the luxury of a door or glass window'. He had, however, often before known the discomfort of being without windows and had brought two with him; so, having plastered the outer walls with mud and laid bamboo mats on the damp earthen floor, he and his family prepared for the rains, 'vainly imagining we were securely sheltered for some time to come'.

But when the 'Burrumpooter' began to rise, it undermined the bank on which this hut was built, 'sweeping away ten paces of the bank three or four times a day, a stupendous mass of earth falling with a crash into the bosom of the stream . . .' The family moved to Butler's court-room, but that too followed the hut into the stream and they took to the jungle. A thatched roof was constructed, but the rain was too heavy to build walls and they had to make shift with canvas screens from tents.

That was only the beginning of the Butlers' trials. The climate of Assam runs to extremes; earthquakes and landslides come like April showers in England. Butler's tent was one night blown away from over his head and when he took refuge in a police-station the building collapsed about his ears. He and his family were transferred three times in the first two years, apart from being constantly on tour. One move, taking four days, was made in a boat roofed over with grass to provide two rooms, each three and a half feet wide by nine feet long and three high. The travellers were not once able to set foot on shore and were so bitten by mosquitoes as to be 'literally scarred from head to foot with sores'. However, they were a family, 'not accustomed to make mountains of molehills' and on arrival they 'enjoyed only the more the comfort of a mud-plastered house without doors or windows'. It was during another such journey by boat that 'we were unexpectedly surprised by the birth of our second son James'.

Captain Butler found that the interest of his work compensated him for all this; Assam was a non-regulation tract and he was Judge, Magistrate and Collector in one. He was 'expected to do everything . . . For six months of the year, the Principal Assistant of a district is constantly travelling about the country, inspecting roads, causing them to be repaired, opening new ones, instituting local fiscal inquiries from village to village, enduring great fatigue, exposed to many perils from climate, wild beasts, and demi-savages in the hills'. But what compensations Mrs. Butler found beyond the intermittent company of her husband he does not say.

Arakan was worse than Assam because of the peculiarly deadly form that malaria takes on that coast. A century later, with all the help of mepacrine and D.D.T., it was not a country that Englishmen could take liberties with. In the first half of the century, it usually killed. An attempt to start a civil station at An lasted four years and was then given up because the first three civil officers sent there died.

Of seventy-nine consecutive Englishmen sent to Akyab, twenty-two died in the station and eighteen were invalided home. Henry Lawrence suffered all his life for the few months he spent in Arakan in the First Burmese War. Fever there was something different from the Madras fever of which Horne wrote: 'When we got an attack, we accepted it as just a go of fever, and all in the way of business. The remedies were boiling tea, unlimited blankets and a thorough sweat.'

Arakan had, too, been devastated by forty years of Burmese rule. Many of the Arakanese had fled; they now began cautiously to come back. By 1852, the population and the revenue of Akyab had increased to about two and a half times what they had been in 1830, while the area cultivated was nearly four and a half times what it had been. This was due to good officers who in spite of fever kept the peace. They had more than fever to contend with. In the early days, there were so many dacoits that the civil administration of Assam was almost a form of warfare. Hardly a month passed without an expedition up narrow creeks or by winding mountain paths against some hidden stockade, which had to be taken like an eighteenth-century fortress by making a breach and storming it. It was done by officers in charge of local levies, a very mixed lot indeed; Fytche, for instance, would not enlist a man unless he was a proved criminal. He thus at one stroke secured the most high-spirited of the population for his own side and reduced the number of his opponents.

To begin with, the old Bengal mistake was made of looking for landed proprietors, but by 1830 that was over and a new system was in force, never to be substantially changed. Village officials collected the revenue and every peasant was entitled to a tax-bill. This being Burma, not India, he could read it. His bill told him that he was taxed on so many acres, that the rate was so much — it ranged between two shillings and four shillings an acre — and that the total was so much. Circle headmen looked after forty villages or so and later carried out a kind of rough survey; they tried small civil disputes and, although their posts were not strictly hereditary, their sons were usually appointed. In Tenasserim there were 'township officers', natives of the country, to supervise the circle headmen.

4. PHAYRE AND LOWER BURMA

There was very little in Burma of either the puritanism or the fervour which the English displayed in the Punjab. But some of that spirit was transplanted at the beginning. Arthur Phayre, for instance, knew what it meant. He went from Shrewsbury to the Bengal Army and as a young man found himself stationed in the North-Western Provinces alongside 'Pickwick' Montgomery and John Thornton, both young civilians learning their work under Thomason. He went out with them in camp, and was so much attracted by the life that, when the chance came of civil employment, he took it eagerly and in the spirit of Thomason and the Lawrences.

He went to Arakan as Assistant to Archibald Bogle, who had settled Kamrup in Assam, and was now Commissioner of Arakan. This was in 1837, and Phayre was nine years on that coast. He had a short spell in Tenasserim under John Russell Colvin, who died at Agra during the Mutiny, but apart from that he was in Arakan till he rejoined his regiment for the First Sikh War. He had been alone a good deal and attained such a mastery of Burmese that Burmans thought he must be a Buddhist and laughingly asked him why he did not do obeisance to a monk when he spoke to him. He came back as Commissioner of Arakan and after the war of 1852 was moved to the new province of Pegu — the delta — where he stayed fifteen years altogether, being for the last five Chief Commissioner of British Burma. He left in 1867 and was later four years Governor of Mauritius.

It was over Bogle's head that Dalhousie sent Phayre to Pegu. Bogle was a man of ability, though he did consider it unnecessary to learn Burmese and after twenty years found he got on well enough without it. But Phayre was outstanding. 'His character stands extremely high in every respect', Dalhousie wrote. He is not, however, an easy man to understand. He lived for his work; he never wrote about himself, there are no convenient letters to sisters or mother. He never married and the Burmans 'could only explain the pure life he led by regarding him as a saint, a superior being, a kind of demigod. . . .'

He was plunged into all the business of organizing a new country, just taken over, and his letters to Dalhousie are full of the difficulties that arise in settling boundaries and securing intelligence, full of town-planning, of rents and revenues, teak and drains. A lightship was needed for Rangoon harbour, a chain of police posts for the frontier, dacoits were alternating with ex-officials in driving away villagers from the British side of the line. Capitation tax, house tax, the appointment of village headmen, rice and wheat for the troops, elephants in the Taungoo Pass, roads, anchorages, cantonments,

committees, the raising of local regiments — all these were his concern and he sticks to them so strictly, stating clear sensible views in
such clear sensible language, backed by such a knowledge of detail,
that it seems impossible he could have time for anything but official
work. Yet he did somehow find time for fossils and archaeology, for
Indo-Chinese philology, for the history and customs of the Burmans.
He wrote widely on these questions and 'his voluminous notes . . .
proclaim him not only a man of scholarly tastes but a researcher who
employed the methods of scientific enquiry'.

All this sounds like a man of mole-like industry and no more. Such
an idea is contradicted both by his portrait and his reputation. An
early description speaks of him as 'tall, gaunt and sinewy', but that
is not the impression left by his portrait, in which he seems tall,
certainly, but not gaunt. Dignified, graceful and well-proportioned,
he stands with the handsome face turned in half profile and looks the
gentleman, the scholar and the soldier that he was. A kindly eye and
a firm mouth were to be expected, but there is a touch, too, of the
dreamer in his look; all his contemporaries speak of his courtesy and
he has certainly the face of a courteous and sensitive man. Some
speak of him too as genial and even jovial, but jovial cannot be the
right word; he was deeply reserved. A friend wrote of him when he
was still in Arakan that while he appeared at first meeting to keep
nothing back, yet on better knowledge he proved unassailably reti-
cent, that he talked readily and easily, but never of himself, that
because he was naturally hot-tempered he would never enter into
controversy and would seldom reveal his views.

He was not a man then to be summed up in a phrase and the few
who have written about him have felt difficulty. Such words as
firmness and justice, courage and liberality, run from the pen and carry
no conviction. He went unarmed and would have no sentry on his
house at night, no guards with his camp even on a newly formed and
very disturbed frontier. It was his custom to see visitors on the
veranda in the early morning; he stood at a high desk and people of
all kinds, Burmese men, women and girls gathered round him; he
listened patiently and tried to find out what was the trouble each had
brought.

In wider affairs, he liked to use existing institutions. He wanted to
develop and improve the monastery schools which taught in Burmese,
but when he had gone — not immediately — his scheme was given up,
mainly perhaps because no inspectors of schools could be found who
understood Burmese and the Burmans as he had done. It was in

Phayre's time that a beginning was made with a new policy towards the forests; it was from now onwards the aim to conserve as well as to exploit. He was thirty years in Burma and no one else did so much as he did to shape the administration of Arakan and Pegu. 'To speak of Burma was to speak of Sir Arthur Phayre.'

But he was not typical and it cannot be denied there were some poor officers. Arakan, in spite of the fever, was lucky; it was almost part of Bengal and an existing system could be applied to it. Tenasserim was too far away to be part of Bengal; it was directly under the Government of India and not often visited. Occasionally of course, even in Tenasserim, someone such as John Russell Colvin or Henry Durand would alight on his way to a career, but the general standard at first was nearer that of Impey, grandson of Sir Elijah Impey. Impey sent in no treasury accounts for nine months and his treasury was at last found to be short of cash by over twenty thousand rupees. He repaid what he could and then disappeared into Siam, taking with him a local wife with whom it is understood that he lived happily ever afterwards.

Another of the same kind was Captain Corbyn of Mergui, appointed to the Burma Commission because, it was alleged, he was a relation of Maingye the Commissioner. There was an inquiry into Corbyn's conduct, of which the most charitable explanation possible is that he did not trouble himself in any way about the condition of the people and that he accepted every statement made by his Burman head clerks. The people, and particularly the Karens of the district, were lamentably oppressed in consequence. But all this changed when Phayre became Chief Commissioner. By the 'sixties, the Tenasserim officers, Lloyd, O'Riley and D'Oyly, are reported to be conscientious and hard-working, most scrupulous to be just to Karens as well as Burmans.

Nor could Sir Arthur be regarded as representative of the early officers in Pegu. By his side must be set his contemporary Thomas Latter, 'as brave a man as ever drew sword', and as a scholar in the Burmese language unsurpassed even by Phayre. He published a Burmese grammar in 1845 and believed every officer ought to pass a language examination. But either he was highly credulous or he believed in leaving his superiors to sort grain from chaff. His intelligence reports brought Dalhousie to write that 'a man such as this upon a frontier eternally crying "Wolf" is a public nuisance . . .' Dalhousie's displeasure however was averted by Latter's death. He was found assassinated in his bed while Deputy Commissioner at

Prome, murdered 'from some private motive never discovered', wrote Professor Hall.

But discover is here used in the Elizabethan sense of 'reveal'. Phayre knew what had happened and left a sealed envelope recording the facts. Latter was on the track of a celebrated dacoit, and no doubt it was in the course of his duties that he first met the dacoit's 'lesser wife'. Perhaps he meant to use her to decoy the dacoit, but it was Latter who was decoyed. He took her to live with him and the dacoit, finding this behaviour intolerable, murdered him on his own veranda. No sentry saw the murderer pass; there were two quite close.

Here perhaps is the place to say that, as everyone knows, the relations of English officers with Burmese women were quite different from anything that was usual in India. In Hickey's day, almost every one in Bengal kept 'a female servant' such as Tippee and Gulab, but these were usually low caste women, a means of satisfying a purely animal desire and no more. There were marriages with Indians of course, and sometimes men were genuinely fond of Indian mistresses, as Hickey was of Jemdanee, but it was not usual. The custom in any case was dying out in Heber's time, had almost disappeared in Northern India by the age of Thomason and the Lawrences and was never general again among officers — though Burton of the *Arabian Nights* found it general in Sind as late as the 'forties. But in Burma it was different; there was no caste and no purdah; women of all social grades went freely wherever they liked. Women talked and laughed with men, managed their own property and sometimes their husbands' as well; women in Burma had to be treated as personalities.

It was not at all unusual then for an Englishman to marry a Burmese wife. It was common, too, for a man who did not actually go through a ceremony of marriage to live faithfully for many years with a Burmese girl who kept house for him, darned his socks and looked after his money. In Burmese eyes there was nothing discreditable in this and it meant a great deal to many men who would otherwise have been desperately lonely. Sometimes, too, and particularly in isolated places, a man who did not want a permanent housekeeper had a friend who came to see him for the evening when his work was done.

There was often real affection or more in these relationships. It was something to come home to an amiable companion who would talk over what had happened during the day, laugh at a man's troubles, and tease him in a friendly way that would restore his sense of proportion. If the Secretariat in Rangoon regarded the custom with apprehension and feared the lady would take money to influence the *Thakin*, why perhaps they were sometimes right, but against that must be set the wide knowledge of his district and of the language which an officer might gain from evenings spent like this. Snooker or whist at the club would never have taught him what he learned from Ma Phyu. And surely a man who had loved a Burmese girl must at least think of the Burmans as human beings, not as columns of figures in his fortnightly returns. All the same, most good officers believed that in the end moral standards were lowered and the way paved for corruption.

Altogether, the more one considers Burma, the more different from India it seems to have been. Even in the border country, before Burma proper was reached, the difference in the people made a difference in English habits. Kisch, who wrote so clearly of the famine in 1874, was stationed a year later in the Chittagong hill tracts and comments at once on the change. The people he met in Cox's Bazar were Arakanese, usually known in India as Mugs; they were Buddhists and he describes the monastery which is also a school, the rest-house, the shrines or pagodas and the wayside jars of water for travellers, which are the features of village life in Burma. He was pleased with the hospitality the people showed to everyone, with the bright colours of their clothes, with the 'air of independence and freedom which is quite delightful'. 'Their women go before anyone without shame or fear', he writes and adds: 'Nearly all the officers who have been stationed in these Tracts like to go about the District and live in the houses of the natives, eating their food, sleeping in their houses and even adopting their style of dress and habits.'

That was something that could hardly happen in India, and among peasants and tribesmen it was wholly admirable. But at a later stage of evolution it led to complications and perhaps there was after all something to be said for aloofness.

5. SCOTT AND THE TRIBES OF UPPER BURMA

Upper Burma consists of the country of the Burmans proper and at least as much again of tribal territory. The Burman part of the country was from the beginning administered by reviving a system of village rule which became law in 1887. The law was drafted by Sir Charles Crosthwaite and described by him in a minute which remained part of the Burma Village Manual till the end. It was a very simple system. For each village there was a headman; the Deputy Commissioner was required to find out who was generally regarded as a leader and appoint him. The headman had power to try small civil disputes and settle them, to report crime to the nearest Magistrate, to arrest criminals, to resist unlawful attacks, to help the authorities by arranging for transport and supplies when officers were on tour, to collect revenue, make roads, and look after the village sanitation, and — like the Deputy Commissioner himself — act as residuary legatee for any other duties that it might occur to anyone to impose on him.

All this, said Sir Charles, 'has been the basis of the indigenous system from time immemorial', and to revive it was the only way to deal with 'the universal disorder which prevailed and could not be suppressed by the ordinary law even when backed by overwhelming military force'. It was an admirable system and it worked; the whole village was held responsible for assisting the headman and duties were prescribed for every villager. It was not however a system which could be applied to the tribes of the hills. Their problems may best be seen against the picturesque career of George Scott.

In the uneasy reign of Thibaw and Supayalat — 'Soup-plate' to the English soldiers — a young journalist, George Scott, turned schoolmaster for the moment, decided to vary by a visit to Mandalay the excitement of giving St. John's College and the S.P.C.K. the best football teams in Rangoon. He went disguised as a Burman and was looking at the girls in the bazar, 'speculating more on the fusion of Aryan and Turanian blood than on the comeliness of any individual, though it was a pleasing study, I don't deny,' when he was gripped violently on both sides and rushed to a secluded spot. Here he perceived that his two captors, naked to the waist, were each tattooed with a dragon. They were soldiers of the Palace guard. 'If you don't come and take tickets at the lottery office,' they said, 'we'll denounce you as a spy and you'll be crucified. . . .'

Scott went with them and on the way passed a drink-shop kept by a Chinese acquaintance of his. He suggested that the three of them should go in and have some refreshment. As he ordered some drinks from his friend, 'I waggled my head at him. Chinamen are very quick of apprehension and Shwee Gwan returned with some *samshu* (Chinese rice-spirit) and "Eagle" brandy, as fiery as a blast-furnace.' A tumbler of this mixture stretched one of the escort on the floor almost at once. The other told Scott his life story before he succumbed and 'Shwee Gwan and I deposited him after dark in a convenient back garden'.

The central episode in the guard's story was an expedition which Thibaw had recently sent against one of the Shan States. What was left of the expeditionary force had come back without achieving very much, beyond providing Scott with an illustration of the dilemma which must face any power in Upper Burma and which he was to spend most of his life in facing. The hills are occupied by peoples ranging from the Shans, who are Buddhists and culturally on a level that can be compared with the Burmese, to the Wa tribes who take heads and go naked. These hill people are on the whole self-contained but from time to time they molest their neighbours. Any power in Mandalay must decide whether to endure occasional raids and insults, which no doubt if unrequited would get steadily worse, or whether to chase the hillman back into his fastnesses and there proceed laboriously and expensively to teach him a lesson. And it must also be decided what lesson should be taught and whether to stay and make sure it has been learnt.

Already the problem had arisen on the Assam side of the hills. There had been raids and punitive expeditions. There had been men who thought the tribesmen should never be trusted; there had been others who had trusted them, gone forward fearlessly and been killed. Already there had been White's disaster at Sadiya in 1839, Lowther's in 1858, Holcombe's in 1874, Butler's in 1875, and Damant's in 1879. They had most of them followed the same lines. The tribesmen had seemed to lose their first distrust. They had come into the camp to make friends. One of them had perhaps laughingly asked to look at a sentry's musket. And when he had it in his hands, he had given the signal and the slaughter had begun.

Governments in Calcutta had taken different views at different times and political agents had differed even more than governments. Some thought it best to interfere as little as possible but to punish sharply when it had to be done, then at once to withdraw. Others believed that this cat-and-mouse policy, known as butcher-and-bolt, was a cruelty unintelligible to the Wa or the Ho, and that contact with the tribes should be developed and grow closer. The result was usually a compromise between two extremes. The troops would be withdrawn after inflicting punishment, but peaceful contact by civil officers became increasingly frequent. It was to be Scott's peculiar success hardly ever to find punishment on a large scale necessary.

Scott joined the Burma Commission in 1886, some five years after his adventure in Mandalay. When the annexation of Upper Burma was proclaimed, the Indian Provinces were asked, as they had been in 1852, to provide civilians. But no province ever had men to spare and not every man was anxious in mid-career to start afresh among a new people and with new languages. After both wars, civilians from India found themselves on the Burma Commission, as on the Punjab Commission, side by side with men who had begun in the Indian Army or in some other calling. George Scott was one of those who came from outside Government service, and a better choice could hardly have been made; he was already a man who knew the ways of the country. He was appointed to the Commission in 1886 and was soon sent to the Shan States.

The Shan country was divided into small principalities, varying in size from Kengtung, twice the size of Wales, to tiny States of a few villages. The princes of these States, who were known as Sawbwas, had owed allegiance to the King of Burma and had sent him from time to time a tribute of gold and silver flowers, dried squirrels, elephants, musical instruments and ponies. To the English it seemed that that allegiance was now transferred to Queen Victoria, but that someone ought to make sure that each Sawbwa understood what had happened. The Shan hills lie where Siam, China and Burma meet and, if no one came to see them, the Sawbwas might well decide to look East or South-East rather than West. It needs an effort now to remember that at that time the French were still spreading their empire in Indo-China and no one knew how far they meant to go.

The story of one Sawbwa must do for many; it concerns Kengtung, the largest and most remote of all the States. It lay beyond the Salween, more than four hundred miles from the railway by a track that crossed many mountain ranges. Scott went with an escort of thirty-six sepoys, of whom eighteen were trained and seasoned Sikhs and the other half local men not yet quite dependable. They were commanded by Captain Pink, and there was a doctor with a 'dash of Gurkha blood'. Tents, food, and ammunition were carried by mules, led by Chinese muleteers. Before the party reached Kengtung, the Sawbwa, a boy of about sixteen, sent gold and silver flowers to meet them, symbolic of the tribute; this was an auspicious beginning but on the third day after the tents were pitched, when the first visit had been paid and before any real business had been done, something happened which might easily have ended the mission.

Scott was developing photographs in a home-made dark-room when news came that one of the Chinese muleteers had been killed and another wounded by the Sawbwa's men. They had been to look for a strayed mule and on the way back had gone into the bazar near the Sawbwa's palace, because there was music and dancing and they wanted to buy some tobacco and a drink. Someone had fired on them suddenly and without provocation; they brought away one wounded man and saw someone emptying a pistol into the back of another whom they had left on the ground.

Scott sent off a stiff letter to the Sawbwa that night. His men, he said, had been wantonly attacked and on account of their employment must be regarded as British subjects. The guilty men must be handed over for punishment without delay. This was bad enough, but things looked worse when it became known, through rumours picked up by the mule-drivers, that the man who had emptied his pistol into the fallen man was the Sawbwa himself. He had often shot men merely for his own pleasure or to test a new weapon; as the expedition's clerk pointed out, he was 'unacquainted with the Penal Code'.

The Sawbwa's Chief Minister came to see Scott and one of those conversations followed in which neither party mentions the central fact of which both are well aware. Scott was uncompromising; till the affair was settled, he could not pay the return call due at the palace. But this would be a public slight on the Sawbwa. 'I said it was a still more serious slight on me that my men should be assaulted and killed.' The Minister was shocked at such language and after some more exchanges asked permission to retire.

Scott consulted Pink; the camp was much too close to the city of Kengtung and quite indefensible. Pink wanted to move but Scott refused. 'Prestige was everything. The slightest hint of nervousness would be fatal.' They must stay where they were, though they were three hundred miles from any possible help. They waited and obtained secret confirmation that the young Sawbwa really was the criminal. 'Of course it would be quite impossible to prove guilt, as no witnesses would come forward, so on consideration I thought that to ask an indemnity was the only thing to do.'

The Chief Minister was recalled and told that compensation would be accepted. It was not an English custom to accept compensation for human life, but for once it would be done. Five hundred rupees for the wounded man, fifteen hundred for the relatives of the dead muleteer. 'The Minister was obviously horrified by the amount, but greatly relieved at the conclusion.'

The Sawbwa appeared to agree to the amount. But when formal

submission and a covenant were proposed, he said he could see no particular advantages in British suzerainty, and, after some talk, postponed all settlement until an opportunity had been taken of consulting the guardian spirits of the town. They were likely, he said, to answer in four days when the state of the moon was propitious. Four days of waiting followed, during which the expedition had to be ready for an attack at any moment. But nothing happened. On the fourth day, the money was paid and the Chief's covenant was formally presented to him in a *darbar*.

'Some years later,' Scott adds in his own account of this affair, 'when the Chief was handing round cakes to the ladies at a garden-party at Maymyo, he mentioned casually that it was only because of the intercession of his wives that he had not massacred the whole party. On the whole, knowing what he now knew, he thought that the ladies had been right.'

There is another version of this episode. Forty-eight years later, an old lady of seventy, the Princess Tip Htila of Kengtung, told Maurice Collis:

'When Scott was at Kengtung, I used to ride across the plain at dusk and dine at the officers' mess, accompanied by a lady-in-waiting and a troop of guards. But my father turned against Scott and decided to kill him. His camp was surrounded; every way but one was blocked with armed men. But I could not let him die and awoke him in his tent, leading him at midnight down the way that remained.' And when Collis asked her why she did this, she answered that she saw that the Shans must have some overlord and she liked the English better than the French.

Now the Sawbwa of Scott's story must have been her brother not her father, and if it had really happened as she said there could hardly have been the peaceful solution which Scott achieved just by showing no sign of nervousness. She remembered perhaps the essence of the situation and came to believe details she had imagined. She was a woman of great character and if, as the Sawbwa said, his wives persuaded him to hold his hand, one can hardly doubt that Tip Htila was the dominating influence among the palace ladies.

There are plenty of other tales about Scott, how for instance finding himself close under the stockade of a strange Wa village, bristling with crossbows and muskets and skulls set on poles, he neither went back nor fought his way in, but stepped forward unarmed and, although forced to speak through no less than four interpreters using five languages, within ten minutes established confidence and walked into the village. He was like a man whom bees do not sting, simply because he assumes they will not.

He looks out from photographs with the face of a small boy, humorous and cheeky but determined to get into the eleven. Beard and moustache seem an incongruous adornment, as though put on for a charade, and there was a boyishness about him that never vanished. He was still playing football at fifty and noting in his journal and letters that the Gurkha orderlies were getting selfish about passing. He collected stamps and the tops of match-boxes and even had measles four times. Untiringly energetic, he compiled the *Upper Burma Gazetteer* for 1890, with its sections on Ethnology, Religion, History, Geology, Agriculture, and a dozen more subjects, an encyclopaedia rather than a book. But he was not the kind of man to consider very deeply where all his activity was leading. He was an ardent believer in the value of the British Empire as a civilizing force; there seemed to him no question that Burma and the tribes were much better off within the Empire than outside; it was enough for him that in the Shan States, where life had been so uncertain, things were peaceful when he left. He was an empire-builder, an administrator, as simple-minded and direct as Malcolm a century earlier, kindly, firm, and practical, but not much more typical of the English in Burma than Phayre in his different way.

Scott, however, and the men of his generation succeeded with the tribes in Upper Burma. The proof was to come in the Second World War, when the English were in deep adversity and the hill tribes showed them a loyalty as moving as any in history. But of the rest of Burma, one must conclude that this mature and self-assured people were much less influenced by the English than the people of India were.

The connexion was in the first place much shorter. Upper Burma was annexed on January 1st, 1886, and in the early months of 1942 the Japanese came into the country. That is only fifty-seven years. But even if the connexion had been longer, influence would still have been slight. The English found in Burma a country already unified under one crown and, although the outlying provinces were at first glad to be freed, in metropolitan Burma the people remembered past glory and forgot past misrule. In India, nationalism was a product of British rule; in Burma it was there ready-made. While Burmans on the whole liked individual Englishmen, they seem from the beginning to have felt humiliated by English government in a way which hardly occurred to Indians until late in the century. Nor did they take to

Western education as Indians did. Perhaps it was because they had had a system of their own when the English came, perhaps it was national pride or perhaps it was just idleness. Whatever the reason, it may well be that the English period will seem to a Burmese historian three hundred years from now an interlude, longer than the Japanese, but not perhaps having contributed much more to the national character and attitude to life. But in the case of India such a conclusion would be out of the question.

CHAPTER VII

SANDEMAN AND THE FRONTIER

1. THE FRONTIER

A YOUNG man appointed to the Indian Civil Service or to political employment did not know where he would be sent. Unless he had a father to follow or some other special connexion with a particular province, he might be appointed to any of the regulation provinces, or perhaps to the Burma Commission or the Punjab. In the latter case he would probably sooner or later go to the Frontier. By the Frontier was understood the North-West Frontier; there was a frontier on the North-East as well, but fewer people were killed there and by other standards too it was less important.

It would be hard to think of two countries or two peoples in sharper contrast than those of Burma and the Frontier. The mountains of the North-West are rocky and arid, there is little rain and very little vegetation. There were more trees a hundred years ago, but then as now it was an inhospitable land. Goats, sheep, camels and mules are kept, but their existence is precarious, their scanty grazing spreads far over stony and precipitous hills. In the narrow valleys, the summer heat is searing; on the bleak serrated tops, the winter is icy. The sparseness of the grazing, the intensity at either extreme of the climate, drive the people to a life half-nomadic. They may sow a crop of millet or barley in a high village in the summer and in the winter move their herds down to more sheltered grazing grounds. Or they may cut a winter crop of wheat or barley and in summer move to grazing that has been covered with snow. In either case, bare subsistence is the most the tribesman can hope to extract from the harsh integument of the hills; for a wife or a rifle, he must get money from another source, from trade, service, loot, or tolls on passing caravans.

The life of a Border cattle-thief was not one that encouraged a vague goodwill for one's neighbours. Nor was there likely to be tolerance in a country where there was no shade but the shade of a rock. A man looked out on the world with suspicion and hostility. But fidelity within the group and between host and guest, this was a point of honour, while courage and patience were never lacking.

One tale from hundreds must suffice to give a picture of these people. It comes from a valley near the Khyber where each homestead is a fort, manned by ten, twenty or thirty rifles. Subedar Amir Khan, an officer of the Kohat military police, had long ago killed two men from another of the valley forts; what made the deed worse, he had done it in his own house. He maintained that they had come to kill him and it was his life or theirs, but his act was regarded by his enemies as a breach of border etiquette and the vendetta was pursued with more than ordinary keenness. So long as he was on duty with his unit he was safe, but when he went on leave he had to move by night and reach his home in darkness. He could never go out by day. At last he retired and settled down, but still he could not leave the fort, which on three sides was within rifle-shot of his enemies. On the fourth side, however, there was open ground, hidden from his enemies by ridges and commanded by the towers at the corners of his own house. It was an open slope, with perhaps a bush or a boulder here and there, but no cover to hide a man and not much for a partridge.

Subedar Amir Khan dug a trench from his home to the open ground, the only place where he could stand upright in safety and look at the hills. He made his prayer ground here and every evening at sunset went there by the covered way to give thanks to his Maker. His enemies of course knew his habit but for a long time they could see no way to make use of it. At last, two of them crept by night to the open ground and stayed there during the whole heat of the following day. They were hidden so long as they kept still but exposed to fire from the towers if they gave themselves away by a movement; they had to lie quite still on burning stony ground. No one saw them; in the evening Amir Khan came to say his prayers and they shot him.

The Sikhs had held this country only as far as the foot of the hills, the border villages being frequently let out on an annual payment not of money but of heads. Knife, rope, or bullet was all that passed between Sikh and Pathan. The coming of the English instead of the Sikh was, then, a pleasure as positive as the end of tooth-ache. Edwardes in Bannu could work miracles and Nicholson seemed an incarnation of the divine. 'Abbott Sahib's heart was like a fakir's,' said the old men, thirty years later. 'He was always thinking for his people.' And Mackeson, whose name they cut short to Kishan, was remembered as Kishan Kaka, Uncle Mackeson, forty years after he was murdered by a fanatic in Peshawar.

The men of that golden age resented any paper work that kept them to their desks, leaving them, they said, no time to associate with the people. This was all very well when the English first came to the country; to decide on life and death in five minutes under a tree, to settle the Land Revenue of a district in six weeks, was still better than anything the people of the country had had before. But it was not much more than substituting one man's whim for another's. The reign of law had to come sooner or later; something had to be done to ensure that what was an offence in Mackeson's district was not rewarded in Abbott's. And nothing John Lawrence did deserves more admiration than his managing of his brother Henry's team of young men on the Frontier.

John himself put an emphasis on finance, on rules, on answering letters, that Henry never could, yet John saw the value of those turbulent spirits and made full use of them without losing one. Coke he told gently that he could not drop his district and run back to his regiment because it was fighting. Nicholson he checked with a wise amiability for trying to command a brigade at the same time as a district, and Mackeson — but in Mackeson's case he confessed a failure. 'No man appreciated Mackeson's high qualities more than I did, but work I could not get out of him. I have written five times officially and three times privately before I could get an answer to an ordinary reference. Everything was in arrears.' The truth, Lawrence believed, was that Mackeson neglected his own district, letting everything else go in order to cultivate the friendship of the tribesmen across the border. There were always men like that, men who did not answer letters, who were always in bad odour with headquarters and worth a dozen careful scribes. But John Lawrence had too many of them on the Frontier to be altogether comfortable.

Lawrence then laid stress on the settled districts and wanted no adventures in the unadministered tribal areas. The English had inherited from the Sikhs a line at which the administration stopped short; up to that line there were districts of the Punjab administered by Deputy Commissioners. Beyond that line were wild tribes and the Queen's writ did not run. Beyond them again came the Amir of Kabul, but where exactly his jurisdiction ended or began, no one could say.

In Sind, it will be remembered, Bartle Frere and John Jacob had believed that their solution could be extended to cover the whole Frontier. There was however the first essential difference that in Baluchistan a wide strip of desert lay between the ploughed land and the hills and the second, that the Baluch tribes were on the whole obedient to hereditary chiefs, while the Pathans were most emphatically not. The Sind system was to patrol the frontier and take instant action when it was violated, to punish individual offenders, to back the Khan of Kalat as head of all the Baluch tribes whenever possible. John Lawrence insisted that the first duty of his frontier Deputy Commissioners was to show the people of the administered districts the solid advantages of British rule; as to the tribesmen, he believed that the first step was to convince them that we had no intention of going into their country. And of course the points he had emphasized were frozen, after he had gone, into stiff and rigid rules. Very soon there were standing orders that no Deputy Commissioner must cross the administrative boundary.

Yet the Deputy Commissioner was responsible for the peace of the border and the tribes confronting him across the administrative boundary were in some undefined way 'our' tribes. They were encouraged to come down for trade; every year they laid down their arms and left their women and children in black tents encamped on British territory while they went down into India with bales of dried fruit, carpets and wool, coming back in the spring with copper, indigo and cotton. There were others who did not trade but relied on loot for their more expensive necessities; these periodically raided the plains, that is to say the administered districts. They had after all nowhere else to raid. Looters and traders alike depended on India.

From his own side of the line, the Deputy Commissioner urged 'our' tribes to repent and reform, but there was nothing he could do until a punitive expedition was ordered. The tribe calculated that they could go a long way before patience would be exhausted, but in the end the moment would come. At last, the Deputy Commissioner would be allowed to cross the line that had been forbidden him so long. When he entered tribal territory for the first time, he went to burn and kill.

Punishment for crime, usually for long continuance in crime, was the object of these expeditions. Punishment took the form of cutting crops, burning villages, blowing up defensive towers. Sometimes a tribe was 'blockaded', but the blockade was seldom without leaks and the tribes were so nearly self-sufficient in the bare necessities that they could last a long time under even a tight blockade. A blockade hardly ever induced them to submit unless combined with an expedition. When the tribe yielded, they were told to pay a fine of so many rifles and the expedition retired. The tribe were kept busy for some time rebuilding their villages and towers and acquiring means to replace their rifles, but it cannot be supposed that they felt either affection for those who had chastised them or inclination to reform.

In terms of lives, labour and goods, the punishment had cost the Queen's Government more than the tribe. The tribesmen it is true had a smaller capital from which to pay, but they were less reluctant than the Government to start again. The Pathan as well as the Baluch was utterly reckless of life, he enjoyed excitement, and when it was all over those who were still alive could resume an existence that was much the same as before. Polygamy was permitted and a widow was on the whole an economic asset to the brother-in-law to whom she lapsed; even the widows were not as a rule inconsolable. Altogether, one need not believe that a fox enjoys being hunted to suppose that a Mahsud found a punitive expedition a good deal less intolerable than it would seem from London.

'A system of non-intervention, tempered by punitive expeditions' was then the traditional policy on the Punjab frontier. On the Sind frontier, now frozen to rigidity in the hands of Sir William Mere-wether, who had won the battle against the Bugtis in 1847, non-intervention in tribal affairs was just as much the rule, the only difference being that a raid was followed up at once and the actual offenders often caught. The system was bound to be modified sooner or later, but it would have lasted much longer than it did if it had not been for one man, Robert Sandeman, and if he had not been appointed in 1866 to one district, Dera Ghazi Khan.

2. SANDEMAN AND BALUCHISTAN

Dera Ghazi Khan is part of the Punjab[1] but is confronted, across the administrative line, by Baluch tribes as well as by Pathans. Sandeman had to deal with raids by Marris and Bugtis, who are Baluchis, as well as by Sheranis, who are Pathans. Sandeman had come to the Punjab Commission from the Company's Army immed-iately after the Mutiny. 'Robert Sandeman!' had been the farewell words of the preceptor of his youth, 'ye did little work at school but I wish ye well. And I wadna be the Saracen of Bagdad or the Tartar of Samarkand that comes under the blow of your sabre.' His back-ground in fact was that of Malcolm and Munro, and he shared with them a forthright, unprejudiced approach to every problem, a grasp of essentials and a certainty of where justice lay.

[1] See map, p. 31, chap. I.

He found himself Deputy Commissioner of a district a hundred and fifty miles long, within which he was: 'Judge of appeal and of first instance, in criminal and civil cases, magistrate, chief of police, gaol superintendent, head of the revenue department, way-warden, chairman of committees, statistician and reporter-general on every topic from land-tenures to dak-bungalow chimneys, from the repression of a raid to the loss of a scarf-pin by some distinguished traveller.' But Dera Ghazi Khan was a frontier district and he was warden of the marches as well as all this and he soon became dissatisfied with responsibility for a frontier he could not cross.

Bruce, his assistant, has a tale of how one morning soon after his appointment a villager came to see him with something wrapped up in a cloth. It was a human head. The owner of the head had been a tribesman, a neighbour from a mile across the border. He had carried off the villager's wife and the villager, a man with a respect for the law, had petitioned the Deputy Commissioner for redress. He had been told that as his enemy lived across the border nothing could be done by process of law. He had accordingly taken steps — outside the law. Now he had come to submit to authority, bringing material evidence to substantiate his report. Bruce, one is glad to hear, decided that no offence had been committed.

But clearly such a state of affairs was intolerable. Things were particularly bad in regard to the Baluch tribes, among whom a situation had developed which Frere had not had to face. The Baluch tribe was divided into clans, known as *tomans*, each under a hereditary chief or *tomandar*. The clan again was divided into sections, each under a subordinate chief, and the tomandar must in many matters take the opinion of the subordinate chiefs. Similarly, Baluchistan was a confederacy of independent tribes who had accepted the Khan of Kalat as their head, on the understanding that he too in certain matters would consult the tomandars and other chiefs. The arrangements worked reasonably well until the accession in 1857 of Khoda Dad Khan, one of whose first acts was to open fire with cannon upon the chiefs who had raised him to the throne. For the next twenty years the country was in a state of intermittent civil war.

It seemed to Sandeman that the English could not expect a quiet border so long as there was no settled authority on the other side. Turbulence would spill over, and turbulence could only be ended by an investigation of long standing custom and a settlement, at some Baluchi Runnymede, between Khoda Dad Khan and his barons.

But on the Sind frontier Merewether repeated the incantation he had learnt from Jacob, that the Khan must be supported, from which it followed that the English could have no truck with men in arms against their king.

This was one radical difference of opinion. There were others which came to a head in a practical way in 1867, when a mixed force of some fifteen hundred armed men, Marris, Bugtis and other Baluch tribesmen, came into the district of Dera Ghazi Khan on a raid. Sandeman and Bruce, with some thirty troopers, raised the country against them and with a force from their own district defeated them and drove them off, killing their leader and a hundred and twenty of his followers and taking two hundred prisoners.

The prisoners immediately became a difficulty. They were sub-ects, in theory, of the Khan of Kalat, to whom the only official channel of approach was Merewether. He, as everyone knew, was adamant that the Khan was the only authority in Baluchistan with whom any British officer could deal. In theory, the Khan ought to be asked to ransom the prisoners and guarantee their good behaviour. But in practice the Khan had no power over the Marris and Bugtis, with whom he was in fact in an intermittent state of irregular war. It was a stalemate which Sandeman solved by sending a message to the tomandars of the two tribes. Having already a good deal of respect for Sandeman, they came into his district, apologized for the wrong they had done and undertook to raid there no more. In return, the prisoners were handed over and Sandeman took into employment a number of tribal horsemen, partly as messengers and partly as patrols, to keep open the main caravan routes from tribal strongholds into the settled districts. This was the beginning of the system of tribal employment.

But no promise had been made not to raid into Sind, and from Sind of course the agreement looked like blackmail. The Marris and Bugtis now regarded themselves as Sandeman's friends; they raided other tribes and Sind just as before. And to Merewether it must have seemed that Sandeman was piling iniquity on iniquity when he settled a blood-feud between the Marris and two other tribes by inducing the Marri tomandar to give nieces in marriage to the others. He was interfering across the border and encouraging the tomandars to persist in rebellion against the Khan.

The controversy lasted a long time. In the end, Sandeman got his way because he was able to demonstrate that his policy worked.

This he did by deliberate disobedience. He ignored the standing orders and went for a three weeks' tour across the border. He lived in tribal territory, he moved with a tribal escort, he visited the headquarters of every clan. He risked not only his life but his career. When he came back he reported what he had done and the tour had been so obviously successful that it was condoned by Sir Donald Macleod, the Lieutenant-Governor of the Punjab.

That was one milestone in the controversy. Another was the conference between the Sind and Punjab authorities in 1871, at which Sandeman's system of employing tribal horsemen and keeping in friendly touch with the tribes was approved. Against this gain must be set the renewed assertion that the Khan was supreme and his barons in rebellion. Also, Sandeman was placed under Merewether's orders when he was dealing with Baluch tribes, and that can hardly have made things easier. The third milestone however marked Sandeman's victory.

By 1875, affairs were worse than ever in Baluchistan, and Merewether suggested a military expedition. 'The Marris,' he said, 'do not understand forbearance . . . the Marri Chief . . . must be curbed, and by a good thrashing if persistence makes it necessary.' Sandeman however proposed a peaceful mission; his views were accepted and he was sent to the Khan's headquarters to carry out his own policy — but under the orders of Merewether.

Sandeman was received with enthusiasm by the tribesmen. Before long however he was overtaken by orders from Merewether to return; since these seemed to him to contradict his mandate from the Government of India, he put them in his pocket and went on. His mission came as near success as it could while Merewether was still Commissioner, and so long as the Khan knew that he disapproved of everything Sandeman did. Sandeman was greeted on his return by a letter severely censuring his conduct but within a few hours received the further news that its writer had been relieved of responsibility for Baluchistan.

That was really the end of the controversy. Sandeman's second mission was entirely successful; next year he was appointed Agent to the Governor-General in Baluchistan. The extent of the victory may be judged from the dispatch of March 23rd, 1877, written by a Government whose servants only eight years before had been forbidden to cross the administrative boundary. 'If it be conducive to British interests,' wrote Lord Lytton's Government, 'as we have no doubt it is, to influence the tribes and peoples who live beyond our border, we must be in contact with them. It is by the everyday acts of earnest, upright, English gentlemen that lasting influence must be obtained, not by spasmodic demonstrations . . .' In Baluchistan, at least, 'masterly inactivity' had gone down before the new policy of 'conciliatory intervention'. Warfare between the Baluch tribes ceased. Tribal raids on the plains came to an end. Isolated crimes of course there were, but Baluchistan had become a country in which law had effect.

It was not the Baluch tribes only that were pacified. In the North of Sandeman's area, outside the sphere of the Khan of Kalat and his confederation, the districts of Pishin and the Zhob became British; further still, the Kurram, in the heart of tribal territory, was taken over and administered. The Kurram was an exceptional case because the people are Shia Muslims, surrounded by Sunnis, and they wanted protection. Still, all these were Pathan countries and Sandeman himself firmly believed that his system could be extended northwards and that the whole Frontier could be pacified just as Baluchistan had been. He thought it ought to be done, arguing sometimes, and mainly to convince others, on strategic grounds, more often on grounds of humanity. 'To be successful on this frontier, a man has to deal', he wrote, 'with the hearts and minds of the people and not only with their fears . . . To be successful requires much labour. I have taken it and have had a hard life, but a happy one, in the feeling that I have helped men to lead a quiet and peaceful life in this glorious world of ours. . . .'

His system was, he claimed, only a continuance of the old ways of Abbott, Nicholson and Mackeson, as they had been handed down to him by James, his first district officer. Tribal employment was the cornerstone; the more amenable elements of the tribe must be encouraged and strengthened. This could best be done by letting the tribal leaders present men for service in the tribal levies, thus providing an alternative to loot as a source of cash, while at the same time a force was available when the leader needed help. Tribal levies could be genuinely useful and should be used constantly. If there was any complaint against the tribe or a member of it, there should be an investigation which must be open-minded; there must be no foregone conclusions. Individuals should be judged by a tribal council; if the tribe, or a section of it, had behaved badly, it must be punished by fine, but the fine must be paid in cash or kind. It was wrong to dock the leaders' allowances to pay for the misdeeds of individuals who might be their bitterest enemies. The punishment of the individuals who were actually guilty was as much part of Sandeman's system as it had been of Jacob's.

All this might be more difficult to apply to Wazirs and Sheranis than to Bugtis and Marris, because the Pathans were less obedient to tribal leaders than Baluchis, but it was — Sandeman argued — only a matter of degree. Both understood the idea of tribal responsibility, both had tribal councils or *jirgas*. The Baluch tomandars had been weak enough when he found them; it was his support that had made them strong enough to arrest a wanted man and hand him over to justice. A *Malik* among the Mahsuds or Afridis could not perhaps yet take so strong a line but he could be brought to it in time. A beginning had already been made with the Sheranis and some neighbouring Pathan tribes from Southern Waziristan.

That was Sandeman's doctrine and 'It is no mere theory', he wrote. 'It is born of the calm confidence which arises from experience and leads to success. We have made a commencement with the Waziris . . . let us avoid nerveless vacillation and maintain a firm continuity of action . . . Let us not think of turning back but . . . knit the frontier tribes into our Imperial system. . . .'

To an outsider it sounds convincing, though no Frontier officer living will admit that the Mahsuds could ever be brought to obey a Malik unless it suited them. If anyone could have done it, Sandeman was the man. His name for this purpose was worth all the troops in India. 'It was a wholesome spectacle to watch the chiefs . . . come up to Senaman Sahib and accost him with a friendly slap on the back and a hearty shake of the hand . . . as if they were boon companions.' But they said too: 'It is no use fighting Senaman Sahib; he knows everything and turns up everywhere.' In his day and as late as the 'eighties there were still tribes asking to be administered. He might have taken the tide at the flood. But he died, leaving the States of Kalat and Las Bela to come near war for the privilege of burying his remains. It was left to Bruce to try the experiment in Waziristan. Bruce however was not Sandeman and he had the grave misfortune to be uncovenanted.

3. BRUCE AND WAZIRISTAN

Bruce was the younger son of an Irish landowner. His elder brother, who was a missionary in the Punjab, secured the ear of Sir Robert Montgomery, and the boy was sent out from Ireland with the promise that he would be appointed an Extra Assistant Commissioner. A man holding the same kind of post in the regulation Provinces was known as a Deputy Collector. In most districts, the district officer had four, five or six assistants, all doing the same kind of work. Some were in charge of sub-divisions, one would perhaps be City Magistrate, another would have charge of the office. One perhaps would be a junior officer of the Indian Civil Service, and the others would be uncovenanted — that is, appointed direct in India, governed by no covenant with the Secretary of State.

It was these posts that the Act of 1833 had confirmed to Indians. The proportion of Indians holding them increased before the Mutiny, suffered a set-back and began to climb again. Hittu Ram, Rai Bahadur and a C.I.E., was Sandeman's lieutenant throughout his time in Baluchistan and by Sandeman was made administrator of Las Bela State. He of course was an Indian but, in Victorian times, many of the uncovenanted were European or of mixed blood. They were not as a rule of an education equal to Bruce's, nor were they usually accepted as social equals by officers of the twice-born civil service or of the Army. Bruce however was a gentleman by birth and married his Deputy Commissioner's daughter; he was soon promoted to be a member of the Punjab Commission. His uncovenanted origin was forgotten, except in Simla and by himself.

Before Sandeman's death, he was promoted to charge of a Punjab frontier district, Dera Ismail Khan, the district north of Dera Ghazi Khan. Here he was responsible not only for his own district but for the tribes confronting him, the Sheranis, whom he had known before, and also the Mahsuds and others of Southern Waziristan, as turbulent and difficult as any on the border. He was, in a sense, in the position Sandeman had held twenty years earlier; he had the immense advantage of Sandeman's achievement behind him and he believed that he could do for Waziristan what Sandeman had done for Baluchistan.

Again, one tale must do for many. In 1893, a European overseer in the Public Works Department, Mr. Kelly, with one trooper of a tribal levy, was shot dead while travelling in the Zhob, just outside Bruce's jurisdiction. But it was soon fairly clear that the culprits belonged to a clan or section of the Mahsuds, who were Bruce's tribe. He called them together and demanded from the tribal council the surrender of five men, two who had shot Kelly and the trooper and three others accused of the murder of an Indian soldier. He brought to bear what pressure he could to help the tribal elders or Maliks in their task. That was Sandeman's principle; the whole tribe was not indicted, but the law-abiding elements encouraged. He was successful; the Maliks brought him the five men.

Bruce directed the tribal council to try them and they were tried by all the leading Maliks. They were found guilty by the Maliks and Bruce sentenced them to terms of imprisonment. He dismissed the council to their hills and within a few weeks three of the leaders were treacherously murdered.

It was a vital moment. If the murder of the three Maliks was judicially punished, there might be some chance of establishing the reign of law in Waziristan. But if these murderers were not brought to book, the Maliks would never establish control. The Punjab Government agreed with Bruce and recommended that, in demanding the surrender of the murderers, he should be empowered to speak in such terms that a punitive expedition would follow if they were not delivered. But the Government of India would not go so far. They believed that such an expedition would endanger their negotiations with the Amir of Afghanistan for the demarcation of a frontier; the local problem had to give way to wider considerations.

4. RUSSIA, THE AMIR AND THE DURAND LINE

Alfred Lyall had perceived that local administration on the Frontier and defence against Russia were in themselves quite separate. They were confused partly because the Afghans were concerned with both and partly because it is not much use defending a frontier unless one is reasonably sure of the country behind it.

There were, as everyone knows, the forward school and the close border men. In each decade, the close border men were fewer in number and less in influence. Hardly anyone, by the time the Second Afghan War was over, believed in so close a border as John Lawrence had. There was talk in the 'eighties of making the frontier of India the line from Kabul to Kandahar, and from the point of view of a staff college exercise it was perhaps as defensible a line as could be chosen.[1] The objections to it were political; it would mean a weak and distracted Afghanistan in front and a wide belt of turbulent and disaffected tribesmen behind.

All this, of course, is a simplification. The two questions of administering the tribes and defending India against Russia were argued interminably and with a hundred variations; this is not the place for a detailed discussion. But two points must be made clear. The

[1] See map, p. 31.

Russian danger was not the bogey of faddists; everyone who thought about the future at all shared in varying degrees the idea that the two empires that were expanding — one westward from the Bay of Bengal, one eastward from the Baltic — must sooner or later either meet, or compress what was between them into a compact and defined shape. And, if Afghanistan was to be maintained as a cushion between the two, some kind of working arrangement about the Border tribes must be made with the Amir. We could hardly hope to be on good terms with him so long as no one was clear where sovereignty lay among these turbulent and undisciplined people.

Everyone understood where the administrative boundary lay. Beyond that, there was a wide belt of tribal territory in which some tribes were vaguely regarded as British, some were vaguely the Amir's, but neither were wholly subject to the authority of either power. The tribes could play off the Amir against the British, while the Amir intrigued among the tribes in order to keep the British constantly busy.

It was of the first importance to settle these ambiguities. In 1894, Sir Mortimer Durand went to Kabul and the Durand line was drawn between the Amir's territory and that of the tribes. The position of the tribes was at last made clear in international law. They were not British subjects but British Protected Persons, living in a belt of independent but protected republics. There was at last an international boundary. But for this a price was paid; the murderers of Bruce's Maliks were left undisturbed. A year later in 1895, Bruce, with a brigade of troops, went as British Commissioner to demarcate the line on the ground; his camp was attacked at night and heavy losses were inflicted on troops by Waziri tribesmen. His experiment in Waziristan had failed.

Probably that would have happened anyhow. Probably that moment in 1893 was not so crucial as he thought. Even in 1895, after the attack on Bruce's camp, the Mahsuds petitioned that we should not merely open a pass through their country but take over the whole territory and administer it. To suppose that at one moment the chance was lost for ever is no doubt to over-simplify. But somewhere in the four or five years after Sandeman's death the chance was lost, if it ever existed. Most people would say it did not, that Mahsud democracy was so near to anarchy that the Sandeman system could never have worked among them.

Bruce believed till the end that it could, but he was handicapped. He had been recommended by Sandeman to act for him as Agent to the Governor-General in Baluchistan; later, when Sandeman died, the newspapers had speculated on whether Bruce would succeed his friend. On each occasion, Simla decided against him; he believed it was because he was uncovenanted. That belief tinged his words with hesitancy; he could not wage paper war with the insouciance of the twice-born, the disregard for consequences of Sandeman, Frere and a score of others.

At any rate, ten years later there were no more petitions that tribal territory should be taken over and administered. It may be that, once the Durand line was marked out, the tribes on the British side ceased to be frightened of the Amir. Perhaps it was no more than that by this time they had summed up the English. They knew now just how far they could go. The rules of the game were beginning to be understood and, although it was a rough game, it was one which both sides found exhilarating.

5. THE RULES OF THE GAME

Both sides were constantly improving their technique. On the English side, the twenty years between 1890 and 1910 were mainly a period of improvement in organization. Lord Curzon formed a North-West Frontier Province, consisting of the six frontier districts of the Punjab and six tribal areas. This was staffed by the Political Department instead of by the Punjab Commission, but that made less difference than might be supposed. Both were recruited partly from the Indian Civil Service and partly from the Indian Army; on the whole, the same kind of officer found his way to the Frontier under either dispensation. But the new Province came directly under the Government of India; it was no longer necessary to send everything through Lahore. That meant the chance of a quicker decision. And it was undoubtedly an improvement, both financial and military, to have drawn back the regular army and reserved it for war against a foreign enemy, leaving the task of looking after the tribes in the main to irregular tribal forces. It was a clear gain, too, to separate the administration of the districts from the task of looking after the tribes.

This was Lord Curzon's reorganization. The tribesman in the same period did not reorganize, but re-armed himself with the breech-loading rifle instead of the matchlock. The first breech-loaders had been stolen from troops or from murdered men and had naturally been expensive. An inferior variety was made locally, but the Pass-made rifle was not in competition with the European article; it was a substitute. After the South African War, however, it became possible to import rifles in much larger quantities and prices fell. They were landed at the small ports of the Persian Gulf and came overland by caravan.

The Arab merchants asked for payment in advance and soon most of the working capital — that is, the sum available for paying fines and buying rifles — of such tribes as the Afridis was invested in Muscat and Bahrein and the other ports of the arms dealers. Then British naval and diplomatic action in the Gulf closed down the flow to a trickle and the Afridis could not recover their money. The Afridis of the Kohat Pass thereupon petitioned for compensation. They had lost money, they said, because naval action had stopped gun-running. It was as though a burglar should claim unemployment benefits because he had dropped his tools when surprised by the police.

Circumstances on the Frontier were altogether so odd that the oddity of this attitude is easy to understand. A few tribesmen in some tribes were irreconcilably hostile, but in most tribes most of the tribesmen credited the Government of India with that infinite mercy that a penitent but recurring sinner counts on from the Almighty. The few were kept at white heat by the *mullahs* or by agents of the Amir. While it suited the English to have a strong and friendly Afghanistan between themselves and Russia, it was no less convenient to the Amir that the tribes between himself and the English should be turbulent and incalculable. And for most of the tribes too the situation was not without its attractions. It suited them to live their old lawless lives in a sort of national park or bird sanctuary, from which they could emerge to commit an outrage and retire in the knowledge that nothing very dreadful would happen.

On the English side, too, it cannot be denied that most Englishmen not in the Finance Department liked the Frontier as it was. To the soldier it presented an unrivalled training-ground with real bullets; the Political Officer as a rule felt an affection for the Pathan, for his courage, his sense of humour, and his perverted sense of honour. And if he was a good officer, the Political Agent soon grew to enjoy his own skill at the game. It gave him pleasure to cap one Pushtu proverb with another in the opposite sense. It delighted him to know that, among the Khyber Afridis, the clan known as the Malikdin Khel are allied with the Kambar Khel by virtue of a common ancestry, and that this alliance overrides their adherence to opposite factions in the strange division of the tribes into Samil and Gar — terms more esoteric even than Whig and Tory or Democrat and Republican. He could reckon with confidence on the hostility of the Kuki Khel and the Zakka Khel and to do so gave him the satisfaction that another man would get from potting the red or solving an equation.

There were now six Deputy Commissioners in frontier districts and six Political Agents who took that extra responsibility for tribal territory that had belonged to the Deputy Commissioners in Sandeman's day. Warburton in the Khyber had been the first Political Agent; he had complained that he was tied all day by paper but at least one of his successors found that half an hour a day at his desk was quite enough and that on the whole the most useful part of his work was done out shooting, by keeping an ear alert for the revealing aside, by simply being among the people and talking to them. Hours were spent every day by a Political Agent seeing tribesmen one after another, hearing what they had to say, doling out 'expenses'.

There was a tale current in the folklore of Indian clubs and messes for which there was perhaps no historical authority but which did enshrine a truth. It concerned a Political Agent accompanying troops on a punitive expedition. After breakfast with the officers, he took his lunch in a haversack and disappeared; they did not see him again till evening when, sipping a pink gin by the light of a lantern carefully screened from snipers, he asked: 'And how did things go on your side today? Casualties on our side were half-a-dozen.'

Of course he never really said anything of the kind, but the tale was repeated because every soldier who went on such an expedition was at first puzzled by this strange compromise between a war and a field-day, and still more by the knowledge that it would be succeeded by a peace no less bogus, a sort of cold peace in which the tribes were forgiven for their misdeeds and paid to be good. No newcomer could understand why, once a tribe had broken its engagements and forced the Government to inflict an expensive punishment, there should be a return to the very conditions which had produced the outbreak. English soldier, politician fresh from Westminster, Indian critic — all these for once were on the same side. 'A friendly native', wrote Lord Minto in 1879, 'is one who only shoots you at night, whereas a hostile one shoots in the daytime as well.'

The answer to their criticism lay in a study of finance. The North-West Frontier Province in 1908 was a deficit Province at a time when all the others contributed to the centre. The deficit was of the nature of a quarter to half a million pounds, to which must be added allowances to the tribes and military expenditure.

If for the cold peace there had been substituted all the critic would have liked to see, the roads, the schools and the dispensaries, the bill would have gone up to a figure far beyond India's means. The allowances would for a long time have stayed the same; military expenditure would have increased because there would have been so much more to protect. So the frontier tribes were left alone — except by the mullahs and the Amir's agents. The soldier had his training ground, and the Political Officer was free to tramp the hills after partridge and keep down the murders as much as he could; to share the Pathan's broad stories and enjoy the guest's portion of the roast kid stuffed with raisins and pistachios; to keep his ears open and run the risk every day of the knife or bullet of a fanatic.

CHAPTER VIII

THE REBELS

1. DUTT AND THE LAND REVENUE

A YOUNG civilian who had been about two years in India confessed one day to his district officer that he was worried by flattery. 'My visitors tell me', he said, 'that I am hard-working and considerate, just, kind and sympathetic. Of course I know it is only flattery and at first I used to laugh. But I find I am beginning to like it and half believe it. This must be very bad for me. What am I to do?'

'So long as they tell you that kind of thing,' replied the district officer, 'you needn't worry. They know the kind of man you would like to be and if the picture they paint is one you approve of, you are on the right lines. It's time to be anxious when the picture begins to change and they congratulate you on nothing else but being a good shot or a wonderful man on a horse.'

This was many years later than the 'eighties and 'nineties but district life changed much less between 1820 and 1940 than is generally supposed. Power, we know, corrupts and although the more obvious kinds of corruption soon became rare among the covenanted, a subtler corruption could not be banished so easily. Constant flattery does corrupt; it breeds complacency and an easy optimism, the closed eye and the closed heart. They were vices to which, at least on the surface, the Victorians were prone. The Guardians were however always concerned about how their rule appeared to their subjects.

Sir Richard Temple spent much time discussing such questions as whether the 'educated natives' were likely to become discontented and whether there was any dislike of British rule. He analysed Indian society and divided it into classes, for each of which he gave a different answer. The largest class, two-thirds at least of the total population, are the peasants and agricultural labourers, who for centuries have let the legions thunder past. They do not mind who rules them. They do however know when they are well off and on the whole they are now better off than they have ever been before. They may be regarded as 'loyal', but passively loyal; they prefer British rule to anything else they have known but regard it without enthusiasm. They are not to be relied on for any great sacrifice in the cause of the Empire.

As to the educated, there was bound to be discontent among those few highly-educated Indians who in British India — but not in the States — found themselves debarred from the highest posts. The Government should not, however, for that reason withhold education nor cease to extend all political privileges short of any actual control; they should 'be just and fear not'; all would be well so long as justice was combined with a sufficient number of British troops.

This is not a very imaginative conclusion and there is not much sympathy either for the peasant, who may have been better off than before but was certainly not well off, or for the discontented intellectual, produced because 'it is our plain duty' but unemployed because 'we must retain the ultimate control'. It was this lack of imaginative passion and of sympathy for the individual that roused the anger and indignation of a growing number of Indians and of a few covenanted civilians. They asked the questions Temple had asked but found different answers. Their protests are sometimes overstated, their suggestions sometimes impracticable or even retrograde, but they did at least keep the more orthodox on the alert.

Take first an Indian, one of the first to enter the service, Romesh Chandar Dutt. He passed the examination in London in 1869, with two other Indians from Bengal, Behari Lal Gupta and Surendranath Banerjea. This in itself was an achievement. It took courage for a Hindu to go to England at all; he had to defy religion and face social ostracism when he came home. Banerjea had his father's secret support but his plans were concealed from his mother till the last minute. Dutt and Gupta had to hide what they were doing from both their parents. Nor can it have been easy in a foreign country to study in a foreign language and be successful in a competitive examination against men answering questions in their mother tongue.

Again, when Dutt came back to Bengal in 1871 and was appointed Assistant Magistrate at Alipur, he had to behave as though he were an Englishman, giving twenty or thirty times a day decisions which to an Englishman would have seemed as natural as breathing but which for him must at first have involved careful consideration, because they were based on a foreign system of thought and yet had also to be justified to people of his own race whose mental habits were quite different.

He overcame all these difficulties and was the first Indian to hold executive charge of a district, becoming Collector of Backergunge in

1883. He went on to Mymensingh; his biographer believes that he was considered a good district officer. He was the only Indian in the nineteenth century to be Commissioner of a division, taking charge of the Burdwan division in 1892 and soon afterwards moving to Orissa, with its many tributary States, a charge which was in the end to be a Governor's Province. He was an official member of the Bengal Legislative Council, he was awarded a C.I.E., and he had only twenty-seven years' service when he retired in 1897. And he had used his furlough to translate various works from Sanskrit or allied languages into modern Bengali; he had to his credit translations into English and historical novels in Bengali as well.

Altogether, when Dutt retired, comparatively early, he had behind him a career which would have been creditable even to anyone who had had fewer problems to contend with. But Dutt did not retire in the ordinary sense of the word. He went to England and settled there. He became a lecturer in history at London University and published a number of books, historical and political, the latter mostly critical of the régime in India. He was filled with misery and sympathy when he thought of the famine years which ended the century. He wrote a series of open letters to Lord Curzon, who was provoked by Dutt's criticism into the famous resolution of 1902 in which the Government of India — ostensibly, but actually the noble lord in person — reviewed Mr. Dutt's arguments and proceeded to overwhelm them.

Dutt was a man of more than average ability but he had few advisers and helpers who understood the revenue system. He had experience as a district officer in Bengal, which was quite different from anywhere else, but he had no experience of revenue work at the headquarters even of a province and he knew nothing about settlement. Lord Curzon had the advice of a dozen settlement officers and a revenue secretary from every province. As a gladiatorial exhibition, it was not a fair contest.

Even his biographer admits that Lord Curzon was singularly insensitive to the effect on a man's feelings of being overwhelmed in argument. There was something of the schoolboy in his complex character, and it perhaps never crossed his mind that such a triumph might convert some of his readers to an emotional sympathy with the overwhelmed. But of his intellectual victory there can be no doubt. Sonorous, pompous and usually acid, the sentences flow from his lordship's pen; every paragraph makes a telling point and every other alienates the reader.

Dutt did not dispute the fact that the first cause of famine was a failure of the rains and he put his points with moderation and courtesy. He credited the English with a desire to improve things. He thought however that expenditure was too high and that Land Revenue could be so far reduced that the peasant would be materially better off and better able to resist famine. He thought too that if the Permanent Settlement of Bengal had been extended to the whole of India many of the evils he saw would have disappeared.

'This hypothetical forecast', said Lord Curzon, 'is not rendered more plausible to the Government of India by their complete inability to endorse the accompanying allegations of fact.' In spite of a better rainfall than most of India, Bengal was not better able to resist famine; the number of people receiving relief and the cost of relieving them were just as high as anywhere else. If landlords were well off in Bengal, they had passed on none of their well-being to their tenants, until they were forced to.

There are more points of the same kind, displaying a masterly comprehension of the subject and scoring neatly off Mr. Dutt; it is as though a battleship should register a few hits with her secondary armament on some despised foe to get the range. Then the big guns loose their salvoes and poor Dutt is blown out of the water. If the Government of India were to accept his suggestions, Land Revenue would everywhere be increased. In Madras it would be roughly doubled. In the Central Provinces, Dutt had wanted to limit the King's share to an average of one-tenth of the total produce. But already the average was less than one-twentieth.

After such a salvo as this, the rest was a mere display of pyrotechnics. Dutt, for instance, had wanted to base revenue on the gross produce, the total takings the farmer would receive, but expenses varied for good land and bad, and obviously it was much fairer to deduct expenses first and base revenue on net produce.

Nor was it really true that a lower Land Revenue would increase the people's ability to resist famine. Either the landlord and the moneylender would get all the advantage or, if the benefit could be passed on to the cultivator, he would simply sit idle, or — in Lord Curzon's language — it would react prejudicially upon his industry. Suppose, however, for the sake of argument, that the money remitted could be forcibly put into that twist in the end of his turban-cloth which serves the peasant for a pocket, what would he do with it? 'Speculative expenditure upon litigation' and 'proneness to extravagance upon festival occasions', would eat it up. A reserve fund against famine was surely safer in the hands of the wise Government.

Cruising thoughtfully among the flotsam to pick up survivors, Lord Curzon conceded that the Land Revenue system was not perfect and indicated possible improvements, all in favour of the peasant, to which his Government would try to give effect. He had had the best of it, and not by mere dialectic. He had tried to understand his adversary's case and had pointed out what he believed were the real causes of poverty. All the same, one is left with the feeling that though his lordship's Government might understand all mysteries and all knowledge there was one thing Dutt had which they had not.

Dutt did not recognize his disintegration and retaliated, but there is not much substance in what he says. His biographer rightly concludes that the benefit resulting from his onslaught was that the Government did carefully re-examine the whole question. Dutt went on to be both Prime Minister of Baroda and President of the Indian National Congress, a combination that would hardly have been possible even twenty years later. He was a man of industry and public spirit on whom it would be pleasant to dwell longer.

2. THORBURN AND THE MONEYLENDERS

Dutt had engaged the Government on a wide front for which his resources were hardly adequate; on a much narrower front an English predecessor had scored some success. S. S. Thorburn knew the Western districts of the Punjab thoroughly; he had confined himself to that area and to one point. Land, he pointed out, had never been owned in India at all; a man had the right to cultivate but he did not own the soil and no one could transfer land by sale to strangers. But the English at a stroke conferred upon each peasant what seemed a priceless gift. He became the owner of his holding. We had turned collective into individual ownership.

The peasant however was quite unused to handling money. The Sikhs had taken as much of the crop as they could get and he had lived on what they left. Now he found himself with a capital asset and he was expected to pay a fixed revenue in cash. There would come a bad year — and in Thorburn's country the rains are particularly precarious — and he would go to the village moneylender who was also accountant, shopkeeper and grain-dealer. This was always a Hindu, a man who up to now had been the servant of the brotherhood and no more allowed to raise his voice in the councils of the village or to ride a horse at his wedding than a new boy at an English public school to put his hands in his pockets. The accountant had been used to lending a rupee or two, to be paid back in a few months' time, but now the peasant found that with his new security he could borrow as much as he liked — and of course uses for the money occurred to him.

In the Hindu parts of India the moneylender was among people of his own kind and amenable to public opinion; here in the Western Punjab, where the peasants were Muslims, alien from him in every way, he had once been restrained by fear and by tradition. He was socially despised and his terms of business were fixed by custom. If he departed from accepted standards, the villagers would beat or kill him. But now he discovered not only that his clients had a security they had never possessed before but that whatever he did the law would protect his person. Furthermore, if he could bring written evidence in support of his claim, the law would enforce even what the villagers knew to be outrageous. So he would lend a few rupees, and then a few more, and say nothing of getting them back — until the total with interest had mounted to a fair sum and then he would dun the peasant for payment. The peasant, who was almost always illiterate, would ask for advice; the moneylender would shrug his shoulders and write a bond — for a round figure considerably above the old total. And to that the wretched ploughman would put his thumb. The sum due on the bond would grow until the moment when a mortgage would succeed to the bond, and then the end would be in sight.

Nor was this all. Bonds were sometimes fraudulent from beginning to end. A moneylender would come to a petition-writer, bringing with him a peasant, and dictate a bond by which the peasant acknowledged a debt of so much — but sometimes it would happen that all the time the real debtor was at home in his village. It was Thorburn's contention that a large part of the land was passing away from the Muslim peasantry into the hands of a rapacious and sedentary class who were detested by the villagers. This was not only unjust but was likely, he thought, to produce before long serious political trouble, the rising of a peasantry infuriated by intolerable wrong.

That there was much truth in this no one denied. What had happened was an immense acceleration of a natural process. About the time that Thorburn was writing, Sir Henry Maine was pointing out that it is natural for man to move from a society in which his status is fixed to a free society in which he finds his own level by a series of contracts. The brotherhood of the Indian village was certainly a good example of fixed status; Victorian England had gone a long way towards the free society of contract. The Punjab peasant however had been asked to do in a year what had taken England many centuries.

Some of Thorburn's figures were contested, but every official in the Punjab was agreed that something of the kind was happening. There was sharp disagreement as to what should be done. 'Only a minority', wrote James Lyall — Alfred's brother and soon to be Lieutenant-Governor of the Punjab — 'have proved fit for the improved status which we gave them; the majority will descend into the position which suits them, of mere tillers of the soil, with enough to live upon but no credit to pledge and no property to lose . . .' This was the conclusion of one brought up in the doctrines of *laisser-faire* that had been taught at Haileybury; Thorburn called it scornfully: 'Mr. Lyall's despondent acceptance of the doctrine that whatever is is right', and proposed a series of measures to arrest the natural process.

They were taken up, one by one. Indeed, in the Bombay Deccan most of them were already law. Here almost the same situation had arisen in the 1850s, some thirty years after annexation — and it was now thirty years since the annexation of the Punjab. Facts had been too strong for the *laisser-faire* theory and an act had been passed in the Deccan restricting the sale of land; in the Punjab, the Act of 1900 divided the population into agricultural tribes and non-agricultural. The traders were not allowed to buy land from peasants and a mortgage lapsed if it was not discharged in twenty years. Credit was restricted, interest limited, precautions against fraudulent mortgages introduced. All this was going a long way from the teaching of Malthus and Richard Jones. What could be less liberal than to divide society into classes according to birth and impose legal disqualifications upon a whole section of the community? To the Hindu trained in English thought it seemed an immoral concession to political expediency. To most Muslims and Englishmen it seemed a recognition of simple facts and elementary justice.

Thorburn was still in service when he began his agitation. He wrote state papers addressed to his Government and followed them up by books in which he sharply criticized the Government and individuals. All that happened was that he was ordered to conduct exactly that detailed inquiry in twelve villages which he had himself recommended, and eventually his recommendations were accepted.

The service was still one in which men felt strongly, said what they thought and, if their criticism was sound, had a good chance of getting their way.

3. WEDDERBURN AND CO-OPERATIVE CREDIT

Thorburn's suggestions were mainly directed at restricting the moneylender. Another way of dealing with the evils he described was of course to provide a better source of credit; this had been suggested by another rebel who had in common with Thorburn a warm sympathy with the peasant. But Sir William Wedderburn was a Radical by temperament, whereas Thorburn was a district officer who went where the facts took him. Sir William — he was not knighted but inherited his baronetcy — had as early as 1881 perceived that co-operative village banks would help to solve the problem of the peasant's debts. He had worked out a scheme and obtained the agreement locally of moneylenders, peasants, and landowners. His scheme was approved by the Government of Bombay and by the Government of India; after three and a quarter years of discussion with the India Office it was turned down by the Secretary of State.

There were already village banks on these lines in Germany, but this was a time of robust conservatism in England and the India Office was a great place for thinking of objections; twenty years were lost and it was not till 1904 that Lord Curzon and Sir Denzil Ibbetson passed the Co-operative Societies Act of 1904. Wedderburn however does not seem to have been reproved for interesting John Bright in his ideas while on leave, nor for addressing meetings about proposals not yet sanctioned by the Secretary of State. Nor was this his only venture into policy while still in a junior position. His scheme for making the collection of revenue less rigid was turned down, and with a sharp rap; in a summary it does not sound a good one. He would have given the peasant a choice between a fixed cash rent and a proportion of the crop paid in kind. But he cannot have found many officers of experience to back this; payment in kind can hardly ever be free from corruption.

Another of his schemes was for a revival of the old Maratha village committees which would settle disputes by agreement between the parties. Elphinstone would have approved of this and in one respect almost everyone's experience agreed with Wedderburn's. On the platform under the tree in the village, truth is spoken, but not often in the law courts; a forged bond would stand no chance before a good village tribunal. But the memory of the old tribunals had died; a new committee created under an Act might be infected with the new spirit of the law courts, and a bad village tribunal would be at least as bad as a court. Once intrigue and party feeling had grown up in a village, a committee might be a positive evil. Sir Richard Temple turned the proposal down; he took the safe and timid line. All he had probably foreseen proved to be true when village *panchayats* were introduced in the next century, but with patience and perseverance they could be improved and if Temple had taken the bold course and agreed with Wedderburn, many years might have been saved.

Wedderburn must have been forgiven; he became a Secretary to the Government of Bombay and when he retired with twenty-seven years' service the Government of Bombay passed a resolution complimenting him on his good services and commending in particular 'his enthusiasm in the cause of education and his anxiety to promote all measures which would in his opinion conduce to the moral and material progress of the natives of this country . . .' Having retired, he devoted himself to the affairs of the Indian National Congress. 'I have been in the service of the people of India', he said, 'and have eaten their salt; and I hope to devote to their service what still remains to me of active life.' He did. He was President of the Fourth Congress and thereafter for nearly thirty years, during seven of which he was in Parliament, he was the representative of the Congress in London, the counterpart in England of Hume in India.

4. HUME AND THE CONGRESS

The Congress had been founded mainly by the exertions of another Indian civilian, Allan Octavian Hume. He was a Haileybury man and had come to India in 1849; he was in charge of a district — Etawah in the North-West Provinces — at the time of the Mutiny. He had fought bravely in 1857, winning as a leader of irregular forces more than one pitched battle; in 1858 he was able to write that: 'No district in the North-West Provinces has, I believe, been more completely restored to order. None in which so few severe punishments have been inflicted . . .' Staying on at Etawah ten years, he had been an exceptionally good district officer, showing particular enthusiasm for education and for agricultural improvement. He started juvenile reformatories, his scheme being taken up by the Government and indeed only in one respect did he show signs of rebellion. He disapproved strongly of the policy of drawing revenue from the sale of liquor; he looked on this revenue as 'the wages of sin', though it is not clear what system he would have substituted.

Altogether, Hume was regarded with favour and in 1870, after three years as provincial commissioner of Customs, he became Secretary to the Government of India in the new department of Revenue, Commerce and Agriculture. It had been intended in India that this should be primarily a department of agriculture, and Hume had been chosen as much for his scientific training as for his long and warm-hearted interest in improving the peasant's life. But the Secretary of State insisted that agriculture should be a subsidiary part of the new Secretary's duties.

Hume was nine years in this post, a long time; offices in Simla were later held on a fixed tenure of five years, but even in the 'seventies it was the custom to change them more often than this. Wedderburn, his biographer, is indignant that Lord Lytton made the change, but it does not seem surprising. There had been a difference of opinion, Hume had been there a long time, and a Viceroy is surely entitled to choose his advisers without being accused of the 'grossest jobbery ever perpetrated', a newspaper comment which Wedderburn quotes with approval. The snub, if there was one, lay in the fact that Hume was not promoted, but returned to the Board of Revenue in the North-West. But since Wedderburn says that he was privately offered the Lieutenant-Governorship of the North-West, which he refused, and that Lord Lytton actually recommended him for Home Member, there seems very little ground for his biographer's display of a somewhat acid self-righteousness.

Hume retired three years later, in 1882. He did not go to England but took up his residence in Simla and began to work for the political development of India. He had in the course of his career acquired the title of 'the Pope of Ornithology', having spent much money on stationing all over India trained observers to secure skins and eggs. He was the joint author of the first great book on Indian birds and his collection was unrivalled. During the rest of his life, he was to earn similar distinction as a botanist while carrying on intense political work.

Hume was a man of ardent spirit, 'not only a great organizer, but the most affectionate of men'. 'With the shrewdness and practical sense of the Scotsman he combined the generous warmth and the fiery impulsiveness of the Oriental', wrote Banerjea of him. It was his contention that a new spirit of expansive nationalism was arising to which some expression must be given if there was not to be an explosion. No one can seriously deny that he was right about the new spirit; it is also true that any proposal for change had to overcome a formidable series of hurdles.

A suggestion from, say, a district officer, must first be examined by the provincial Government. This meant as a rule that it was submitted to a Secretary to Government, accompanied by a long minute discussing every precedent, however remote, and every foreseeable objection. This was prepared by a staff of clerks whose lives had been spent in headquarters, under the supervision of someone usually of the unconvenanted service who, if he had any district experience, seldom intended to have any more. Minute industry, a most persevering consideration of all orders and rules, and a determination to make no mistakes, were the usual features of these discouraging documents.

The office note usually suggested rejection; it was the safest course and the least trouble. A great many proposals of course it was right to reject and it was easy to make a habit of saying no. If however the Secretary had the strength of mind to select the right case and the tenacity of purpose to support it against the objections that would be raised by other departments, each anxious to make its mark, if the Governor of the Province approved, if the proposal survived a similar and still more meticulous scrutiny at the hands of the Government of India, it must still face a Secretary of State who had his eye on the House of Commons and was advised by the Council of India. This was the body of retired Lieutenant-Governors and Members of Council who had replaced the old Court of Directors. The whole system was admirably devised for detecting unsoundness, but the last in the world to encourage a daring and statesmanlike experiment.

Against this background, Hume wrote to all the graduates of the Calcutta University asking for fifty volunteers to join in a movement to promote the mental, moral, social, and political regeneration of India. 'There are aliens, like myself, who love India and her children . . . but the real work must be done by the people of the country themselves . . . If fifty men cannot be found with sufficient power of self-sacrifice, sufficient love for and pride in their country, sufficient genuine and unselfish patriotism to take the initiative and if needs be devote the rest of their lives to the Cause — then there is no hope for India. Her sons must and will remain mere humble and helpless instruments in the hands of foreign rulers. . . .'

The result of this letter was the first Indian National Congress of 1885. It had been decided before that date, by Hume on the advice of Lord Dufferin, the Viceroy, to put political reform first and social second; only a government with some popular backing could enforce social reforms in such matters as child marriage. After full discussion, the party was 'absolutely unanimous in insisting on unswerving loyalty to the British Crown as the key-note of the Institution'. It held '. . . the continual affiliation of India to Great Britain, at any rate for a period far exceeding the range of any practical political forecast, to be *absolutely essential* to the interests of our own National Development'.

The first session of the Congress was held at Bombay and it was proposed that Lord Reay, the Governor, should preside. Both Lord Dufferin and he felt that this would be a mistake and that an Indian should be elected. It was in this atmosphere of friendly encouragement that the first Congress asked for a Royal Commission on the working of the administration, a suggestion which would have continued the series of Parliamentary discussions which had taken place every twenty years in the days of the Company. They prayed for a reduction of military expenditure and deprecated the annexation of Upper Burma. They would abolish the Council of India as an obstacle to reform, and develop provincial Councils on the lines actually made law in 1909. But the longest and most detailed of their resolutions concerned the method of recruitment to the Civil Service.

There was hardly anyone, English or Indian, who in 1885 envisaged a country ruled by a parliament and by the majority of votes in a wide electorate. What some Indians of the university class did picture was a continuation of the existing system, but with Indian officials gradually replacing English. To them the age-limits for the examination were of vital importance. At twenty-three a young man from the Calcutta University could compete in written English with Englishmen of the same age. But at nineteen, in his first year after leaving school, he could not. In one of the periodic re-assessments the age had just been lowered, and politically minded Indians feared this was meant to keep Indians out. The Congress therefore put in the forefront of their programme the two proposals that the age-limits should be raised and that the examination should be held simultaneously in England and in India.

Nothing was said in these resolutions about a new caste of Indian Guardians, the Statutory Civil Service, which had been proposed by Lord Lytton's Government and had now been in existence for six years. Appointments to it were to be made by nomination from any Indians thought fit. The status of the new service was to be that of the I.C.S., and it was hoped that the younger sons of princes and nobles would offer themselves; as soon as they were trained they would hold some of the I.C.S. posts. This was all very well, but no one can make people give equal esteem to a service for which there are not sufficient candidates and to another of men picked by keen competition. Nobody really liked the statutory civil service; only sixty-nine appointments to it were made and after 1886 there were no more.

But it is Hume and the Congress with whom we are concerned. Hume was its general secretary until the twenty-third annual Congress, which met in December 1908. The resolutions of that twenty-third session begin as usual with loyal homage to the King Emperor, express the deep and general satisfaction of the country at the reforms announced in that year, and end with a message of cordial greetings and congratulations to Hume, 'the father and founder of the Congress'. The delegates sent a similar message to Wedderburn, who for twenty years had carried on in England the work at that end which Hume was doing in India.

The resolutions that came between are framed in the spirit of Mr. Gladstone; they have a flavour of the nonconformist meeting-house, earnest and well-meaning, perhaps a trifle doctrinaire, fundamentally warm-hearted. The delegates disapproved of violent outrages and hoped for constitutional progress. They protested against the treatment of Indians in South Africa and against what they described as *lettres de cachet*. By this they meant the power still held by the Government under Regulation III of 1818 to confine without trial persons known to be hostile to the Government. The world's history shows few governments who have denied themselves this power, but it is repugnant to the principles of Simon de Montfort and the Great Revolution of 1688. The men of the Congress had been brought up in the mental atmosphere of English Liberalism and they were genuinely shocked by this power. It was a criticism that would never have occurred to their grandfathers, and the Government of India, who might claim to have brought them up, might well have exchanged the self-congratulatory glances of intelligent parents who perceive that their child has begun to criticize them.

The twenty-third Congress was also in favour of an extension of the permanent Settlement — a proposal of which one can only say that a permanent opposition is bound to display a certain amount of permanent perversity. They wished also to separate the executive and judicial functions. Here was another peculiarly English idea, or more strictly a French idea about an English institution; it was

Montesquieu who had noticed that English judges were independent of the individual who happened at the moment to be King, and had exalted into a principle what to the English was a working arrangement. In India, where all functions had centred in the King even more completely than in France, the English had introduced the first stage of the distinction, a written law instead of personal whim. The second stage, of judges who have no function except to judge, they had treated more cautiously. Cornwallis had gone a long way towards it but his ideas had not worked well and there had been a step back towards the older system. The non-regulation provinces had as a rule no separate judges till some twenty or thirty years after annexation. And even when there were separate judges, the district officer was the head of the magistracy and could himself sentence an offender to two years' imprisonment.

In England, too, the magistrates were responsible for the Queen's peace, but they were amateurs and there was no one among them in whom executive power was concentrated as effectively as in the hands of a district officer in India. Nor was it necessary that there should be; it was some time since the most apprehensive had felt seriously perturbed by the thought of riots in England. In India, every religious festival was an occasion when tempers might flare up and lives be lost. There was every reason for the slight modification of constitutional principle involved in the district officer's powers. Nor could it reasonably be argued that judges and High Courts were influenced by the views of the executive.

The Congress asked for the separation of judicial and executive functions because the principle was liberal and because there were no doubt men among them who had heard of some case which sounded unjust. They would have surely been on far firmer ground if they had argued that India had already an overdose of the principle, that people had been far happier when Malcolm and John Lawrence did what they thought right under a tree, that what was needed was something more Indian, some compromise perhaps between the Maratha system of arbitration by committee and the Mogul system of punishment by executive order. But they were English Liberals, with that rigid conservatism in doctrine which seems native to their party.

A more arguable point was that judges should be recruited from the bar instead of from the I.C.S. The plea was that such judges would have greater legal knowledge and fewer prejudices. Legal knowledge of an academic kind was, however, surely less needed than industry, common sense and integrity, with some knowledge of the country. Judges recruited from the English bar were sadly lacking in knowledge of India, nor had they always been conspicuous for sympathy with Indians. As for the Indian bar, it was not, in the nineteenth century, a profession that encouraged honesty of intellect; it was not easy for a man to make a living there and retain his integrity.

In those early days, then, some of the resolutions passed in succession at every annual Congress were ill conceived and if put into force would not have helped the villager. They seem, to one looking back with the advantage of experience, too English for India. All the same, they were one of the healthiest signs of the times and the mere fact that they were made is something of which both England and India may be proud.

5. RACIAL ESTRANGEMENT AND BANERJEA

If the Congress were too English in the remedies they suggested, it was none the less true that something was wrong. It was all very well to say that the peasant was better off than he had been under Akbar; he was still nothing like so well off as an ordinarily humane person would wish to see him. It might not be easy to say what ought to be done for him but it could hardly be denied that something should be done, that his material progress was very slow. The educated Indian saw this and criticized the administration, not always very constructively because he had no administrative experience, but with good cause all the same. And the new and rapidly growing class of intellectuals might, as Temple said, be few but they counted in influence for much more than their numbers. It was their existence, more than anything else, that led to that harshness and estrangement between Englishman and Indian which was perhaps worse in the 'eighties than at any other time.

This may be illustrated by the story of Surendranath Banerjea. He, with Dutt and Gupta, went to England in 1868 and next year the three were successful in the I.C.S. examination. There were four Indians that year, these three from Bengal and another man from Bombay. Once before and once only, in 1863, an Indian had overcome the immense obstacles he had to encounter and been successful. Now there were four, and all over India, and particularly in Bengal, there were loud rejoicings.

It transpired however, after the results had been announced, that three of the four candidates had given an age for a school examination four years before which did not agree with the age they had given for the I.C.S. examination. Two of them, including Banerjea, were over age for the I.C.S. if the age they had given before was correct. The Civil Service Commission rejected their explanation that, according to their own way of reckoning, the three candidates were nine months old when they were born. They refused to hear evidence on this point. They refused to consider horoscopes, which for another seventy years at least were usually the best evidence of age in India. They declared Banerjea and the other man disqualified and their seats vacant.

This no doubt was due to nothing more sinister than an obstinate pedantry; the Commission was perhaps too judicial in its outlook and too much divorced from executive functions. But the India Office took no step to put things right. Banerjea sued the Secretary of State in the court of Queen's Bench and won his case. He and his companion were reinstated. There could hardly have been a worse start to a career.

On arrival in Calcutta, Banerjea was posted to Sylhet, then in Bengal, later in the province of Assam. Here he was under the orders of a man of mixed European and Indian blood, in whom Banerjea thought that feelings of racial superiority were very strong. This may or may not have been so, but at any rate friendliness between them soon came to an end and Banerjea found that he was constantly called on for reports and explanations. A day came when he sent in a false return. It was a list of cases in which no action had been taken because the accused could not be arrested. To include a case in this list was sometimes a convenient way of avoiding explanations for delay, and unfortunately he sent in another list in which he gave a long explanation of the delays in a case which also appeared in the first list.

If a young Englishman in his first year under an English Collector had done such a thing, it would have met with a friendly reproof. 'You can't of course always check everything you sign', he would have been told, 'but you can check a percentage and keep your Court Clerk sufficiently frightened to stop this kind of thing. Don't let it happen again.'

Banerjea's Collector however reported the case to the Bengal Government. The Bengal Government ordered an inquiry by three senior officers, who came to the conclusion that Banerjea had known what he was doing and had deliberately meant to deceive his Collector.

Banerjea was a person of intelligence and it does not seem very likely that he would have been such a fool, but they had studied the evidence. They were themselves surprised when they found that the sentence recommended by the Government of India and approved by the Secretary of State was dismissal. Banerjea became a dismissed Government servant, branded for life.

It is not necessary to suppose that anyone concerned acted of deliberate malice, but deep in the minds of the commissioners and of those who decided on the punishment there must have been a feeling of distrust for Indians, a belief that they were not straightforward, that they could never take the place of English district officers.

Some years later a Lieutenant-Governor of Bengal said: 'I have a soft corner in my heart for Surendranath; we have done him a grievous wrong, but he bears no malice.' It came to be generally believed that he would have been treated differently if he had been an Englishman. That he did bear no malice, that he remained always moderate, that in a life of agitation and political work he always attributed sincerity and high motives to those who opposed him, shows a remarkable nobility of character. But that such a thing could have happened at all needs explanation.

It has been fashionable lately to put down to the Mutiny most of the strained feelings between English and Indian ever since. Of course the Mutiny was a memory never wholly effaced, but most contemporaries write as though that wound scarred over with surprising speed. There were set-backs; trouble which before the Mutiny might have been looked at with a tolerant sense of proportion was felt afterwards to be perhaps the beginning of something much bigger. An example of this was the Cowan episode in 1872. A party of about a hundred Sikhs of a fanatical sect known as Kukas attacked a town in State territory. They were defeated, some being killed and sixty-eight being taken prisoner. These sixty-eight were handed over to L. Cowan, the nearest British deputy commissioner. Cowan was not a member of the Indian Civil Service; he was uncovenanted, like Bruce, but he had been trained in the tradition, stronger in the Punjab than anywhere else, that a quick blow at once will save ten later. The prisoners had been taken with arms in their hands 'waging war against the Queen'; there was no doubt about their guilt nor that under Section 121 of the Indian Penal Code the punishment for the offence was death. Nor, at that time, does there seem to have been any likelihood that the penalty would not have been inflicted. But

Cowan decided that the moral effect of immediate executions would be overwhelming and would end any possibility of the trouble spreading. He blew away forty-nine men from guns, illegally— because his legal powers did not extend to death—and in the face of explicit instructions from his Commissioner, Forsyth, to wait. Forsyth, true to the Punjab tradition, approved what he had done. The Government of India found that his illegal action was 'not palliated by any public necessity' and dismissed him. The English press thought he had been unjustly treated.

That incident could hardly have happened in quite that way before the Mutiny. Yet it is wrong to suppose that the Mutiny was always in men's minds. It was for another reason that things subsequently grew worse. Henry Beveridge, writing to his wife in the 'eighties, felt that relations between the races were worse than ever before. Sir Henry Cotton thought the same. 'It is a grave symptom', he said, 'that the official body has now succumbed as completely as the non-official to anti-native prejudice.' In the 'sixties, nine civilians out of ten were on the side of the ryot against the planter; by the 'eighties, nine out of ten were against Lord Ripon over the Ilbert Bill. It was the Ilbert Bill that brought the feeling to the surface, but the Bill was not the cause. If all had been well between the races, no one would have been afraid of an Indian Magistrate.

The real reason is not far to seek. It is easy to forget, if one has only known Delhi or Calcutta, the immense gulf between the educated Englishman and the Indians whom he met in a district, even in the twentieth century. In a small district, even in the 'twenties of this century, an Englishman in the North, apart from peasants, met only the men who were leaders of the district, landowners and business men, of whom few spoke English. There would be a few pleaders, but he must be particular not to become intimate with pleaders. Hardly any of his clerks spoke English and in the nineteenth century hardly any of his tahsildars. The mental background of the Indian gentlemen who came to visit him was still that of the Hindu epics or of Firdausi's Book of the Kings. The civilization to which they belonged had stood still. It was as though John Stuart Mill were to be discovered in conversation with one of the chiefs in whose hall Homer sang.

Between people so different there could be courtesy, kindliness and liking, there could be affection, but no dealing on equal terms. The relationship was paternal, accepted on both sides. It was fixed and settled, like caste; the district officer and his family were one kind of human being, the people of his district another. There was no thought of equality. The earliest Head Clerks, the earliest Deputy Collectors and subordinate Judges, however subtle and polished their minds, never felt themselves to be made of the same stuff as the English covenanted servant. It was easy enough for Bartle Frere to sit down by his head clerk on the ground and call him 'Uncle'. There was not the least likelihood of that elderly Brahman calling him 'Frere, my boy'.

In the 'seventies and 'eighties, things began to be different. In the districts, the gulf — with rare exceptions — was just as wide as ever. But in Calcutta there were Indians of a new kind who could not be regarded as beings of another order. 'Men who speak English better than most Englishmen, who read Mill and Comte, Max Müller and Maine, who occupy with distinction seats on the judicial bench, who administer the affairs of native States with many millions of inhabitants, who manage cotton mills and conduct the boldest operations of commerce, who edit newspapers in English and correspond on equal terms with the scholars of Europe' — such men as these, urged Sir Henry Cotton, cannot be expected to salaam every Englishman they meet in the street, to dismount from a horse or lower an umbrella when they see him coming, to remove their shoes when they enter his house.

The educated Indian had stepped right across the gap; now it was his father and his brothers who were a different order of being from himself; he had come inside the enclosure. He thought and talked like an Englishman and claimed to be judged by English standards.

It was a shock then to Englishmen used to the old paternal relationship to find themselves confronted by Indians who claimed equality. It meant the end of the old fatherly dominance in which everyone did as they were told. It meant also social stresses and difficulties in a society which had been simple and which had involved no great effort. This shock roused a great deal of irrational anger.

To this sense of shock at having to concede equality must be added the genuine difficulty that there were still very few Indians with whom it was possible to share a meal or a drink; there was also something else, the Hindu, and to a lesser extent the Muslim, treatment of women. There was genuine feeling on this point; no doubt also there were people who seized on it as a rational explanation for an emotion they may have felt to be not entirely respectable. But with the best will in the world — which seldom existed — it was difficult to be really friendly with people whose women were segregated and who still practised child marriage. Annette Beveridge, a woman of education who came to India unmarried, with the purely altruistic purpose of helping Indian women, wrote to the newspapers about the Ilbert Bill, taking the side against her husband and opposing the jurisdiction of Indian magistrates over Europeans on this sole ground of the treatment of women. Perhaps the Age of Consent Act of 1891, or rather the evil it was intended to cure, was a more important factor in the feelings of this time than is generally recognized. It had its origin in the case of a child wife who died of injuries received on her marriage-bed; Indian Liberals supported the bill — which raised the age for consummation of marriage to twelve — but it aroused bitter opposition among many orthodox Hindus who regarded it as an interference with religion. It was this agitation which started Tilak on his career.

Indian social customs with regard to women had not of course changed for the worse — indeed they were already beginning to change for the better. But they were brought into prominence by the growth of education. How could you be intimate with a man whose wife you were not allowed to see? How could talk be anything but guarded between you? It is surely facile to judge by the standards of today and to suppose that the easy intercourse of 1950 could have been possible in 1880.

No one can deny, all the same, that there were things at this time of which an Englishman should feel ashamed and at which an Indian has a right to feel bitter. There was resentment because Indians were beginning to claim the equality the English had promised them. There was resentment because Indians were beginning to criticize the way the country was run. There were cases of rudeness to fellow passengers by train; there were cases — not many, but a sprinkling — of British soldiers injuring or even killing Indians when drunk and escaping with inadequate sentences. There was a feeling in the air summed up in a sentence overheard by Mrs. Moss King. At the outbreak of the Second Afghan War, 'a young artillery officer put the present popular feeling in a nutshell. He said: "I know nothing of politics, but I do know that if a nigger cheeks us we must lick him." '

Racial arrogance there was then, and it was more widespread than at any time before or since. It was less necessary than it had been to meet Indians and to understand them, because there was more English society in India than ever before, because it was cheaper and quicker to go to England and because leave was taken more often. There was less isolation and there were more English women to talk to. 'Among women, who are more rapidly demoralized than men, abuse of "those horrid natives" is almost universal', wrote Sir Henry Cotton. A process that had begun in the 'forties was accelerated; fewer and fewer Englishmen were identifying themselves thoroughly with the country. At the same time the English as a nation felt utterly secure, their pre-eminence in wealth and naval power unchallenged, their works manifestly approved by the Almighty.

These are generalizations; against all this it must be remembered that there were many districts where things were just as they had been fifty years before. And in every province there was an ardent minority of the service who hated arrogance in every form and who believed that justice was not always done as between English and Indian. These men were life-long members of a public service, among whom some common doctrine was essential. Yet it was still a commonplace for men in the service to write to the papers on political subjects. Continual, unconstructive criticism of course did not help a man's career; Boanerges Blitzen

> Languished in a district desolate and dry,
> Watched the Local Government yearly pass him by,

but a great deal could be said with impunity. Sir Henry Harrison, as Chairman of the Calcutta Corporation, 'boldly stood out for the Corporation and fought the Government', says Surendranath Banerjea. In the darkest days of the Ilbert Bill controversy, Harrison and Cotton arranged a mixed dinner for Indians and English and Cotton 'made a speech breathing the spirit of equality'. Both these men stood up for the Bengali against the Government repeatedly; it did not stand in their way to high office and knighthoods. Perhaps it is even more remarkable that R. C. Dutt in 1882, while still in service, wrote to *The Statesman* a letter reviewing the career of the retiring Lieutenant-Governor, Sir Ashley Eden, very fair to his virtues and very critical from the point of view of an Indian liberal reformer.

The racial bitterness was to improve before long, partly because English people became used to the idea of Indians educated in Western ways, partly because Indian women began to emerge and join society, but surely also because Indians knew that there were men as generous and warm-hearted as Cotton, Harrison and above all Hume. 'Do you', Hume appealed to his own countrymen, 'at all realize the dull misery of these countless myriads? From their births to their deaths . . . toil, toil, toil; hunger, hunger, hunger; sickness, suffering, sorrow; these alas! alas! are the keynotes of their short and sad existences.' It was a picture that Lord Curzon could no doubt have disproved with statistics acidly marshalled, but there was some truth in it. And it was just because there were some Englishmen who sounded that note — and many more, the majority, who felt a warm if less passionate sympathy — that on the political side the quarrel that was now beginning to develop was so much a family affair.

In Banerjea's long story of struggle he speaks often critically, sometimes bitterly, of abstractions such as the system, the service and bureaucratic rule, but not often in the same spirit of individuals. 'Mr. Charles Allen, an officer of great promise . . . and a personal friend' — 'Sir Charles Elliott, with whom my personal relations were friendly and even cordial . . . but a typical bureaucrat . . . who believed the people could not be trusted to manage their own affairs' — 'Sir Edward Baker, strong, generous and impulsive . . .' — those are the kind of references that fill the pages of Banerjea, who had a right to be bitter if any man had. But the family nature of the whole discussion is seen most clearly of all perhaps in the comment made on R. C. Dutt by his biographer, Gupta, another I.C.S. Indian, who could write: 'Through him, more than through the medium of any other Indian, has India learnt the value of the rarer gifts of the English character — the love of independence, truth, patriotism, and an unflagging sense of duty . . .' And, to bring the question up to date, consider the dedication of Nirad Chaudhuri's *Diary of an Unknown Indian*, published since independence. 'To the memory', he wrote, 'of the British Empire in India, which conferred subjecthood on us but withheld citizenship, to which yet every one of us threw out the challenge *Civis Britannicus sum*, because all that was good and living within us was made, shaped, and quickened by the same British rule.'

The young Congress movement was in short a quickening of the spirit, a child both of England and India. It should not be forgotten however that in the background, excluded as yet from the Congress, lurked a dark spirit linked with the more reactionary side of Saivite Hinduism. While Wedderburn and Hume, with Dutt and other Indian leaders, were talking of Montesquieu and George Washington, of John Stuart Mill, Cobden and Bright, Tilak was praising Sivaji for stabbing a Mogul general in the back at the moment he was about to sign a treaty of friendship. While the Congress were welcoming the mild reforms of 1908, Tilak was preaching that if burglars — that is to say, *mlecchas*, non-Hindus, Christians or Muslims — come into your house, you have a perfect right to shut the doors upon them and burn it down with them inside. Ram Mohun Roy had believed that

Hinduism must reform itself by a synthesis of the best from Asia and Europe; as that reform began to take effect it bred a new resistance, an angry rejection of the West, that grew from just that confident questioning spirit the West had created, that looked bitterly and defensively back, determined to find good only in the East. That spirit in varying degrees was for the next seventy years also a part of Hindu nationalism, always in conflict with the other element which has so much in common with the English nonconformist radical movement.

It was that bitter spirit that alienated the Muslims. Sir Sayyad Ahmad perceived that to apply liberal principles, such as majority rule and selection by competitive examination, would mean Hindu rule; it was perhaps because he already detected the seeds of Tilak's doctrines that he rejected the prospect. At any rate, the conflict was clearly stated in those early days, the first days of the Congress. A beginning had been made to the recession of British power, a healthy and natural development. But no one yet perceived that this involved a struggle for the inheritance that was to split India and to destroy the great achievement of unification.

CHAPTER IX

A SENSE OF PROPORTION

I. PIGSTICKING AND THE PURGATION OF LUSTS

ONE F. B. Simson of the Bengal Civil Service, who retired in 1872 as Commissioner of Dacca, was sitting one day in his court when a villager entered carrying the mangled leg of his son. This he laid before the court.

'What sort of a ruler are you?' he cried — and one may guess that in his rage and grief he used the familiar 'thou' to which the villager always does revert when he is excited. 'What are you doing, sitting here arguing with lawyers when a tiger is eating my son?'

It was a view of the Magistrate's duty that agreed with Simson's own. He left his court and shot the tiger. But it was not a view that fitted in very well with the plea of the National Congress some fifteen years later for the separation of judicial and executive functions.

The resolutions of the National Congress and the opinions of Radicals such as Hume and Wedderburn were all very well, but three-quarters of the service at least, and perhaps more, would have laughed at talk of the separation of powers and if you had spoken of India's right to govern herself they would have agreed that some day this must come. 'But India will not be ready for it in our time or long after', they would have added, 'and we have more important things to think about.'

The District Officer was thinking, for instance, of the best way of dealing with Brij Mohan, an inspector of Land Records, widely reputed to be corrupt but so far too clever to be caught; of how to raise the money for an extension of the hospital at headquarters; of whether a new primary school at Gopalpur was really essential or whether it might not be better to concentrate the scanty funds on existing schools; of the state of the road to Ramnagar at the thirteenth milestone; of the murder case from Gwalabad and how the defence could be prevented from tampering with the evidence; of what should be done about the pipal trees on the Moharram route at Pitampura.

This last was a problem that occurred again and again. On the tenth day of the month of Moharram, images of the tombs of Hasan and Husain, the grandsons of the Prophet, slain at Karbala, are taken in procession to be buried. They are gaudy towers of tinsel and papier mâché. They jolt, swaying on men's shoulders, through the narrow streets and along the sandy rutted roads between the fields. And then comes a sacred pipal tree, surrounded perhaps by a brick platform on which there may be a coloured stone or a shrine no bigger than a doll's house. Either the gilded tower or the pipal tree has grown since last year; the image will not pass unless a branch is cut. The Hindus of the village with their six-foot bamboo quarter-staffs have collected and wait grimly for the first insult to the sacred tree. The Muslim escort of the image will not agree to deviation by a yard from the usual route, still less that the tower should bow its head or be carried aslant.

It was a problem that called not for naked force — which indeed was seldom available — but for a quality for which there is no exact single word in English. But there is a word for it in Hindustani, *hikmatamali*, a judicious mixture of finesse and tactful management with a hint of force in the background. An Indian inspector of police, confronted once unexpectedly with this dilemma of the tombs and the pipal tree, by hikmatamali persuaded the leaders of the village to call out the landless labourers and dig the roadway deeper, so that it was possible for the tombs to pass without disturbing a leaf. But of course the most skilful use of hikmatamali lay in never letting things come to such a pass — or rather, *impasse*. In a well-run district, the authorized height of every tomb was recorded in a police-station, and, between festivals, the route could be prospected and opened up discreetly. E. H. H. Edye — in the twentieth century, it is true, but the problem was unaltered — arranged between festivals for two elephants to graze near an offending pipal tree; elephants are not exactly sacred but are under the special patronage of Ganesh and no one would grudge them a branch or two from a pipal. And next year, to everyone's surprise, the tomb passed easily where before it had stuck.

This skilful management was needed because there was very little force available. There was about one British soldier and four Indian soldiers in India to every six thousand of the population. In most districts there were no British soldiers; in very many there were no soldiers at all, British or Indian. There might be none within a hundred, two hundred or three hundred miles. There might be seven or eight hundred police in a district to a million or so inhabitants; they would all be Indian except for the Superintendent, a covenanted officer, and the Inspector who trained recruits, a kind of regimental sergeant-major. A man had to rely on his own wits, his own power of command, his hikmatamali, coupled with the immense confidence he felt in himself and the system of government. And the reverse is true; so little force was needed, partly because there were very few people who suffered from any strong general sense of injustice, and partly because as a rule the district officer was a man of humour and human understanding, tact, common sense and above all a sense of proportion.

It was surprising that so many were equipped with a good share of these qualities. They were, the majority of them, brought up directly or indirectly in the tradition of Arnold of Rugby and *Tom Brown's Schooldays*, a tradition which had spread by now to half the schools in England. They had all had to work hard to pass their examination; they were all used to the ideal of hard work and hard play. And many of them believed that it was the hard play which, in a life of much loneliness and of very heavy responsibility, kept them sane and balanced and helped them to retain a saving sense of proportion.

The game of games, easily first in the estimation of all who practised it, was pigsticking. It was generally encouraged and, though it would not be true that a man had to hunt pig to be thought well of, there is no doubt he had a better chance if he did. To be good after a pig a man must be a horseman, which was in any case a great asset to a district officer. And he must also have just the same qualities — the power of quick but cool judgment, a stout heart, a controlled but fiery ardour and a determination not to be beaten — that are needed at the crisis of a riot, or for that matter of a battle. The kind of man who has those qualities needs to exercise them; it was an old saying in India that pigsticking had saved many a man's liver but it had saved much more than that. The danger and excitement, the ferocity thus harmlessly given an outlet, sweetened men who might otherwise have been soured by files and hot weather and disappointment, as lime sweetens grass soured by poultry. Ugly lusts for power and revenge melted away and even the lust for women assumed — so it was said — reasonable proportions after a day in pursuit of pig.

The civilian, but hardly anyone else, often hunted pig alone. And to kill a pig with a spear by oneself is an achievement. A boar can go faster than a horse for three or four hundred yards; a man must drive in his heels and gallop as hard as he can to keep the beast in sight. This first gallop, at a pace unknown to fox-hunters, was always through thick country with long grass or tamarisk bushes and usually cut up by water-courses. After that first burst, if his horse is still on its feet and if he still knows where the boar is, the hunter must use judgment, hustling it perhaps at a hand gallop through broken country but not pressing too close among the tamarisk, going as hard as he can the moment an open patch is seen, trying all the time to tire the pig, so that he can catch it when he sees it clearly, or so that it will turn at bay. When it does turn to fight — and the bigger the boar the sooner that will be — he may advance at a walk, relying on straight eye, strong arm and keen spear to keep the sharp tusks from his horse's legs and his own, or he may meet its charge at the gallop, or perhaps spear the defiant beast as he gallops past, as men spear tent-pegs at a horse-show.

It is no use pretending that this sport contributed directly to good district management. There are much better ways of preventing the depredations of wild pig, and a district officer who thought of nothing but pig would hardly be a good officer. But in fact the good pig-stickers were usually very good officers. The district officer who spent all his time with his nose in files on the other hand did not always have his district in good order; some recreation was needed to keep a lonely man sane and stamp-collecting or carpentry were little better than files. Pigsticking and shooting did take a man among the villagers, to whom the pursuit of animals seemed less irrational than most forms of amusement, and a journey in pursuit of snipe, tiger, or pig seldom failed to produce a petition perhaps, or the news of some oppression, or perhaps it would be a sidelight on a chief's character or the proof that a well, a dam or a school was really needed. Most important of all, good officers were eager to stay as long as they were allowed in districts where there were tiger or pig. If all civilians had been thoroughly civilized, everyone would have competed to avoid those lonely districts that were mostly jungle and — worse still — would have done what they could to get away once they were there.

Pigsticking and tiger-shooting were the two first sports of the civilian. It was hard to raise a team of civilians for polo tournaments; in the North-West, which became later the United Provinces, teams were always entered for minor tournaments, sometimes even two teams, but they never had any practice together and were usually out-classed. In other provinces teams were not as a rule even entered. Everyone played polo when not in camp though few reached a high standard. But in pigsticking the I.C.S. could hold their own; their contingent for the Kadir Cup, the supreme event of the pigsticking year, when as many as a hundred spears might be competing, was big enough in 1898 to give them a camp of their own, making a third to cavalry and gunners; members of the service won the cup twice and were several times in the final. In 1919 P. W. Marsh scored the double triumph of winning the Kadir Cup and one of the two cross-country races held at the same meeting. In 1898, C. E. Wild and P. V. Allen were both in the final of the Kadir Cup, both having been first in the competitive examination in their respective years.

But it is not victory in competitions that constitutes the point. What has to emerge is the picture of a man who gets through his files quickly because he wants to be out of doors and because he wastes no time on looking up the rules; who writes short decisive judgments because he is clear in his own mind where the right lies and does not seek to justify himself; who expects his subordinates to do their own work and trusts them until he has reason not to; who likes to get about his district and see things for himself and sees no reason why he should not chase a pig in the course of the day. He does not want transfer or promotion; he does not want to catch anyone's eye by flashy work; he wants to stay where he is and, though he would like another Waler and another Sowter saddle, really asks no more of Fate than that his Commissioner and the provincial Government should let him get on with his job his own way. And incidentally, being a fair scholar, a man who perhaps got a good second or just scraped a first, he is quietly getting on, whenever he has a spare moment, with the *Gazetteer* describing the history, antiquities, crops, castes, sects, marriage customs, land tenures, soil, and occupations of his district.

It is, I think, true to say too that the men who hunted most among civilians were the men who were remembered in their districts. In the last years, three names in Northern India are particularly remembered in the annals of pigsticking, F. L. Brayne from the Punjab, with over three hundred first spears to his credit, Percy Marsh and Charles Hobart from the United Provinces. Everyone who has heard of India in the last thirty years has heard of Brayne's work for village improvement; Percy Marsh was known by every villager in Aligarh and Meerut. Charles Hobart won one of the two Hoghunter's Races in 1920 and broke his neck pigsticking — but did not lose his life — and of Hobart: 'Look,' they would say years later, wherever he had served, 'this is where Hobart Sahib sat.' When he came back, even for a few hours, to any district where he had served, there would be a hundred visitors to see him. He was often in trouble but received a C.I.E. when at last he retired; the letters, he remarked thoughtfully, must stand for: 'Charles's Indiscretions Excused.'

A SENSE OF PROPORTION

The North-West Provinces became the classical centre, the Leicestershire, of this sport; it had been practised from the beginning throughout the old Bengal Presidency and to a lesser extent in Bombay. In Madras the country was seldom suitable, but there were bison and buffalo to be stalked as well as tiger, while in Assam there were rhinoceros, which seem to have been still quite common in the middle of the century. But none of these beasts called for quite the same qualities in their pursuers as the boar.

2. ZEAL WITHOUT SENSE

What exactly is meant by sanity and sense of proportion can best be illustrated by its absence. Aubrey Pennell was a man of brilliant intellect whose career at one time seemed most promising. He was a Bengal civilian who volunteered for a spell in Burma; he was picked as Private Secretary to the Chief Commissioner and after some time in Government House went to a district as a settlement officer. He was an able young man and he came to the conclusion that the settlement might be run much better on quite different lines. He said so, with some cutting comments on his seniors; it was arguable that he was right but the upshot was that he ceased to be a settlement officer; the Government of Burma had really to choose between Pennell and the rest of the Settlement Department. He became a Deputy Commissioner in Burma but there was a scandal which he wished to expose and everyone else to bury — and Pennell came back to Bengal with a recommendation that he should be employed as a judge.

He began in this new capacity at Mymensingh, where he made some remarks about the conduct of executive officers in general which the Calcutta High Court ordered to be expunged from his judgment. He then went as judge to Chapra where he almost at once found himself involved in a case which became notorious.

In this part of Bengal, the rivers are often banked up between high earthen dykes, and when the waters rise their level is sometimes many feet above the surrounding country. Incalculable damage is done if the dyke breaks and the country is flooded. It is not at all easy to get villagers to take any steps about a leak, and when there is a threat or break any official who happens to be near forgets everything else until the crisis is past. Two young Englishmen, one a policeman and one an engineer, were one day trying to deal with a breach. They collected villagers, headed by village watchmen; one man refused to help, and he was a person of some slight local consequence. The two young men gave him a thrashing and subsequently, thinking perhaps that he would bring a complaint against them, they proceeded against him by law. He was tried by the District Magistrate — a Muslim — and sentenced to two months' imprisonment. His own complaint against the two Englishmen was dismissed.

Now it was a general maxim that no Englishman should strike an Indian, but if ever there was a case where the misdemeanour was excusable it was surely this one. The young men were working desperately in the public interest; everything hung in the balance and one recalcitrant might well turn the scale. The man seems to have been regarded as a leader of some kind; if he hung back unpunished, why should anyone work? Some drastic action was quickly needed; to have had the shirker arrested and taken away was not only less dramatic than a beating but meant the loss of at least one reliable man as escort, at a time when none could be spared. It depends on the nature of the beating, but a wise district officer would probably have regarded the shirker as already sufficiently punished and given the two young men an official reprimand, accompanied probably by a private word that it need not be taken to heart so long as they did not do it again.

Pennell, however, not being a pigsticker, was not a wise man. When the shirker appealed, he took up his case as a matter of principle. A man had been beaten without fair trial; it was oppression. He certainly ought not to go to prison and the case against his assailants must be started afresh. These orders were promulgated in a judgment which included biting criticism of the Bengal Government, of the High Court, of a good many officers, and particularly of various steps that had been taken to keep the matter quiet. The judgment reached Whitehall, questions were asked in Parliament and Members subscribed for a gratuity to the shirker which set him up in idleness for the rest of his life.

The High Court in Calcutta on this occasion agreed with the substance of Pennell's judgment, though they condemned his language as intemperate; the *Westminster Gazette* said it was 'needlessly picturesque'. It may be imagined that the newspapers enjoyed themselves even more in Calcutta than in London and it was, Pennell thought, on account of this affair, and certainly it was soon after it, that he was transferred to Noakhali, then regarded as the most undesirable station in Bengal. Here, too, he soon found evidence of the iniquities of the Government.

A moneylender disappeared. After some days his son found his body floating in a village pond. He reported the matter to the police but no progress was made with the investigation until one day the murdered man's son met the acting District Magistrate on his morning ride. This young man, whose name was David Ezechiel, set to work to find out what had happened. He formed the opinion that the inquiry was not proceeding very fast because the persons thought to have committed the murder were near relations of the Sub-Inspector of Police, one Osman Ali. Osman Ali seems to have been one of those real villains who are very occasionally found among the police. When they do occur, they are very hard to detect and Osman Ali in particular was an adept at deceiving his superiors. Reily, the Superintendent of Police, was apparently an idle officer, widely thought to be the most incompetent of his service in Bengal; he believed all he was told by Osman Ali.

Ezechiel however insisted that, in spite of Osman Ali's report of insufficient evidence, the case should be tried. But before the trial actually began, Ezechiel reverted to his cold weather rank and his place was taken by Cargill, who held the post substantively and had been on leave. Cargill had already formed an opinion on Osman Ali and no doubt described him in his reports in some such terms as these: 'A darogha of the old school, somewhat rough and ready in his methods, but energetic and efficient; he gets his man and has a saving sense of humour.' At any rate he agreed with Reily that Osman Ali was to be believed and there was really no case.

The trial however had by now begun. Pennell conducted it at his own leisurely pace. Reily was called in evidence and the Court spent four days examining him. He had from pure idleness accepted as correct a sketch-map which was misleading. He had not himself visited the scene of the crime, but, relying on the sketch-map, he was foolish enough to say he had. He was soon exposed and at the end of the trial Pennell charged Reily with perjury, insisted on his arrest and refused him bail. He then spent three weeks writing a judgment in which he analysed the evidence with subtlety and shrewdness, sentenced one of the accused to death and two to transportation for life and acquitted the fourth. Into this searching analysis, however, he wove a scathing, intemperate and sometimes witty indictment not only of Reily and Cargill, not only of almost everyone in Bengal, but also of no less sublime a figure than Lord Curzon himself.

It was silly to call Lord Curzon a guinea-pig Viceroy, it was irrelevant to dwell on Cargill's[1] notorious meanness and altogether

[1] Among his equals at the Club, Cargill had the reputation of being mean, but since this book was written evidence has been sent to me that he spent sparingly in public in order to have more for secret charity, to which he gave generously. I am glad to make amends to his memory.

there is much in this judgment not worthy of Pennell's intelligence, but there are moments too in the spirit — and faintly in the manner — of Junius if not of Burke. An English judge for instance should display 'a strenuous resistance to every appearance of lawless power; a spirit of independence carried to some degree of enthusiasm; an inquisitive character to discover and a bold one to display every corruption and every error of Government'. A leader of Her Majesty's Opposition rather than a judge, one might have said, but Pennell had no doubt that judges should be watchdogs over the throne and goes on to contrast this ideal with the reality of the Calcutta High Court. But there is no room to quote him at length.

Having spent a very enjoyable three weeks writing it, Pennell delivered his judgment in Court, gave one copy to the reporter of a Calcutta newspaper and stepped into a boat — the best way of getting about in Noakhali — in which he spent more than a week on a visit of inspection to a subordinate court at the other end of this watery district. During these days no one could get in touch with him; as he took with him his judgment and all the connected papers it was technically impossible for anyone to move in the case at all. Reily was in jail and the district police without a Superintendent, while in Calcutta the *Amrita Bazar Patrika* published Pennell's judgment as a serial and was read in circles from which it would normally have been excluded.

When Pennell came back, he refused to let the High Court or the Government have copies of his judgment on the grounds that his few copyists were fully occupied in making copies for the accused. It was three weeks from the delivery of the judgment before the *Patrika's* monopoly ended and the High Court could read what Pennell said about them without borrowing a newspaper from their clerks. He was suspended from duty and spent two months trying to find out what were the charges against him. What these were to be was of course the problem that was puzzling everybody; Pennell had gone beyond all limits, but to speak his own mind had always been a prerogative of the service and it was not easy to frame a charge that would not seem illiberal. In the end, he solved the problem; tired of doing nothing, he took ship to England and enabled the Secretary of State to dismiss him for leaving India without permission. He received neither pension nor compensation. And incidentally, his irrelevancies resulted in a miscarriage of justice; they caused so much delay that it became out of the question to carry out the sentences. All the same, when he left his last district men lined the road for miles to see him go and to say goodbye.

A SENSE OF PROPORTION

Pennell was an extremist in both methods and opinions. He died a man of some wealth, but a miser, described as too mean to eat and as looking like a man who sold matches in the gutter. He was perhaps a little mad, but with a certain nobility because the principles for which he stood were noble principles if temperately pursued. He recalls Snodgrass of Madras, who sixty years before had refused to hand over his district until troops were sent to dislodge him and who, when denied a pension, set up as a crossing-sweeper in Leadenhall Street and touched his hat to the directors every morning until they relented.

There were many others at either end of the scale of normality who must be mentioned to complete the picture. Consider first the men of more than usual ability. No one as a rule sat for the examination unless he had shown some signs of intelligence; about one in five of those who sat succeeded. Of these, some stagnated mentally but some made steady progress and in every year there were one or two giants. But the empire had now developed to a pitch where one man could not leave his mark on it, as Metcalfe or Munro had done. It can hardly now be said that if one of these men had not lived the system would be different.

If Charles Aitchison, in his ten long years as Foreign Secretary, had not compiled *Aitchison's Treaties*, someone else would have been found to describe the relations of the Crown of England with every State in India — and the result would have been no less ruthlessly discarded in 1947. Again, Aitchison, as Chief Commissioner of Burma, was shocked to find so many of his officers intimate with Burmese women; he suggested to Lord Lytton that promotion should be stopped when this intimacy was known. Lytton would have none of it, but when Aitchison moved on to be Lieutenant-Governor of the Punjab and to found the Aitchison Chiefs' College at Lahore, another Chief Commissioner of Burma made the same suggestion to another Viceroy. Lord Ripon accepted the recommendation; the practice did not change.

There are men in each generation worthy of biographies. Auckland Colvin, for instance, a brilliant young civilian of the North-West (later the United Provinces) was in his youth sent to a dull and isolated district as a punishment for articles in Indian newspapers which criticized his seniors; he survived and was deputed to Egypt, where, under Cromer, he put Egypt's finances on a firm footing, and by his articles in the *Pall Mall Gazette* forced Gladstone's Government to accept responsibility in Egypt. He came back to India as Finance Member and is the hero of Kipling's *Rupaiyat of Omar Kalvin*. He was a man of imposing stature but there were others to take his place. The system had taken control, and there were plenty of men to keep it moving.

> And One, long since a pillar of the Court,
> As mud between the beams thereof is wrought;
> And One who wrote on phosphates for the Crops
> Is subject-matter of his own Report.

wrote Kipling, and continued:

> . . . Do those who live decline
> The Step that offers or their work resign?
> Trust me, today's 'Most Indispensables',
> Five hundred men can take your place or mine.

And yet each of these men had his own enthusiasms, his pet hobbies, his tricks of temper, carefully noted in the districts and discussed when each appointment was made. Look him up today in the works of reference and you see Antony MacDonnell as a list of high offices, Chief Commissioner of the Central Provinces, Member of Council, Lieutenant-Governor of the North-West, Under Secretary of State in Ireland, and much more; he sounds like the administrative machine of John Lawrence's ideal. But the man lived, warm, fierce and dominant. 'If Antony and another man are cast away in an open boat and only one of them can live, it will not be Antony who is eaten', said a friend. He was remembered in Lucknow fifty years later as a friend of the Hindu, there the underdog. And the words with which he rose to answer Lord Morley in the House of Lords are not those of a bureaucrat. 'I have played', he said, 'upon that stormy harp whose strings are the hearts of men; the noble lord opposite has spent his life writing books about books.' Yet history was hardly changed by MacDonnell.

Look at the imposing figure of Sir Denzil Ibbetson, 'untiring in administration, fearless in doing right, a scholar and a man of affairs'. There is humour and warmth in his face as well as pugnacity and the power of command. 'No one to whom Sir Denzil Ibbetson was known,' wrote one of his successors, 'can ever forget his personality, his tall and commanding presence, his vivacious and original conversation, his constant sense of humour, his quick indignation and his equally quick sympathy.' Yet, for all his special knowledge of rural indebtedness, his service on the Deccan Agriculturalists Relief Commission, someone else could have been found to frame the Co-operative Societies Act of 1904. He would, it is true, be remembered by a small circle for his Settlement Report on the Karnal District if for nothing else, and by a wider circle for his Census Report on the Punjab and the *Handbook of Punjab Ethnography* into which he subsequently condensed most of it; these are brilliant works of scholarship, permanent contributions to ethnology, yet if Ibbetson had never lived someone else would have collected the material, assembling it perhaps less dexterously, discussing it less profoundly, but still serving the Government's purpose. There was no task left comparable with Munro's, which affected everything that the Government did in Madras for the next hundred years. And though scholars such as H. H. Risley and William Crook will not be forgotten, it is not by them that the English in India will be remembered.

It would be a mistake, then, to dwell on those brilliant men who were successful in the last part of the century; they governed India, they went on to the Council of India, sometimes they went on to other appointments, but they cannot be used to illustrate a development which was hardly taking place. It is at this stage the rebels, not the governors, who illustrate development. Yet one is the complement of the other; if Thorburn and Wedderburn talked about co-operative credit, Ibbetson in fact framed the bill which became law.

The work of the architects, in short, was almost complete and in the time that remained to the empire it was in one sense maintaining the fabric that mattered. This was done by the district officer. It was his character and his ideals of conduct that the people of India saw, not laws that were already becoming too complicated to be understood.

It was of the first importance then that for every man who became a member of the Governor-General's Council there should be a dozen of the calibre of say, Sir Evan Maconachie in Bombay, of R. Carstairs in Bengal, men aware of the narrow road the administrator must walk between on the one hand such folly as Pennell's and on the other that other abyss, in which sloth or cynicism or both urge acceptance of things as they are. Whether inspired by legalistic pedantry or by humanitarian zeal, the folly which distrusts a subordinate and shows the distrust will paralyse the administration; sloth and cynicism allow the momentum to die away. It was men who would take the middle way who were needed.

Maconachie had a short spell in Simla as Under Secretary but spent the rest of his time either in his Province or in States; his recreations were gardening, photographing Indian architecture, of which he knew a good deal, and making drawings of insects that are both exact and beautiful. He took any chances that came of shooting and fishing too, but the garden and architecture came first, sandwiched between income-tax appeals, aboriginal tribes, survey and settlement, and reflections that the paternal form of government was not producing enough men of the calibre needed for the Prime Ministers of the larger States.

It is in Maconachie's book that written record remains of Frederick Lely. In his early days Lely had been administrator of Porbandar State in Kathiawar, and a ballad was made about him of which the last four lines are:

You removed the old Servants of the State and made New ones;
You abolished the old Stocks and built Police Stations;
You did away with Hand Looms and introduced Mills;
You destroyed old Carts and brought the Railway.
  Mad, impious, Lely.

The song was sung at the wells forty years later, but long before he left they had learnt to know him better and used to repeat a rhyming jingle on his name: 'Lely, Lely, raish na beli — Lely, Lely, protector of the peasant.' And a missionary has a tale of how, preaching one day in the market square of Porbandar, twenty years after Lely had left, he was describing the life of Jesus, speaking not of a teacher, but of a man with no fixed home, who went about among the people doing what good he could find to do. An old peasant came up, listened for a moment, and then his eye brightened and he began to nod his head. He knew who this must be. 'Lely, Lely', he said quietly to himself.

Carstairs served in Bengal for twenty-nine years, 'with credit, but without distinction', he says himself. He published several books, pleading for the better local government of Bengal, criticizing the effects produced by the permanent settlement, describing with loving interest the world he knew. But of all his time, that which he most enjoyed was among the Sonthals, a people not strictly aboriginal, but who were in India before the Hindus. Here he was in charge of a district about the size of Yorkshire, in which there were certain special customs.

It would be pleasant to dwell on them, to remember the great days of Yule, who founded the administration of the Sonthals, writing on two sides of a sheet of paper rules which lasted unchanged for thirty years; to consider how Richard Temple knocked the bottom out of the system, by amalgamating with the stroke of a pen the Sonthal Commission with the provincial list for Bengal, so that instead of staying ten years a magistrate moved on after twelve months; to think again of George Campbell, who when the Government of India would not let him have what he wanted for the Sonthals replied that in that case he must have soldiers to shoot them — and got his way.

But there is no room for them, and just as much to the point perhaps are such men as Frederick Grant. Grant carried out in a part of this hilly country a quick cheap settlement based on a look and a guess; he found it worked. But when he had finished his rent roll, by which titles to land were decided, it did not at all agree with the papers and measurements on which it was supposed to be based. So after some puzzled hours trying to reconcile the two, Grant burnt the papers, preserving only his conclusions and no evidence by which they could be upset. And being ordered, after a famine, to dispose of surplus rice by sale, he was so ashamed of the poor price it was fetching that he brightened the market by buying eighteen tons himself and feeding the poor of his sub-division on it for a year. He was uncovenanted, like Bruce; his salary cannot have been high.

And there was Boxwell, 'very tall, with a stoop and a lovable Irish face — untidy in his ways, unmethodical in his work . . . and a lover of trees almost to superstition . . . When he was making a road (he was a great road-maker) he would often turn it aside from the straight line to save a tree, or if that were inconvenient, he would leave the tree standing right in the middle'. 'He was beloved not only by the Sonthals but by his officers. He drove them; he scolded them; but he was intensely loyal to them, defending them from the censure of higher authorities and even taking on himself the blame for acts done against his orders. . . .'

These were warm-hearted men who often seemed to themselves to be struggling with a cold impersonal machine at the centre. No doubt there were cold impersonal men in that machine but they are forgotten, the indiscreet are remembered. Every district officer in some degree was at war with authority; most men cloaked their warfare in polite words, but some had a genius for making the solemn look ridiculous. Such was Tawney of the Central Provinces, who quite early in his service was rebuked for not appearing punctually when summoned before a superior. He must come at once, whatever he was doing, he was told. It was a rebuke quite foreign to the traditions of the service and Tawney made the most of it. Next time he was summoned he appeared naked, borne shoulder-high in a tin bath-tub by four orderlies.

But it was pure impishness, provoked only by solemnity of demeanour, that made Tawney spoil Bampfylde Fuller's experiment in crop cutting. Fuller was Director of Land Records. He wanted to estimate the crop in an area of one square chain in an average field; the area was measured and posts driven in at the corners; a team of Gond women with sickles were collected to cut. They would begin when Fuller arrived — and no doubt they would have begun, if Tawney had not warned them at the last minute that, when the wizard who was coming put a glass in his eye, any woman at whom he looked would become barren. And Fuller no sooner felt for his monocle than they fled to their homes.

CHAPTER X

THE END OF AN ERA

I. THE WAR AGAINST PAPER

IT was an India then in which personal relations counted for everything, an old-fashioned aristocracy, very loosely centralized, in which the provincial Governments consisted of perhaps a Lieutenant-Governor and three Secretaries, and the Government of India was on a hardly larger scale. To this empire, based less on system than on the individual characters of Scots, Irish and English men, came the young man in a hurry, Lord Curzon, trained for the Vice-regal purple by years of self-discipline, study and travel, determined from the day he arrived to carry out his list of twelve major reforms.

It is strange that the Governors-General — there were only thirty-two of them — should have included three men so strangely alike, so strangely un-English, as Wellesley, Dalhousie and Curzon. Curzon resembled Wellesley more closely than Dalhousie; there is the same inability to comprehend another point of view or any attitude from an inferior — and the world included many inferiors — but one of grateful and loyal subservience. There are in both the same strong personal emotions, in both an introspective but intermittent humility behind an outward arrogance, a fanatical industry and attention to detail, an almost neurotic inability to delegate power. But most of these qualities Curzon possessed in a higher degree.

Lord Curzon to himself seemed undoubtedly the 'Most Indispensable'; nothing was ever right unless he had drafted it himself. 'It is no good', he wrote, 'trusting a human being to do a thing for you. Do everything yourself.' It was a principle that if universally applied would have destroyed the Indian Empire. 'Now in what manner was this wonderful thing done?' asked 'a grizzled long-haired Central Asian Chief' in Kipling's story, and the answer was by obedience. 'Mule, horse, elephant or bullock, he obeys his driver, and the driver his sergeant . . .' and so on up to 'the general who obeys the Viceroy who is the servant of the Empress.' But of course that was not really how this particular Empire did work. It was only one side of the truth and it was not the characteristic side, the side which distinguished this Empire from others. It might better have been put that the Viceroy on the whole trusted his Lieutenant-Governors to get on with their work, but checked, encouraged and inspired them now and then, that the Lieutenant-Governors did the same by their District Officers and so on down to the patwari. The machine worked only because the Service as a rule understood how to delegate power.

This Curzon never did. And therefore he alienated the services and Indians alike. Where he gained a point by intellect and industry, he lost another by doing the right thing in the wrong way — as for instance when he detached the North-West Frontier Province from the Punjab in such a way as to wound the Punjab civilians deeply; as for instance when, for admirable reasons, he divided Bengal and infuriated its inhabitants. He was too self-centred to see how his words or actions would hurt other people — witness his speech contrasting the Western and Eastern ideas of truth — and the same lack of perceptiveness led him to believe that the Congress and Indian Nationalism in general were about to die. He could not see that most people — not only Lord Curzon — prefer on the whole to do things their own way for themselves.

Of all he did, that which most concerned the Guardians was his reform of the way business was done in Simla. It must be pictured against the background of the place. Simla is the knot where half a dozen ridges of high ground meet, a starfish or an octopus of narrow ridges. There are roads along their crests; below the crests, there are more roads, cut out from the hill-side before it gets too steep. Seen from the air, little roads wriggle and writhe like the veins on a horse's neck. They are too narrow today for cars; they were always too narrow for carts or buggies. In Simla, you had to ride or walk or go in a rickshaw, which was a large perambulator, pushed by four men, usually at a run. But gentlemen did not travel in rickshaws in Lord Curzon's day; they rode and the ladies went in rickshaws.

At intervals along these little roads would be a garden gate, from which a steep and winding path led to a bungalow. The path was often too steep for a rickshaw; on either side of it were usually little shelves hewn from the hillside where zinnias grew, blue lupins and many-coloured dahlias and everywhere, like a weed, pink cosmos. The bungalow was built as a rule largely of wood; ferns hung in wire cages from the veranda roofs. Inside, it was darker than a plains bungalow, all the woodwork being stained and blobbily varnished; the rooms were much smaller. The floors and the low ceilings were usually uneven; in the tiny bathroom that went to each bedroom there was a wooden washstand with a hole in it for a wash-basin, as in seaside lodgings; there was a ewer full of water that was strangely cold after the plains and there was a moist earthy smell, like a potting-shed in an English garden. It was not at all like India; there was a parish magazine, and if only there had been thatched roofs instead of corrugated iron, it would have been possible for a few minutes to think you were at home. The feeling was strongest with your eyes closed when the chestnut leaves were falling in the autumn.

That was for family men who lived in bungalows: for A.D.C.s and bachelors at the Club the illusion would hardly be so strong. But for everyone there was something a little fantastic about Simla. It may have been the architecture of the larger buildings, which ranged from the ponderous railway-station Gothic of the main Secretariat through the brewer's Tudor of the Commander-in-Chief's house to the pure nightmare of Army Headquarters, which was as though a number of trams had been piled untidily on top of each other and bolted together with flying steel rods. It may have been the mixture of Surrey and Tibet, the perambulator on its way to the circulating library passing a slant-eyed woman with lumps of raw turquoise in her nose-ring, the baby slung like a tiny mummy on her back bumping against the wooden tube in which she mixed tea with salt and butter. Or it may have been the far vision of the snows, faintly reproachful alike of frivolity and toil. Whatever the reason, it was not easy to remember the earthen baulks between the little squares of rice and millet or the look of a mud village when twelve inches of rain have fallen during the night. It was not easy to remember India — and that was really more important than the fact that it took eight or nine hours behind 'the clacking tonga-bar' to get down to Kalka where the railway began.

Lord Curzon was conscious of Simla's mental isolation; he was not at all insensitive except where other people were concerned. He would not, he said, himself have chosen to make his summer capital there, but he looked forward all the same to Simla as a place where with very little interruption he could absorb an immense amount of information and, having pondered it, construct, mould, and polish his reformation of the shape of things. Here he planned to reorganize the way the Government of India did its work; here he framed a formidable charge.

Lord Curzon, of course, was the last person to see that on almost every head of his indictment he was himself the worst offender. 'Thousands of pages, occupying hundreds of hours of valuable time, are written every year by score upon score of officers, to the obfusca-

tion of their intellects and the detriment of their official work . . .'
This no doubt was true. All wrote much — but no one wrote so much
as Lord Curzon. 'He appeared, indeed,' says his biographer, 'to
derive positive satisfaction from the mere physical act of writing.'

Paper too was increased by his anger at anything done without his
knowledge. When a political officer built a road from Gilgit to
Chitral without sanction it seemed to Lord Curzon 'the irresponsible
zeal of a petty captain'. He did not perceive that this was the way the
Empire had been built, nor that it was also the way Lord Curzon
behaved to the Secretary of State. Mr. Brodrick, however, was
philosophical about the fact that he was expected to act as 'George's
ambassador at the Court of St. James'; 'don't think I am complain-
ing', he said, 'I knew it when I took the post.'

Too much paper, too much ink, and still the Viceroy was insuffi-
ciently guided and not told enough. In long scarlet gowns trimmed
with gold lace, the orderlies at Viceregal Lodge walked every evening
in procession to the Viceroy's study, bringing his lordship's evening
task. There might be a hundredweight of papers a night; sometimes
there would be more. A cubic foot or so of previous references,
weighing fifteen or twenty pounds, would come with quite a simple
proposal. And to a newcomer, they were papers among which it was
easy to lose one's way. 'I have perused these papers,' wrote Lord
Curzon — but everyone knows the story — 'for two hours and twenty
minutes. On the whole, I agree with the gentleman whose signature
resembles a trombone.'

The custom went back to the days of the Company. Everything
had to be justified to Leadenhall Street; Philip Francis and Warren
Hastings recorded their views on every point in writing. In Simla,
everyone in the Secretariat knew everyone else; the signature like a
trombone was as familiar in the next department as the number of his
bus to a suburban Londoner. And someone might want to verify the
exact wording of Lord William Bentinck's dispatch, so all the papers
might as well go together. If Lord Curzon had been a different man,
it would have been easy for his private secretary to give him a summary, but if Walter Lawrence had been the kind of man to do that,
he would not have been Private Secretary for long. It is easy to
imagine the majestic indignation that would have fallen on any suggestion that His Excellency should be spoon-fed.

As it was, His Excellency was never consulted enough. He was
brilliant at the expense of those who discussed a proposal at length
before venturing to lay it before him. 'Round and round like the

diurnal revolutions of the earth went the file, stately, solemn, sure and slow; and now, in due season, it has completed its orbit and I am invited to register the concluding stage. How can I bring home to those who are responsible the gravity of the blunder . . .?' Many people have enjoyed that minute but can any of them be sure that, if he had seen the file earlier, Lord Curzon would not have been equally disturbed that so ill-digested a proposal had been submitted to him? He ought, of course, to have been told sooner; there can be no two opinions about that. But it was partly his own fault that he was not. And it is worth remembering that he did in the end adopt the proposal here pilloried — the partition of Bengal — and that it was one of the most unfortunate acts of his reign.

What Lord Curzon was trying to do was, after all, exactly what every good officer tried to do when fresh to the Secretariat — and Lord Curzon's results were probably as long-lived in their sphere as the average. He could hardly produce a permanent effect because he did not try to change the basis of the system, which was a unit of one expensive man and ten cheap men who were clerks. If the ten cheap men had been replaced by two expensive men with good prospects, it would no doubt have been possible to produce something more concise. Committees, as in Whitehall, would have taken the place of long notes. As it was, no one could spare the time for committees and, as everyone knows, it is easier — and for most people quicker — to write a long note than a short one.

Where Lord Curzon did achieve something was in regard to the tenure of Secretarial posts. And here he was altogether right. That Secretariat appointments were confined to too narrow a circle was the weakest spot of the whole system. It had happened very naturally. It is easier to keep on the man who is known and who knows the work; it takes time, whether in Simla or Whitehall, to learn enough about procedure and personalities to get things done. Secretaries to the Government of India had thus developed the habit of staying in their posts until they were moved up to something better, and no doubt they grew a little dull. Secretariat life did not always attract the most adventurous in the first place; men were chosen partly on their examination record, which sometimes meant precocity and bookishness, and once they were in Simla it was easy to forget India and to revel in words.

Lord Curzon introduced a definite tenure for each post; he made it a rule that, between Secretariat appointments, a man should go back to his province and if possible to a district, where he would meet someone with a plough. The rule was not always honoured, but it was something that it was there and that from time to time, through the chill white clouds that blanket Simla in the monsoon, there should come the sharp reminder that, far below in the sunshine on the other side of Kalka, India was still patiently waiting.

2. THE GREAT DURBAR

Lord Curzon lost, by one act after another, the admiration which Indians had at first been ready to bestow on him. India has, all the same, reason to forgive him for much, because he did love India, he did perceive the poetry and the glory of his position, because in short he was as different as anyone could be from Lord Auckland, who was bored. And perhaps because of his shortcomings, even more than his good qualities, his reign seems to sum up and close the era which began when the Crown took over direct rule. He was the last who could regard the mighty structure with a pride that was hardly mixed with apprehension.

The structure was indeed mighty. A political unity had been imposed that had never before been equalled and had not been approached in the Christian era. Roads, railways, bridges, canals, were far ahead of anything else in Asia; there had been internal peace for half a century, the raids of bandits were no longer a feature of everyday life and robber chiefs had one by one submitted.

It was true that there were conflicts of stress and tension in the most essential parts of the building. 'To educated Hindus', wrote Alfred Lyall, 'the incongruity between sacrifices to the goddess Kali and high University degrees is too manifest.' And Kali may stand for caste and untouchability, purdah and child marriage. That was a stress within Hinduism, while Muslim India had already begun to display a deep distrust of the undiscriminating liberalism which, the Muslims believed, would mean the reign of the moneylender and the Brahman. Finally, Indians were beginning to perceive that, even in his own Western field of examinations and newspapers and the ballot-box, the Englishman could be met and forced to suffer a reverse, while in arms the Italians had been checked in Abyssinia, the Russians were to be defeated by Japan in 1904. The dominance of the European could no longer go unquestioned.

These stresses, which seem so obvious now, were less apparent in 1901; to Lord Curzon, whose powerful imagination was poetic rather than analytic, it would have seemed that they were no more than those balanced stresses that lock the keystone of an arch in its position. It was his own idea to sum up in the Great Durbar of 1903 the splendours of the era which as yet he hardly realized was at an end. There was to be a parade of troops, a state entry, an investiture, a ball, scenes of magnificence never equalled before; not least in the eye of the artist who designed this week of 'becoming pomp and dignity' was a display of Indian painting, jewels and goldsmiths' work, of tapestries, carpets and manuscripts, summoned from every corner of the Empire in the splendour of whose past he delighted. To him the Durbar was the outward and visible sign of an ideal, the heavenly pattern of an Empire to which his life was devoted.

'Is it nothing,' he asked, 'that the Sovereign at his coronation should exchange pledges with his assembled lieges of protection and respect on the one side, of spontaneous allegiance on the other? . . . Is it nothing to lift an entire people for a little space out of the rut of their narrow and parochial lives and to let them catch a glimpse of a higher ideal, an appreciation of the hidden laws that regulate the march of nations and the destinies of men?'

To Lord Curzon the Durbar was an 'overwhelming display of unity and patriotism'. It was real to him and to many who were there, but to the peasant — concerned with canal dues and rust in the wheat, with locusts and rats, his debts to the moneylender and his neighbour's ineradicable tendency to take a short cut across the corner of his field — to him it is not easy to talk about the march of nations and the destinies of men.

It is strange to read now that Lord Curzon rejected the hymn 'Onward Christian Soldiers' — he must of course approve every hymn chosen for church services during the Durbar — not because the opening words would be out of place at the proclamation of a sovereign most of whose soldiers were not Christian, but because it contained the lines: 'Crowns and Thrones may perish, Kingdoms rise and wane' — an unbecoming note of pessimism. But the English in India — even the many who were conscious of a personal irritation when they thought of the Viceroy — were most of them at least as obtuse as he, almost as impressed by the brilliance of the spectacle and the magnificence of the structure of which it was the symbol. A very simple account conveys the feeling exactly, a journal written for the children in England by Mrs. Macpherson, the wife of an officer of the Bengal Service — as men still said, though it had been one Indian Service for fifty years.

There was a special train from Calcutta for those who were going to the Durbar in the party of the Lieutenant-Governor of Bengal. It left on Christmas Eve, December 24th, 1902, and halted at Dinapore on Christmas morning. A few miles from Dinapore and a hundred and forty years earlier, two hundred English had been massacred by the order of Mir Kasim; it was fifty miles nearer Delhi, and less than fifty years ago, that the little house at Arrah had survived its memorable siege. This Christmas Day, however, was ineffably peaceful in the thin sunlight of early morning. 'We walked to the little station church, where Mr. Moore, one of the party, held a service . . . Dad and I loved to hear the Christmas hymns and to feel that a few hours later you would be singing them too — "As o'er each continent and island The dawn leads on another day".'

Christmas Day wore on, the long, long day of an Indian train journey. 'Dad did some work and there were more meals and we rushed through a barren and thirsty land and saw the peasants watering their fields and the blue jays sitting on the telegraph wires and the mud-walled villages and the buffaloes going out to the water with bare brown boys driving them and the bamboo clumps . . . Can you remember the look of it all?' A second night in the train, and by midday on the day after Christmas they crossed the Jumna, close to the place where the mutineers, now incredulously jubilant, now desperate with terror, had crossed it from Meerut fifty years before. A little railway, specially laid for the Durbar, took the guests to their camp, where 'our tents are most luxurious. We have a bedroom, sitting-room and office room, all furnished very completely, and lighted with electric lights and a charcoal stove to keep us warm at night.'

There was a rehearsal for the great review, there was Church on Sunday in the Viceroy's camp — where the troops, disappointed perhaps over their favourite hymn, did not sing as heartily as had been hoped — there was dinner with the Lieutenant-Governor, when Mrs. Macpherson wore her emerald, a stone engraved with a Persian inscription and given to her husband's great-grandfather, Colonel Allan Macpherson of Blairgowrie, by Shah Alam, the last Mogul Emperor. There was New Year's Day, 'a red letter day for us', because a message came of congratulation on Macpherson's C.S.I. 'Dad . . . thought it was a mistake — But it isn't, it isn't, it isn't! . . . His name has been sent up for it seven years running . . . We are so pleased and proud and I am especially delighted that it should have come now and here . . . and he will be actually invested here in Delhi in the palace where his great-grandfather, the founder of the Blairgowrie family, received decorations and honours. . . .'

There was too the State Ball, held in the Dewan-i-Am, the Public Audience Hall of the Great Mogul. 'The Duchess of Portland's dress was of soft white material, the skirt had insertions of a sort of open-work pattern, the edges of which were ornamented with diamond drops, there were perhaps six of these rows of diamonds, and she was wearing lovely ornaments . . . Mrs. Grant Gordon and I stared for all we were worth!' Mrs. Bourdillon danced with Lord Kitchener, who confided in her that this kind of thing was not much in his line; 'the Duke of Marlborough wore his Garter — diamonds and emeralds . . . ; we wandered round the splendid ball-room looking at the many lovely dresses and uniforms and the Native Chiefs simply smothered in jewels . . .' Supper was in the Dewan-i-Khas, the Private Audience Hall, 'with its marble pillars inlaid with jade and cornelian and much gold tracery — at one end the marble screen through which the ladies of Shah Jehan's Court were allowed to peep at his receptions . . . You must try to imagine a fairy palace, for that is what it was like.' Mrs. Macpherson wondered whether her emerald felt at home in this revival of forgotten pomp and of course she read: 'or at least *he* did — the inscription on the wall in Persian characters:

> If there is a paradise on the face of the earth
> It is this, it is this, it is this.'

To the Macphersons the ball seemed the crowning event of the Durbar ceremonies. But there are two other events which happened earlier and which for us must take a higher place. The State Procession went from the Red Fort, the Mogul Palace, to the Great Mosque. There was of course some waiting; 'at last the guns told us the great man had arrived and . . . at last they began to appear. First, mounted police, then five regiments of cavalry, then artillery, then the heralds, grand in yellow and gold, blowing a fanfare as they reached the mosque. After them, the Imperial Cadets, a corps of young natives, sons of noblemen, all mounted on black chargers with leopard skins, and dressed in white uniforms and pale blue turbans — they were really lovely! And then came the elephants . . . and it was just a dazzling procession, one more splendid than another . . . Six came together first, three and three . . . then a splendid creature covered with silver and gold and carrying a silver howdah in which sat His Excellency Lord Curzon and his lovely lady . . . they came slowly and majestically along, followed by a train of forty or fifty more magnificent animals, all decked and painted and bedizened with cloth of gold and dazzling frontlet pieces and great hanging ornaments over their ears, some wearing silver anklets which clashed and all having bells which sounded boom-boom tinkle-tinkle and made one think it really couldn't all be true, it was so lovely.' Then came more cavalry and more elephants, a hundred and twenty this time. 'But there was hardly any noise and no cheering to speak of.' And Mrs. Macpherson adds: 'the trying thing at all these shows is the great difficulty of finding one's carriage to go home.'

The crowds, the cavalry, the swaying elephants, the bells, the silver howdah and the cloth of gold — and silence. That is one picture to remember. The other is at the amphitheatre, a little way beyond the Kashmir Gate where Nicholson fell. Here into a great amphitheatre came the Shan chiefs from Burma 'like walking pagodas glittering with cloth of gold', fierce long-haired Pathans from the West, princes from the North and the South, 'with ropes and tassels of pearls and masses of emeralds and diamonds', all come to do homage to the Emperor's Viceroy. Here too marched 'the surviving veterans of the Mutiny. There were Europeans and natives, old tottering fellows, some of whom had to be supported on each side . . . The massed bands played "Should auld acquaintance be forgot" and the people shouted and hurrahed till they were hoarse. Most of us had big lumps in our throats and some of us were crying so that we couldn't shout at all. The thought of those old fellows and all they went through and how they stuck to us at a time when we were in sore straits and in very different scenes to yesterday's triumphs was quite overpowering. It was the best thing Lord Curzon ever did to give the veterans their share in the triumph . . . and they must have been glad and proud beyond words of the nation's acknowledgement of them yesterday. . . .'

There was good cause for a lump in the throat and a prickling of the eye. Three hundred years had passed since Queen Elizabeth's proclamation and now the last stone had been placed on a noble building. The time had come to take away the scaffolding, to clear up the heaps of lime and rubble, to leave the imposing fabric to its inhabitants. The architects and the masons however were as yet hardly aware that they had to go and they were not unnaturally impressed by the cost.

It had cost a great deal. Two million graves of Scots, Irish and English, were scattered through India. There were many small records of a loss that to one pair was a blinding grief, to another a few days of heartache, to a third a sadness long remembered in prayer; there were graves of wives and husbands, soldiers and civilians, boys just landed and men worn out with work. Nor were graves all the cost; much endurance must be counted in as well, much loneliness, hardship, and separation, much toil, much loss of faith, much hardening of the moral arteries.

For all this the Mutiny veterans stood as symbol. Eight thousand spectators inside the amphitheatre cheered them till they were hoarse; there were forty thousand outside who could not get in and they cheered, too, perhaps less fervently. It was a nation's acknowledgement — but who exactly was the nation? There were three hundred millions who no more raised their heads at that faint huzza than at the first the islanders had uttered when they first charged home on Indian soil. The Empire whose material achievements seemed so magnificent to Lord Curzon had not stirred their hearts.

Not that hearts were unaffected on either side. Few Englishmen could leave a district without regrets and when the time came to retire there were servants whose eyes filled with tears, there were masters too who turned hastily aside. There were soldiers who would die without flinching for their officers, there were Indians everywhere — landowners, clerks, lawyers, orderlies — who remembered with affection kindly Englishmen who had helped them because they liked them. There were men too to whom the Western ideas of political freedom, justice and tolerance, had given a second motherland for which they felt a real love. But few of these men were stirred by the pomp of Empire.

The Great Durbar was, indeed, as Lord Curzon had thought it would be, a landmark in the history of the people. It was the end of an era. When it was done, the tents were struck, the light railway was taken up and 'the nation' — the eight thousand within the arena, the Princes and the English — dispersed to their palaces, to their offices and court-rooms and to camps that were less luxurious. 'The trying thing', many must have said, 'at all these shows is the great difficulty of finding one's carriage to go home.'

II

THE DEMISSION OF POWER

Tell me, my daughters,
Since now we will divest us both of rule,
Interest of territory, cares of state, —
Which of you shall we say doth love us most?
                                        King Lear

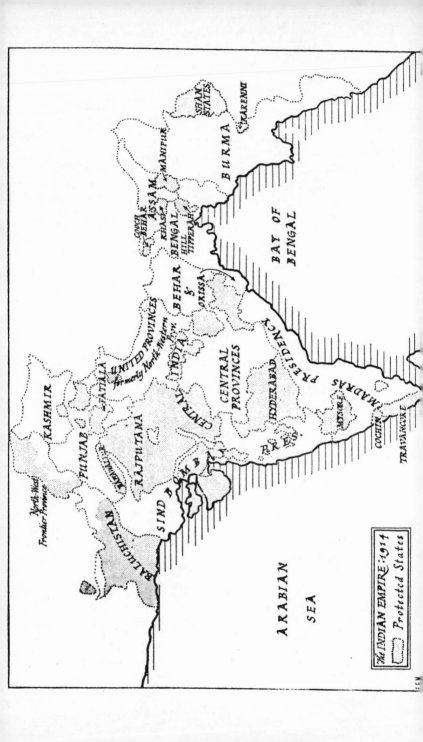

The INDIAN EMPIRE : 1914

▨ Protected States

KASHMIR

North-West
Frontier Province

PUNJAB

PATIALA

UNITED PROVINCES
formerly North-Western

RAJPUTANA

CENTRAL
INDIA

SIND

BALUCHISTAN

BOMBAY

CENTRAL
PROVINCES

HYDERABAD

BOM. PRES.

MYSORE

COCHIN

TRAVANCORE

MADRAS PRESIDENCY

BEHAR
&
ORISSA

COOCH
BEHAR

ASSAM

MANIPUR

KHASI

BENGAL
HILL TIPPERAH

SHAN
STATES

BURMA

KARENNI

BAY OF
BENGAL

ARABIAN
SEA

CHAPTER I

TWO DISTRICT OFFICERS AND
REFORM

I. REFORM

ADOZEN miles from Delhi, where the nation had cheered the veterans at the Durbar, lie the ruins of Tughlakabad. Mighty ramparts of ponderous stone, pierced by vast gates, embossed by massive bastions, enclose a jumble of ruined masonry among which here and there the fragments of a guard-house or a tower emerge, but in most of which it is possible only to guess at the builder's intention. The city was not sacked, it was abandoned within a few years of its foundation because water was insufficient; it is now a lair for hyenas and a nesting-place for owls. The plain around it in every direction, as far as man can see, is strewn with the tombs of dead kings and the remnants of forgotten empires.

Perhaps it was some apprehension of the thoughts these ruins might inspire that had induced Lord Curzon to say so clearly that there must be no hymns at the Durbar which mentioned the passing of kings and thrones. But this caution was hardly necessary. Metcalfe, a hundred years before, had mused on the insecurity of empire; to most of the Guardians of 1903 such thoughts would have seemed fanciful. To most of them the fabric seemed very firm. Yet among them were men who would see the English Parliament shake from itself all the cares and business of this Empire, divest itself of rule, interest and territory. To none of them would it have seemed possible at the time that the change could be so swift.

This demission of power was not accomplished, like Lear's, by one regal gesture, but by four, each conceding far more than its predecessors. To understand the reactions of the Guardians to what happened, it is necessary to be clear about these four steps, though of the later three only the barest outline is needed at this stage.

First came the Morley-Minto reforms of 1909. Lord Minto succeeded Curzon in circumstances very similar to those in which his great-grandfather had succeeded Wellesley; in both cases a masterful Governor-General had become rather too masterful. The second Minto came with few preconceived ideas except the general reflection

that in training a horse it was as well, now and then, to give him a
rest in his gallops. He was, in fact, a conservative by temperament
and now a conservative by party, though he had been born a Whig.
His mind was modest and practical. He gave little thought to his own
fame or reputation; he had developed late, having spent his time at
Eton and Cambridge with, says his biographer, a notable economy of
intellectual effort. He was one who 'saw things clearly and simply
without the irrelevant subtleties with which the practice of law or
politics clogs the most honest minds. . . .' Having a humbler intellect
than Lord Curzon's, he saw much that the more brilliant man had
missed and perceived almost from his first arrival that 'the fellow-
service of British and Indian administrators under a supreme British
Government is the key to the future political happiness of this
country'. It was the remedy for Indian troubles which had been prescribed by Metcalfe, Frere, Lyall and many others.

His partner at the India Office was a man as different as could be
in training and habit of thought. A Liberal intellectual, a brilliant
civil servant, who had 'spent his life writing books about books', it
was strange that Morley should have formed so real a friendship and
found so wide a field for agreement with Minto, of one of whose
closest friends at Cambridge it was said that a visitor to his rooms
could not find one single book with which to pass the time. But the
two men were agreed in their practical, experimental approach to a
change which from their end of the half-century looked much larger
than it does from ours. 'The only chance . . .' said Morley, 'is to do
our best to make English rulers friends with Indian leaders and at the
same time to do our best to train them in habits of political responsibility.'

Their authors, then, did not think of the Morley-Minto reforms as
final. Still less had they any clearly conceived idea of the end at which
they were aiming. The reforms grew out of the past and were rather
a means of keeping abreast with the present than a path to the future.

As long ago as 1888, Lord Dufferin had proposed that the legislative councils in the provinces should be larger, that some of their
members should be elected, and that members should be allowed to
ask questions and record opinions on a wider range of subjects than
those laid before them by the Government. Needless to say, the
Governor would agree with them or not as he thought fit. Part of
these proposals — but not the public election of members — had been
conceded and embodied in the Act of 1892. It was from this that the
reforms of 1909 proceeded.

They do not seem revolutionary from the viewpoint of 1954. The legislative councils were to be enlarged to a membership of sixty at the centre and of fifty in the larger provinces. They were thus still glorified committees, which were to be partly official and partly non-official, the Guardians being in a majority at the centre but not in the provinces. Of the non-officials — that is to say the Indian members, for there were not many Indian officials yet — about one-fifth were nominated by the executive power; the rest were elected, some by voters who were organized in general but small and highly qualified constituencies, others by special constituencies such as municipal boards, universities, chambers of commerce, landowners — and members of minority religions.

Here of course was a sharp point of controversy and one that was to grow sharper. The Muslims are backward in Western education and must have special help if they are to hold their own — thus ran the English argument. True, the Hindu conceded, but to give them a separate constituency is to perpetuate the differences between us. No Muslim will be elected unless he oozes communal bitterness. Give them indeed the right to so many Muslim seats, but let the candidates for those seats be elected by a general constituency. Then the Muslim to be elected will be the one who is ready to sink communal differences and meet the Hindus. Then we shall have a chance of becoming one people.

That kind of Muslim is no use to us, replied the faithful. You would elect a traitor, one who is no more than a Hindu with a beard. We need a true Muslim, who will protect our rights.

Those were the two arguments. To such a man as Minto, concerned to get over his next hurdle and win this race not the next, the Muslim argument was bound to appeal. Hindus, however, came later to believe that this introduction of separate constituencies was a deep-laid, subtle plot, aimed at dividing the communities and providing an excuse for extending British rule for ever. Nothing could be further from Minto's character and to Morley the idea could only have occurred to be instantly rejected.[1]

The new councils were far from popular bodies; they were less democratic than Parliament in England before the Reform Bill of

[1] There are two careless sayings of the Mintos which, to those who do not understand his character, seem to support the Hindu view that his acceptance of the principle of separate electorates was Machiavellian. But I am sure the Hindus misinterpret them. Minto and his wife did think that what he had done would make for the continuance of British rule – not because it would cause division but because it would mean that everyone would be satisfied. He is open to a charge of naïveté but not of duplicity. This however is not the place for controversy.

1832. But they were a step forward for India; what was more, members could not merely discuss the budget and bills placed before them, they could also ask questions and move resolutions on any subject of public interest. The councils did provide a means of testing and creating opinion, some check on a Platonic system in which the Guardians alone knew what was good for the people.

At the same time — and in Minto's eyes it was more important — Indian members were appointed to the Secretary of State's Council and to the Executive Councils of the Viceroy and the Governors.[1] It was what Minto had wanted from the beginning of his term of office.

In the spring of 1909 few responsible Indians asked for more. To most people, both Indian and English, it seemed that responsible and representative institutions on the English or American model were still out of the question, being only possible where the minority was prepared to accept the decisions of the majority. 'Suppose', asked Pandit Moti Lal Nehru at a meeting in Agra in 1909, 'we attained the goal of our aspirations, the colonial form of self-government, would that, without purging the many social diseases that your body politic suffers from, convert you into a united Indian nation?' And the argument was widely used that it was wrong to transplant Western institutions to an alien soil.

No one then knew where the 1909 reforms would lead. Morley 'almost passionately' disclaimed the idea that they were leading to responsible institutions — though of course they were. But what even to the Congress had seemed enough in 1909 was very soon felt to be a dose that called for repetition. And among the 'chemical changes' of the Kaiser's War, which 'left no element of the whole unaltered', Lord Hardinge made the thoroughly un-English suggestion that it might be as well to define the object of English rule in India. In 1917 it was defined, as:

'the increasing association of Indians in every branch of the administration, and the gradual development of self-governing institutions, with a view to the progressive realization of responsible government in India as an integral part of the British Empire.'

The drafting, strangely enough, was Lord Curzon's. It was this declaration which led to the reforms of 1919, by which the legislative councils in the provinces were more than doubled in size, about two-thirds of their members being elected. They became small assemblies instead of large committees, while from the elected members were

[1] Indians had been on the legislative councils since Frere's day.

to be chosen Ministers who would advise the Governor on certain 'transferred' subjects. This was the second of the four great steps and it requires explanation.

The Governor now presented to the world two persons. He became 'the Governor acting with his Ministers', a constitutional figurehead, in respect of what came to be called 'the nation-building subjects', education, agriculture, the control of municipal boards and the like, while in respect of the protective subjects — finance, police and general administration — he remained the Governor in Council, the apex of an oligarchy, just as he always had been. His right hand was despotic, his left was very nearly responsible to an electorate — but not quite, because he need not take the advice of his Ministers in the last resort. And it was still an electorate for which there was a high qualification.

The English have always taken pleasure in institutions which at first sight seem quite unworkable and, if they had departed from precedent by the decision to say where they were going, they certainly restored the balance by this strange device. It would be fascinating to consider in detail what might have happened if this proposal for dyarchy — the technical term for handing over the steering-wheel and retaining control of the accelerator, the gear-lever and the brake — had been adopted in the original form made by Lionel Curtis. He had suggested that each province should become a kind of federation of self-governing units. A group of six, eight or a dozen districts would become a State, with an assembly and Ministers, administering such subjects as education and agriculture with full responsibility. The Governor in Council at the head of the province would deal with his reserved subjects as one person, unhampered by Athanasian distinctions. He would lose certain subjects to the smaller units but in the subjects that remained he would act as before. If the suggestion had been adopted in 1919, such an organization in three tiers, like a cake-stand, might have provided, a quarter of a century later, a chance of preserving unity. The map would already have been carved up into more or less homogeneous fragments. But in 1919 one practical difficulty would have been to find enough Ministers and another was finance, while Edwin Montagu always felt that it was a mistake 'to alter the map at the same time as the constitution'. The three tiers then never came into being.

The 1919 reforms were carried a stage further by the 1935 Act, of which it is for the moment enough to say that it provided that the provinces should be governed by Indian Ministers responsible to an

Assembly. In 1937, the provinces did in fact pass to the control of elected Ministers, each province being under a Premier. The last stage was reached in 1947 when the Central Government 'pared its wit o' both sides and left nothing i' the middle' — but that, one should remember, was only the Fool's comment on Lear's act of demission.

In the course of thirty-eight years, then, political power, which under Parliament had been absolute in the hands of the Viceroy, was entirely made over to elected representatives of the people. Those thirty-eight years were a strange and unexpected test for the caste of Guardians, who up till now had ruled this Platonic empire. They had come to a world in which they had been unquestioned masters, flattered and courted on every hand. Now they breathed a new and harsher air. They were supposed to be training Indians to be 'fit for self-government', they must give advice instead of orders, and they met constant opposition, slander and abuse. To most of them it was axiomatic that political change should come almost as slowly as biological evolution, just as it had in England. But the people to whom was assigned the role of grateful pupils had behind them a history in which the death of every king was a revolution. They saw no reason why change should be gradual. They were impatient; they did not want to be taught. They wanted to drive the car themselves.

The Guardians had therefore to deal with a changed world, though it was less changed than anyone would have supposed from reading the newspapers. It is impossible to generalize about their reactions, because each man had his own views. At all levels — Governors, Secretaries to Government, district officers — may be found men who saw in the reforms nothing but doctrinaire folly and men to whom the object, if not the detail, seemed profoundly wise. Few, certainly, perceived that if a period of tutelage is prolonged beyond an ideal point it makes the ward not more, but less, fit for responsibility. The best course, as before, is not so much to generalize as to exhibit samples. Here is a district officer who cannot be called typical, because he was peculiarly himself, but who did possess rather more than most people of some typical qualities.

2. A PROGRESSIVE

E. H. H. Edye went from Harrow to Balliol with a classical exhibition, and came to the United Provinces in 1909. He left India in 1936, having spent very little time away from a district officer's work.

He left two books, both written at the request of friends; their publication was prevented by the war of 1939.

Edye was an able man, but a man with less vanity than most and what he had was at the mercy of his sense of humour. In his fifth year, he found himself suddenly in temporary charge of a district, one of his first duties being to sign and dispatch the confidential reports which his predecessor had drafted. His own was among them. Now there was at that time one of those shortages in the judicial branch which did occur from time to time, because judicial work appealed to some men but not to enough. Edye enjoyed executive life enormously, not only the work but the opportunities for shooting and pig-sticking. He did not want to go to the judicial. He added to his own confidential report the words:

> Judicial capacity beneath contempt.

Lack of vanity is a likeable trait, but it was one that undoubtedly hindered Edye's promotion. He believed that 'if you are abroad three hours before your neighbours, you gain more than three hours start on them.' But he did not say this aloud; when his friends congratulated him pointedly on having so little work to do and on always having time for golf or polo, he smiled and reflected: 'It may be easy to win a name for laziness, but to keep it up over a period of years is a laborious process.'

He certainly did all that he could to keep up the reputation, partly perhaps as a good-tempered reproof to the pompous or priggish, partly because he was too honest to indulge in eyewash, of which he noted that the kind you buy at the chemist is meant to clarify your own vision, the bureaucratic lotion to obscure other people's. But his idleness was wise, far-sighted, and in reality far from cynical. His mind was at the same time unusually detached and unusually practical; he could see another man's point of view without losing his own powers of 'clear thinking — and, what follows from clear thinking, easy and rapid decision'. Through all his writing, there runs one principle. 'If you tell your gardener to shoot a cat,' he wrote, 'and then hold his hands while he aims at it, you cannot hold him responsible if he misses.'

He insisted therefore that his officers should do their own work. 'I have said to each of them in effect — "This is your sub-division or your job. These are the lines on which I want it to be run. Now go and run it. If you make a really serious mistake I shall have to overrule you. Otherwise I shall not interfere. If you want advice, I am here to give it. If you want a definite order, you are free to ask for it. But if you make a habit of wanting either, you will be very little use to me." '

This method, he claimed, worked in nineteen cases out of twenty — and it was easy to get rid of the twentieth. 'If you spend your time holding the sub-divisional officer's hand,' he wrote, 'you will have no leisure to think about your proper job . . . certainly no leisure to initiate anything — and a district officer should not be content to leave his district no better than when he found it.'

Now this principle was the backbone of British rule, and was in danger of becoming obscured. Jacquemont had noticed a century earlier that where there would have been twenty Frenchmen there was one Englishman. This was only possible because the Guardians learned to delegate power. It was this that distinguished the Anglo-Indian empire from other empires, it was this that distinguished the Indian administrative services from the fighting services or the civil services in Whitehall. Supervision remained but power was delegated.

A tahsildar or a sub-inspector of police was in the main trusted to do his work. He lived alone in the centre of his small kingdom, far from any Englishman; his power was such that far into the twentieth century the unsophisticated villager could think of no more comprehensive blessing than: 'May the Lord make you a Sub-Inspector!' — and he would sometimes bestow this blessing even on an Englishman supposed to be the Sub-Inspector's superior.

And here let me include a personal memory. In 1930, when I had been eighteen months in India and was for the first time in charge of a sub-division, I mentioned in conversation that the Muslims in a certain village objected to a Hindu procession simply on the ground that it was new. 'It does no one any harm,' I said. 'It will go nowhere near a mosque or a house. But it has never been done before, so they object'. It seemed to me pointless and selfish, mere spite, and I said I was going to allow the procession. It seemed to me a principle that one ought to allow any activity that did not harm other people. I was not asking for advice, but telling the district officer — my superior — what I had decided to do.

'You are wrong,' he said. 'You will have trouble in that village if you allow a new procession — not serious trouble, but something. But you must learn for yourself. If I interfered, you would think me a crusty bureaucrat and you would not be convinced. And in a year or two you would make the mistake on a larger scale and lose lives. So have it your own way and see what happens.'

That was Michael Nethersole, a born leader, a wise teacher of other men. In no other service would that have been said.

Delegation of power, combined with confidence and trust — the confidence that orders would be carried out, the kind of trust Edwardes had shown in Bannu — these had been the distinguishing marks of this service. Of course the trust was sometimes abused; it was the point of every satire in the nineteenth century that the district officer was in the hands of his subordinates. Occasional abuse, however, was a price that had to be paid. And of course there were men who were too timid or too small to trust anyone. Edye was not different from his fellow-countrymen, but simply had more than most of their distinguishing quality, and one they were losing as the century advanced. He did not find many of his superiors who quite came up to his standards.

It was his argument that 'if you are fit to run a district at all, you will run it best when you are given your head. If you are refused your head, you will have to fight for it.' And he adds that 'fighting for your head is a very pretty art and can be great fun'. He had served, he says, under thirty-one Commissioners, only one of whom he did not like and only two of whom he did not find considerate. But there were only four of whose methods he could whole-heartedly approve.

These four 'were men who had thought out their function, who recognized that if I were charged with a duty I could only be held responsible for the result if I were left free to discharge it in my own way. . . .'

There remained 'a round two dozen of Commissioners whom it was necessary to handle, though seldom two of them on the same lines'. The more difficult were 'men of strong character, who for years had run their districts efficiently and well, but on promotion failed to realize that their function had completely changed, who assumed their new job to be not the administration of five districts as a group, but the direct charge of five districts instead of one'. This no doubt happened because a Commissioner was usually a district man, who had probably held charge of several districts in succession — including perhaps at least one of those in his charge on promotion. He had learnt to delegate just so much; he had lost the flexibility needed for the next step.

There is no room, I am afraid, for Edye's methods of dealing with Commissioners; he was probably cleverer than most at keeping his superiors in their place, but his experience was general. The common noun of assemblage for Commissioners was an interference and for their wives an umbrage.

Edye's attitude to rules might be deduced from his general principles. One of his earliest — and best — Commissioners advised him not to have any manuals of government rules near his desk. 'If you learn to rely on those books, you will never get through the day's work. And if you can't manage without them, you are grossly overpaid.' With this he agreed, as all good district officers would; he had spent years inspecting and supervising the work of tahsildars before he found out that there was a manual laying down how it should be done.

Like all good district officers, too, Edye felt some impatience at the growth of centralized departments, though with his usual tolerance he recognized that it was inevitable. The district officer could not for ever be policeman, engineer and sanitary expert as he had been a century ago; one by one the departments had to be formed. But he would have agreed with Bartle Frere that within a district the representatives of a central department should report not on, but to, the district officer. And he was sometimes regrettably flippant about their activities. Ordered to fill up a pond where mosquitoes were breeding, he replied that in a perfectly flat country it was impossible to fill up one hole without digging another. The protest was overruled; a year later an official of the department reported that the pond was still there. No, replied Edye, a new pond, formed by filling up the first. He had, of course, his own ideas about malaria and mosquitoes and very sound they were.

He had — he was bound to have — a contempt for the Secretariat, where 'you deal, not with men, who may give trouble, nor with things, which may be awkward, but with paper, which cannot answer back'. And he neatly summarizes all Secretariat procedure:

Secretary to Office	— Any precedent?
Office to Secretary	— No.
Secretary to Governor	— Turn it down?
Governor to Secretary	— Yes.

Not always quite true, of course, but very often it was very like that, and Edye recognizes that something of the kind is likely in a centralized bureaucracy. It is quicker to say no, and men are caught in a maze of increasingly complicated routine from which no one has time to consider the means of escape. Indeed, the maze becomes more and more complicated, until no one understands it well enough to plan an escape except the few so used to it that they no longer want to get out — and would have no livelihood if they did.

Metcalfe had seen the dilemma a hundred years before. 'Many first-rate men,' he had written, 'with the power and inclination to initiate and carry out great schemes of amelioration which would be of incalculable benefit to the people are necessitated to spend themselves in the work of mere routine.' And in Edye's day of course it was getting rapidly worse. He points out that in 1909 the provincial government consisted of a Governor, three secretaries and three under-secretaries — seven men. But in 1936 the Governor had to advise him six Ministers, six secretaries, six deputy secretaries, an under-secretary and three assistant secretaries, with four officers attached on special duty — twenty-seven men. Meanwhile, 'no one, I think, would deny that as an engine for the direction and control of the administration it has lost a high percentage of its efficiency'.

He was speaking of the United Provinces, whose population was then roughly that of Great Britain. In Great Britain, of course, the spiral of secretarial inflation is much sharper, and Whitehall would think the Governor's a very moderate staff to administer fifty million people.

It would be pleasant to linger over Edye and his ways of dealing with plague and cholera, his Gambit of the Second Reminder — an infallible device for providing oneself with an excuse for disobeying unreasonable instructions — his views on mobs and crowd psychology and his habit of reaching a decision in difficult cases while fishing or pruning roses. There were the floods, too, when he stopped every passer-by not wearing a shirt and with no legal authority ordered him to work on the embankment — and was fortunate enough to encounter no Pennell. It is pleasant to meet in such good-humoured company the moneylender who 'looks as if he had had a morning swim in warm batter', the district officer whose 'value is in inverse ratio to the wear on the seat of his trousers', and the tahsildar whose attitude to his duty is: 'Perish India but the Commissioner's camp must not be short of potatoes.' Admirable, too, is the fairness of the half-rueful glance over his shoulder at the choice he made when he refused a Secretariat appointment and chose a life in which he could be very nearly his own master.

But it is his attitude to reform that is important. It is really implicit in his guiding principle that most men can be trusted to exercise responsibility and will rise to the occasion if it is offered them. 'If

... India has benefited by a hundred years of the control and guidance of the British services, that is no argument ... that she should acquiesce in, or would benefit by, similar control and guidance for a further period. On the contrary, if in a hundred years the services have not trained India to stand without support ... they have so far failed in their fundamental task.'

He was perfectly clear, however, that though in this respect there had been some failure on the part of the British in India, it had not been deliberate. No one had set himself to emasculate Indians by refusing them responsibility; what had happened was that very few Englishmen had thought of standing back and making Indians do things themselves. He gives as an example the work of District Boards, of which, in most parts of India, the district officer was Chairman until the reforms of 1919. 'As a rule he was in fact practically dictator; and the members were quite content ... Such tasks as seeing that the roads of my district were maintained and improved and flanked with avenues of shade, as getting a drainage scheme for a city financed, designed and executed or building it a market-place, gave me ... the very keenest enjoyment. It certainly never occurred to me at the time that it would perhaps have been wiser to stand aside and insist on a sub-committee of the board making what it could of these undertakings.' 'We have dry-nursed our Indian colleagues and subordinates,' he added, 'not to order but through the human proclivity to follow the line of least resistance.'

He was thinking, when he wrote of District Boards, mainly of the days before 1919. Of the 1909 reforms, he makes no mention; they hardly touched the district officer, although in the Secretariats men wondered how it would be possible to carry on government at all. Indeed, all through the reforms period, the district officer took things less tragically than his masters. Edye, looking back on the time between 1919 and 1937, the period of dyarchy, when one partner had the wheel and the other the accelerator and the brake, felt that it had been worth while and that a staggering and zig-zag progress had been made. India in thirty years had become a happier country. 'Everything is changed — and everything for the better,' he was told by a friend, a Colonel in the British Army, revisiting India after twenty-five years. 'What he had foremost in his mind was a journey from Bombay on which he had shared a railway-carriage for two days with an educated Indian and had found him a delightful companion. Such a thing would have been hardly thinkable thirty years ago.'

Elsewhere, too, Edye speaks of the growing comradeship between

Englishman and Indian. All through his time it had never been wholly absent, but it was ripening, he thought, as conditions forced each to see that, from a different approach, 'we both have the same aim — the well-being of the people of the country'. 'Outside India,' he goes on, 'a very false picture has been conjured up of the relations between the two races . . . There has been grievous misunderstanding, but our instinct has never been to dislike each other. I have no better friends than among those Indians with whom I have been in almost lifelong conflict . . .' 'Relations have never been really bad and were never better than now. For this we have to thank, in the Indian his natural courtesy and kindliness, and in the Englishman, what the Indian recognizes, his fairness and the transparent benevolence tempering the stupidity. . . .'

That was one change for the better, but there had been many others and Edye thought that in the ten years from 1926 to 1936 hardly any country in the world could show more material improvement than India. He instances domestic architecture and the rapid spread of improved varieties of sugar-cane, cotton and wheat.

All this was true. In less than twenty years, the face of the countryside he knew had changed. The old short red-stemmed sugar-cane, not as high as a man, had given place to a noble ten-foot crop with stems as thick as a child's wrist. The leather bags, in which water had been hauled up from wells since the days of the Moguls, everywhere disappeared in favour of Persian wheels, which give a far greater flow of water for less effort on the part of the bullocks. Bicycles appeared in every village, electric torches, and cigarettes; it became the custom to drink tea, a thing unknown among the peasants before 1914. This was material progress of an intelligible kind.

Edye's conclusion on the political future — in 1936 — was that popular government and the gradual elimination of the English from the services were inevitable. This would mean, at first, 'a perceptible fall in the standard of efficiency, due to lack of administrative experience and tradition. There will also be instances of unfairness and nepotism, due to various social pressures. These drawbacks constitute the price that will have to be paid for a fundamental advance . . . The price will fall from year to year but in my view it will not prove too heavy to be paid now.'

'We are passing on a torch', Edye concludes, 'to hands well trained to receive it . . . The receiving hands might arguably have been trained more quickly and the torch passed sooner. But what is a matter of ten or twenty years in the history of a continent?'

THE DEMISSION OF POWER

3. A DIE-HARD

Of course everyone did not think as Edye did. Nor was everyone consistent in his thought. But whatever they may have said in moments of exasperation or disappointment, most men when in a position to think with detachment would have agreed that reforms of some kind there had to be. Sir William Marris told Edwin Montagu as early as 1917, that 'the Indian Civil Servants were very sorry that their day was done; recognized that it was inevitable and were willing to go ahead'. Even from an earlier generation his view would have found support. Horne of Madras, for instance, who retired in 1913, might have been expected to be resolutely on the other side. He had come to India because: 'I had to earn my living and having strong open-air tastes, a love of all sport, a whole-hearted detestation of desk work, I thought the I.C.S. would suit me. I should have preferred the Army but the pay was not good enough.' Looking at the reformed India fifteen years after he retired, he does not criticize the fact of reform, but only the pace. 'Change', he wrote in 1928, 'was no doubt inevitable, and new wine had to be introduced into the old bottles, but it is possible to think that it might have been poured with a gentler hand.' And again: 'We are making a political experiment, the boldest, perhaps the most reckless that any nation ever has made, because in such matters there is no retracing of steps and very little standing still . . .'

More positive was Evan Maconachie, who retired in 1921. 'Questions as to racial equality', he wrote in 1926, 'seem to me beside the point. What race is there should claim superiority to peoples that gave the world a Buddha, an Asoka and an Akbar, religions and philosophies that embrace every religion that has ever existed, an epic literature perhaps unrivalled, and some of the greatest masterpieces in the realm of human art? But there is a difference between Indians and ourselves . . .' 'It is absurd to suppose that a handful of foreigners from across the sea can continue to rule indefinitely hundreds of millions of Orientals on the patriarchal lines pursued . . . down to the time of the recent reforms. Apart from questions of elementary right, there are the repeated promises and solemn assurances . . .' And he goes on almost in Edye's words: 'The only way to fit men for responsibility is to place responsibility upon them. . . .'

That was written in 1926 and was, as Sir Evan says, by then the view of the majority of the Indian Civil Service. But there were men — a few — whose politics were those of Hobbes, who believed that 'the cause which moveth a man to become subject to another is the fear of not otherwise preserving himself', and that force and the fear of force were ultimately the only factors in any situation. There are always minds to which this simplification of something highly complex seems unanswerable. But these were a minority of a minority; there were more who saw the whole question in essentially practical, and indeed personal, terms. They could not believe that people such as — and here would follow a few examples — could run the district as well as themselves.

Every revolution throws up not only men with high ideals but scoundrels on the make. India from 1919 to 1947 was going through a revolution in slow motion and in every district, behind the idealists, there were unscrupulous and designing men, careerist lawyers, small landowners in debt and the like, who in the nineteenth century would have been lickspittles of power — that is, of the district officer. In the twentieth century, such men more and more put their money on the nationalist cause and lost no chance of embarrassing and opposing the executive power — that is, the district officer.

To some officers, then, it was intolerable to think of their district at the mercy of such rascals as these. There were others who could not see the point of spoiling a system which seemed to be working very well and in which the great majority of the people cheerfully acquiesced. Let us consider someone who thoroughly disapproved of the reforms. Unfortunately, he wrote no statement of his creed; there are the memories of a friend and there are a few letters, that is all. The choice is random, in that memories of him came pat to my hand when the argument required them; it is, of course, arguable that to be entirely fair I should have chosen a less agreeable person.

Alexander Loftus Tottenham is a sharp contrast to Edye, though they would certainly have enjoyed each other's company. Loftus Tottenham — he was widely known as Loftus — had been a brilliant classical scholar and might have been expected, as Edye might, to become a Secretariat man. But he remained a district officer in spirit, though he held a Government of India appointment of a rather technical kind in the last ten years of his service. The contrast with Edye lay in his way of life; no polo ponies, no pigsticking, no shooting, fishing, or gardening beguiled him. Talk and books seem to have been what he most valued, but bathing too came high and he thought he could have lived for ever at Madras with not too much to do and constant bathing.

'A confirmed bachelor and never a club man or a player of games, he always, wherever he was, maintained open house and a magnificent table. His house was full of beautiful things, good furniture, much of it designed by himself, blue and white china which he and Charles Cotton had discovered in Madras, and masses of books . . . The first half of the day — hot weather made no difference — was spent out of doors, either in some inspection, often after a long ride, or if there was nothing else to do, in cutting down some unwanted tree. He was not an expert horseman or axeman but made up by energy what he lacked in skill . . . Lunch about the middle of the day was a large and excellent meal, accompanied by a constant flow of wit and, so far as Loftus was concerned, by one or two large bottles of cold beer and a glass of Madeira. He then reclined in a long armchair and piles of files were brought in by a procession of orderlies. With these he wrestled till they were finished, whatever the time. Nothing was left over for the next day and most of the work was done in the long armchair, but every now and then a long note or a draft would send him to his office table and typewriter. A short stroll followed, if there was time, before dinner and then another leisurely meal with excellent food for both mind and body and again there was beer, and two glasses of port, neither more nor less.'

This cannot really have been the way he spent every day, for he must have had visitors to listen to and appeals to hear sometimes. But it begins to give an impression of the man. And since it is not easy to take wit on trust, the motto he proposed for the Secretariat— 'First start your hare, then split it' — deserves to be recorded, together with one good-humoured riposte. He entertained the Governor and his wife while they were on tour and, when they had become good friends, Lady Pentland ventured to ask, with a delicate and attractive stammer, whether Mr. T-tottenham did not find b-beef and b-beer rather b-brutalizing. To which he replied: 'Well, I don't myself, Your Excellency. But of course if you do, you're quite right to keep off them.'

In spite of his dislike of the Secretariat, he devised a system of reference and office management which was widely adopted, and he became eventually one of the two members of the Central Board of Revenue. Here he had to deal with opium, among other things, and his views are worth mention. He knew, of course — everyone in India knows — that opium in moderation is no more harmful than aspirin. Many an Englishman remembers the prodigies his servants or the men of his company performed on a pill or two of opium when there was no food to be had or no shelter in cold and wet. It becomes a vice when taken regularly as an indulgence, as by the Rajput nobles in Tod's day, or when smoked — but that is a Chinese custom, rare in India. It had been exported to China and since it was a Government monopoly this export made up a part of India's revenue that no government would like to lose.

Loftus wrote: 'My own view is that they ought to stop exporting opium altogether, except medicinal opium to England, not because I believe half of the hectic statements made ... they talk about India being scourged and ravaged and all the rest of it by opium, which is absolute nonsense except possibly in some small areas in Assam — but because export is absolutely inconsistent with the position we have taken at the Hague and Geneva ... Of course people say — If we don't sell opium to these countries, Persia and Turkey will, so why sacrifice revenue for the advantage of less conscientious countries? But to my mind that is a rotten argument, from any point of view.'

These are random thoughts, jotted down in his regular home letter to his sister, but more revealing perhaps than his official writings. Loftus retired after thirty-five years service in the I.C.S. and then came back to the South of India as Prime Minister of a small State, where he died as he was beginning his fiftieth year in India. It was not an official career of great distinction, but 'he had more friends and fewer enemies than any man I ever knew'. 'He read widely and possessed real knowledge about many things. Botany, Indian art and archaeology, Medicine, Philosophy, Music and Religion were among his subjects ... but he could sing music-hall songs or recite the Cautionary Tales of Belloc with as much enjoyment as he could quote from Homer or Milton. . . .'

He could, of course, afford to be generous, because he was unmarried, but he was surely more generous than most. He mentions, in one of his letters written during Hitler's War, that he claimed no rebates of income-tax due to him in England and was giving the interest on all his savings to the War Fund in England, as well as about £250 a year in India. This might not be remarkable by itself, but in another letter he mentions casually that he has been spending £500 a year on a holiday home for convalescent officers; in another that he has put the beggars who used to receive odd doles at the gate on to a regular list, which costs him another £100; and in almost every letter there is mention of some considerable sum, two or three hundred pounds, sent to a relation in England, or of some kindness to a servant.

He was a kindly and genial man, then, though with a strong dislike of sentimentality or pretence, a man to whom 'sin is lack of consideration for others'. 'I hope you aren't going all anti-Semite', he writes to his sister. 'I take people as I find them, Jew or Gentile, Hindu or Muslim.' Young people, too, sought his company because he was witty and unpretentious. But he thought democracy would only work in a Greek city-state or a Swiss canton, where everyone knew everyone else. 'Now the idea is that every race is fit for "self-government", — really very few are — and certainly not the oriental races. If you want to see the state that "self-government" reduces one of them to, look at the state China has been in ever since it became a Republic.' And again: 'To talk as if the people of India were down-trodden slaves is ridiculous and meaningless. And what does our "yoke" amount to? Little more than keeping the peace internally and protecting them externally . . .' And again — slipped in with friendly gossip about the victory of his bearer's son in a badminton tournament —'. . . The vast masses of people are too hopelessly primitive and ignorant to be even *as* able as the masses at home to form a rational opinion about anything. . . .' Or again: 'For us who profess to be fighting for democracy (which itself is rot) to contemplate handing over the people of India in the name of democracy to be governed by an oligarchy of people whose outlook would have been up-to-date in the time of Assurbani-pal or Esarhaddon and who are more oppressive and more selfish than anything you can conceive . . . is really funny if it weren't tragic.'

That last sentence was written in 1918 and he was thinking no doubt of the Brahman monopoly of power, which as a district officer in South India he had spent the best years of his life in trying to mitigate. It was a feeling widely shared. How can we leave these people, who have trusted us, to the mercy of the moneylender and the landlord? That was the question many asked; the answer, of course, was that we could not for ever continue to interfere between the peasants and men of their own race whose power over them was partly an artificial growth that we had allowed to flourish. The peasant, said Edwin Montagu, must be awakened from his pathetic contentment. There were many like Loftus to ask why, men who felt doubtful whether the great majority of mankind were ever likely to attain any state preferable to contentment.

Faith is needed to let a boy go for his first bicycle ride or to release eggs from the tyranny of coupons. In this sense, every bureaucrat has a wolf by the ears and it takes courage to let go. It is a matter of temperament whether you say, with Edye, that the price must be paid, that, even if it costs a finger or two, you and the wolf cannot stand staring each other in the face for ever — or with Loftus Tottenham, that it is much better to hold tight and a little tension is better than going through life maimed. There were, of course, many who shared the view of Loftus; it is my contention, first, that they were not so many as those on Edye's side and secondly that the surprising thing was that there was anyone on Edye's side at all. If India had been ruled by a caste of Guardians who were, let us suppose, Spanish or Roman, French, Portuguese, Turkish or Dutch, can one believe that many would have been found who saw the need to go?

Loftus, of course, generous, witty, genial and friendly, concerned about his bearer's grandson, taking everyone as he found them, utterly unpretentious, noting that the only good thing about the 1919 reforms was that he was no longer called the Honourable for wasting his time in the Assembly — Loftus is not the conventional picture of a die-hard. But he was, I believe, at least as representative as the noisier kind.

CHAPTER II

THE CHANGE OF HEART

1. DISAPPOINTMENT AND DISTRUST

'I HOPE,' wrote Lord Minto in 1909, 'that public opinion won't take the unreasonable view that the deeds of a few anarchists are proof of the doubtful loyalty of all India.' He was thinking of course of public opinion in England, and he had good reason for making the point. An attempt to assassinate him with a bomb had just been made and it was the year which saw the murder of a public prosecutor in Bengal, of Sir William Curzon Wyllie and Dr. Lalkaka in London, and of Mr. Jackson, Collector of Nasik, shot at a farewell party given in his honour.

Lord Minto's view was that which until 1919 most people would have taken. The cult of blood and violence, of which Tilak was the chief prophet, Tilak's teaching that truth should be disregarded by fighters in the nationalist war, all this was still confined to two centres, Bengal and Maharashtra, the home of the Maratha Brahmans — and to a very small minority there.

Most educated Indians, that is to say perhaps one million out of three hundred million — were mildly nationalist but their dream was of an India governing herself within the Commonwealth. When they thought on political subjects, they still used English terms; they still regarded English ideals with affection, but for that very reason they wanted to govern themselves and to emerge from Platonic slavery. The masses were still indifferent to the forms of government and, if not exactly enthusiastic about English rule, were inclined to regard it as preferable on the whole to anything else they could imagine — unless it might be rule by their own group.

That this was the truth was shown by the war. The Germans had some excuse for their belief that in a European war India would prove a liability to England, but they were wrong. India was in fact an asset of the first importance and not a material asset only. In the First World War, most educated Indians still felt that they shared the ideals for which sacrifices were being made.

These, of course, are generalizations which many will question. India was growing up and changing, one may say loosely; but it was individuals who were changing and they did not all change at the same time. Nirad C. Chaudhuri has described, in his *Autobiography of an Unknown Indian*, the feeling of his boyhood that there was a kindly and protecting government, something warm and fatherly over his head, a feeling in which a change took place after the Boer War. Other Indians speak of the same change. The old desire to rule for the good of India vanished, they thought, and its place was taken by a desire to exploit and to rule for the sake of domination. 'We felt we could hope for justice no longer', they will tell you. But Campbell-Bannerman and Asquith represented England as well as Joseph Chamberlain and perhaps a change in the Indian way of looking at the situation was at least as important as any change on the English side. A sudden impatience at any continued control came to different Indians at different times; it became general in 1919.

What had been true till the summer of 1918 seemed to change almost over-night. Seemed to change — for a few years later the first force of that sharp disappointment had spent itself and there was an appreciable reaction, not to be fully realized until events in 1947 showed that between India and England there was the kind of tie that exists between a man and a woman who have long been married, and — what is more — married with intervals of happiness. The violence and suddenness of the change of feeling at the end of the war however can hardly be exaggerated. In early July of 1918, for instance, Mr. Gandhi was still speaking of equal partnership within the Empire; he was engaged in a recruiting campaign, urging peasants to attain self-rule by joining the army and winning the war. But a few months later it seemed to him axiomatic that the Government of India must be opposed.

The Acts known as the Rowlatt Acts, which provided a special machinery for dealing with conspiracy, have by some been supposed to be one cause of this change of feeling. But it had taken place before they were drafted. Turn to Mr. Gandhi's autobiography and you will find, sure enough, a chapter headed: 'The Rowlatt Bills and my Dilemma.' But the dilemma is nothing to do with the Bills. More than half of the chapter is concerned with a tenderness in the writer's anal tract and the dilemma in which he was placed by a vow not to drink milk. He happened to read an account of the report of the Rowlatt Committee in the newspaper, just when he had reluctantly decided to solve his dilemma by drinking goat's milk instead of cow's. The committee's recommendations did not seem to him to require discussion; he immediately proceeded to the attack.

Now Mr. Gandhi and his friends were agreed with the English in condemning assassination as a means of political argument. Nor was there anything very terrible in the shortened procedure suggested in these Bills for trying conspirators and would-be assassins. It is arguable that the Acts were unnecessary and in the event they proved to be so. The powers they provided were never used and they were soon repealed. But the Acts were opposed with passion, and passion is not roused by redundancy. The reaction was so bitter and so immediate because the Acts were a sign of mistrust — one sign of many, and of mistrust of a particular kind.

All over the world men thought that when the First World War was over the millennium would come. Self-determination — everyone not at the Peace Conference knew exactly what it meant. It meant what every man wanted for himself. In India, men had been proud of their country's part in the war and they wanted their partnership in the war to be recognized by some act of royal generosity which would place India at once on a level in the councils of the world with Canada and Australia. Their immediate concern was with status — rank, prestige, fair name in the world's eyes — at least as much as with democracy or responsible institutions. They would have been content if these had come more slowly.

The proclamation of 1917 had used the words 'gradual' and 'progressive'. There was no quarrel at the time as to what these words meant. 'That India could not advance, as the Dominions had advanced, by one step to full responsible government was generally accepted', wrote Lionel Curtis in 1916. It was however a shock and a disappointment that there was no sudden accession of status and prestige, while in the discussion which took place from 1916-18 certain assumptions were made that were deeply wounding to Indian pride. If doubts had been confined to the inexperience of Indian leaders and electorates, not much harm would have been done; it soon became clear however that what was really in doubt was the good faith of Indian leaders as trustees for the people, and particularly for certain minorities. The moment this was expressed, bitterness was inevitable and co-operation became impossible between the Government and a large section of Indian Nationalists.

Withdrawing then to a distance, so that India can be seen from far away, it is possible to say that in 1918 the system of the Guardians was still intact to the eye. The State was still ruled by trained rulers according to their own idea of what was good. But the system was to last no longer. It will appear to go on for another quarter-century, but it did really end in 1919. This was not because the war had strained and wrenched the system and reduced the ranks of the Guardians; they could have recovered. It was because Indians were no longer prepared to accept the passive role of being ruled. Nor were they willing to be taught. India's partnership in the war had raised hopes of Indian progress which might have been realized in amicable partnership if it had not become clear that one partner felt a distrust for the motives of the other. Indians, aware that they were distrusted, returned the sentiment, became impatient of the old system and irritated by delay, and progress therefore had to come by conflict instead of by partnership.

There was another factor of vital importance, a change of heart in England, too, though it was not the change of heart the nationalists believed they detected. Neither Morley nor Minto had ever doubted that England would fight to keep India. By 1919, that had ceased to be true. No party in England was prepared to use force on a large scale to keep a partner who wanted to go. If this was not a temporary quarrel, if there was a real desire for separation, then separation there must be. The ultimate sanction for the system had once been bayonets; they had been kept in the background but they were there. Bayonets were now to be worn for ceremonial purposes only and for the next quarter-century the system continued largely by its previous momentum.

It would be fascinating, though of course infructuous, to speculate what might have happened if in 1919 both parties to the suit, England and India, had been generously ready to trust the other; if English people had had faith enough to let go without reservation, to fix a date twenty years ahead and work whole-heartedly to make India — not only British India but the States and the Indian Army — ready for that day; if Indians had been willing to co-operate in the constitutional experiments of 1919 and 1935 and learn all the English had to teach. But, in fact, neither trusted the other.

2. THE KAISER'S WAR AND THE GUARDIANS

The Kaiser's War showed that many Indians on the whole still preferred English rule to anything else they saw any immediate chance of obtaining. But the case for this opinion was then overstated and evidence put forward which is quite inadmissible. India did not need to declare war but became automatically at war as soon as His Majesty was; that India provided troops which helped to delay the first swift thrust for Paris, that she provided so many million shells, rounds of small arms ammunition and boots — all this is beside the point. It was the result of decisions by Englishmen. It is relevant to an argument as to whether India was well organized by her Guardians; it has nothing to do with the wishes of most Indians, because they had no say in the actions of the Government.

That every ruler who maintained troops placed them at the disposal of the Imperial Government is less significant than that many princes personally volunteered for active service. That in the first months of the war hundreds of letters and telegrams poured in, offering assistance; that at the first meeting of the Imperial Legislative Council, member after member rose to his feet to demonstrate his attachment to the Throne — this is significant and still more that it was felt safe to reduce the number of British troops throughout India to fifteen thousand. Fifteen thousand among three hundred million; that figure alone proves that at the lowest reckoning India acquiesced in her share of the war. But it was more than acquiescence. In India as in England, men thought it a noble act to help a small nation attacked by one much larger. This does not apply to the masses, who as usual were mainly concerned with the price of grain. It does apply to many of the educated.

Among the people who were recruited for the army, reactions of course were simple. There was still no question of commissioned officers; the appeal was to the peasants and a man went to the colours in India for much the same reasons as Marlborough's or Wellington's recruit. His brother perhaps had his father's cottage and bit of land and there wasn't room for two; here was a shilling and a warm coat, a kind word and a handshake from the squire, instead of black looks and the danger of the stocks. It is easy to turn that into Indian terms. Food and a regular wage called, the *zamindar* and the sub-inspector of police urged. There was one other factor present in India, professional pride; here a soldier was proud of his calling, and held in honour as he never was in England. It was a voluntary army — but there was, if you care to put it in abstract terms, some degree of social and economic pressure to obtain recruits.

Pressure of course varied in degree; it was never so acute as was needed for Nelson's navy. In some villages, and particularly in the early stages, none at all was needed and more men were ready to go than could be taken; this was always the case in peace. In other areas, competition was stirred up between large landowners to 'give' recruits; there was a badge and a certificate on vellum, signed by the

Lieutenant-Governor, for the man who 'gave' a hundred. No sensible district officer would ask questions about a recruit who came forward voluntarily and took the oath without visible compulsion; on the other hand, he would feel bound to protect a man who complained of being ill treated because he would not join the army. But it would take some hardihood to complain.

It was then a voluntary army, voluntary in much the same sense as most voluntary armies. The number recruited from start to finish was 1,300,000, to be added to a strength at the outbreak of war, of 280,000. They fought in France, Belgium, Gallipoli, Salonika, Palestine, Egypt, the Sudan, Mesopotamia, Aden, Somaliland, the Cameroons, East Africa, North-West Persia, Kurdistan, South Persia, Trans-Caspia and North China, 'forcing every sea and land to be the highway of their daring'.

This is not the place to discuss the Mesopotamian Campaign and the bad organization with which it began. It is enough to say that it was Whitehall which — against the Viceroy's view — had decided that the army in India should be controlled by the Viceroy's sole adviser in military affairs; it was Whitehall which in peace had confined India's role in any future war to limits which were disregarded within a month of Germany's ultimatum. Brilliant success in Palestine and Mesopotamia sponged out that memory and by the time of the Armistice, India's main sentiment with regard to the war was one of pride and anticipation. There was pride in what the Indian Army had done, in the financial contribution India had made and in the munitions of war she had dispatched. Mica, saltpetre, rubber, skins and tea; guns, jute and bandages — all that India had done is recorded elsewhere. In all of it she felt pride mingled with a good deal of pleasant curiosity about the form gratitude would take.

That was the feeling of many. There were others in whom the change of heart had already taken place, who were conscious mainly of an angry despair because getting rid of the English seemed as distant as ever. Both feelings were there; perhaps at different times and in varying degrees, every educated Indian was conscious of both.

The old system, that is, government by the Guardians, was strained and wrenched by the war though it was not for that reason it came to an end. It was natural that at the beginning of the war the men of the administrative services should have wished to fight; it was more surprising that they should have been allowed to go, but then that First World War was an amateurish, slaughterous, ill-organized affair,

One-sixth of the Indian Civil Service, that is two hundred out of twelve, were permitted to take commissions in the Indian Army. Some were not permitted to go, being too old, or because enough had gone already; some resigned the service in order to go. Political officers, of whom two-thirds had been through Sandhurst, were even more dangerously reduced. Those two hundred odd did, in general, neither more nor less than other Englishmen of their age and class. Those who stayed were able to say, as Loftus Tottenham wrote in another war: 'Thank the Lord I have not been tried too high; I do not know if I could have borne it.' They were neither bombed nor rationed; they usually had long separations to endure, they were sometimes worried about money because they had no rises in pay, as most services did; they were overworked and would not have wished it otherwise. But they came off lightly.

Recruitment to the service virtually stopped and there was of course no leave in the ordinary sense of the word. There was much new work; a man might become Controller of Prices or Munitions, Commissioner for Wheat or Foodstuffs, Director of Civil Supplies or Home Indents and Priority. Fewer were left for the districts, where work was naturally heavier than usual because of recruiting, rising prices, rumours and general unrest. Most men no doubt emerged in 1919 feeling, as Loftus Tottenham put it, 'slightly vermiform' — but so did most of their compatriots.

All this was soon put right. Arrears of leave were quickly wiped off and arrears of intake were met by the addition of young men from the armed forces. There were improvements in pay — nominal of course; no one could hope to retain his old purchasing power — and men no longer had to meet the cost of their own passages. There was no reason from the side of the service why the old system should not continue; the stress had been taken and the fabric was outwardly intact.

In one sense, however, a failure on the part of the English rulers of India did contribute to the coming change of heart. The Guardian caste was used to ruling without assistance from the public; when letters and telegrams came offering help, it was the instinct of almost everyone to acknowledge politely, to take no action. Many Indians felt aggrieved and disillusioned that their offers were not made use of. In every English village there were hospitals, knitting guilds, co-operative savings societies, a host of activities, mostly organized by volunteers, which may not have done much to win the war but did make it possible for everyone to feel he was taking part. In

India, officials were too busy or too unimaginative to start such ploys and there were not enough Indian middle-class leaders with the necessary habit of mind. And enthusiasm unharnessed soon sours.

More important was the ferment, general throughout the world, produced by this cosmic stirring of the pot. Rising prices, new ideas, men who had seen the world coming back to their villages from the war — it is a familiar tale, apt enough to cause unrest anywhere but particularly so in India, where not one man in ten could write his name, nor one in a hundred say he had crossed the sea. It was into this atmosphere that the announcement of August 1917 was launched, raising hopes sharply, preparing the way to disillusionment, ending the system.

3. THE DISCUSSION OF DYARCHY

'Yes,' said John Lawrence in the 'sixties, 'India is quiet. As quiet as gunpowder.' That was exactly the position in those days just before the end of the war when political India was waiting to know what would be the practical outcome of the announcement of 1917. Discussion was in progress. It did not perhaps cause much thought to the man in camp, whose copy of *The Pioneer*, *The Statesman* or *The Times of India* came out to him by runner, with a cauliflower and the bread, two days late, tied up in a twist of the thread used for sewing files together. He would look at the war news and the local gossip but not always spend long on political speeches or on Letters to the People of India.

Some members of the service are however on record, though anonymously, as having taken part in the discussion. When Lionel Curtis, fresh from The Round Table and constitution-making in South Africa, put forward the idea of dual rule, of a long step forward with half the body, he consulted some senior officials of the Indian Civil Service and published their views. No doubt he consulted men who had listened to his ideas with sympathy. It is unlikely that they make a representative batch, but the way they think is typical if the result is not.

Every one of the nine agrees that some forward step is needed. The first quotes much from the wisdom of Munro and contrasts his natural easy liberalism with the stiffness of writers in the years after the Mutiny, the great Victorian period when there was so much to do that hardly anyone had time to think. And he quotes from Hobhouse: 'What is spontaneous in a people . . . is always the source of life' and fears that our administration, though conscientious, has proved too heavy a burden.

But though all the nine agree that something must be done, while all but one feel that Indians should be given far more of the higher posts, all in varying degree feel some doubts about dyarchy. Their approach is different from Curtis's. They think of what they have seen. They would build upwards, rather than reform downwards. 'In my district of over one million people,' writes one, 'only one graduate lives outside the headquarters town . . .' And he continues, of the landowners who ought to be the political leaders: 'As there is no public opinion, there is no restraint on their morals and it has been a frequent disappointment to find men of good reputation, when entrusted with the control of co-operative societies, making use of them for their own advantage.' He is afraid that separate electorates will mean the election of extremists in religion, who will make poor trustees. He would therefore proceed, not to introduce democratic government, but to bring Indians into the services and control the various departments of the Government, not by Ministers but by small Boards of nominated Indians.

There were variations on this theme. One from South India is afraid of Brahman domination. He had spent his life trying to make sure that this community, less than three per cent of the people, did not obtain every post in his office and throughout his district. And he had not seen much sign of altruism when they were in power. He wished to begin reform by giving far greater powers to local boards administering small areas, smaller than a district — just as Lord Ripon had suggested — areas of perhaps two hundred villages. He would base his scheme on village panchayats — in the manner of Munro — but with a Board to control the Area and one most impor-tant difference. He would provide for every Board an elected but highly paid Indian President, thus attracting a full-time man of real capacity. This would be an experiment; if it was successful, he would agree to dyarchy.

This was in a way typical; five out of nine agree to the principle of dyarchy, four make alternative proposals for delegating power, but all express doubts. These are directed not only to the inexperience and apathy of the electorates, about which everyone agrees; a deep distrust is also revealed of the good faith of the elected.

It would be tedious to go through all the nine, but one more must be quoted, because his way of considering the problem is typical of the district officer. He had thought about it a good deal when 'threshing water and getting no fish', and he put down his thoughts in a staccato style not at all like the Secretariat's:

> I start from bedrock. What do you cater for?
> The odd million literates
> The three hundred million others
> You must cater for the 300 million others.
> I am all for
> One man, one vote.
> Age 25 and over.

He then proceeds to organize and administer the polling-stations on polling day, with red and blue tins for votes and coloured screens. He would have States about the size of a Commissioner's division, with an electorate of five or six million and an assembly of one hundred or one hundred and thirty members, and these States would rule themselves in their own spheres of action. He goes into a good deal of detail: 'Language of the Assembly to be local. English barred. But the first thing to put down is this racial antagonism which has sprung up.' He is adamant however about one thing; there must be no watering down the civil service while this experiment is being introduced. It is thin enough already and every man will be needed to carry through so tremendous a reform. There must be no electoral colleges. 'Every delegate would be bought. Very important, one man, one vote.'

It is easy to picture him, casting his lure a long way out over the tail of a pool, pipe gripped firmly between his teeth, saying to himself: 'Very important, one man, one vote.' No one took any notice but there was a great deal of sense in it; the more votes, the harder it is to buy men one by one. And it is surely better to bribe villages with schools than men with rupees.

4. O'DWYER

In England it was generally believed that the services in India were opposed in principle to the 1919 reforms. Of course some were; a few thought of Aristotle and believed the Indian was doomed by his temperament always to be a bondsman. But the idea that all were opposed to advance was perhaps mainly due to two books, *The Lost Dominion*, and Sir Michael O'Dwyer's *India as I Knew It*. The first is written with discursive learning in a style of an attractive peppery brilliance but the second carried more weight because the author put his name to it and because of the part he had played.

Michael O'Dwyer was one of the fourteen children of an Irish landowner of no great wealth, as much farmer as landlord. He was brought up in a world of hunting and snipe-shooting, of threatening letters and houghed cattle, where you were for the Government or against it, where you passed every day the results of lawlessness in the blackened walls of empty houses. It was a world very different from the mild and ordered life of southern England.

O'Dwyer passed the I.C.S. examination from Wren's and, like most of his year, spent his two years' of probation at Balliol, but had 'more friends in other colleges'. He stayed up a third year to get a degree, read a three-years' course of law in one year and obtained one of the five firsts. He distinguished himself also as a linguist; one gets the impression of a man who seldom opened a book without a purpose, whose keen hard brain acquired quickly and did not forget but had little time to waste on subtleties.

He went to the Punjab, and that too is important. The Lawrence tradition had not died and in the Punjab more than anywhere it was the first article of faith that the man who is most ready to use force at the beginning will use least in the end. It was the second that juniors must be given a free hand and backed up with unswerving loyalty. And the attitude of the English was still taut. In the rest of India an Englishman alone in a village was usually physically larger than anyone he met and men were in awe of him. But in the Punjab, Sikh, Jat and Muslim are all big men physically, taller than most Englishmen, and the visitor must assert himself to hold the mastery. Further, Punjabis made more than half the Indian Army. The civilian in the Punjab was·at the fountain-head of power and could afford no laxity.

Nor was it a country with any slack to take up. Before the canals, there was famine or scarcity almost every other year; every fifth year or so there would be trouble of some kind on the Frontier calling for every camel and bullock that could be scraped together. A hardy, virile and warlike people to control, fierce tribes beyond the Border to be watched; that was the civilian's task in the Punjab.

O'Dwyer went to the Western Punjab, Thorburn's country, and quite early he became a settlement officer. He was in daily touch with the Muslim peasantry. He saw the villagers swarm round himself and his assistants with their disputes; he lived among them in tents for nine months every year, with no Sundays or holidays, spending most of the day in a good-humoured chaffing battle of wits, they trying to persuade him that all their land was poor, he looking for the best crops with an eye sharpened by the knowledge that the tallest sugar-cane might hold a boar or a partridge. No one who has ever been a settlement or a record officer can forget those months in camp; he comes to think of the peasants as his children, and the more masculine his character the harder he finds it to believe that anyone else can look after them. And there could be few characters more masculine than O'Dwyer's.

It was Thorburn's country. The burden of debt to the Hindu moneylender was heavy. O'Dwyer heard of it everywhere. And he went next to the Frontier Province, where there is even more hostility to the moneylending Hindu, who to the Pathan is an idolater, an eater of cowdung, a parasite on society engaged in a trade forbidden to the faithful. O'Dwyer, like amost every British officer, had a liking for the Frontier Pathan and for any merry rogue. To cattle-lifting and banditry he was severe, because he wanted an orderly district. 'You are wasting your time praying here', he heard a fellow Muslim say to a prisoner waiting outside his tent, 'reserve your prayers for the appellate court where they may do some good.' But liking and a grim understanding went with the severity; if the boot had been on the other foot, O'Dwyer would himself have been a cattle-lifter — and as cunning and as lucky as any on the Border. For the moneylender he could have no such feeling. For the moneylender O'Dwyer — and for that matter nine Frontier officers out of ten — felt dislike, contempt and distrust.

There were two measures in the first ten years of the century designed by the Punjab Government to improve the position of the Muslim peasant in the West. One was the Punjab Land Alienation Act, meant to prevent the peasant mortgaging or selling to a moneylender. The other was not merely an Act but the administrative action that followed it, all that went into the steady development of Co-operative Credit. This meant that a peasant known in his village to be reasonably reliable could borrow money at 12 per cent or 15 per cent every year, instead of one anna in the rupee every month — which is 75 per cent. Both these Punjab measures were opposed by politically active Hindus — on the purest grounds of Victorian liberalism and with a tinge of outraged smugness at the corrupt favouritism of the administration. That opposition to benevolent measures, all he had ever heard of moneylenders, came to O'Dwyer's mind when he heard mention of Hindu politicians.

Michael O'Dwyer, being Irish, knew his friends from his enemies and let humour temper justice; he was the ideal king of Sadi and the Persian poets, who cuts off the tallest poppy-heads and keeps order by checking the spring of sedition before it has grown into the river of revolt. He was a man to be admired, utterly courageous, both morally and physically; he had been in many a Border skirmish and was a fine horseman who had been the death of many a boar. He was a man of compassion for his children, proud that while Akbar had reduced the King's share to a third, the British had reduced it to an eighth or a twelfth; it was part of his compassion that he would not spare the rod.

He had of course the defects of his qualities. He was not likely to see the point of view of a Hindu politician; he could not weigh such imponderables as freedom and spontaneity against the visible benefits of a peaceful country-side and a low assessment to land revenue. And his natural habit of mind was accentuated by his war-time experience; his was the province that found the fighting men for the army and it was his province too that had to face the *Ghadr* conspiracy, started among Sikhs in America.

Not more than a few thousand men were affected from first to last, but they had been in touch with German agents, they came into the Punjab with plans for revolutionary outrage, assassination and destruction by bombs. They murdered Indian police officers and Sikhs well-affected to the Government, but the conspiracy was dealt with; it never spread. There were other conspiracies with German backing, but this was the most dangerous. Another had looked even more formidable. We were at war with Turkey, whose Sultan was recognized as the Khalif of Islam; the possibilities in a mainly Muslim province were as obvious to the Germans as to us. Though the Khilafat movement never became strong during the war, it was always a threat. All through the war, accounts of conspiracy and of murderous plots formed the Lieutenant-Governor's daily reading — and he knew from his boyhood what conspiracy and outrage mean to peaceful folk. The Frontier and the tribes hung always over his head. But he never slept the worse.

This was the man who ruled the Punjab in April 1919. And here it is important to remember the order of events. The report of the Committee recommending dyarchy appeared in July of 1918. Soon afterwards came the report of the Rowlatt Committee, recommending that certain special provisions for accelerated trial, in force during the war, should continue after the war for cases of assassination and conspiracy. In November, Mr. Gandhi, recovering from illness, happened to read an account of these recommendations and determined that if they were given effect they must be resisted. In March the Acts were passed; on March 30th the first blow in Mr. Gandhi's campaign was struck. He had proclaimed a day of mourning and general strike; in Delhi this resulted in rioting and firing.

Somewhere, then, between July and November 1918 the change of heart had taken place and the majority of Indians who had political views had made up their minds against co-operation in the reforms.

Mr. Gandhi himself realized very soon that he had made what he called 'a Himalayan blunder' and he said so. He realized now that the people of India were not educated to the point of discipline necessary for peaceful civil resistance. But it was not so easy to turn off the tap as it had been to turn it on and, before it could be turned off, things had happened which hardened opinion for a generation.

O'Dwyer always referred to the events of those few weeks as a rebellion. He had reason to believe that Hindus of the extremist or Tilak school were trying to incite both the police and the Indian Army to mutiny and at the same time were making advances to Pathan tribes on the Frontier, while the peasants of the Punjab, though not disaffected, were making ready to attack the towns if anarchy and disorder grew. Intelligence reports of this kind present every ruler with a problem. Believe them, act on them—and they are proved false. Disregard them—and they may come true. Whatever judgment is passed now on the validity of those reports, O'Dwyer believed that they indicated a genuine danger. The facts are that there were outbreaks of mob violence at a number of places, of which those at Lahore and Amritsar were the worst. At Amritsar, the railway station, post offices, banks, the Town Hall, mission schools and mission buildings were attacked, looted and burnt; Europeans were murdered. The mob took control of the city. In the few days that followed, telegraph lines in many parts of the Punjab were cut and trains derailed and attacked. The police for two days had to be withdrawn from Lahore.

O'Dwyer was steeped in the Punjab tradition. He quotes more than once Sadi's couplet:

The spring at its source may be turned with a twig;
When it has grown to a river it cannot be crossed by an elephant.

He quotes, too, exactly the same doctrine, expressed by Sir Henry Maine in a different literary convention: 'The Governor who waits to recognize a rebellion till it looks like a war will probably find that he has waited too long.' He at once asked the Government of India for the introduction of martial law. Martial law, of course, to a jurist means no law; it means that the military commander has the right, as in an occupied country, to do whatever he considers necessary to preserve order; he is governed only by military law and the conventions of civilized people. In spite of his first in jurisprudence, O'Dwyer had hoped to retain control of the situation himself, calling in the soldiers as a reinforcement and freeing himself of delays in procedure. This could have been done by giving him and his officers military rank, but the Government of India replied pedantically: 'Military authorities consider it impossible to place officer with executive military authority under orders of Lieutenant-Governor' and more to the same effect. O'Dwyer from this point onwards could only advise; he did however concur in almost everything that was done.

This is not the place to discuss the detail of what was done. There was the Hunter Commission and a report from which, apart from Amritsar, nothing very terrible emerged. No one who has lived through two wars and has a sense of proportion can today be seriously disturbed to know that between two and three hundred people, having been found guilty by a court, were caned to save sending them to jail, or that a few more were made to skip and touch their toes. But Amritsar — and even more what was said about Amritsar — is another matter.

Amritsar city from April 10th to the 12th was in the hands of a mob. On the 11th Brigadier-General Dyer arrived and, the situation being obviously beyond police control, the Deputy Commissioner made over charge to him. Dyer took great care to make public by beat of drum orders forbidding meetings and warning the inhabitants that meetings would be fired on. On the afternoon of the 13th, a meeting was held in defiance of these orders. Brigadier-General Dyer found himself personally in command of a small force — fifty rifles and forty men with *kukris* — all of the Indian Army, confronting a crowd estimated variously at between five thousand and twenty thousand strong. They were in a square, an open place enclosed by houses with few and narrow entrances. In his first military report, and verbally for some days afterwards, Dyer said that he expected the mob to attack and believed that his first duty as a soldier was to preserve the force under his command; he therefore dispersed the mob. He fired one thousand six hundred and fifty rounds, killing over three hundred people and wounding over a thousand more; he stopped when no ammunition was left. That evening the city was completely quiet.

General Dyer's first report implied that he had used so much force as he considered necessary to disperse the mob — and no more. The mob was being addressed by men who later were held by the courts to be dangerous agitators. It was made up mostly of peasants who had come in for a fair, Sikhs armed with the six-foot quarterstaff and many of them with the *kirpan*, the short Sikh sword. Sikhs are a violent people, quick to flare into fury; it was potentially as dangerous as a mob could be. If Dyer had kept to his first report, it would have been difficult for anyone who had not been there to impugn his judgment. But he changed his ground and it may well be that his second statement was at least as near the truth as the first. At such a moment, every influence in a man's life may play a part and it may be relevant that Dyer had been educated in India at Bishop Cotton's School, where most of his companions were the sons of European subordinates or people of mixed blood. It is a soil in which racial intolerance grows very freely, as Kim found at St. Xavier's.

What perhaps lurked in Dyer's mind was brought to the surface by letters, speeches, and press agitation from the English side. 'It was not till April 13th that people realized that the Government was in earnest and that it was determined to protect them even against their own will . . . I held many meetings and heard on all sides that this incident had saved the situation, and that is my own private opinion.' So wrote an official from a neighbouring district. Much to that effect was said in much less temperate language, and General Dyer came to think himself the saviour of India. He no longer confined himself to what he had said in his first report. In his evidence before the Hunter Commission, he used language reminiscent of Cooper's when he was Deputy Commissioner of Amritsar and took the fleeing mutineers on the island in 1857. Dyer said, as Cooper had said, that he had determined to influence the whole of the Punjab. This was more than he had any right to do as a local military commander.

That he was influenced by 'resentful retaliation' — a phrase used a few days later to describe the spirit in which martial law was *not* to be administered — is shown by other actions, notably his notorious order that any Indian passing that way must crawl along the street where an English woman, a missionary teacher, had been attacked by the mob and left for dead. This order was withdrawn as soon as it came to notice and Michael O'Dwyer took Dyer severely to task for it. It was apparently only once enforced but it must be mentioned because of its effect on Indian feeling.

Dyer's continuing to fire for so long, his crawling order, most of all perhaps his words later before the Hunter Commission, filled politically minded Indians throughout India with bitterness. They had expected at the end of the war a sudden recognition of their nationhood, an instantaneous partnership. They had been offered instead the position of an articled clerk, which might in the course of a life-time or so lead to partnership if they were good. 'Never use that offensive word sympathy to us', a Bengali friend said to Harcourt Butler, 'it is a word of superiority.' And the reforms of 1919 were based on an attitude which, from the Indian point of view, was at its best sympathy, at its worst distrust.

Many Indians had been hurt and offended by such an offer. In a mood which to many Englishmen seemed childish and petulant, they had determined to have nothing to do with it. It was a mood which might not have lasted long. Dyer's words, however, as much as his deeds, hardened their resolution. They felt, said one after the Punjab rebellion, that the English had come to regard them as a foreign people with whom they were at war.

That hardening of Indian opinion was one effect of the events at Amritsar and what followed. Another was a temporary loss of confidence among the men of the Guardian caste. Hardly one would have agreed with Dyer's crawling order, but many, and not only in the Punjab, believed that by opening fire without hesitation and continuing to fire longer than the strictly local situation seemed to demand, Dyer had saved lives in the end. They observed however that Dyer forfeited his career — and many other officers too who had acted much less questionably. They lost confidence in England's will to support them.

O'Dwyer himself drew a contrast between this rebellion, in the province potentially the most dangerous in India, and the Moplah rebellion a year later. In the Punjab, which was handled firmly from the start, the total number of lives lost, altogether, from start to finish, was, he claimed, less than five hundred, of whom two-thirds were at Amritsar. The Moplah affair, on the Malabar Coast, broke out in August 1921, at a time when it was most important to make the reforms a success; the Government of India tried at first to conciliate the rebels and were gradually forced into measures more and more rigorous and finally far harsher than anything in the Punjab. In the end, 'more than two thousand Mohammedans were killed by troops and thousands more in other ways . . . while the number of Hindus butchered, . . . skinned alive and made to dig their own graves before slaughter, ran into thousands . . .' with other horrors not to be told. There were twenty thousand brought to trial against two thousand five hundred in the Punjab.

No one of course can be sure that O'Dwyer was right and that if the Moplah business had been dealt with on the lines of the Punjab there would have been any economy of misery. Nor is this the place for a long discussion of either. It is however essential to make it clear that from now onwards the whole situation was changed. Government had been carried on with the consent — usually apathetic and half-hearted, but still consent — of the governed. That consent was now changed to active mistrust. And for the rulers a new dilemma was in existence. The officer confronted with the prospect of riot had been brought up to avoid loss of life at all costs. He had been used to having very little force at his disposal and he had known he must therefore use it or display it quickly. He had acted at once with complete confidence that he would receive support, because the first object of the Government was to keep order.

From now on it was not the first object of the Government to keep order. To the district officer this often seemed in some way dishonest or immoral, but Parliament and the English people were committed to handing over power and to training Indians to govern themselves. From now on they were bound to be responsive to Indian opinion. And Indian opinion, inexperienced in administration, was not yet convinced that firm steps were needed at the first sign of trouble — or, perhaps, was not prepared to admit they were so long as power was alien.

CHAPTER III

DISTRICT OFFICER, NEW STYLE

I. CONFUSED PROGRESS

IN the years between 1919 and 1937, India moved forward like a sailing ship beating up in narrow waters against a moderate wind and a strong tide. Seen from six thousand feet above her, the tiny ship seemed to gain a little on almost every tack and slowly pass one marked reef or buoyed mud flat after another. But from the deck it was not so easy to discern progress, and every time the ship came about there seemed to be hesitation and contradiction, so that she would hang in the wind with sails flapping before she came round and filled on the new tack. It looked from close quarters as though both captain and crew were thoroughly confused about the whole affair.

And so in fact they were. There was confusion between the strategy of the voyage and the tactics of avoiding each reef as it drew near, not only among those who had once been the Guardians, but also among those they had formerly ruled. This was perhaps inevitable. India — to abandon the metaphor of the ship — was proceeding from an authoritarian to a popular government, not by the Russian or French method of violent revolution, but by the English method of prolonged argument and crisis upon minor crisis. Her progress was bound to be uncomfortable. It is not easy for a Guardian who has been trained in knowledge of the good to make over his charge to someone who manifestly has not; on a different level, it is hard to serve where you have ruled.

Everyone in the Indian Civil Service and the Political Service had been brought up to hear both sides patiently, to arrange a compromise if possible, and if not to impose one. The solution was imposed as a rule simply by a firm manner of announcing the decision, occasionally by a display of force, very seldom indeed by the use of force. Everyone in a district or a sub-division did this in some form two or three times a day. Here is an example, from a letter written home in 1933 by a young man in his fifth year in India:

'I have had an exciting and busy week, which I thoroughly enjoyed. Monroe has gone on a fortnight's leave and I am in charge of Lucknow. He said before he went that everything was perfectly quiet and so it was, but two days later things boiled up. The Kotwal — the police officer in charge of the city — came to tell me there was trouble between Sunnis and Shiahs — the two main sects of Muslims, you know. One side had published a poster announcing a speech and a meeting to which the other bitterly objected and there was likely to be rioting. Most of the city of course is Muslim and the sects are pretty even in strength — even enough for both to be ready to fight. I won't bother you with details of the argument. But I talked to the leaders of both parties for hours and at last I got the party who had published the poster to agree to a statement that they'd had no intention of being provocative, and that if they had hurt anyone's feelings they were sorry. They agreed to this reluctantly and withdrew, but two hours later they were back to say their followers had repudiated them. They hadn't done anything wrong and didn't see why they should apologize. I argued for more hours and said that *if* they hadn't meant to tread on anyone's toes — which they assured me was the fact — *obviously* they were sorry if they had. It was only a conditional apology and blackened no one's face. But they wouldn't have it. It was an apology and the others had scored off them and their face was black.

'I saw at last it was no use going on, so changed my note. Very well, I said, have it your own way. Don't be sensible if you don't want to. No public meetings on either side for a fortnight. No assembly of more than twenty people. For the next three days — to cover the time when this chap had been going to speak — we'll have lorries of police dashing about the city armed with cut down polo sticks — thick canes which hurt but can't break a limb — and they will break up a meeting as soon as there's any sign of one. And troops will be ready to move in at once if there's any need. There are plenty of troops here and — I told them — I am going straight to the brigadier to see that a battalion of British troops is kept ready for the next three days. And if they do come I shan't hesitate to tell them to shoot.

'It worked like a charm. The brigadier grumbled at having to keep his troops ready — they were at one hour's notice — and it was a strain on the police, but it all passed off peacefully. They obeyed orders and there were no meetings.'

That particular quarrel broke out again twelve months later and for some years was an anxiety. There was occasional rioting and loss of life. But for the moment it had been plastered over. A temporary solution had been imposed by a threat of force. A reef had been avoided. It was the kind of thing that was being done all over India.

Everyone was trained to this technique. It was the right technique for the local situation, and the District Magistrate who did not do it was no good at his job. But tactical lessons cannot be applied to strategy without modification and when the issues were much bigger, when the Secretary of State and the Viceroy took the place of District Officer and City Magistrate, the technique could not be applied in quite the same way. You can impose a decision if you are staying to work it yourself. But if you have said you are going, you must find a solution that someone is prepared to accept, because someone will have to work it when you have gone. The Secretary of State needed much more patience than a City Magistrate.

But many of the district officers, the superintendents of police and the battalion commanders expected their Government to behave as they themselves would have behaved in a local situation. They were often inclined to call their Government weak because it did not, because it behaved — as it was bound to — with the strategic object in view. No doubt they were right sometimes, but it was not, for instance, weak of Lord Irwin to meet Mr. Gandhi and try to secure his co-operation. It was both wise and courageous.

There was confusion then among the English, who sometimes looked at what was happening 'less with the pleasure of a parent at the independence of a son than with the irritation of a nurse at the crying of a fractious child'. There was even greater confusion among Indians, who were inclined to look on every step towards self-rule as a triumph wrung from the unwilling English. They had not heard, in the districts, of trusteeship, but of the stark and simple word which means rule. No one — reasoned the peasant — gives up power unless he is forced to, or unless he is renouncing the world and planning to live as an ascetic, which the English manifestly are not. Therefore if the District Board runs a school which the district officer used to run, it is a concession forced from him, a victory for the nationalists. If the Congress colours fly instead of the Union Jack on a school building, that is a blow in the face to the district officer. And that Indians thought it a blow made it very difficult for the district officer not to think the same. Thus misapprehension was mutually intensified.

All this confusion of mind rose from the confusion in the situation. Dyarchy was meant to be a bridge from authoritarian to popular government; the Guardians were supposed to be instructing their wards in their art, and both were supposed to be going about their business in a spirit of friendly co-operation. But that sudden change of heart had taken place in 1918 and most of the wards were obstinately refusing to be taught. The district officer was too often forced to consider not how much he could hand over but how much he could cling to, while members of the district Congress Committee did not always think of how they could benefit the district and hardly ever of how they could gain administrative experience. But they did think very often of how they could score a point against the district officer.

No one in the average rural district could picture a party system and an opposition which might one day be the government. No one therefore could separate in his thoughts the government of the moment, the actual human government which made plenty of mistakes, from the ideal of government, the principle of law and order as opposed to anarchy. Opposition to the ruler in the traditional systems of India, whether Hindu or Muslim, is a crime and a much more serious crime than gang robbery. No one could understand why the English had suddenly become so tolerant of one form of crime, and it occurred to some people that it might be worth an experiment or two in other kinds.

Those who wanted political progress — and who therefore wanted to change the actual human government and perhaps put themselves in power — thus found themselves in the same camp with those who were against the principle of government and on the side of anarchy, and also with people who were criminals in the Western sense, gang robbers for their own gain. There were also gang robbers who robbed to get political funds with which to fight the British. In the mind of the peasant and the policeman there was not much distinction between any of them; they were all the party against the government. To such a party the district officer and all those on the side of law and order were necessarily opposed and the district officer therefore found himself forced into waging a kind of intermittent and partly surreptitious civil war with the nationalists of his district — the very people whom, according to the will of Parliament, he was supposed to be instructing and to whom he was, some time soon, to hand over power.

All this was more or less the case in most of the Hindu part of India, that is the United Provinces, Behar, Orissa, the Central Provinces, Bombay and to a much less extent Madras. In the Punjab, Sind and Bengal, and intermittently in Assam, there were parties ready to co-operate with the administration.

THE DEMISSION OF POWER

2. COLD CIVIL WAR

The first years of the new period were the worst. From 1919 onwards for three years Mr. Gandhi's influence was perhaps stronger than it was ever to be again till 1947, and he was in alliance with the Muslim movement for the support of the Khalif known as the Khilafat. Non-co-operation was his declared policy; he had many active supporters, while many more who were doubtful of his wisdom dared not express their doubts. District officers and police did not find things easy; it was for instance difficult to get supplies in camp or to move tents. Forests were burnt, liquor-shops were picketed, every form of government activity was hampered. There was a brief outbreak of political murders in some parts of India.

This extreme phase passed and it would be tedious to try to recount the waves of pulsating opinion which broke and washed back between 1919 and 1937. Nor is this the place to consider the sequence of Round Table Conferences, Commissions, Delegations and Pacts which caused them. Sometimes the struggle came into the open and the district officer was encouraged to take firm action. This meant that he was instructed to ban meetings at which the people were incited to violence and to arrest those who did the inciting. Sometimes too it was his duty to arrest or disperse people engaged in some economically fatuous but symbolic act, such as breaking the Government monopoly of the sale of salt. Often enough there would be opportunity for the display of physical as well as moral courage. In some ways — and certainly to many of the service — those periods when the fight was on were preferable to those which would follow, when the leaders of the Congress would be released and the district officer must make uneasy friends with those he had been fighting.

'The non-co-operation movement,' wrote Macdonald-Tyler, Collector of Kistna, to the Government of Madras in 1923, 'may not ineptly be considered as a form of warfare and certain of the principles of warfare have undoubted application . . . A purely defensive attitude on the part of Government is unlikely to have the effect of deterring the masses from supporting the movement . . .' He goes on to enumerate the methods by which the campaign may be countered, ending a full and detailed discussion with the remark that on the whole he would be sorry if the movement came to an end; its place would only be taken by something worse. And being of the opinion that the efforts of the non-co-operators could often be met more effectively by a smile than by 'the too ponderous operation of the penal laws', he had found that the whole business provided 'a lighter background to the dull routine of a Collector's daily task'.

Until far into the 'thirties, the district officer in most parts of India could usually count on a good deal of support, quite apart from that he always received from the police. Some of this came from landowners to whom Congress radicalism seemed a threat; more came from men who were old-fashioned and simple, who saw only bad men opposed to the Government and were glad to do something to show their fidelity. Here and there, perhaps, one man took a longer view and calculated that the English did not really mean what they said, that they never did give up anything and never would; it would pay to be on their side. There were Muslims too who did not yet see much sense in the Muslim League and were prepared to do a good deal to avoid rule by the Hindus and money-lenders.

Altogether, then, there was backing available in most districts most of the time and the police and officials were unfailingly stead-fast. The bluff still held — though by now it was so thin that it was hardly a bluff at all. The district officer's power was already much less than it had been. There were still titles and gun-licences in his gift but patronage was dwindling. Once he had been able to reward a zealous official or a helpful landowner by making his son a patwari, a clerk or even a tahsildar. But now everything must be done by merit as the result of examinations; what had seemed the most natural thing in the world was now held up to execration as a kind of corruption. In a sense of course it was true that this was corruption; it was part of the whole system of bluff and hikmatamali — judicious management — by which the country had been ruled. But it was, none the less, a saddening and humiliating thing for a district officer to have to explain to a nice old man who had been faithful all his life. The reward you have expected, he must say, will not be paid and in the competitive examination your son will get no favour at all com-pared with the son of a Congress lawyer who has spent his life stirring up hatred and contempt for the government and inciting people to riot and disorder.

It was a matter of temperament. Some people could take the situation lightly; some could remember that it was by the will of Parliament that the English were retreating, not because of a tactical defeat. Many could be friends with Congress opponents, as Edye could, for instance. Maconochie, too, has a tale of a barrister 'who had always been a very good friend', and who 'asked if I had any objection to their holding a meeting and passing a vote of censure on me. I assured him that I had none whatever . . .' That kind of relationship was common, almost universal; few however could equal Lydall's detachment. . . .

'One of my friends . . . spent much of his time denouncing me . . . as a satanic and cold-blooded murderer . . . In the front row of the audience, carefully taking notes for my edification, would be a police sub-inspector, interrupting now and then to ask for a repetition of a difficult passage. Then, the meeting over, the Sub-Inspector would come round to my bungalow with his version of the proceedings. But my perusal of his report would be interrupted by the arrival of the orator himself. . . .

' "I'm sure you'll be interested," he would begin, "in these rather beautiful old Assamese paintings. Illustrations to the Mahabharata . . ." And the small hours would find us still talking hard. . . .'

And he has a story of a political leader — this time on the North-West Frontier — who called on him secretly late at night and begged to be sent to prison. 'I am losing face with my followers,' he said. 'They say I am not suffering for the cause.'

'I issued a warrant for your arrest,' I pointed out. 'Won't that do?'

'No, Sahib. You know you told the police not to execute it and as a result everyone is saying that I am in your pay.'

'Well, so you are.'

'That,' he said with dignity, 'is not the point.' He was in the end accommodated, being led out after sentence 'with a final cry of "Up the Rebels!" and a broad wink at me'.

But farce is seldom really tolerable unless it is played with some delicacy and not everyone had the lightness of touch for this kind of thing. There were honest men with minds too straightforward to see anything but the tactical situation; to them there were no two ways about it, we were letting down our friends and appeasing our enemies, failing in courage and honour. Such men were happier when Congress leaders were in jail and when, in the words of the circular letters, Government was resolved not to tolerate disorder. Others disliked this open hostility because they felt it was getting neither side anywhere and yet they were hardly happier in the intervals when Mr. Gandhi was released and had made a pact with the authorities.

It was not easy for a district officer in those interludes. The English were morally on the defensive — and they had been used on the whole to feeling rather self-righteous. They had been incorrupt-ible, their word had been synonymous with truth. It had once been assumed on all hands that they were just and, within reason, benevo-lent. Now everything they did was questioned. Anyone who did not like the district officer's views would go to the District Congress Committee, who would send a telegram to the Government com-plaining of tyranny and high-handedness. The Committee would conduct an inquiry of their own into an affair which the district officer had himself investigated. They would themselves hear evidence — not always taking pains to make sure both sides of the dispute were represented — and produce a report contradicting the district officer's. Politicians, lawyers, the press, and sometimes, it appeared, the judiciary — all seemed to take it for granted, that the district officer was not to be trusted.

The judiciary, it was true, had always cherished certain conven-tions about preserving an impartial mind which seemed to many executive officers designed to defeat justice. Judges had even been known to hold impartiality so tender a plant that it could not survive a visit to the scene of a crime. But though in its name they certainly did much that to the district officer seemed puzzling, no one minded the judicial assumption that the district officer was some-thing of a tyrant and not much to be trusted; everyone had read enough English history to have heard of the Stuarts and to under-stand English fear of the executive. But that the Congress should pretend to take the same view, should take it so smugly and express it so violently, did very often rankle — and particularly when one was so seldom allowed to hit back.

It cannot be said too often that the cold civil war had to be sur-reptitious, that the district officer was supposed to be guiding and instructing those who opposed him in every act, and that although the rank and file of the Congress movement included some people who did not live up to their leaders' ideals, it was not permissible to say openly what scoundrels some of them were. Nor was it possible to give official encouragement to those simple-minded people who were ready to support the cause of law and order in the only way they understood, by taking a six-foot bamboo pole and hitting those wicked folk the rebels. All this was because of the absurd confusion which had arisen. The whole situation looked quite different from Whitehall and from a district; Delhi and the provincial capitals alternated un-easily between the two points of view.

THE DEMISSION OF POWER

All this time, while conferences were held, while delegations went to and from London, the district officer had his district to run. And apart from people's feelings, the greatest difference in what he had to do was in connexion with District and Municipal Boards. He had, as Edye said, been Chairman and virtually dictator. It had actually been much easier for him to act as Chairman than for anyone else, because in any case he pitched his tents in every part of the district and could look at every bridge and road and school in the course of his work. But now he must be very careful. Everyone who thought there was anything to be gained by it would ask him to put right matters that had become the concern of the elected Chairman; it was not easy to be helpful without seeming to be officious. It was painful — and to some temperaments humiliating — to explain to a petitioner that some manifest wrong could not be righted at once, that application must be made to someone else, but it often had to be done. Sometimes, of course, the elected Chairman would welcome a friendly note mentioning the state of a road or a school building, but it must be carefully worded. It must be clear that it passed on information, and was not a complaint; the Chairman must not be allowed to feel that he was being treated as a subordinate. That was usually the case; sometimes of course the characters of the two men were such that in fact the Chairman could be treated almost as one of the District Magistrate's officers, but that did not happen very often. And sometimes there was continual friction.

The Congress Party was more ready to enter district and municipal politics than provincial or national, because there was more responsibility at that level. But at a time when the Congress were refusing to co-operate in the government of the province, a Congress majority on a Municipal Board certainly made things no easier for a district officer.

The standard of local politics in the early 1920s was often one through which the municipalities of England had passed in the seventeenth or eighteenth centuries. If the factions were evenly balanced, a member would be locked into his bathroom just before leaving home and the crucial vote taken while he was still trying to get out. Or the office clock would be advanced and one party, but not the other, warned to be present ten minutes early. Far more interest was often taken in intrigue, in personal appointments, and in achieving a personal triumph, than in administration. The smaller towns sometimes got themselves into a hopeless tangle, their dues heavily in arrears, their streets dirty and unlighted. Such boards would have to be superseded and handed back to the district officer, who for three years or so would ruthlessly collect arrears of taxation and see that money allotted to services was in fact spent. And then the Board would be re-constituted.

It was all discouraging but it did work. No one could deny that on the whole municipal and district boards were better in 1938 than in 1920. Edye remarked that in the first stage of local democracy a man votes for A instead of B because A has promised the voter's cousin a job for his nephew and B has not. But in the final stage he votes for A because he thinks A is the man who will mend the parish pump. He might have added that there are parallel stages for the candidate; at first he stands because he is a big man in the town and wants no one else to look bigger; in the end, he stands because the pump needs mending and he thinks he can mend it better than anyone else. By 1938, there was an element, if not a very large one, among both voters and candidates in local elections who had got into the final stage.

Far more of a civilian's time was now spent in supervision and training of semi-technical workers outside his own mysteries of land tenure and general administration. Co-operative banks, village forest management, town planning — all these he was expected not merely to understand but to teach. And it was refreshing — if sometimes a little annoying — to note how quickly the devil came to quote scripture. 'No,' said an old and illiterate villager, shaking his head at a proposal made by his S.D.O., '*silvicultural principles ke mutabiq nahin.*' It was not in accordance with what he had been taught — he, who ten years before would have happily cut every tree he wanted!

The emergence of local bodies made one change since Trevelyan had described a civilian's day. Another was the increase in loneliness. Of course, in one sense, there was never any loneliness; no I.C.S. officer was ever very long away from people. But a kind of loneliness it is — though a pleasant loneliness if not too protracted — for anyone expensively educated to be for months together surrounded by people who either cannot read at all or who read only the Ramayan or the Koran. In the nineteenth century, a man came in from camp to the headquarters of his district with a feeling of pleasure almost as keen as the anticipation with which he had left it. He looked forward to seeing half a dozen men with whom he had shared the last hot weather, whom he had perhaps grown heartily tired of, but whom he knew well enough to talk to without any kind of reserve. There might be a judge, a policeman, a canal man, a doctor; he might be tired of their company again before May was out, but he did all the same want to see them after his months in camp. He did after all share with them experiences and assumptions about life that he shared with no one else round him.

In the new India of the reforms, that particular kind of unguarded companionship was much less likely to occur. In a small district — and most men spent a great deal of the first half of their service in small districts — there were hardly ever to be found so many as four or five officers of the old Guardian services—what were now called the Secretary of State's services. The district officer himself was as likely, by the 'thirties, to be Indian as English. There might be a Forest Officer who, it was several chances to one, would be an Indian; the policeman again would probably be Indian if the District Magistrate was English, and the reverse; if anything, there was rather less likelihood of friction than if both were English. Either Forest Officer or policeman might or might not be a congenial companion, but, in the political circumstances, it was by no means always possible for Englishman and Indian to talk with unbuttoned ease. Perhaps the judge or the doctor would belong to the provincial service; that is to say, he had been promoted, after twenty-five or thirty years of toil, to the kind of post in which a young man of the higher services might officiate after five or six years. Of course, there was plenty to learn from the provincial service, and there was plenty to talk about, tales of crime and village life, of successful scores off the Secretariat, of shooting and the ways of animals. But it was not always that there could be wholly unrestrained talk. The provincial service man had seldom been out of India and too often there was a fear of causing offence on one side, a determination not to be patronized on the other, that was fatal to ease and to real friendship. This constraint was perhaps more often present between the two grades of service than between Englishman and Indian. As to friendship with Indians who were not officials, in a really small place there were often none of any education. But it did happen now and then.

Nor was it probable that there would be anything like so much in common as before, even among the English members of those who did belong to the Secretary of State's services. In the years immediately after 1919, the majority of the entrants were Indians; four or five years later the pendulum began to swing back and there were more English, the declared intention being to recruit half and half.

Those who were of British birth had in common one thing at least, that they were all men who had come to their career knowing that it meant co-operation with Indians. But they represented a greater variety of social background than before the war and there had been much less eager competition. There were not so many among them who might have been, as Trevelyan said, fellows of Trinity or of All Souls. There were not so many who had played for their colleges, nor so many who knew people of influence in London. In their early years at least, they often found that there were surprising differences in mental approach between them. These soon wore off and they were soon delighted to meet each other; it may even seem absurd to mention such differences. But the smallest difference begins to count when you come in, from two months in camp, to a place where there is only one other man of your own nationality, with whom you are going to spend six months in a shade temperature varying between 80° and 120°. There may be friendliness, there may even be friendship in such a case — but there may still be mental loneliness.

From the end of the 'twenties onwards, there were an increasing number of young Englishmen in the I.C.S. who felt very strongly that their predecessors had been lacking in sympathy for Indians. 'I belonged to the generation', wrote Hugh Lane, recruited in 1938, 'that thought it was our job in life to live down the land-grabbing nigger-beating sins of our fathers.' After his first eighteen months of settling down, he was sent to Lucknow, where for the first time there was an Indian Deputy Commissioner, Jasbir Singh, a man widely liked and admired; he came of a noble Indian family and ought to have been in the I.C.S., but through some misfortune at the time of the examination had spent far too long in subordinate posts. 'I was soon an ardent worshipper of my D.C.', writes Lane, 'who trusted me with so much and seemed so wise and experienced himself . . . To me he was always a guide, philosopher and friend and when he died, I felt as though I had lost my own father.' 'An Indian D.C. who treated me as a favourite pupil was, of course, an ideal trainer. I would sit spell-bound in Indian Clubs while he gossiped with the strange mixture of types that only India can produce. . . .'

It would not be true to say that this example is typical of the relations within the service between English and Indian; it was a case of a young man happily in love with India. Lane's was a new generation, but even in an earlier generation there was almost always friendliness, particularly between those recruited after 1919. There was usually a relationship which would permit friendly jokes at each other's expense. Indians of Lane's generation used Christian names to their English contemporaries and they stayed in each other's houses. This had sometimes happened in earlier generations — particularly on the Frontier — but not often. There was sometimes a real friendship, but usually a certain reserve. An Indian was bound to feel in his heart that self-government was better than good government — indeed, he might wonder whether a government by foreigners, however well intentioned, could really be good government at all. It was easy for him to be over-sensitive and to suppose that he was being snubbed because he was an Indian, when in fact he was being treated with the lack of ceremony usual to the English. Conversely, he did sometimes feel that his English senior was over-careful to be polite to him, where he would have called Smith a young fool and left it at that. But it would be easy to exaggerate such feelings and probably more typical was the experience of A. D. Gorwala, an Indian who since independence has written of the old service in terms almost too generous to be quoted:

'More important . . . was the informal part . . . of the training of a young officer . . . A good Collector's house was often a second home to the young administrator. He was encouraged to drop in of an evening. Hardly ever was the Collector so busy or preoccupied that he would not have time for a few words with the young man. In addition he might ask the new magistrate to come and have tea with him one evening a week. Almost in passing he would suggest that it would perhaps be a good thing if he brought along any particular cases which were perplexing him . . . . Seated on a comfortable sofa . . . plied with good tea and excellent home-made cake, the touchiness and arrogance so characteristic of the intelligent, inexperienced young prize-winner . . . would fall off like an old garment. Differences of kind or race would sink to insignificance and the young man would, sometimes to his surprise, find himself talking freely, listening with attention . . . pleased at the praise, not hurt at the warning and advice. . . .'

'The young man imbibed standards, sometimes without even being told. Automatically he learned there were certain things one did not do. However awkward the circumstances . . . however grave the consequences to oneself . . . one did not lie. In all emergencies it was one's duty to stand firm. However frightened one might feel, one did not show it. In all one's dealings, the rule must be probity. The throwing of one's own responsibility on one's subordinates degraded one not only in the sight of one's fellows but in one's own eyes. One's work must have preference over all other interests. While one showed deference to one's elders, one was not frightened of them. If one differed, one expressed one's views frankly . . . Thus was built up the morale of the general administrator, that state of mind in which men seek to apply their full powers to the task on which they are engaged, by reason of the satisfaction they derive from their own self-realization and their pride in the service.'

Gorwala wrote these words in 1952 and delivered them to an Indian audience. Perhaps to English hearers he would have expressed more criticism of the old service, but there is no doubt of his sincerity. 'It was a great merit of government in this period [that is, up to 1947] that it neither punished frank expression of opinion from its officers nor even resented it.' And he tells three stories to illustrate this point. 'This, then,' he continues, 'was the measure of some of the men who held power. Is it any wonder that they were well served?'

Another Indian member of the service, a few years younger, Dharam Vir, spoke in almost the same words. 'I often disagreed with my superiors', he said. 'An Indian was sometimes bound to feel differently. And I usually said frankly what I thought, but I do not think it was ever held against me or taken amiss.' And he went on: 'It was curious. We were all men of the same calibre and background. Sometimes it was chance that one man got into the I.C.S. and a classmate into the provincial service. There was not much in the formal training of the I.C.S. The training lay in being given a job and being told to get on with it. But because we were given that trust and responsibility we soon found ourselves ready to tackle anything in a way they — the provincial service — seldom were.'

4. RIOT

With these new preoccupations, the district officer in most of India and through all this time had to consider almost every day one abiding danger. Feeling between Hindus and Muslims was getting steadily worse. Almost anything might serve to touch off angry feeling into riot, loot and murder. As a rule some political incident, something in the national press, heightened feeling and then some local incident, or perhaps the rumour of an incident, started a panic. Crowds would gather, sometimes perhaps in fear and for self-protection, sometimes with the idea of defending a mosque or a temple or of rescuing people of their own community. And if two such crowds met and stones began to fly, the gangsters and ruffians would come out with knives. But an example is best. It happened in Benares in the spring of 1939, but in most of the essentials the same riot took place in half the cities of India between 1919 and 1940. The fact that it happened after the reforms of 1937 did not alter the character of the rioting. I had the tale from R. V. Vernède who was the District Magistrate; he told it me after looking up such facts as he could check, but some of it depends on memory after a twelve years' interval. The facts and the pictures are his; I have done no more than put them into writing. There is nothing unusual about the story; two hundred men at least could tell it. He said:

'There is a kind of situation that just gets steadily worse, but there's nothing you can put your hand on and call a cause for the actual outbreak. Feeling all through the Province had been getting worse ever since the Congress came into power, mainly because they wouldn't have a Muslim in the Cabinet unless he was a Congress Muslim — and therefore no Muslim at all in Muslim eyes. We asked for more police but they didn't come, and we could do nothing but rehearse and revise our riot schemes in consultation with the military. That year Moharram came at the end of February and the tenth day, when they bury the tombs of the martyrs, was about the last day of the month. We had been keyed up for Moharram of course; the police had been doing extra patrolling all the ten days and the magistrates had all been taking turns at the police stations, so that one would be available at each of a dozen key points as soon as he was wanted.

'We had all been keyed up — and I had wondered once or twice whether I had taken stringent enough precautions. Before Moharram began we had arrested some of the main gangsters — one always does, just to keep them out of mischief. It's easy to hold them for a few days as known bad characters, under the security sections. I think now that perhaps we should have pulled in a few more. It was always a matter of very nice judgment but I don't know that it would have made any difference in the end.

'Moharram passed off without any serious trouble and I suppose we all relaxed; we had a few days, about a week I think, before we were wound up again for the Holi festival. The Hindus, of course, are the majority in Benares, but not by so many as you might expect in their sacred city. There's a big group of Muslim silk weavers, all illiterate, fanatically religious and very excitable. It's about two Hindus to one Muslim in a population of not much under a quarter of a million. So in a way Holi, when the Hindus were more likely to be excited, was more to be feared than Moharram.

'The riot came just between the two, just when we were relaxed. It came out afterwards that both sides had stored up petrol and kerosene in their houses; the Muslims were probably the aggressors in the first place but I'm not sure that proves they'd deliberately planned it to prevent the Hindus celebrating Holi. They were after all the minority. They may have just been frightened. Anyhow that's guess work and we never did know exactly how it began.

'I got a confused message about five o'clock on March 3rd. It came at second-hand by telephone from the police-officer in charge of the city, and was only enough to tell me that rioting had begun. I had of course talked things over with the Superintendent of Police very thoroughly beforehand; he was Kazim Raza, a Muslim in the Indian Police Service and a good chap; he was first-class, all the way through, though a bit impatient with politicians. We'd decided we could take no risks — our forces were too small. As far as I remember, we had three hundred civil police, armed with batons, and a hundred and eighty armed police with smooth-bore muskets. I haven't been able to check those figures but they're not far out; not much to control a quarter of a million people in a built-up rabbit-warren of a city, all narrow lanes and little closed courts. In reserve was one company of British infantry — the Berkshires, they were. Since we had so little, Kazim Raza and I had agreed to call in the military as soon as trouble began. I rang them up at once and their C.O. kept a platoon at half-an-hour's notice and the rest at two hours' notice; warnings went out to put the riot scheme in operation and I went off to see what was happening. The riot scheme in its first stage was, of course, mostly orders and warnings; orders to the public not to assemble in crowds or carry arms; warnings to the police to requisition lorries and take charge of all arms in the dealers' shops; warnings to the hospitals to be ready for casualties, to magistrates to get to their posts, to the fire service to man the fire-engine. We only had one, a creaking old thing, but it did wonders.

'By about half-past six or seven that evening we had all the warnings out and all the magistrates and police at their posts. It was clear already that we were in for something pretty bad; there were several big outbreaks of fire already and that of course showed that there had been preparations; you don't usually get arson on that scale in the first few hours. About half-past seven I got news that the fire-engine with its small escort of armed police was held up by a hostile mob who wouldn't let it get near enough one of these fires to take action. I got in touch with the Berkshires and started off for this fire with one platoon under a newly joined second lieutenant. We had to provide transport for them; the army, believe it or not, hadn't a lorry to spare in 1939 for aid to the civil power. So we were in commercial buses, which had been commandeered from the city as soon as the riot scheme came into force.

'We passed another fire on the way; a group of huts by the roadside between cantonments and the city. You know the sort of thing there is near every Indian city; thatched sheds, shops selling tea and mineral waters, the houses of vegetable-growers and milk-men. Perhaps thirty or forty families lived there. It was all one blaze and not a soul was to be seen. Thatched roofs — and dry as tinder in March. It was too late to do anything. We drove on.

'The fire we were going to was in the silk spinners' quarter. It's odd the way the famous Benares silks are made. The silk is spun by Hindus who sell the spun-yarn to the Muslim weavers. That's been so at least since Aurangzebe's day. There was one section of the city where the Hindu spinners lived and worked and all round them were Muslim weavers. And of course it was there the trouble now was. We left the buses in the main street and went down an alley that led us into a close, a small square with houses all round. It was bright moonlight and houses blazing on every side; you could have read a newspaper. But it was like watching a silent film; the flames drowned every other sound. We could see men on the roofs of houses not yet burnt, clear against the flames; we could see them getting stuff out and throwing it to friends below. But all in dumb show. It didn't seem real at all.

'There was no time to spare and it was useless to shout or give warnings. I had settled with the subaltern on the way from cantonments what we would do. If I told him to disperse the mob, he would begin by firing one controlled shot at them. Firing over their heads merely infuriates a crowd and causes more casualties in the end. I gave him the word as soon as we had taken in what was happening. He ordered a corporal to fire one round at the mass of men in front of us who were picking up the stuff as it was thrown out of the houses. It was spun silk on bobbins, done up in parcels. The looters were all Muslim weavers who as a rule had to buy it and pay for it.

'By a miracle that one round went right through the crowd without hitting anyone. But it had a miraculous effect — more like a film than ever. In less than sixty seconds we were alone in the close. There were more fires somewhere behind this close and I went with the officer and a section under the same corporal down a side alley. In twenty yards — no, less; it was barely ten yards — we were in another close with the same scene before our eyes. Flames, moonlight, silence — and dark figures at work against the glow. They hadn't heard the shot; everyone that night was as good as deaf with the roar of flames. I told them another round was needed for this lot and I pointed out to the corporal a man on the cornice of a roof, throwing out bales of stuff. He was clear against the blaze behind him. The corporal was ordered to fire one round and he did; he killed that man.

'There was a stampede. That close was a dead end, though we didn't know it at the time. They could only escape into the houses or out by the alley where we stood. Some went over the roofs, some into the houses. A group rushed straight at us. The corporal didn't wait for orders this time but fired another round at a big man who was brandishing what looked like a thick heavy crank-shaft. I was very glad he did fire; in three more strides he would have been on us. The shot brought him down; it took him high in the shoulder and he survived. The thing he was waving proved in the end to be loot, not a weapon; it was a spindle with bobbins of spun silk on it which gleamed liked steel in the light of the flames and of the moon. The rest of the charge jostled past us or melted into the doorways. We realized afterwards they couldn't have seen us; we were in the shadow.

'News of the firing was all round the city in fifteen minutes. Don't ask me how, but I know it was so by the telephone calls. They were coming in to the *kotwali*, which you might call Riot Headquarters, continuously. That incidentally was one of the problems. We had to find police to guard the telephone exchange and to give protection to linesmen repairing the lines, but we sometimes felt we'd be better without telephones at all. Internal calls on the Benares exchange were normally about four hundred an hour. During the riots they went up to a thousand and most of the extra six hundred in every hour seemed to come to us at the kotwali. Everyone with a telephone could be called middle class and had property to be protected; what was easier than to ring up the police and say a hostile mob was on the door-step? Police would come to see if it was true and that would be enough to keep the gangsters away.

'I went home after the silk spindle incident to get my bedding and re-organize myself with Riot Headquarters as my headquarters. We had proclaimed a curfew of course, but had not had time to make the news known. We hadn't a loud speaker van; there was only one in the province, and — would you believe it? — that belonged not to the police but to the Rural Development Department. That was an anxious night; I suppose I had about an hour's sleep. I went out a good deal to see what was happening, but never very far from head-quarters, unless it was to a known strategic point where I could be reached by telephone.

'I won't try to describe the next four days in detail. We were all the time ludicrously short of men and equipment. For example, we were never able to get a second fire-engine — except for one Heath Robinson affair pushed and pumped by hand — because every other city was afraid of riots too. The man in charge of ours, a Parsee, did magnificently; he had to deal with eighty major fires in the course of five days, and usually in the face of violent obstruction and stone-throwing by the people who'd started them. As to men, I've told you our numbers; with less than five hundred police all told, we had to find guards for every essential service as well as patrolling the city. Corpse collecting, for instance, and the wounded. The people who ought to have gone round as ambulance bearers ran away. We had to find people to do it and protect them as they went round. And with all those small parties dispersed, we had to find men to keep the main streets clear.

'I imposed a twenty-four hour curfew after the second night; pretty stringent, I know, but I'm sure it was justified. That made it possible to keep the gangsters to small parties in the alleys and closes; after that, large parties hardly ever ventured into the main streets and we had very few pitched battles. We did a good deal of bluffing; when all the lights are out and curfew imposed, an ordinary bus with a civilian driver is pretty impressive at night. Lights blazing and engine roaring, we kept them at it all night long, up and down the main streets; no one could tell there was only one constable inside with a stick.

'The night that stays in my memory is the second. They began shouting war cries. You'd hear the old Muslim war cry go up from the weavers' quarter. *Allah Ho Akbar!* or *Din! Din! Din!* they would shout, all together. And then you would hear *Jai Ram!* or, *Har! Har! Mahadeo!* from the Hindus. I suppose we were a bit jumpy by then; I remember Kazim Raza saying to me: "Every time I hear those cries go up it is like a blow upon my heart!" It sounds melodramatic but I knew exactly what he meant. It kept everyone on edge. It was next morning I shut down the curfew and said there would be fines on the whole quarter if there were any more war cries. I think as a matter of fact they were defensive; they were meant to show the other side that there was someone awake and ready for them.

'Odd incidents are still very vivid. I remember seeing a big Sikh come out of an alley in broad daylight, obviously expecting no one there. He was almost stark naked, not even a turban and his hair knotted up as Sikhs have it. There was a strap round his waist and a *kukri* slung on it, bumping on his naked backside. The sheath was broken and I could see blood still dripping from the weapon. He must have murdered someone in the minute or two before he saw me. I drove the car straight at him but I couldn't get far along the alley. It was the wire stay of a telegraph pole that stopped me. I jumped out of the car and ran after him. But without shoes or clothes he had the legs of me; perhaps it was just as well because I had nothing but a cut-down polo-stick. He looked over his shoulder, saw he was gaining and grinned. I can see the white of his teeth now. He lengthened his stride and began to go away from me and just at that moment my hat fell off, which somehow made me see how ridiculous it was. So I stopped.

'A sad thing happened on the fourth day, when an armed police constable, no doubt very short of sleep, saw something move in the mouth of an alley and thought it was someone lying in wait for him. It proved to be a harmless old woman, but he had shot her before he knew that. The gangsters reckoned on police fatigue; they let the whole thing die down on the third morning and then towards evening, when we were off guard and very tired, they slipped out and it flared up again. They incited men from the villages to make for the city, a most dangerous development. But it wasn't a big riot, of course, as riots went in those days. In the old days, yes, but by 1939 standards it was parochial. Altogether, the rioters killed 42 and injured 159; most of those were pretty bad, dangerous stab wounds. Nearly all those were stabbings in alleys when a gang caught a man alone. There were eight cases of firing, two by the military, one of which I've mentioned, and six by the police.

'One case of police firing is worth describing because it shows what we were up against. On the third day, the Benares Hindu University began to join in the rioting. There should have been examinations that day; after much discussion the authorities decided not to hold them and in the afternoon a body of Hindu students attacked a Muslim village on the edge of the city. It was on fire — I think they set it on fire — and people were being hurt. A small party of armed police arrived; a corporal who happened to be a Muslim and three constables who happened to be Hindus. The students grew more and more threatening and began to throw stones. The corporal had his forehead badly gashed and things really began to look dangerous. He ordered his men to fire at the crowd; the constables fired over their heads. He alone fired at them and wounded five students. The rest fled, taking the wounded with them. One was seriously hurt and died later.

'I'm sure those constables wouldn't have behaved like that earlier. But they were so tired that discipline began to fail and communal feeling to show its head. I heard of this soon afterwards and knew there would be trouble. "Police fire on fleeing students" — that sort of thing in the headlines. I held an inquiry myself, on the spot, as soon as I could — within four days. I hadn't a moment before then, though I knew it wasn't the sort of case you could leave. They tried to prove the wounded boy was running away when he was wounded but that didn't square with the medical evidence. And they had a lot of evidence about a tree with marks on it which were supposed to indicate the same thing. If the marks had really been made by buckshot and by the police, there might have been something in it. But there was no doubt the marks on that tree had been made with a penknife — I think the night before the inquiry. It was manufactured evidence.

'There were eight cases of firing and eight inquiries, not to mention the big inquiry into the whole thing afterwards. They didn't blame me for anything except running about too much; they thought I should have stayed more at headquarters. There may be something in that; it's very difficult to get it just right. I'm sure the District Magistrate should be at the kotwali or wherever he makes his Riot Headquarters, not at his house. I'm sure he must go out a bit to see what's happening. So-and-so, you remember, was broke for not going out enough. I had to see how my officers were doing and what the place looked like and above all I had to keep in touch with the soldiers.

'All the reinforcements we had were another company of British Infantry, the Queen's, from Allahabad, and eighty armed police. No other District Magistrate dared spare anything, you see; no one knew when his own turn would come. The evening of the third day I managed to collect a peace meeting and form peace committees of the leading citizens. They were a very ill-matched lot; the Hindu leaders tended to be philosophers and the Muslims butchers. It was often a toss-up whether to put a man on a peace committee and trust him to restrain his own side or to arrest him as a fomenter of trouble. Sometimes we began one way and had to end by arrest. The peace committees helped when the back of the thing was broken, but they were always a nuisance in one way. They insisted on having gangs of "peace volunteers", who often turned into communal rescue parties and made things worse. The Congress party of course claimed to represent both sides, and that didn't help.

'But the Premier[1] was good. He came to a meeting on the fourth day and did his best to back us up — though there was of course a sort of implication, never quite stated, that any good we'd done was by virtue of the Congress government. He accepted, improved and put forward in his own name our suggestion that in any case of stabbing or arson the other community in that section of the city should be collectively fined. We could never collect the fines, of course, but it helped. People at the meeting accused the police of bias and it was then Kazim Raza lost his temper. He was wrong, of course, but he'd had no sleep for four days and he himself couldn't have been fairer. He had all my sympathy.

'That fourth day, when the Premier came, was the second day of the twenty-four hour curfew and the worst was already over. There had been thirty cases of arson the second day and sixty-nine casualties; by the fourth day it was ten cases of arson and only twelve killed or injured. We'd arrested four hundred and fifty or so for looting and arson by then. Next day we lifted the curfew two hours morning and evening to let people buy food and after two more days I lifted it altogether in the day-time.

'That's really all. As a matter of technique, I think the three most difficult things are timing the precautionary arrests, which you make beforehand as a preventative; being in the right place at the critical time — and knowing which communal leader to trust and which to arrest. You need general experience and a knowledge of that particular city. Another most important thing of course is good relations with the soldiers. They are always hampered — from our point of view — by some doctrine based on Clausewitz or someone about the concentration of force. People at Army Headquarters write about it with almost theological passion. We want a line of pickets along a main street to confine gangsters to their own quarters; the soldiers don't like breaking up into small parties which — they imagine — may be overwhelmed in detail. They think it more suitable to be kept in a strength of at least a platoon and marched out against a hostile mob — which is just what we want to avoid. Well, it makes a good deal of difference to the interpretation of their instructions if you know your man.

[1] Pandit Govind Ballabh Pant.

'Subsidiary points are dealing with the Press, who of course want to exaggerate, and dealing with educational authorities, who are not always realists. We had five thousand students in Benares. And of course there may be a Commissioner to deal with. But I was lucky and my Commissioner left me alone.

'It was my only big riot as a District Magistrate. I was in several as City Magistrate, and of course I'd been — I suppose dozens of times — in the sort of situation when one is just on the edge of a riot but by listening to both parties for hours one either persuades them to compromise or imposes a solution. And of course, I've talked riots, both with policemen and our own people, by the hour. Except for the odd way it began, with no warning and no ostensible cause, it was a classical riot with all the usual features.'

CHAPTER IV

THE THIRD STEP FORWARD

1. A CHANCE MISSED

ONE thing at least the keenest critic could not deny. The English had given India a political unity she had never had before. But the English talked of going; there were really only two possible heirs to political power, the Congress, and the Muslim League; they eyed each other with sharply rising jealousy. There were also the Princes, who did not wish to be subordinate to either heir and each of whom had for several generations been bound to England by a treaty which involved obligations for both parties. To settle that jealousy and preserve the estate undivided ought, surely, to have been the first concern of the testator.

Here a digression is necessary. Anyone who has taken part in the administration of British India and believes it was right that the centuries of effort should lead to independence must feel a deep regret that independence did not take a form in which both religious communities could feel secure. We are bound to look on it as the failure of our main task that it did not. But that does not imply that most of the old administrators do not feel a friendliness for both successor states. Most have friends in both; a man who has always been in one province may have friends only in one. But all wish well to both.

Partition however registered a failure. That failure was not entirely the fault of the British, but already it is possible to see where they made mistakes. Probably, though no Pakistani will agree, the introduction of communal electorates in 1909 was the first. The step forward in 1919 was as long a step as was politically possible at the time but surely a mistake was made then in that far greater pressure was not brought to bear on the Princes to bring them into tune with the age in which they lived. They too ought to have been in training for constitutional democracy. But they had not been made aware of the changing times and to that unawareness must be attributed at least some responsibility for the chance that was missed when the Act of 1935 was introduced.

Parliament in 1935 passed a new Government of India Act, a successor to the long line stretching back to 1833 and 1783. The 1919

Act had introduced dyarchy, the step forward with half the body, in the provinces; the 1935 Act went further and introduced self-government in the provinces with another, and rather complicated, half-step forward in the Government of India. It was not the same kind of half-step; it is enough here to say that it provided for a government in which the Governor-General would on most subjects normally — that is to say, except in crisis — follow the advice of Executive Councillors who would be members of an elected Assembly, to whose views they would have to pay a good deal of attention. The constitution was one for which there is no exact parallel, because federal India was to consist of provinces as well as States, the States having a greater degree of independence than the provinces. The States, whose position up till now had been governed by various treaties with the Crown, were not to be forced into the new federation; they were to accede voluntarily. If they acceded, they would be represented in the Federal Assembly.

What would have happened if something else had not is always matter for dispute, and no one can be sure. But here one can perceive a balance of probabilities. The Assembly under the 1935 Act was meant to provide an elected body in which some compromise would have been essential between the different interests, because no one interest would have been able to dominate the others. Sikhs, land-holders, women, Christians, labour — all were to be represented as well as the three big blocks of the States, the Muslims and the Hindus. There were 250 seats for British India and 125 for the States; of the 250, only 86 were general constituencies, open to any candidate. The party overwhelmingly in the majority in the country — which was the Congress — might win every one of those 86 and be faced by a solid block of 82 Muslims; they might, of course, win more than half the special seats, those reserved for women, labour, commerce and the rest. Though it would not be at all easy, they might get a majority in the house so long as the States were not there. But if the States came in with their 125 seats, whatever British Indian party was in a majority would have had to make a bargain with a body of opinion likely to be distinctly conservative.

The Congress Party might well have refused to come into such an Assembly and that might have spoiled the Federation. All the same, there was here a chance, perhaps the only chance, of unity. It brought the States much closer to the fabric of India than ever before and provided thereby a flywheel of conservative opinion encouraging to the Muslims, who might have reflected that it would be difficult in such an Assembly for the Congress to carry an outrageous measure against them. What was much more important, the Act if fully implemented would have started a federal government of a kind, and the burden of proof would have rested firmly on anyone who proposed to disrupt it. Everyone was suspicious, but it might have worked if it had been tried. Everything however depended on the Princes — not because they were the Princes, but because the federal part of the Act did not come into operation unless they acceded. And they had to be brought in; they had to be coaxed, persuaded or driven. Their status had been frozen since 1858 and few of them saw any reason to regret it.

Picture, then, a Viceroy who in 1935 firmly believed that the declaration of 1917 was the will of England and who wished above all things to carry it out, who believed wholeheartedly in the Federation and in the Act of 1935. Such a Viceroy, peering into the future, would surely at once perceive that it was essential for the Princes, if they were to preserve their States at all, to make a bargain with the heirs to British power. He would surely warn them in the strongest terms that the English would not permit the unifying work of two centuries to be wrecked. They would leave no loose ends when they went. The Princes would have no chance of independence and the terms on which they would be permitted to come into the Federation on that day of wrath would certainly not be so good as those now offered.

Such a message would not be easy to deliver. But picture a Viceroy with humour and courtesy, with insight and understanding of another's point of view and a core of hard realism to the whole, the kind of man who can tell unwelcome truth without giving offence because he likes the man he is talking to and shows his liking. Such a man might have brought the Princes into the Federation and might — but it is only a dream — have preserved the unity of India.

There had been plenty of men fit for this task in the history of the British in India. Nor was the breed now extinct. The Guardians themselves were debarred, by a convention usually justified, from the supreme post, but one of them, specially empowered, might have carried out the task on behalf of a Viceroy temperamentally unfitted for it. There was more than one man who could have done it if given a free hand and yet backed heart and soul by the Viceroy, if known to be speaking as his mouth, if encouraged by him to be ruthless in the substance, but not the manner, of what he said.

All this however is fantasy. Nothing could be further from the reality of the personalities and of what actually happened. It is too soon, of course, to make a final judgment. The papers are not yet available; one can judge only by outward actions, public utterances, hearsay and impressions, crude unmatured material for history, still fermenting in the vat.

But, judging as one can, it seems that the advice Lord Linlithgow received was formally impeccable and that intellectually he was wholly convinced of the need for haste. There are things left unsaid however in all advice, wishes, perhaps below the level of conscious-ness, which can make themselves felt. However that may be, one is conscious in the sequence of events of a lack of warmth and urgency. It is less easy to be sure whether it lay in the Viceroy, in the advice he received from the Political Service, in the control of the India Office, or in all three.

For many years now, the Political Service had been recruited two-thirds from the Indian Army and one-third from the Indian Civil Service. They were picked men, picked from picked men. The Service presented the possibility of a career which, as Lord Curzon had said, might be as fascinating as any the history of the world could offer. But the kind of service Lord Curzon had in mind was mainly on the foreign side; there were not, in theory, two branches but in practice once a man had been a certain time in the States he became Political rather than Foreign, he tended to stay among the States. That was something different from service in the Persian Gulf or on the Frontier. In this narrower sense, in the States, political service usually involved less toil at gritty detail than life in a district. There were exceptions, of course, and certain men were always being moved to places where there was detailed work to be done. But for most of them, and for most of the time, the very nature of the rela-tionship with the States dictated a life calmer and less harassed than a district officer's. The Resident did not administer; he was in the State to guide, to advise, to suggest. The less directly he interfered the better. He needed rare qualities; he must not let leisure degener-ate into idleness nor forbearance into indifference. There were many great men among the Residents, men who wisely and gently guided the rulers of the States to which they were accredited. But theirs was not a training to prepare men for revolution.

The political officer was inclined to look at his colleague, the dis-trict officer in British India, with a touch of patronage, as a dull dog and perhaps not entirely a social equal. The district officer gazed back with a spice of envy at a life usually more pleasant and picturesque than his own, but with a certain grim pity, too, for one who had — as it seemed to him — deliberately chosen less work and a less arduous responsibility. The political officer was perhaps less inclined to talk shop than his colleague in British India; it would be fair to picture him as usually more amiable and agreeable, more often witty and an excellent companion. But there certainly were some political appointments in which it would have been eccentric to work after lunch; there were many political officers who had never dealt with a riot. If there was more consciousness among them of all the coloured diversity of India, of the poetic reality of a past living in the present, there was perhaps less awareness of the political reality of a future clamorous for recognition. It was, in short, more common among political officers than in the administrative service to find a tendency to complacency with things as they were, a certain cynicism as to political progress.

It was no doubt a mild and agreeable cynicism, wittily expressed, and pleasant to listen to, directed with classical good taste to human destiny in general and in particular to the destiny of India as a democracy. It was backed, too, by genuine feeling on a valid point. Political officers had noticed that the peasants in the States, though they might be poorer, usually seemed to be happier than in British India. Most political officers had come to find in the States much that they liked and admired. Many genuinely did not want the States changed and for reasons admirably altruistic. Cynicism, then, combined with genuine conservatism in a feeling perhaps not often explicitly stated; it had been a comfort to remember all through these difficult years that even if democratic experiments in British India went wrong, there was an autocratic reserve of power to fall back on in the States.

The Political Service were clear enough intellectually that change had to come and that the Princes must be advised to come quickly into the house while there was a house to come into. But they had spent all their lives considering each Prince's treaty, his exact degree of precedence; they liked the Princes as a rule, they liked the States they could not help sympathizing with the men they argued with.

The influence of the India Office was different. Of course the India Office was not really at all like the picture of it framed by most officers in India, a place of cobwebbed and shady corridors, where life stirred only drowsily, like a hedgehog awakened from winter sleep, where the *élan vital* had given up all hope and men thought only in terms of files, reminders and reasons for inaction. No one who had met Sir Findlater Stewart could preserve that picture. But that the con-

sideration of legal forms and constitutional precedent, the elaborate
enumeration of possible dangers, took a high place among the functions which the India Office carried out, its warmest defenders would
agree. It put forward in fact the kind of views which it is proper for
a solicitor to put; but it was also in control, and a business managed
entirely by solicitors is likely to proceed with caution.

A Viceroy ruled whose most loyal friends would not claim that he
had a gift for establishing personal relations quickly. His advisers in
the Political Service saw the need for haste and stated it without
hesitation, but their advice was delivered against a background of
personal regret for what must be lost if it was taken. And from the
India Office came counsel that was sombre with caution and legal
exactitude. Five men, all of proved ability, were chosen to convince
the States. But they were hampered in what they did by clumsy
machinery and quite obviously they did not get instructions as whole-
hearted and as ruthless as they needed. They were sent round to
deal with the States one by one; they were to discuss with each State
its treaty rights and obligations; they met everywhere objections,
bargaining points, conditions for coming in. The situation was, it is
true, extremely complicated because of the variety of the treaties.
And it was, of course, in the end, the Princes' own fault; they had
been warned, they had had their chance. But it is difficult to resist
the feeling that they were warned in a voice so cold and impersonal,
so muffled with historical exactitude and legal complications, that
they were virtually invited to bargain and wait and stand out for
better terms.

2. UNDER THE CONGRESS

Federation never came into being and thus one chance of preserving unity was missed. The Princes and the British share the blame
for this chance missed; for the other it is impossible to blame anyone
but the Congress Party. Their mistake too may well have been due
more to pedantry — an insistence on a theory — than to malice.

Provinces became self-governing on April 1st, 1937, and in the
Hindu provinces the Governments which — after a short interlude —
rather hesitatingly took office were Congress Party governments. The
Congress claimed to be the only national party and to represent the
whole of India, even those who did not agree with them. The Muslim
League on one side, the Hindu Mahasabha on the other, were, the
Congress believed, communal organizations, narrow-minded and

fanatical, out of tune with the new secular state. The Congress would include Muslims in their Cabinets, yes, by all means. But not communalists, not men determined to represent only their own community. Only Congress Muslims need apply.

Congress Muslims of course were anathema to the Muslim League, who believed that Muslims should represent Muslims and who could not accept the ominously totalitarian doctrine of the Congress. So the split grew, and the hope of unity fell back.

In the districts, the change of government was viewed by the former Guardians with feelings resigned and wary. On the whole, however, the change proved less startling than might have been expected. Officers had been used for some time to a provincial Government which, though not responsible, was at least responsive to public opinion, and which in composition had been largely Indian.

A scene still vivid in the memory is the installation of an Indian Governor, the Nawab of Chhatari, in 1933. It was in April and already hot; light and air were carefully excluded from the Council Chamber. In the half darkness, the new Governor advanced to take the oath, a tall and imposing figure in white breeches and silk stockings, resplendent with gold lace and sword. He was a man who would have been judged handsome in any company in the world. He was followed by his Council, three Indians and one Englishman. The Chief Justice awaited him on the dais in scarlet robes and white wig; he too was an Indian. The formal archaic words of the oath were read by the Judge and repeated by the Governor in tones slightly alien to an English ear; among the cocked hats and morning coats of the spectators, more than one man must have wondered with what feelings a Roman official heard his language used by some such chief as Cogidumnus of Sussex, who was styled *Legatus Augusti in Britannia*.

The old government had usually included three Indians to two English; both had as a rule been inclined to meet Congress objections, when they could, by anticipation. And the Congress in office found at once, as any opposition is bound to, that proposals which had seemed easy enough from the other side of the house now presented all kinds of difficulties. The change therefore proved in fact to be, from the point of view of most districts, not very much more terrible than a change from Conservative to Labour in Great Britain.

For the Governor and the Chief Secretary of course it was from the start much more difficult than that. Both were met at every turn by suspicion; Congressmen had worked themselves into a state of

mind when they believed that to uncover the nakedness of government would be to reveal a tangle of writhing monstrosities. Finding
few monstrosities, they felt sure they were being deceived. The
Governor had the heavy burden of discretionary powers which he
must use only as a last resort. It was only by persuading the Congress
that these powers might never need to be used that he had induced
them to take office at all, yet he had responsibilities which might force
him to use them. He must then be a constitutional monarch relying
on confidence and friendly advice, but his advice must be given to a
Cabinet who suspected him all the time of having a whip up his
sleeve — as in fact he had.

The Governor was a constitutional monarch and the head of the
services; he was regarded as their one certain protector. Yet his
advisers wished to introduce a special tax which was aimed directly
at their own servants as an indirect way of reducing their salaries,
while to begin with every adherent of the Congress Party thought it
was now within his powers to give orders to the district officer.

The Governor usually found his Cabinet ready enough to support
executive authority when disorder began. Indeed, he had as often as
not to restrain them. 'Why don't they shoot sooner?' was the question
one Governor was constantly asked by his Premier. But he found the
same Premier most reluctant to prosecute for speeches which to an
Englishman would seem direct incitements to riot.

The Chief Secretary was the channel through whom the orders of
the Government were conveyed to their officers. He was traditionally
the source of postings and transfers; to most district officers he was in
fact the Government. He had now to serve a body whose basic
assumptions on almost every point were exactly opposite to those in
which he had been brought up. He had been taught, for instance,
that the district officer was in the last resort responsible for his district, must be given a wide discretion and where possible supported.
And the Chief Secretary usually knew the administrator very well
and just what his words meant. But the new Government began with
a feeling of distrust; they suspected that the district officer was more
concerned about maintaining his own prestige than about the welfare
of his subjects.

The Chief Secretary therefore found himself engaged in continual
remonstrance on account of district officers, still more on account
of officers of the provincial services. There were some of these who
had been regarded by the old Government as particularly trustworthy
because they had not been afraid to give sentences to men who were

supporters of the Congress. Were they now to be overlooked for promotion and good districts, were men to go over their heads whom the late government had regarded as unreliable dabblers in politics? Every Chief Secretary must decide how far he should go in their protection. The new Government might wish to be fair but their conception of fairness was not always the same as his.

It worked, somehow or other. There was enough Congress idealism and desire to be fair, there was enough British goodwill to the new Government, to keep it moving. One example will illustrate better than generalizations the odd dilemmas that arose, and the way the machinery was kept moving. It is reluctantly I choose an experience of my own, but I have heard no story more to the point.

I was posted to Garhwal as Deputy Commissioner in November of 1936; it was the district I had wanted above all others and I was very happy to be there. The first impression might well have been that things had hardly changed since the days of Mr. Traill; it was still three days of normal marching into the hills — about forty miles — between any road fit for wheeled traffic and the headquarters of the district; it was more than twenty days' march from Pauri, the headquarters — a village of four thousand inhabitants — to the highest village on the Tibet frontier. Everything was limited to the pace of a mule, and there were many villages, even some groups of villages, where a mule could not go.

But that impression could not survive the first day's march. The population was now more than half a million, certainly three times Mr. Traill's; they had cut down their forests and let goats and cattle graze among the seedling bushes; in all the lower part of the district, erosion was serious and the hunger for land, for grazing and for fuel was acute. The people too had changed. They were still friendly, humorous, courageous and simple. But, though everywhere glad to welcome an Englishman, they no longer looked towards the Government with the whole-hearted gratitude that Bishop Heber had noticed when Gurkha rule was a recent memory. They had grievances, mostly of a physical kind, and the first grievance was that they had no road.

There were so many people now that the district imported grain and to pay for it they had nothing but army pensions. A road would make the grain cheaper to import and would make it possible to export fruit, potatoes, tea — crops that could be grown much better than in the plains, but which now must go down on the backs of mules, so that their cost was trebled before they reached the railway.

But the road meant more than that; it had become a philosopher's stone, the elixir of life, and when it was built, both women and ewes would bring forth more plenteously, the morning star would sing and the hills skip with joy.

The District Board had asked the old Government to build a road. The Government had instructed their Public Works Department to prepare an estimate. Their estimate was so high that the Government turned down the project; they could not afford it. There were not ten people in the district who understood the idea of a change of government, but there were plenty who understood the idea of voting for someone who would represent their grievances. The election in the early spring of 1937 was fought by the Congress on a simple platform, of which the main plank was the road. As the other side had no platform at all, the Congress candidates were elected.

Meanwhile, however — and before the election — the District Board had decided to shame the Government into helping them. They thought the Government's estimate was excessive and announced that they could themselves build a road for less than one-tenth of the amount. Even this was far beyond their means and they did not pretend that their road would be up to the standard of the Public Works Department. But they made a start. The Chairman added, as a point for my ear only, that he knew very well that, owing to the nature of the ground, the first three or four miles were much the least expensive. But by the time he had got into the more difficult part he hoped that the Government would be so deeply humiliated that they would have to help him.

The Congress came into office and found that all over the province awkward promises had come home to roost. They simply could not do all they had said they would do and it took some time to decide how they should divide what money was available. Their decision about the road was announced at the end of February 1938, after nearly a year's delay. They noted with pleasure the self-reliance displayed by the District Board in starting the road on its own initiative; they would allow it to complete the work and would make a grant of £2250 in the current year and £1500 a year thereafter till the road reached Pauri, the capital. On the District Board's estimate of the cost, which everyone knew was highly optimistic, this would get the road to Pauri in about fifteen years, if the Board was not bankrupt before then. On the Government's own estimate it would take two hundred and forty-nine years. And to the other end of the district on that basis would take well over a thousand years.

As may be imagined, there was some dissatisfaction. But the full depths were not realized at first. I went on four months' leave in 1938 and came back to find the District Board threatening to proclaim civil disobedience and non-co-operation against their own autonomous Congress Government. The first sum of £2250 had not been claimed within the financial year, of which only about a month had remained when the decision was announced. It had therefore lapsed and could not be claimed. The second instalment could still be claimed — but not until the Board had paid the Public Works Department's little bill for preparing their fabulous estimate. At the usual percentage, this came to more than the £1500 of the grant for the second year and the upshot was that on the first two years, the Government's scheme for helping the Board had resulted in a loss to the Board. The Board were annoyed at this and unless something was done very quickly they were going to incite everyone in the district to stop paying Land Revenue, to cut the telegraph wires, and to disobey the forest laws. That was really all the damage they could do in Garhwal.

The provincial service officer who had acted for me was, I think, glad to be rid of this situation. My own first reaction was regrettably flippant. I told him I was a civil servant now; I was no longer a Guardian, a ruler of the state. It was not for me to get politicians out of the difficulties in which they had embroiled themselves by hasty promises. I would do whatever the politicians told me to do, but it was for them to give me instructions. In the meantime, I proposed to go at once into camp and get on with mapping the fields and making records, my main task at the time. I should watch the situation develop with some amusement. 'Amusement?' he said with horror. 'You will not be amused when you hear how the Premier looks at this.'

Of course, I could not really persist in this attitude. The Government asked for my opinion. I replied by recounting the history of the case; from the facts set out it seemed to me inescapable that the grant offered to the Board in 1938 was ludicrously too small, that it had been a blunder to let the first year's grant lapse on a technicality and that it was a pedantry to insist on departmental charges for an estimate the Government did not themselves appear to accept. The anger and disappointment felt in this district seemed to me not only understandable but justifiable and the only recommendation I could make was that the Government should make a fresh offer and a very much better one. I suggested that I should summon the District Board and put it to them that their best chance of getting a road was to make peace and ask for reconsideration. But before doing this I should like to know that the request would be favourably considered.

I dare say this letter was not very wisely expressed; I had been brought up by a District Magistrate who advised me always to draft really intemperate letters to the Government on the grounds that they took no notice of any others. And after a day checking field measurements on steep hillsides, one is not inclined to linger polishing phrases. The Premier, however, took it on the whole very well, recognizing no doubt that I was actuated, like Mr. Pattle in the eighteenth century, by a warm partiality for the people of my district. He replied, in a personal letter, that he agreed in general terms to most of what I said. But I was not to summon the District Board; their behaviour had been turbulent and rebellious and the first move must not appear to come from the Government or its representative. I must not summon them, but the news might be allowed to seep round unofficially that if they withdrew their threats and petitioned to be allowed to approach the throne, there was a chance that there might be a bag of sweets for someone in the cupboard.

Now it is all very well to let things seep round unofficially in a big city, but in Garhwal some members of the District Board took a week or a fortnight on the way to a meeting and went over their knees in snow. It would take a great deal of seeping to reach them. I acknowledged this letter in non-committal terms and wrote to the members a personal message. I said I was writing not as the Deputy Commissioner but as a friend. I had been trying to think what we in the district could do to get our road; would they meet me to talk it over? I gave them a date and said I would come to their committee-room to meet them; in India, the man who comes to another man's house is a petitioner and at a disadvantage. They might easily have refused to come to my court or my house.

They all came. I heard the night before that they were saying among themselves that they would never give in to the Premier. However, when we met next morning, I suggested that we should approach the problem in a practical way. How were we to get our road? What would happen if they destroyed the telegraph wires? They would be cutting off their noses to spite their faces. Once they launched their civil disobedience, the Premier would never give in till they were crushed. But he must — I could only guess — he must be concerned that they should not start the movement. It would be highly embarrassing; everyone in India would laugh at the Congress. Surely he would do anything to avoid that? I could only guess, but it seemed to me that if they would ask him to receive them and discuss the matter again, they would be in a very strong position.

They said they would like to talk it over by themselves. Two hours later we met again; they thanked me for my advice and agreed that there was a good deal in it. They were sure I meant them well. But it was the Government which was in the wrong. The Government had behaved abominably and it was for the Government to make the first move. If the Premier would invite them to Lucknow, they would go.

I sent the Premier a telegram in cipher, saying that I had had a long unofficial talk with the members of the Board. They were anxious to meet him and ready to do so in a constructive and reasonably submissive spirit. They had made the first move. Would he name the day — in cipher, please?

He gave me a date and I told the Board that the Premier had invited them to meet him in Lucknow, when he would be ready to discuss the matter in a constructive spirit. He had made the first move — would they go? They went — and the first thing they did after their interview was to send me a telegram in the kind of terms which in England are used after the Boat Race or a Cup Final. They had reached a satisfactory solution.

It remains to be added that they came to see me, one by one, delighted with themselves and with the world, and assuming that I had heard all about the solution from the Premier, whose agent I was supposed to be. I had in fact heard nothing and did not for nearly three weeks, when I wrote a letter even more intemperate than the first, an ungenerous letter I now think. I ought both in this letter and the first to have been more polite. I ought to have recognized that it was inevitable that an untried opposition should be embarrassed when it found itself in power — and particularly so when it had never really expected power. I was right to speak frankly but I had been wrong to put into my letters one or two barbs meant to wound, things the people of the district were saying about the new Government. They said a good deal which it gave me a malicious pleasure to repeat; it was a change to hear criticism of those who had criticized us so constantly with such smugness and sometimes with such venom — and I passed it on.

When I next met Pandit Govind Ballabh Pant he told me I had been wrong to tell him such things. I see now that he was right; even then I admired him and still do, as a man with much greatness about him, a sincere and magnanimous man with the obstinacy that is required to stick to ideals in the face of the disappointments of office.

The circumstances of this story were peculiar to Garhwal; what is typical about it is the relationship. We, the former Guardians, could not forbear some rejoicing at the difficulties in which the Congress were placed; we laughed at their misfortunes and some of us delighted in pointing out mistakes. But we did what we could to help. The King's Government had to be carried on and Vernède, for instance, conducted his riots at Benares in exactly the same way under a Congress government as he would have done under a Governor.

CHAPTER V

THE SAME INDIA

1. THE TWO SCHOOLS

WHILE Governments changed, the same India went on. In the twenty years from 1919 to 1939, there was a political, an economic and a social revolution; step by step society became more secular, the state more democratic, the towns more industrial. But in the greater part of India the life of the peasant and of the district officer went quietly on. Men still heard disputes under a tree, still checked land records in the fields.

There were still tents beneath the dark green leaves of the mango-trees and the camp might still be pitched by the side of such a road as Hawkins had travelled three hundred years before. Perhaps there was a festival and the peasants from near and far must go to bathe; early in the morning, before the first light, the carts would begin to pass and a sleeper would wake to the creaking of wooden wheel on wooden axle, a long-drawn creak, rising and falling as the bullocks lurched in the ruts, dying at last in the distance as others took up the tale. Lying there, kept from sleep by the shrill chorus of creaking wood, he would hear the peasants singing as they went to the river, men's voices and women's, singing songs they had sung in Akbar's time. Or later, when the sun was low again, he would see them at the ferry, waiting to cross, the women brilliant in their best clothes, apple-green and black, scarlet, deep crimson, yellow ochre and black again, the colours taking a deeper and a richer hue in the evening light.

Or perhaps the river had changed its course and a score of villages had been robbed of their fields. The villagers had made a one-sided bargain with the Government; if the river gave them new land, they need not pay on it till the next assessment, but if the river took their old land, the bargain would be re-considered and they might be excused their taxes altogether. There would be long mornings in the flat sandy ground by the river, when the dew was still pearly and the white blossom still damp among the silver-grey foliage of young peas and wheat; there would be a late breakfast in the shade of a tamarisk bush when the sun was high and the white sand by the river as bright as the water; there would be, perhaps, the chance of a snipe or a quail before the ride back to the tents, and certainly there would be long hours checking the patwari's papers, hearing how Ram Kalan had agreed to let Jodhu use the field for a few years only on condition. . . .

You could still see, in the village where you went to check and to encourage the work of one of the new village committees, a scene unchanged since Akbar's day, the shrine beneath a fig tree, a yoke of bullocks tied in a corner by a manger of mud, a cart with its shaft pointing to the sky. In April, in the level evening light, you would still see the muzzled bullocks treading the straw, a man standing on a platform with hands raised to let the grain fall and the wind winnow away the chaff; grain and straw alike would be palest gold in that warm apricot flood. There might still be one flame-of-the-forest, late in blossom, dusky orange against the sky, filling the air with scent; along the roadside, the *neem* trees, planted in a double avenue by some forgotten district officer, would spread fresh young leaves, their green as delicate as young beech, against boughs darkly contorted.

You would suppose, from a novel so brilliantly and delicately written as *A Passage to India*, that the English in India lived in a state of semi-hysteria, resolutely suppressing a fear that the Mutiny would come again. Perhaps it was so in Bengal, where three district magistrates of Midnapur were murdered in succession; it was not so in the North or in the South. In 1928, Charles Grant, District Magistrate of Saharanpur, was roused from the brief and hard-won sleep of a night in June by someone trying to undo his mosquito-net. He woke angrily to find a petitioner intent on explaining some trouble which for the moment Grant did not attempt to diagnose; he could not understand why the sentry who was supposed to keep watch on his house had let the man disturb him. Then he remembered that he had been kept awake one night by the sentry's boots and had banished him to the stables to guard the horses' corn — something far more in need of a guard than the District Magistrate. He turned to the petitioner who, it transpired, had lost his railway ticket and, being persecuted by inspectors, had escaped them and fled for succour to his father and mother.

In camp, of course, a man slept unguarded in his tent; why should he not? He knew that in every village of his district he would be welcomed with grave courtesy. And in the South, in the intervals of settling the peasants' rent as Thomas Munro had taught them to, civilians placidly continued the tradition of Bignold, turning into light verse the instructions which Munro had issued a hundred years before to junior civilians regarding their behaviour to Indians.

If peptic noises punctuate
    The flow of conversation,
Politely pause till they abate;
No gentleman should deprecate
    An honest eructation. . . .

wrote J. A. Thorne and again:

To passer-by who makes salaam
    Don't raise a finger meagrely
With air of contumelious calm;
But with entire uplifted palm
    Reciprocate it eagerly.

G. H. B. Jackson chimed in with:

In talk, the characters discussed
    Should be, as all agree, males;
If lovely woman pierce the crust
Of studied reticence, you must
    Refer to her as 'females';

and a dozen more. And noting that an official leaflet urged 'the prompt disposal of old dry cows', Jackson wrote:

We who taught the ryot how to grow his rice,
    Taught him how to sow his seed, also how to plough,
Cheerily present him with further good advice
    Re the prompt disposal of his old dry cow.

Thorne, indeed, wrote verses all his life, remembering the classics while he governed 'the friendly folk among the vines and palms of Malabar' and turning Horace into lines with a local flavour.

No need, my boy, to look so coy,

he wrote, translating: 'Ne sit ancillae tibi amor pudori', and continuing:

I'd risk a bet your dark-eyed pet
    Can claim affinity (paternal)
With stock as fine as yours or mine
    Of Judge, Commissioner and Colonel.

Not many would have guessed, hearing in the Assembly in Delhi his composed exposition of a reasonable but uninspiring policy, that he had to his credit the triolet:

I intended a quarrel
It turned to a kiss. . . .

nor his poem on 'The Senses Five', with its echoes of Brooke and
Hopkins, or the clear ring of Housman in his 'Spring in Simla':

. . . And faint the cuckoo singing
From Tara Devi sounds.

Mark how again the season
Apes English clime and bent
And woos with kindly treason
The exile to content. . . .

That men still wrote verses does not prove they were free from
anxiety. And of course they were often anxious, about riots, about
the future of the world. Who indeed since 1914 has been free from
anxiety? But perhaps because they were detached from what was
round them, perhaps because the habit of responsibility usually brings
with it the power to put it aside, they were — as a rule and in most of
India and whatever novelists may say — rather less anxious than their
countrymen in England. There were still *Weeks* in every station of
any size. There was Christmas Week in Lahore, not very different
from when Kipling had written: 'They were picking them up at
almost every station now — men and women coming in for the Christmas Week, with racquets, with bundles of polo-sticks, with dear and
bruised cricket-bats, with fox-terriers and saddles.' There were
Weeks for the polo or the Races, where everyone met everyone else
and 'talked shop joyously'. Everyone, after all, still knew everyone
else, you were delighted to see the man you had quarrelled with last
hot weather, and His Excellency would drive on to the course . . .

Formal dinner-parties were much fewer than in Jacquemont's day
though perhaps not less dull; the guests would always include
Indians as well as English and one no longer brought one's own
servants. In Delhi cocktail parties had largely taken the place of
Dinners and here too the guests were sure to be mixed. But Delhi
was still largely official.

Every year at the Viceroy's House there was a Ball at which something of the splendour beloved by Lord Curzon might still be seen.
There was the scarlet and rifle-green of the infantry, making with
blue velvet and black a recurrent pattern, sombre and gorgeous, lifted
into gaiety by the apricot of Skinner's Horse, by facings of light blue

and French grey, by waistcoats of silver lace and aiguillettes of gold, by the more delicate finery of the women, by the brocades and jewels of the Princes. To the eye, there was not much difference between the guests who had attended Lord Curzon's Ball and those who now wandered among the fountains of the Mogul Garden, in the summer-houses of stone tracery and among the staircases and corridors of an architecture massively polite to a variety of traditions. There were more Indians in uniform and in tail coats; there were more *saris* to soften and vary the colours. The guests had perhaps less difficulty than Lord Curzon's in finding their carriages to go home, and now, of course, the carriages were cars; they drove along spacious uninhabited boulevards, flanked by long avenues of stone lamp-posts, stately, scholarly and very expensive, round circles intended to control a traffic that would one day need control, past the cold statues of the Viceroys, and the long empty processional way, to palaces, bungalows and tents.

There was Christmas Camp, too, with partridges and jungle-fowl and hopes of a tiger in his royal winter coat, with wonderful picnics of cold turkey and chestnut stuffing, cold game pies, and cold brandy butter with the pudding. Still mornings there were too in the cold forest before dawn, every leaf, every blade of grass cold with dew, the air sharp with the fragrance of bruised leaves and of dust wet with dew, the deer hooting in voices shrill with sudden fear, the jungle cocks crowing as darkness grew thin to the East. And there was the mixed soupy smell of elephant and driver, the breathless scramble into the tree above the tiger's kill, the sharpness of dusk when you counted the birds and went into the tents for tea and Christmas cake. And sometimes there was a Christmas tree, but that was a sham because there were hardly ever any children.

Every Commissioner, every Collector, still had his *shauq*, his pet subject, as the rulers of Bengal had in Bignold's day, as Binks of Hezabad had in Kipling's. The district notable who was really assiduous for honour still felt it wise to contribute a hundred rupees to the Commissioner's fund for midwives and the same to the Collector's for playing-fields, keeping twenty-five for the Joint Magistrate's experiments in village bee-keeping. And in fact many a pet scheme which had been the unofficial love of some patriarch of the past was now an honest woman with her marriage lines, asked to Government House and made much of. Brayne's village uplift, once a heresy, was fashionable in the 'thirties; all over India, men were trying to persuade villagers to make dunghills outside the villages instead of inside, to clean the streets and open the windows, to conserve humus and use better seed. Co-operative Credit, once mistress of Thorburn and Wedderburn, had now been wife in succession to Strickland and to Malcolm Darling. And among contributions to human well-being made by man, few perhaps have achieved more than co-operative credit.

Soil erosion too was something about which once only a few faddists had been concerned. When the British first came to the Punjab, they found hillsides which had been kept as game preserves by the kings and princes before them. But the new rulers had been brought up by disciples of Malthus, they had read Bentham and James Stuart Mill; they believed in reducing the burden of government and letting men pursue the greatest happiness of the greatest number. They remembered William Rufus and found it shocking that, for the occasional sport of a few, a whole hillside should be closed to the villagers who lived at its foot. They threw the forests open.

The peasants cut grass, they grazed cattle and goats, they cut down trees for houses, cattle-sheds and fire-wood. The goats gave the seedlings no chance to replace the timber taken away; the population increased and the cattle and the goats. Soon the hillside was bare and once a southern slope in the Himalayas is bare it is subjected to a stress that is severe, varied and continuous. It is cracked and riven by frost for six months in every year, scorched by the sun for three, and for another three subjected to intermittent rain-storms of appalling violence. Not only is the hillside itself stripped of soil, but the rain is lost which would have been stored, by the spongy leaf-mould of the forest, to emerge in springs and to be used months later for irrigation. Instead, it rushes at once to the plains, where the torrents become more sudden in their onslaught and more impetuous in their destruction. Sir James Penny speaks of 'flat-topped stumps and pinnacles standing out as in gigantic borrow-pits to mark the original level of the land' and again of trees from which the surrounding soil had been washed away to leave the naked roots forming an arch five or even ten feet high.

Public spirit did nothing to check the yearly loss of thousands of acres of top soil; little things were done here and there by individuals, reports were made by district officers and pressure applied, notably by Baden Powell, a civilian who for years was Conservator and for a short time Inspector General of Forests, but the Government of the Punjab were slow to move. They did move however: in 1900 they passed an Act which made it possible to resume areas already devastated, to close them to the public and give vegetation a chance to form once more a rich mat that would protect and renew the soil and store the water. But powers were not enough; men were needed to plan a wide campaign and to persuade villagers to co-operate. In 1900, the conception was sterile and negative; it had once been the aim to let people do as they liked; now the first remedy for evil consequences was to stop them doing something. The villagers at this time thought of the Forest Department as enemies who from sheer greed and perversity would not let them cut down trees or feed their goats.

By the 'thirties this spirit had changed. Much hard work had been done, committees had sat, commissions had reported, but the real change lay in the spirit. Now the peasant was urged to protect himself and others; the Co-operative Movement came to help and co-operative societies were formed to establish village reserves of grass and fuel, small forests run by the villagers themselves. Brayne, once a lonely prophet living on locusts and wild honey, was now bishop of an established religion — and if the religion now attracted some humbug, that is a penalty of establishment.

That was the course of events in the Punjab, but not only in the Punjab. In the United Provinces, villagers in the foothills had become enthusiastic about forest panchayats. It was done partly by the efforts of forest officers, partly by district officers, but in both cases by a spirit of confident optimism that had survived from a former period and taken a new and more positive content.

There was then still something of the spirit that had burned so clearly in the 'sixties, when Trevelyan had written of the civilian's enthusiasm for his work. But there was much difference. Then there had been two types of men. There had been the protectors of the poor, such as John Lawrence and in a different way Richard Temple, who had usually been radical in their outlook, hostile to Indian chiefs, busy, bustling men, whom some thought inclined to go too fast for India. And there had been thoughtful, philosophical men, Henry Lawrence, Bartle Frere, Alfred Lyall, who saw the value of Indians as individuals and of Indian institutions, who were distrustful of applying Western doctrines wholesale. They had come to be known as protectors of the noble, because they had often come to believe in some kind of indirect rule through chiefs. Their descendants of both lines can still be traced in the 'twenties and 'thirties; the spiritual pedigree runs clear through Thomason to John Lawrence, to Thorburn and his moneylenders; to F. L. Brayne, teaching the peasant to use a plough that went too deep and increased evaporation. But it was a dwindling line; in the last generation, hardly anyone was sure enough of anything to preach it as a gospel.

The other dynasty too had changed, but it continued, and no one more clearly belonged to the school of protectors of the noble than Harcourt Butler. His had been a brilliant career even before he rounded it off with ten years as head of a province, of Burma twice and the United Provinces once. He was a man of whom many tales were told; he had the knack of talking with easy friendship to anyone and everyone, usually on the other man's subject. He liked talking and he liked people; he was interested. His mind was in some ways more French than English; he was not particularly concerned about democracy or freedom but he was concerned that people should be cheerful and enjoy themselves. He liked Indians, particularly if they were gentlemen. He loved Lucknow and under his rule it assumed in an odd way some shadow of the fantastic air it had borne in the days of the Kings of Oudh. He beautified the city with flowering trees and fountains; he made it once more a city in which people at once thought of pleasure. His principal viziers — it would be wrong to call them ministers — were Sir Ludovic Porter and the Raja of Mahmudabad; the triumvirate were widely known by a rhyming vernacular jingle — '*Nawāb, sharāb wa kabāb*' — that may be loosely translated: 'Food, wine and a lord.' But let him speak for himself; he is talking to the young men of the I.C.S. who have just come to Burma in 1927. One at least of them was sufficiently impressed to keep a copy of what he said — but remember that in this speech Sir Harcourt is on his best behaviour.

He spoke of the open mind, of the danger of forming an opinion too soon or on insufficient grounds and of not testing it. 'There is really no limit to the degree in which facts lend themselves in appearance to foregone conclusions.' 'By inquiry you will get to the facts. When it comes to action, you must think what will be the results . . . What next? is a question which you should keep constantly before your mind.' 'The most important thing is to be accessible to the people . . . to be not an official only but a friend . . . To gain co-operation should be the object of every administrator . . . If you can get anyone to take up your idea and make it his own . . .' — and the flow continues, almost every sentence quotable, shrewd and tolerant. 'It is not enough to do the right thing. You must do it in the right way.' If only Lord Curzon had listened to Sir Harcourt! 'There are few questions which cannot be settled in personal discus-

sion over a cheroot and a cup of tea' — though here one may guess
that Sir Harcourt did not originally write tea. 'Keep principles
clearly fixed in your mind so that you may escape the snares of
personalities . . . Get rid of unessentials in your work . . . there are
generally only one or two points in a case or in a proposal by which
that case or proposal will stand or fall . . . Above all, avoid doing
other people's work over again . . . As regards your superiors,
express your opinions frankly and obey all orders loyally . . . Administration means service. You have to serve the people and the
Government which represents the people . . . and is more the government of the people than it has ever been before in Burma, than it is
in many countries in the West . . . Keep your sense of humour and
proportion . . . the business of Government has been described as
getting out of one damned hole after another. . . .'

It reads perhaps a little like the Book of the Wisdom of Solomon,
but it is none the less true for that. In his own life, he had been open
to criticism for not avoiding 'the snares of personalities'; he liked the
Taluqdars of Oudh personally and was perhaps too ready to believe
that they all behaved as gentlemen in quite the same sense when they
were on their estates as when they were in Lucknow.

> And I tickled the tail of the Taluqdar,
> I tickled his tail so successfully
> That now I am Sir Harcourt and the next L.G.

a jealous contemporary had written long ago. And perhaps he more
than most should be held guilty for that increase in the prestige of
the Princes that was so fatal to India's unity. But that was the school
to which he belonged; he was an *amir-parwa*, a protector of the nobles,
and if the type had grown worldly and *bon garçon* since the days of
Henry Lawrence, it had also grown genial and human.

It is not so easy to assign to the school of Thomason and John
Lawrence the greatest figure of the 'twenties and 'thirties, Malcolm
Hailey. Certainly he would seem in strange company with Brayne;
in administration, his heart did not run away with his head. In a
sense he combined the best of both schools. He escaped deliberately
from Simla and the Government of India in order to get back to the
fields and settlement; he became Colonization Officer in the Shahpur
District, putting peasants on to the squares of new land reclaimed by
irrigation from the desert. Brought up then in the Punjab school,
by the time he was Chief Commissioner of Delhi he had the plough
and the bullocks, the threshing-floor and the corn-bin, before him in

all he did. They were always there in the blood of his brain. But the brain was too clear, the grasp of detail and principle too tenacious, to let the figure of the peasant blot out everything else. Realism and common sense made the picture he looked at as clean, as detailed as a Dutch interior. It was no doctrinaire liberalism that made him support Lionel Curtis's proposals in 1917, but a shrewd perception that educated opinion is bound to spread to the public and that public opinion cannot be fought indefinitely on behalf of a benevolent democracy seven thousand miles away. Minute, industrious attention to detail, the sudden revealing glimpse of the whole — to describe his mind is to describe the ideal scholar or lawyer.

It sounds inhuman, but it was not, because with a commanding intellect and a commanding presence went humility and humour and the hall-mark of a good Indian Civilian, the power to let another man do his own work. 'You will have a trying day tomorrow,' he said when Chief Commissioner of Delhi to the District Magistrate. 'You will be on the alert all day and will probably have a riot. But I have discussed all your arrangements and I approve of them. One embarrassment at least you shall be spared. I am going fishing.' That could have been said in no other service. And one evening in Lahore when he was Governor, he escaped from the A.D.C.s and went for a walk by himself in the pouring rain with his dog, taking no mackintosh because it was too hot and letting his shirt and shorts get soaked. He saw a procession pass, peaceful but in protest about something, shouting slogans; wondering how the police really dealt with such a gathering, he joined it. Nothing happened, but it was with delight that he read next day in the police report that at such-and-such a spot and such-and-such an hour the procession was joined by 'a disreputable European with a dog'.

He governed the Punjab for four years and the United Provinces, the highest post in the service, for six. He could govern a province with firmness and restore order, keeping exactly to the narrow way that avoids a pedantic legalism on one side and on the other a cynical connivance at brutality; he could at the same time preside over a Committee with a genial, an almost paternal, indulgence. He knew individuals — indeed, he made notes as it were with his left hand while he talked to them and wrote up his notes afterwards into a gigantic Who's Who for each of his two provinces — yet he was never caught in the 'snare of personalities'. He will be remembered as a Governor; if he had not been a Governor, he would be remembered for the outstanding grasp of constitutional principle which he showed in the discussions before the Act of 1935. And if for none of these things, he would be remembered for the work of scholarship on Africa which he undertook after retirement, nothing less than to make himself an expert on every aspect of the life of a new continent.

But he is not an easy man to write about. Whoever tries is faced with the difficulty which confronted the biographer of Bartle Frere. You cannot find a fault; there is no dark shading to bring out the high lights. And if the portrait seems flat, it cannot be helped; one can hardly expect a man to cultivate vices for the benefit of his biographer.

2. THE SAME FRONTIER

There were still men of stature then in the 'thirties. Another constant was the Frontier. Here the tribes were still treated like tigers in a national park. They could kill what deer they liked in the park; they risked a bullet if they came outside and took the village cattle That had been the position in 1900 and it was still a fair description in 1947.

Some Frontier officers are inclined to speak as though there was a change of principle in the development of *khassadars*, or tribal police, after the Kaiser's War. The khassadars were servants of the tribe, not of the Government; they were ordered by the Government to guard a stretch of road, a pass, or an officer but they acted on behalf of the tribe. They were responsible to the tribe — and for the tribe; if the tribe misbehaved, the Government could dismiss the khassadars even though as individuals they were blameless. This was different from the old system of Sandeman; his levies were governed by a contract between the Government and the individual. The *khassadari* dues were considerable — a khassadar received a good deal more than the wages of a sepoy in the Indian Army — and although the individual's khassadari was paid to him direct, in practice each man's pay was divided and sub-divided into complicated fractions and the whole tribe was hit when payment was withheld.

To an outsider, however, it does not seem a change of principle. It was traditional, throughout India, to employ members of criminal tribes to guard property. It worked well enough; you became a patron of the tribe and the watchman directed intruders to someone else's house. But it was, all the same, blackmail, and that word becomes no less ugly if the watchman is responsible to the tribe instead of to the householder. Indeed to most people this arrangement would seem to recognize the real nature of the payment more frankly.

Life on the Frontier still had an immense appeal. No one suffered more continuously than a Frontier officer from that slight mental derangement that afflicted every officer throughout India more or less. Lydall noticed it in himself when he came back from a tour among Assamese headhunters to the company of planters. He found he could not join in their conversation at all; random thoughts and pictures came to his mind from the world he had left, where it mattered supremely if a hare crossed your path from left to right or the reverse. Everyone knew the feeling, when he first came back from camp and stared in astonishment at the cold unnatural pallor of his own face in the glass. With most people it wore off and soon it was that other world of bullocks and moneylenders that came to seem like shadows on the wall of a cave. But to some Frontier officers, the *jirga* and the bloodfeud were always the reality, the club and the polo tournament the shadows.

It was the opinion of the Mahsud tribesman, wrote Evelyn Howell — and he added that it was an opinion not altogether on the subconscious plane — that a civilization must surely be designed to produce a fine type of man and must be judged by its success. By this standard, their own social order, bloodfeud and all, must surely be allowed immeasurably to surpass that of India, with its lawcourts and its assemblies. 'Therefore let us keep our independence and have none of your law . . . but stick to our own customs and be men like our fathers before us.' And to this plea the writer, 'after prolonged and intimate dealings with the Mahsuds', was inclined to agree.

It was the opinion of almost every Frontier officer. There were no long hours at an office desk, and although there was always the chance of a bullet and often a good deal of discomfort, it was a life that everyone on the Frontier enjoyed. Everyone liked the Pathan, his courage and his sense of humour; far from being aloof, many of these Frontier guardians were, like Howell, half inclined to accept tribal standards. And it was all still oddly personal; allegiance was given, if at all, not to a Government but to a man. Nothing illustrates this so well as the tale of a man whom I will call Aslam Khan.

Aslam Khan was a *havildar*, that is a sergeant, in the Guides Infantry. He had been promoted young; he had his Army Certificate of Education; he was a man who stood well with his officers and was sure of a Viceroy's Commission before long. On one leave his father told him that a moneylender was constricting him — hemming him in, turning the screw, making things tight for him; there is no exact equivalent in English. Aslam Khan went and talked seriously to the moneylender. On his next leave, his father told him the moneylender had not listened; he was constricting him as tightly as before. Aslam Khan killed the moneylender and reported to the police-station.

At his trial — for this was administered territory — the district officer and a selection of his regimental officers came to give evidence in his favour. No one denied the murder, but it was urged that his behaviour had always been excellent and that everyone liked him, whereas — though this perhaps was not part of the evidence — no one likes moneylenders. It was hardly the kind of evidence one would expect to hear in a murder trial, but the Frontier had its own standards. Aslam Khan did not hang but was given a seven-year sentence. In prison, his behaviour continued to be excellent and he was out in five years, wanting a job. Everyone liked Aslam, but it would hardly do to employ a convicted murderer in British territory. In the end, he was made orderly to a Political Agent across the administrative border — in the bird sanctuary. No one would look askance at him there.

It so happened that about this time the Faqir of Ipi announced a personal feud with this Political Agent. The Faqir was going to have the Agent killed — or failing the Agent, his wife, who of course was living in administered territory, outside the sanctuary. The Agent thought this should be taken seriously; he wanted his wife to have a permanent personal bodyguard who would lie across the door of her bedroom with his rifle loaded and ready to his hand. He sent Aslam Khan, because he considered him completely trustworthy. And he was right; Aslam Khan, convicted murderer, was utterly worthy of trust. He guarded the lady for a year.

That Agent was transferred and a new Agent came, an able man, but eccentric and independent in his judgments. The new man did not like Aslam Khan. He did not say so, he did not degrade him or dismiss him, but the new feeling was there; everyone was aware of it. Aslam Khan felt his honour impugned and went over to the other side. He became the right-hand man of the Faqir of Ipi.

It was a personal world then, fascinating to those who lived in it, as utterly absorbing as a boy's game of stalking on the hill. It was still played with good humour on both sides. A raiding gang of Pathans, intercepted on their way back to the hills, found themselves for the moment held up; the pursuing party were firing on them, but were too few to surround them and unable to rush them over open ground. It was stalemate till dark, when they would get away; meanwhile, a sniper's battle began, such as the Pathan loves. But the regulars were firing low and hating to see ammunition wasted one of the gang rose and signalled them the range, as though they were practising at a target. He had after all been in the army himself.

There was chivalry then, humour, and fidelity to an obligation. The escort with Charles Duke, once when he was Political Agent in North Waziristan, ran into a party who fired a few random shots at them. There was an exchange of shouts and Darim, the *subadar* commanding the escort, came to know that his son was leading the other party. 'But the sahib is in my charge,' Darim shouted, 'I shall shoot you unless you go home.' And shoot him he did, knowing he was his son.

There were still Frontier officers in the tradition of Abbott and Sandeman, men whose lives were dedicated to the masculine excitement of this barren unrewarding game. Parsons — all the world knew him as Bunch Parsons, but it was as undescriptive a nickname as ever was coined — had decided when he was a boy that he would go to the Frontier as a political officer. An uncle's tales had inspired him and he went up to Oxford, his immediate aim being the I.C.S., his ultimate the Political Service and the Frontier. But for family reasons he had to leave Oxford after two years, without a degree and with no hope of the I.C.S. He went to the Sherwood Foresters, hoping now to get to the Indian Army, the other source of recruitment to the Political Service; he achieved the Indian Army and with his eyes still on the one goal besieged Simla. Having no success at first, he managed to be seconded to the Scouts, the Pathan levies; it was the next best thing to being a Frontier political officer. It was not till 1919 that at last Simla relented and he became a political officer at the age of thirty-five.

The appointment came too late for Parsons to hope for a career like that of Roos-Keppel, who had been head of the province from 1910 to 1919 and had left a lasting name as a good friend and a bad enemy. What was he like? Rather like a battleship, one is told; a large man with a chin like the ram of a fighting ship, cheeks like the sheer of its sides; but he had been loved as well as feared. He had spoken the language like a Pathan and in the 1908 expedition against the Zakka Khel, the Zakka Khel men in the Khyber Rifles fought their own people because of their faith in Roos-Keppel; when the fighting was over, the Zakka Khel leaders crowded round their recent enemy to ask if they had fought well. 'I wouldn't have shaken hands with you unless you had!' was his reply. Roos-Keppel was perhaps the last man among the Guardians who could in practice make or end a war by his own decision. Parsons, without that career, did leave a name, mainly perhaps because he was so entirely a Frontier man.

He never married; the Frontier and his friends on the Frontier were wife, child and home to him. He could keep up with a Pathan youth on his own hills; he seemed impervious to heat or cold, wearing in all climates — and on almost every occasion — shorts of khaki drill and a coat of the same, the simplest clothes possible, and yet contriving always to look the same trim ascetic figure. Nothing pleased him more than a day spent moving fast over the hills with a few Pathans, young men of the Scouts perhaps or tribesmen, talking to them and finding out what they thought. They transformed his name from Parsons to *Paras*, which means a touchstone; and some applied that meaning to the name; he was the stone, they said, by whose touch truth was known. Certainly he had a look that might abash a liar, the look of a man who belongs to an order, a look you sometimes see in a naval officer and sometimes in a monk.

Not all on the Frontier lived this spare dedicated life. There was another school of whom perhaps the best examples were Packman and Sikandar Mirza, one of the first Indians to pass through Sandhurst and into the Political Service. Both were men who enjoyed the Frontier and the Frontier game in rather the same way as the Pathan; they enjoyed getting the better of a man by a cunning trick, intercepting, for instance, a piece of intelligence that had been bought by the other side, buying it back before it was delivered and substituting something else that would deceive the enemy and if possible mislead him into some mistake that would turn the laugh on him. Both were *bons viveurs*, neither very concerned about what might happen in five years, opportunists hoping to get over the next hurdle and perhaps obtain some amusement. It was Ṣikandar who arranged that a procession which he thought might give trouble should be entertained to tea, quite early in the course of its route, by a party of sympathizers, who had — as it happened — included in the strongly sugared tea one of the most powerful and rapid of vegetable laxatives. The procession dispersed before reaching its objective. This of course was in administered territory; there were no processions among the tribes.

Those are the extremes on either wing; in between came the majority, among whom one man in the last twenty years is outstanding, largely because he occupied a position so completely central. because he was so utterly imperturbable, so tolerant and so calm,

Cunningham had been Personal Assistant to Roos-Keppel and Political Agent in North Waziristan; he really made his name — it is sometimes said with a touch of friendly malice — by never saying a word when he was Private Secretary to Lord Irwin. It is true that he was not a man to speak unless he had something to say; it is probably true too that he never was a reformer nor a creator. But he was something else, as valuable as the great reformer. He was the holder of the balance, accessible, wise, ready to be friends with Mammon if there was the least chance of Mammon conceding a point, trusted, admired and liked by all, a shrewd judge of men. He was in sharp contrast with Parsons, an edged blade, a man of close friends but not without enemies, intolerant of the second-best, a reformer and a zealot. As Agent to the Governor-General in Baluchistan, Parsons set about purging the country of the anomalies that had grown up since Sandeman's day, things everyone else accepted, indefensible in logic or to an Auditor, but unquestioned because they had been there a long time. Cunningham would probably have let them bide. Parsons believed that in administered country the system of trial by jirga had outlived its usefulness; he would have swept it away. Cunningham preferred to let it die its own slow but natural death. There was nothing at all intolerant or sharply edged about Cunningham, who, though reluctant to generalize, would in practice act on the maxim that the best is enemy of the good.

He was Governor of the North-West Frontier Province from 1937 to 1946 and again, at the invitation of the Governor-General of Pakistan, from 1947-48. For the first three years of his time, he had the strange problem of a Muslim Congress Ministry. Everything was topsy-turvy on the Frontier and when, in the 'twenties, the people of the settled districts — not of course the tribesmen across the border — came to know that they might play a new game called politics, they began with enthusiasm. They were a healthy and high-spirited people and their idea of politics was to embarrass the Government. It was easy to form an anti-Government party; what was not so easy was to find a programme of grievances — or, turning it into jargon, an ideology — and someone to quarrel with.

There was really only one genuine political question in administered territory; the Khans or chiefs retained some feudal privileges which were out of date and they were still in a position to exercise a good deal of influence. It was possible to draw a kind of party line between the friends of the Khans and their opponents and the new anti-Government party took the side of the opponents. Sir John

Maffey, an amir-parwa, a protector of the nobles, had made a belated attempt in the early 'twenties to increase the power of the Khans and that had sharpened the feeling. And in villages where that distinction had no meaning at all, two factions who opposed each other for the mere sake of strife would choose one party or the other. In the 'twenties and in that part of the world, the Muslim League was a decorous and law-abiding body; the opponents of the Khans and of the Government therefore chose to affiliate themselves to the Indian National Congress and in that improbable partnership they remained until politics suddenly became serious in August 1947. It was as though, in Victorian times, the Southern Irish of the shille-lagh and moonlighter school had decided to join the Primrose League when the Conservatives were in opposition; it might be a convenient alliance for the moment, but their ideals were different. In 1947, the affiliation to Congress India ceased to be convenient and disappeared.

When this strange party came into office in 1937, they were led in the Frontier Province by Dr. Khan Sahib, a man who had been sur-geon to a regiment of the Indian Army and had not the least personal animosity either to British officers or to European ways. Like the other Congress premiers, most of his views were a good deal modified when he came into office and it was seldom that any real controversy seemed likely with the Governor, who was on the whole a protector of the poor and felt some sympathy with him over the Khans. When difficulty did arise, Sir George Cunningham would ask him round to play bridge and lose a few rubbers amicably, after which it was usually possible to come to an agreement.

In 1947, when the new Dominion of Pakistan was set up, Sir George, who had been a year in retirement, was invited to come back as Governor, being the man everyone trusted. The time that followed he found the most interesting, and also the most peaceful, of his career. It was so much better without the Government of India; there was so little paper, so few instructions. Mr. Jinnah, the Governor-General, wrote to him, he thought, once only. This of course was ideal; every Frontier officer was a district officer at heart, and every good district officer detested hearing from his superiors. With one exception, everything went on just as before; the bird sanctuary was maintained, the allowances were paid. It might be logically indefensible, but it worked.

Indeed, looking back over the fifty years since 1897, it had really worked very well everywhere except in Waziristan. It was only among the Wazirs and the Mahsuds that the system had involved much beyond raids and skirmishes; the new Government of Pakistan solved that problem by withdrawing troops from Waziristan and now lady missionaries found that they could summer peacefully and without protection at Wana, where no woman had been allowed when the place was full of troops.

The Frontier then did not change much in the first half of the century. The Frontier officers — thought Sir George — came to know their tribes steadily better and better, till at the end they knew them better than ever before; but not everyone would agree with that judgment. The administrative border, except for purposes of justice, came to matter a little less every year, but there was no change of principle. There was, however, a change of technique, the introduction of bombing.

There was some argument about this, both from a purely technical point of view and from one which admitted moral and political considerations. And you could look at it either strategically or tactically. If it was decided that a tribe should be punished for some atrocity they had committed in the administered area, it was much cheaper to send a few aircraft than a brigade. There was no painful marching over inhospitable hills, no losses from snipers and dysentery. It was also much quicker and much less preparation was needed. The Pathan on the other hand thought it unsporting. 'A great tyranny,' he would say, shaking his head. 'But if you were in our place, wouldn't you drop bombs?' 'Oh, of course we should,' he would answer, with a merry peal of laughter. The Government of India recognized the unsporting nature of the technique, and — in the spirit in which certain water is limited to dry fly — ruled that only small bombs must be used and then only after due warning. Leaflets were dropped to give everyone time to go away — white first and then, borrowing ideas shamelessly from the Inland Revenue, red notices. That was 'proscriptive air action' or 'denial of an area'; over a whole area bombs would be dropped occasionally for a long time and tribesmen were supposed to keep out of the way and live in caves. 'They don't like it because they get lice,' one used to be told. Another kind of punishment was to destroy houses and terraced fields, but destroying a man's peaceful means of livelihood is surely a punishment in which the reformative element is at its minimum.

Most Frontier opinion held that air action alone might punish but without ground support would not bring an unruly tribe to surrender a solitary Hindu or a rifle — just as blockade by itself had been ineffective. And 'proscriptive air action' was not in the true Frontier

radition; what all parties enjoyed was a brisk fight and then to be
riends again afterwards, talking the battle over and congratulating
:ach other on shrewd manœuvres and well-aimed shots.

Looked at from quite a different point of view, strategically, the
rgument Loftus Tottenham had used about opium applied. The
ocal advantage had to be weighed against the moral loss at Geneva
ind in the face of world opinion, where it was no use explaining that
/ou dropped red leaflets and only used twenty-pound bombs. No one
›elieved it. And to use bombs at all against 'British protected persons'
lid not look well. On the whole, however, neither on the Frontier
ior at Simla was anyone much concerned about Geneva. But there
vould have been Frontier support for the view that it was better not
:o bomb tribesmen at all unless it was really a big affair and part of
general military action. And then, of course, with the gloves off.

CHAPTER VI

HITLER'S WAR

I. TWENTY YEARS OF REFORM

IN September 1939, the period of Reform came to an end and until 1947 war was, in a sense, the main thing in everyone's minds — but in a different sense for English, Hindus and Muslims.

The Reform period had begun with the declaration of 1917 which had promised 'the increasing association of Indians in every branch of the administration' and also 'the gradual development of self-governing institutions'. Of these promises only the first was entirely within the power of the British to carry out and in the civil part of the administration on the whole a good deal had been done. For twenty years, recruiting to the I.C.S. had been about half and half British and Indian; as there had been very few Indians taken before 1919, most men with over twenty years' service were British, and there was therefore still a preponderance of British officers — 760 to 540 out of 1300. And, since there were in proportion more senior officers in the Secretariat than elsewhere, there was a greater preponderance in that branch, 147 to 71. But that part of the promise had been carried out fairly enough, although it seemed to Indians that they would never be rid of the English altogether. They were still coming, 'wave on wave', as Burke had said, and it would be thirty years or more before the last of them retired. Transfer to Indian hands had been carried out much more thoroughly in the Forest Service, in the Public Works Department, and in the services under Provincial Ministries, rather less in the Police. Of the Police and Indian Civil Service it was said that it would not be safe to make them entirely Indian; they were a steel frame, necessary to keep the whole together. That and much more that was said in England undid much of the good of what had been done.

Among the Indians of the I.C.S. were men of the highest calibre. No civil service in the world could hope for abler men than Bajpai, Hydari, Trivedi, H. M. Patel, Gorwala, and others. They were — not unnaturally — a little more like civil servants in England than the old Guardians had been; pigsticking and shooting seldom played much part in their lives. They were more often townsmen in their outlook and when they thought of the daily labourer were perhaps more inclined than their British forebears to think of the industrial labourer; they were perhaps less sympathetic with the peasant and certainly less sentimental about him. In districts they were sometimes a trifle more high-handed. But the difference between English and Indian was really less than the gulf between the officer who had been in a district all his life and one who had served even for a short time with the Government of India; there a real difference of outlook arose. Between Englishman and Indian, over work there was little difference; how often, for example, did one hear from military officers, who had hardly ever before met an educated Indian, high praise of Mohammad Ali, now Finance Minister of Pakistan, once a Deputy Financial Adviser in Military Finance — the natural and as it were hereditary enemy of every soldier! Good-humoured and humorous, wise, friendly and likeable, he carried out a task as unpopular as a dentist's or an Income Tax collector's and was liked, admired and respected in spite of it. And Trivedi, smoking the foulest of cheroots and saying, 'I tell you, work is its own reward' — no one could have wished for a more loyal or a more able chief. Hydari, too, son of Sir Akbar Hydari of Hyderabad, uniformly cheerful, tolerant, shrewd — no one could be better fitted to be a constitutional Governor. He went on to be Governor of Assam and Trivedi to Orissa, the East Punjab and Andhra.

Whether in the districts or anywhere else, there was nothing at all between the best English and the best Indians; there was more difference in the tail on both sides. Whereas the Englishman whom no one could call brilliant would sometimes become a picturesque eccentric or a conscientious plodder, there had been rather more Indians who were definitely misfits. That was probably because the method of selection was not yet quite right; there was material in India. Indeed, it was a true criticism of the system that human material was wasted because if a man just missed getting into the I.C.S. he would take a very long time to catch up. Any time in the last thirty years, in one district out of three, you might find a young man who might well have been in the I.C.S. struggling to rise to the rank of tahsildar. When that was achieved there would be another long struggle until with twenty-five or thirty years service he would find himself where his schoolfellow had been in his second year.

On the whole, then, the first part of the promise had been carried out, at least until the third step forward, the stage of the Act of 1935. Then surely it would have been wise to stop British recruitment and show India — as nothing else could have done — that England meant to keep her word. Still, what had been done was well done. The second part of the promise, the gradual development of self-governing institutions, had not been so successful. For the greater part of the twenty years, there had been no co-operation at all from the largest political party. In the last three years, that party had accepted power, doubtfully and grudgingly, and had learnt a great deal; there was certainly more clear thinking on painful subjects among them than there had once been and many eyes had been opened among their supporters. Lane, recruited in 1938 in the last batch but one, had been a warm well-wisher of the Congress ministry; he wrote that, many months before they resigned, the Indian Deputy Commissioner to whom he had given such admiration and devotion had become disillusioned, 'as he discovered how much the Congress Ministers and still more the Parliamentary Secretaries and Members tried to use district officers to further private or political aims. By the time they came to resign there was little that he could find bad enough to say about them. This from an Indian who had reputedly been posted to Lucknow as a slap in the face to the British was doubly impressive. . . .'

Progress had all the same been made by 1939. The Congress were far better equipped, when they came to take full responsibility, than they had been in 1937 — simply because they had more experience. There was improvement by 1939 in local government, Municipal Boards, District Boards and village committees. In the Punjab, where the Muslims were just more numerous than Hindus and Sikhs together, a coalition had been formed, on the whole a conservative body, which included all three communities and whose aim was to maintain the unity of the Punjab and avoid a party division along purely religious lines. In Madras, the ministry had been a marked success. But everywhere the progress so hardly won was threatened by the immense overhanging crag of dissension between the communities.

As for those who had once been the Guardians, they had — most of them — learnt new ways. They had become teachers where they had been rulers; some of them had learnt to speak in Assemblies and had become to some extent politicians. Not much enthusiasm had been displayed for that development; Malcolm Hailey, Denys Bray, Ernest Burdon, and Charles Innes had spoken in the first Central Assembly with point and gusto but, on the whole, those who spoke effectively and with any appearance of enjoyment had become fewer.

It was difficult enough in any case for men with real work to do to feel much interest in an Assembly where votes could be disregarded; in later Assemblies, with the Congress away, the whole affair took on the air of an undergraduate debating society. Criticism was often ill-informed and the same criticism would be put forward again and again, without much attention to facts which had been explained. From the Government benches, speeches tended to consist of facts and figures, perfunctorily repeated and without the fire that a counter-offensive must have. They were too often dull and decorous, appealing to the head of a civil servant much more than to the heart of anyone on the popular side. But certain conventions were happily established; whatever they might say about each other in their speeches, on the floor of the House and on the way to the division lobbies members met with good humour and friendly chaff.

In the districts, things had not changed so violently at any one moment as might have been expected. Over twenty years, however, the change had been great, and above all in emphasis. It had been the basic assumption that India was a poor country which could not afford luxuries, that a district officer must concentrate on the first essentials — public order, the swift administration of justice, the prompt payment of taxes moderately assessed, the maintenance of accurate and up-to-date land records which would prevent disputes. Those had been the four first things. After them came minor matters, salt, stamps, opium, excise, and all the District Board work, roads, bridges and schools. The rest were luxuries, excellent if you had any time or money to spare when the real work had been done.

By 1939, the emphasis had changed and rural development, co-operative banks and village committees were inclined to come first. Since 1919, there had been an increase of forty-four officers in the I.C.S. the total rising from twelve hundred and fifty-five to twelve hundred and ninety-nine. This was for the three and a half hundred million of India. The Secretariat had increased by more than forty-four; the districts were weaker in strength than in 1919. Yet the district officer must add to his innumerable duties the maddening and infructuous business of answering questions, whether put down for formal answer in the House or sent informally direct, the host of subjects included under the head of Rural Development, and the labour of persuading where he had been used to command. It was not surprising that he did not always find it possible to check land records as he used to do, that cases were taking longer and longer to be settled.

That was why to some at least of the service it seemed that it was time to go. Rule of the old kind was running down; districts were being run in a new way, which might be better, but was not the British way and it did not seem right that the British should go on taking responsibility for direction essentially not theirs.

The point was brought to everyone's notice by the Bengal Famine, but long before that it was clear to many district officers. And it was not mere pedantry that made a man cling to the four first things — a peaceful district, in which justice is swift, the land revenue paid promptly and the land records accurate. He found, perhaps, when he had time to look, that a peasant had been brought in to head-quarters a dozen times over a period of twelve months before his case reached even the first formal hearing, at which the points were decided on which he was to bring evidence. Or he would find that someone had been forced to spend all he had to defend his holding against some fabricated claim, simply because the land records were not accurate and up to date. As to Rural Development, most British officers would have agreed that a great deal of what was proposed was admirable if the villagers would do it themselves. Some suggestions however were not suitable to village life at all, and there was un-doubtedly a sickening amount of pretence and self-glorification. It was not — every district officer would agree — that Rural Develop-ment was less than important. But it could not be a success without paid staff, properly trained; the training would take time and cost money; it should not be done inadequately and at the expense of justice and public order. And surely, if the tremendous expense of this experiment was to be undertaken, it should be clear where the responsibility lay.

The system was really out of date. In the nineteenth century it was enough to keep the peace and to see that every man had his own. That could be done by a small number of platonic amateur despots and it had been done admirably. And for such an ideal of govern-ment a foreign government was perhaps better — because more im-partial — than any government responsible to the people. But that ideal was no longer enough. Something more positive was needed and it could only be provided by a government native to the country whose responsibility was clear-cut.

That then was a feeling already held by some in 1939 when war came and every Englishman knew that now the first thing to do was to win it. As in 1914, so when Poland was attacked, there was among educated Indians a wave of sympathy for England and of hostility for

Germany. Indian political opinion almost without exception traced its pedigree from Mr. Gladstone; in the 'thirties, it had been no less reluctant than the British Liberal and Labour parties to criticize His Majesty's Government both for speaking soft words to Hitler and Mussolini and for spending money on what might induce them to hear strong words. Bellicose but defenceless they would have had us be — but when war came there was hardly an Indian of education not on England's side as against Germany.

A great deal of that initial goodwill disappeared in the first weeks of the war. As in 1914, there was technically no need for India to declare war; she was automatically at war as soon as His Majesty was. This was not the case with the Dominions; Canada came loyally to His Majesty's aid and India would have liked to do the same.

For a year, Delhi and Simla had been preparing for war, considering every contingency and in particular what legal powers would be needed. In a year, that technical point could surely have been dealt with and some arrangement made whereby India could declare war herself. But no one thought of it. It was not malice or arrogance that committed India to the war without consulting any popular leader. It was insensitive, no more than that; no one thought of it — and if anyone had, you may be sure the thought would at once have been killed by legal pedantry.

2. THE WAR IN INDIA: THE '42 REBELLION

Whatever the reason, India was automatically in the war and after some discussion the Congress ministries in the provinces resigned. In the Punjab, the coalition stayed on; in Bengal and Sind, ministries mainly Muslim continued to keep themselves in power by the same curious methods as before. In the Congress provinces, the Governor ruled as in the old days.

Many senior members of the service believed that this made no difference to the part India played in the war. Not another shell, not another pair of boots, not another recruit would a Congress decision to support the war have produced. It is not, all the same, easy to persuade an outsider that to have the people behind you in a war can be anything but a help. The question however is academic; from now on, the energies of the Viceroy and the British members of the services were concentrated on the war and many of them were angry and bitter at the Congress attitude. The English view was that during those critical years the people of India had freedom to say and write what they liked, freedom to associate, freedom to go where they liked — all to a far greater extent than the people of any European country and in many ways than those of the United Kingdom herself. For political freedom surely they could wait till the war was over and till it was clear that there was some likelihood of any freedom at all continuing anywhere in the world.

The Congress did not see it like that. Mr. Gandhi began the war with a real emotion, weeping at the thought of Westminster Abbey and the Houses of Parliament reduced to ruins. As the war progressed and the worst had not happened, his attitude changed. The war could be looked on as a European civil war; the deep Indian dislike for Hitler's racial theories receded, and by 1942 it became possible to contemplate without tears a Japanese victory. Japan, after all, was an Asiatic nation and there were indeed reasonable grounds for supposing that Japan would win; Mr. Gandhi was able to persuade himself that if only she was dissociated from Britain, India would have nothing to fear from Japan. In 1942 then he asked the British to withdraw entirely from India. Of the Congress in general it might be said that their attitude was not dissimilar from Mr. Churchill's, though the object was very different. Each meant to win his war and was not particular about his allies — but the Congress war was not with Germany or Japan, not even with England, but with English rule.

The English and the Congress then were intent on their war aims. So too were the Muslims. Some years before, the suggestion of a separate Muslim State within India had been put forward as a debating point in a students' society. The Muslim League had played with it — again as a debating point, as part of the ritual of bargaining. Now in 1940 the Muslim League officially adopted it. Now each of the three parties to the argument had declared its purpose.

Against this background, most of the ex-guardians continued a routine which in a world at war became fantastic because it was so little changed. There was a general rule that none would be allowed to put on uniform, not even the former soldiers in the Political Service. This was relaxed for a very few; Tull, for instance, being very young and a qualified pilot, was released to the R.A.F. and won a D.S.O.; Ian Bowman took casual leave and travelled third-class to Pondicherry to enlist in the French Foreign Legion; after various adventures he was brought back but eventually released to the Army as incorrigible. Even these two were dragged back into para-civil formations in the end. But for almost everyone the war meant simply going without leave, getting very few letters from England, doing much more work, and, if in Delhi, taking part in what *The Statesman* described as Lord Linlithgow's 'laboured continuance, apparently for reasons of prestige, of opulences that seemed unrelished'.

Here, for instance, is the letter of a young wife, herself a teacher by profession, helping an I.C.S. husband to do his work in the Punjab, in 1941. But not all wives worked so hard as this one.

'In Ferozepur we have been on the run all the time without stopping. I have visited four schools and enrolled 110 Guides besides attending a Guide Rally at which about 250 mothers and innumerable children were present. We have given two dinner-parties, one entirely Indian and one European, and been out to dinner three times — twice Indian and once European — to lunch once and to tea four times — all Indian — and have spent three mornings judging ten villages, one morning inspecting a Lady Welfare Worker, one afternoon inspecting Health Centres, one evening at a play in a Hindu girls' school and one at an Indian film. Archie of course has done a whole lot of additional things. . . .'

And again, camping near Moodkee, the site of the battle in the Sikh War:

'That day Archie went straight to his destination by car, so as to have time for some work, while I made a detour on horseback and rode sixteen miles to inspect Mudki and a couple of other villages en route. I was accompanied by the Revenue Assistant and a bevy of *Zaildars* and we had a most interesting ride and I had the feeling that we had got right off the beaten track, for we were inspecting villages which were absolutely typical — not on a motorable road, lacking schools or hospitals to be inspected . . . such villages are almost entirely left to themselves and are still living in the nineteenth century if not earlier . . .' It is not surprising that the writer found she must continually impress on herself the reality of that world war.

Meanwhile, the Japanese overran Malaya and Singapore and the British suffered their greatest disaster in Asia since Dr. Brydon had reached Jalalabad alone just a hundred years before. The Japanese drove them out of Burma, Japanese ships for a week sank what they chose in the Bay of Bengal; their aircraft raided Ceylon, and Colombo was left next morning with two Hurricanes still fit to take the air. There was not one division in India fit to attack. Hardly anyone knew quite how bad things were — but anyone could see they were bad. And to the Congress it seemed that an opportunity had come. Mr. Gandhi had moved rapidly between April and July of 1942.

From an invitation to the British to leave India 'to God, or in modern parlance to anarchy', he proceeded to his statement in July: 'There is no room left . . . for withdrawal or negotiation . . . After all, it is an open rebellion.' And again, 'We shall do or die.' It is difficult to read the utterances and resolutions of the Congress without concluding that they meant in August 1942 to do all they could to help the Japanese by disrupting communications in India and if possible seizing power themselves. They pictured — it would appear — something swift, a short violent campaign. This may not really have been their intention, but that is what it sounded like and what it looked like from the districts.

The English, however, as Suraj-ud-Daulah two centuries before had failed to realize, are impatient of distractions when engaged in a major war. The Congress leaders were arrested on the eve of their rebellion and, within ten days, the back of the thing was broken. But, for a short time, in the eastern part of the United Provinces and in Behar, things were like they had been when the small house at Arrah was defended.

Lines, a young man of twenty-seven or twenty-eight, went to Darbhanga in Behar to take charge of his first district on August 10th, 1942, the day after the arrests. 'The Congress High Command', he wrote, 'had planned well and the execution of the plan was good. No time was wasted.' On the 11th, the schools and colleges were empty; on the 12th and 13th, the villagers, 'some hopeful of easy loot, some urged by what we thought at the time misguided patriotism, others again just carried away by excitement, cut all the roads and railways. The roads were cut where they were carried over embankments several feet high, trees felled across them, masonry bridges demolished, pontoons of the pontoon bridge on the main road sunk; railway lines torn up, 40-foot spans of the bridges removed and dropped into the rivers, the delicate and at that time irreplaceable electrical signalling apparatus at all stations destroyed; telephone and telegraph wires everywhere cut, rolled up and carried off home. Copper bracelets and bangles for years to come.

'By the 13th, they were working up to the redoubts for the storming of the citadel itself. Police stations and government offices in outlying places were occupied.' Post offices, he points out, had no choice but to surrender — and what choice did a police-station have? A sub-inspector, perhaps an assistant, a head constable and five or six constables — they had not much hope against a mob of thousands. Yet some did escape or defy the mob. 'The man in charge of Laukaha, on the border of Nepal, saved by a couple of hundred Nepalis, beating saucepans and armed with spears and battle-axes, driving the Congress attackers from the attack. The Brahman Dube at Jainagar, shooting dead the first man in the mob who tried to enter the police-station, and then with the help of reinforcements holding his own. The stout Rajput at . . .' and so on. A few survived and won through — 'but mostly they lost — as at Singhia with a dozen spears through the assistant-sub-inspector . . . Of the twenty-three police stations in the district, hardly six remained in police hands.'

All this of course Lines did not know at the time. 'Telegrams coming in at all hours of the day and night while the wires lasted, then messages by hand — one carried in a man's ear, another in the hem of a woman's sari — these kept us too busy disposing our meagre forces to meet each new threat . . . Our police were staunch enough, once they knew they were expected to be, but a total police force of five hundred men to cover a district with close on four million inhabitants, a district in an uproar, was on the thin side . . . There was a rumour that troops of some kind had reached Samastipur. So Salisbury' — Salisbury was the district judge; he had unofficially reverted to the executive, as judges did in 1857 — 'and I slipped out one night with his Pathan orderly and a handful of armed police and reached Samastipur before dawn — to get the loan of ten British soldiers and one officer! But others were coming and now waverers wavered no more and the police took fresh heart . . . The tide had turned and the people generally were by now as certain as we had always been which way it would finally flow. . . .'

Lines goes on to speak of the pleasure of getting out into the district again, of seeing 'the early morning sun on the snows, in the clear atmosphere after the heavy rains — the friendliness in so many places and the almost universal relief at the re-establishment of law and order; the cheers for the Collector at Singhia, where not a month before the mob had murdered the Sub-Inspector . . .' And he looked back on the whole affair with feelings very like those of Alfred Lyall, ninety years before: 'The relaxation of being constantly taut for many days and nights, driving out all need to think or worry about anything but what was thrust most violently under one's attention; the elevation of hearing of and witnessing instances of heroism and devotion to duty; the comradeship that tense action generates; the delight of mere action itself; the unlimited friendliness and kindnesses from European and Indian' — all these, he felt, were something without which life would seem a little flat.

In the Eastern United Provinces, Hugh Lane was now Joint Magistrate at Benares, under 'Bill Finlay, the finest man I have ever had the honour to serve'. Lane had watched his Indian Deputy Commissioner become disillusioned with the Congress and had come to share his feelings, 'as I witnessed their paltry speeches and even more paltry resignations from office'. He and two young policemen lived in Finlay's bungalow, Mrs. Finlay being in the hills. 'We got on together very well; I think it was because we all liked and respected Bill Finlay so much. His main obsession (which we gleefully shared) was an almost pathological hatred of all Secretariats. Communications to District Officers from Lucknow and Delhi were nearly always the subject of biting scorn or ribald mirth . . .' However, they obeyed orders and on the appointed day 'the well-known and mainly moderate Congressmen in Benares were escorted to jail, leaving those whom we later found were the real plotters of the Rebellion happily plotting away. . . .'

It was two days later, the 11th, that huge demonstrations were arranged, the object being to provoke police and magistrates into acts that would allow 'feelings of self-martyrdom to develop'. 'I vividly remember how an aged crone, holding a Congress flag in her shaky hands, was pushed to the front of the crowd and almost on top of me in the hope that I would get rough with her.'

It was later that day that crowds began to pull telegraph poles down and railway lines up; in the latter case, 'they used special spanners, removed the fishplates and lifted the lines bodily, proving how carefully planning had been done'. Culverts, where main roads carried on embankments crossed a ditch or river, were destroyed by digging up the foundations; the mob attacked wayside railway-stations 'taking great care to wreck the valuable control and signal machinery . . .'

This was in the country; meanwhile in the city of Benares, 'I was put in charge of the mounted police, with a European police sergeant, and given a roving commission to break up all unlawful crowds . . . The students had organized huge crowds, flushed with their successes of the previous evening and ready to attack all Government buildings . . . My mounted police charged hither and thither and proved most effective. We were only about a dozen but we put literally thousands to flight, as there is nothing so terrifying to pedestrians as a line of horses cantering up a street. . . .'

'In a day or two, the back of the Rebellion in Benares City was broken and there remained the far more serious problem of the

villages.' The police were confined to their police-stations, guarding
them against the mobs; none apparently were lost in this district.
As soon as the city was quiet, parties of police were sent out to the
villages; they found rural post offices had been looted and — 'a typi-
cally short-sighted piece of folly' — Government seed stores. 'The
very peasants who had taken part in the looting complained bitterly
next year that they could get no seed.' But now reinforcements
arrived of armed police and some troops, under the general control
of Michael Nethersole, and in Benares the tide turned, and, as
Edwardes had said in Peshawar, in May of '57, 'friends were thick as
summer flies now'.

In Ballia, however, a little North and West of Benares, and not
far from Buxar and Arrah across the border in Behar, things had been
more dramatic. There was no Englishman in the place; Nigam, the
District Magistrate, had lived through three years of Congress rule
and knew the Congress would rule again. He knew that even if the
Japanese did not win the war the English were committed to giving
up more and more power. Lane, in spite of his disillusionment with
politicians, had been 'revolted by Lord Linlithgow's heavy-footed
dealing with the Congress Ministries', and he says that Finlay too,
with sixteen years' service and no theorist, felt the Congress had
been wrongly handled. An Indian district officer was likely to hold
these opinions even more strongly. It is not surprising that Nigam
wavered; the astonishing thing, in the circumstances, is that so few
police and magistrates did waver.

Nigam carried out the arrests as he was told, just as Finlay had,
and no doubt he too disagreed in his heart. Next day he, too, carefully
forbore to disperse meetings or processions and thus give provocation. But on the third day of the trouble, Finlay, perceiving that
this was really a rebellion, forbade meetings and dispersed them when
they occurred; Nigam forbade them but did nothing when his orders
were defied, and then, as things got worse, gave up all hope, released
the prisoners from the jail as a gesture of appeasement and ordered
the notes in the Treasury — £35,000 worth — to be burnt. How
many actually were burnt, no one ever knew, but they all disappeared.

The Congress flag was hoisted over the Courts and the leader of
the mob proclaimed himself Collector and Magistrate; he ruled for a
few days only 'before Nethersole's avenging force arrived'. In Ballia
town, nearly every Government building was destroyed, the damage
including hospitals, dispensaries, seed stores and A.R.P. shelters; in
the district two police stations only remained intact. The tahsildar

of Rasra wrote that he was 'persuaded and threatened in turns to sur-render to the Congressites. My reply to them was in emphatic negative. The situation was very grave. There was a handful of armed guard police whose loyalty too was of a doubtful character. Such being the situation I sent my personal servant with a letter sewn in the seat of my cycle to the officer commanding the forces stationed at Mau direct for help. The poor boy was put to serious search by a gang of these lawbreakers but he tactfully managed to reach Mau and military aid reached Rasra at midnight. The law-abiding public very much rejoiced at their arrival.'

And one sub-inspector of police not only beat off the rebels but imposed collective fines on the worst villages, successfully collected them and eventually remitted the proceeds to headquarters, having during his brief reign assumed something not far short of sovereignty, issuing decrees over his own seal and signature and assuming the style and title of a brigand chief who had been famous in the province thirty years before.

Ballia after the rebellion 'rather resembled a country that had been fought over and conquered. Not only were there numerous signs of material destruction, but the attitude of the people changed almost overnight from rebellious truculence to abject fawning. Personally I dislike fawning and I did my best to discourage it . . . ' It should be mentioned that for seventy years Ballia had been a penal district; if a good officer was sent there, he was promised he need not stay long; more often the officer who came to Ballia had some contempt to purge or some misdemeanour to be forgiven. The district had hardly had a fair chance to form a good impression of British rule.

Lane ends his account of the rebellion with its effect on Europeans: 'It was very reminiscent of what one reads about the Mutiny. They drew closer together, kept very careful watch on the women and children and eschewed Indian society . . . Tolerance was rather at a discount; the ghastly fate of two Canadian Air Force officers who were almost literally torn to bits by a mob at a railway station in Behar was described more often than was necessary. Fear always breeds preju-dice but we felt also a great measure of honest anger at the wanton damage, especially as it was impeding the war effort, and thus incidentally any hope India had of becoming free.' 'I freely confess that in those few months my own feelings towards Hindus became very far from charitable and it took me some time to recover.'

Few people in the rest of India realized how serious the rebellion had almost been, but most Englishmen knew enough to share Lane's anger. From the more detached point of view of ten years later, one may feel that the Congress were as much justified as anyone else in pursuing their war aims but that they were fortunate in not achieving them.

3. THE WAR IN BURMA

Burma, as different as could be from India, had been an uneasy appanage of the Indian Empire. The country being rich in oil, teak, rice, silver, copper and rubies, everyone in Burma felt it would be better to be free from an India primarily agricultural and barely self-supporting. Again, Indians are a serious and hard-working people and many of them had come to Burma to do work which the Burmese preferred to leave undone. This did not make them popular. For a long time, then, Burma's chief political wish was to be unyoked from India. The wish had been achieved by the 1935 Act.

A great many of the Burma Commission however had belonged to the Indian Civil Service. In spite of this label, some of them had hardly set foot in India; they travelled between England and Burma by steamship lines which did not go to India and they hardly met people from India even when they went on leave. All the same, their story in the last years is part of the whole story of the rise and fall of the rule of the Guardians.

Much has been written about the invasion of Burma and it would be possible to fill many volumes with a day-to-day account of all that happened between Japan's attack on the American fleet at Pearl Harbour in December 1941 and the evacuation of Burma by the last British and Indian forces in the summer of 1942. In those six months, the daily life of every official in Burma was a feverish improvisation. To each might be applied the words used by R. H. Hutchings, an I.C.S. officer from India who was Agent for the affairs of Indians in Burma. He was writing of the problem with which he was specially concerned, the evacuation to India of those Indians who wanted to go — as most of them did, fearing the Burmese at least as much as the Japanese. 'It is difficult', he wrote, 'for people who have not worked under war conditions to visualize what they mean in loss of time, lack of precision and demands on nervous energy. Most of the refugee work would have been much easier if things had been normal in the sense that offices were in their usual places and fully staffed, that letters and telegrams reached their destination with their usual certainty and promptitude, that stores, petrol, labour and all the other things we take for granted were to be had as usual. But . . . nothing was simple, nothing was normal. Every danger, every alarm, every inconvenience, that made refugees into refugees was also . . .' a danger, an alarm, an inconvenience for those improvising the exodus.

A picture of what happened may be drawn from the notes of one district officer and of one judge. There were of course some civilians who in the course of the retreat became soldiers; George Cockburn served with 4 Corps, Robert Peebles took part in the rearguard actions on the Chindwin, William van Wyck fought 'in the ding-dong warfare between Buthidaung and Maungdaw in Arakan, was cut off in 1944, when 7 Indian Division formed the famous box which held the Japanese attacks, and was killed by our own forces while trying to make his way back to our lines, disguised in Burmese dress'. But that is really outside my story, which is concerned with their work as civilians.

W. I. J. Wallace at the time of Pearl Harbour was Deputy Commissioner of Amherst district, with headquarters at Moulmein. It is part of Tenasserim, the long coastal strip of Burma that runs South to the Kra isthmus and has a frontier with Siam. He notes, thinking it over afterwards, that personal responsibility was the keynote; there was no getting orders, once the invasion had started, from anyone else. A man had to decide what needed doing and do it himself. He had to improvise the means, using any man he could lay hands on, whether he had any training for the job or not — forest officer, excise superintendent, engineer or schoolmaster — it did not matter. Wallace held charge of three districts in succession and then — as the British remnants were pressed back upon themselves further and further north — in three more helped as an additional District Magistrate. It was always possible, he explains, to move about the country with confidence. The people of Burma were even less inclined than Indians to regard the war as any business of theirs, but they 'were still the same people one had worked among for years, sympathetic and helpful, but bewildered and frightened, not treacherous. There was always the risk of air attack and much worse, towards the end of one's time in each district, the fear of being outflanked and killed or captured'.

Wallace had been in Amherst district two years and his life had been much like that of a district officer in India, the work increasing almost month by month and with some special problems peculiar to the district. He had controlled prices and tried to increase the production of everything, particularly salt; he had requisitioned buildings for the Army and the Air Force, found land for the extension of airfields and had done much else to make things ready for the armed forces. He had organized various forms of civil defence — a coast-watching system, air raid precautions and all those measures, with which most people are sadly familiar, to prevent landings on any open space by aircraft or even parachutists. Bamboo spikes, the traditional defence of jungle paths and villages, came largely into his plans. Being right on the Siamese frontier, all this was specially important in Amherst.

Pearl Harbour came and an uneasy month waiting for the first air raid. There were orders, later cancelled, that in the event of invasion the Deputy Commissioner must stay with his people, to look after them under Japanese rule. From Moulmein, the wealthier Indians began to leave for home, and some of the wealthier of the peoples of Burma. For the latter, there was no real evacuation problem. Moulmein, after Rangoon and Mandalay the largest town in Burma, had only seventy thousand inhabitants and, when the raids came, 'ties with the countryside were so close that Burmese, Mons and Karens simply melted into the surrounding countryside'. Special arrangements however had to be made for the Indians — and while Indians had no home in Burma to go to in an emergency, they were some of them essential to the working of the ports.

The Government of Burma was now a Government of Burmese Ministers, who had seen no reason to resign as in the provinces of India; they had for some time been engaged in a wrangle with the Government of India about the Indians in Burma and were reluctant either to let them go or to admit that they were essential to the economy of the country — which would have spoiled the arguments they had been using for some years. It was the part of Hutchings, the Agent of the Indian Government, to play Moses to their Pharaoh without any of the special powers delegated to the original Moses. But it is Wallace's story we are telling. Early in February he successfully passed on most of his Indians from Moulmein to Hutchings in Rangoon; he stayed behind and, being in addition to everything else Civil Defence Controller, 'usually took charge in the control room at any hour of the day or night when the air raid siren went; my wife used to go down with me and take charge of the Civil Defence Canteen'.

Tavoy, the next town down the coast, was captured in mid-January and with it the Japanese captured the Deputy Commissioner, who was interned till the end of the war. The next week, they were in the Amherst district; from Moulmein the women were evacuated and 'the town began to take on that typical look of emptiness, later to become so familiar to us all over Burma'. Only small staffs of essential services remained; the rest had been permitted to go — but 'a faithful few remained on my personal promise not to leave without them'. The orders about staying on under the invaders by now were cancelled.

There were about ten days to a fortnight of this bare, stripped existence, which Wallace records laconically. He paid visits to the telephone exchange and the telegraph office, the jail and the hospital, all mainly to encourage the staff. He was often at the headquarters of whatever military formation was in the neighbourhood, collected what news he could and passed it on to Rangoon, gave out three months' pay in advance to Government servants allowed to leave, distributed arms to trusted persons who were going to stay behind, spent hours fighting fires after each raid. He does not say so — his account keeps strictly to facts — but he must by now have been in that state of partial anaesthesia when the mind and will direct the body to the next task but there is no energy, even if there were time, to look any further ahead.

At last it was clear that the worst would come to the worst very soon. Wallace spent the last hours destroying secret papers and codes — not that the Japanese would have found much to interest them there, unless the contents of a Deputy Commissioner's safe were very different in Burma and in India. He burned all the notes in the Treasury and dropped the coin in the river, and finally 'evacuated the faithful — the jail staff and convicts getting away in good order on the last afternoon when mortar shells were already falling in the town'. The Japanese were in Moulmein the next morning, which was January 31st.

Wallace was then put in charge of Thaton, the next district. The air raid warning system had broken down here as soon as Moulmein fell, but it was essential to get it going again for the benefit of Rangoon. That was done. And then it was Amherst over again. One example illustrates the way men were still building walls of sand against the tide. There was a big quarry in this district, from which the stone was extracted by convicts. It was working hard to produce material for airfields further back in Burma, but both the staff and the convicts were very jumpy — as indeed they might well be, for they were on the wrong side of the Sittang. By a personal visit, the Deputy

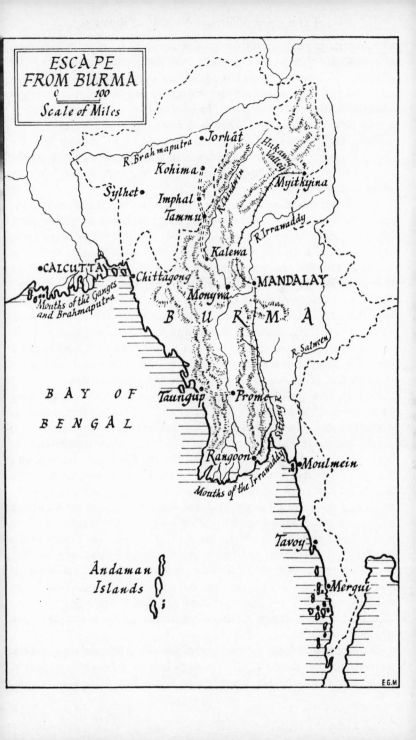

ESCAPE
FROM BURMA
0   100
Scale of Miles

• Jorhât
R. Brahmaputra
Kohima •
Sylhet •
Imphal •
Tammu •
Hukawng Valley
Myitkyina •
R. Chindwin
R. Irrawaddy
Kalewa •
• CALCUTTA
Chittagong •
MANDALAY
Monywa •
Mouths of the Ganges
and Brahmaputra
B   U   R   M   A
R. Salween

BAY   OF
BENGAL
Taungup •
• Prome
Sittang R.
Rangoon •
• Moulmein
Mouths of the Irrawaddy

Tavoy •

Andaman
Islands
• Mergui

E.G.M.

Commissioner persuaded them to agree to work on provided a means of retreat was there, visible for all to see, ready and waiting. How he did it Wallace does not say, but a train, the engine attached, the steam up, was put in position. Everyone could see it and the convicts worked on till the last moment. The expedient, says Wallace, obviously a true district officer, was 'kept dark from higher authority'.

Pegu, third invasion district, was the same again, though here the 'heart-breaking problem' was crowds of Indians, setting out on the long journey to India; they were late in starting and 'the war was now close on their heels'.

This is not the place to describe in detail the evacuation of Indians from Burma; the whole achievement might well make another book in itself. Everything that was done was an improvised expedient, carried out with an improvised staff. A bare list of such expedients would be tedious; one must stand for scores. In Mandalay, camps for thirty thousand people had been prepared, hastily and piecemeal; they were transit camps for people on their way North and they were kept filled. Cholera broke out. It became necessary to make fresh camps, move thirty thousand people into them — during the epidemic — and destroy the old camps. Mandalay had been raided and a great part of it burned to the ground. All the time, sick people had to be looked after, those who were fit must be fed, inoculated, and sent on their way, new people received daily. It was done; the camps were moved — and the whole was done by a voluntary staff of forest officers, doctors, missionaries, school teachers and others.

And one scene on the route, one of thousands, recounted by Hutchings. A young Indian couple are on the road between Kalewa and Tamu. They have a bundle of a few clothes and the food given them at the last camp, enough to last them a few days. They must get on while the food lasts. They have two children, a boy of six and a toddler of two. The wife is tired out. The husband takes the boy by the hand and the bundle on his back. He walks on, three or four hundred yards. Then, leaving the boy to rest and guard the bundle, he goes back for his wife. He picks up the child, gives her his arm, and helps her to where he left the boy. He has a hundred and fifty miles to cover to Tamu and no certainty of a lorry when he gets there. Those who went later by the Myitkyina route had a longer and more difficult march.

Wallace was at least improvising in his own trade as he went back through his six districts. The judges had to forsake their special skills more extravagantly; one of them, Gledhill, will do as a sample.

He had come into the I.C.S. after service in the Kaiser's War, 'because he wanted to be a judge'. In Hitler's War, he says that until Pearl Harbour 'we in the districts in Burma regarded ourselves as among the world's more fortunate inhabitants'. Then came disaster upon disaster, and not much that a judge in Mandalay could do to help. Gledhill undertook to distribute propaganda, but there could be few less rewarding tasks; the material sent him was patently out of date before it arrived and soon dried up altogether. Blow fell on blow until there was nothing he could say except that the side the Americans were on was sure to win in the end — which was true, but poor comfort in Upper Burma.

He sent his wife and daughter to India and turned the house into a hostel for people passing through. But that period came to an end with the air raid on Good Friday. 'There was no warning except the throbbing hum of the engines. I was in court at the time . . . Then in a shower the bombs fell . . . the court house was not touched and we heard the dying throb of the retreating planes.' He sent off his staff to see what had happened to their relations and himself went to the stricken area. He found that the General Hospital had been temporarily put out of action and a great part of Mandalay was on fire. Many of the houses were of wood or of grass and bamboo and the fire was never really extinguished till the rains. The Mandalay fire service of course was too antiquated to deal with a catastrophe on this scale, the place was almost deserted after the raid and fresh fires kept breaking out here and there. 'I saw fire one afternoon streak across an open space covered with dry grass and set light to a wooden building, and there was not a soul except myself within half a mile.'

That afternoon Gledhill settled into his house, 'in addition to the refugees from Lower Burma I had left there that morning', a number of others, mostly Anglo-Burmans from the stricken area, and then set out on a tour of the town. 'It was decided that the corpses must be removed and with two wagons and some A.R.P. volunteers I set out on this grisly task. I remember the corpse of a pretty Anglo-Burmese girl with terrifying wide staring eyes lying beside the corpse of a grey-haired relative, a good easy Burman decapitated while sitting in a deck-chair under the trees . . . We hurriedly loaded our dreadful cargo and as the light faded directed the driver to the cemetery. The loading was bad but the unloading was too much for my stomach — and for others too.'

Next day Gledhill concentrated on his court, where a peculiar problem had arisen; he had charge of the assets — securities, jewels and the like — in various administrative cases. The bank which had held the assets now repudiated responsibility; it was not always clear who were the beneficiaries and in any case it was difficult to get in touch with them. When they could be found, they were usually prepared to leave the matter to Gledhill's discretion. 'To such as I could contact I said that if I left for China and got there, I would deposit them with a British consulate, if . . . to India . . . with the High Court in Calcutta.' He does not comment, but the beneficiaries showed, surely, a trust that is reason for pride.

Another pressing problem was payments from the Treasury. The bank which usually made these payments had closed down; a Treasury Officer had then been provided but he and all his staff had been victims of the raid. Litigation being at a discount, Gledhill agreed to pay out money, impressing each day someone, a friend or one of the claimants, to sit by his side and write down all he did. There were new problems every day for an amateur; one that was constant was dealing with a mob of claimants who 'did not understand the queue habit'. There might be the accountant of a hospital, with his staff pay-bill to be met, an army pensioner drawing his few rupees, or the representative of an important firm with a cheque so considerable that he needed a suit-case to take away the five-rupee notes. Fresh air raids constantly occurred, when the payees fled to slit trenches but the cashier felt he could not leave the money spread out, so sat on the floor in a corner of the room and hoped for the best.

Those contrasted duties, collecting corpses and paying out on behalf of the Treasury, are typical of the odd things everyone did; in between, Gledhill sat on courts martial and took out the fire brigade. At last he was told to go; he went up the river, loading boats with Indian refugees and distributing rations to them. Eventually he walked out by Tamu and deposited the securities with the High Court in Calcutta. In Calcutta he met with an unexpected difficulty as his bank at first refused to divulge his wife's address, but this too was overcome in the end.

After a brief reunion Gledhill asked the Government of Assam for work and, as they had plenty of judges, he became an Additional District Magistrate. He found the districts in Assam startlingly big and the police force, he thought, inadequate, while everyone was expected to do whatever task came to hand in a way which reminded him of the old court of Ava, where the Poet Laureate might suddenly find himself Commander-in-Chief. He shared a bungalow with his first Deputy Commissioner, by birth an Oudh Taluqdar; Mr. Morar not only made him very comfortable but aroused his warm admiration by the patience and courage he showed in dealing with a mob at Sylhet.

After only six weeks, Gledhill moved on to Silchar, where he was himself Deputy Commissioner. Here he was surprised by much that was familiar to every district officer, but new to a judge. He found that, if he had complied with all the regulations about the Treasury, if he had counted the money and checked every payment exactly as prescribed, he would have done nothing else. He found his office staff startlingly good and startlingly trustworthy. He found that the least part of a district officer's work is done at his office and that he was besieged night and day by importunate visitors and petitioners.

Here Gledhill's story merges in Assam's and the story of Assam in the war is another that could fill many books. But before going on to Assam, mention must be made of Waterfall, Chief Commissioner of the Andaman and Nicobar Islands. The islands contained a convict settlement from India, a few police and jailers, and a company of British Infantry from Rangoon. In preparation for war, the garrison was withdrawn; Waterfall and his Deputy Commissioner, Radice, were left with an islandful of homicides in the face of the approaching Japanese. No help could be sent him; there was nothing to send. A moment came when he ordered Radice to leave, which he did, slipping down to a launch on the West coast of the island and making his way to India. Waterfall remained and was captured; he was in Japanese hands till the end of the war. A year later his execution was described in great detail by an eye-witness to a military intelligence officer, but in fact he survived, paying in full the penalty for his fidelity.

4. THE WAR IN ASSAM

Civilians in Assam and the eastern parts of Bengal were plunged into the war in a way that happened to no one else in India. It is not important to the main story that they worked hard at getting coolies to the airfields or that some of them showed courage; all Englishmen throughout the world were doing that kind of thing. What is important is their doings among the tribes, the Nagas, the Lushais, the Kukis and the rest of those people of the hills between Burma and Assam. This was their distinctive contribution.

The first encounters with these people had not been markedly successful. Since the days of Captain Butler, there had been many incidents when small parties had been attacked and murdered. But these had gradually become rarer; in every group of tribes, sooner or later, a situation arose when the Government, whether of Burma, Assam or India, yielded to the repeated requests of local officers and decided that to keep the peace the hills must be taken over and some elementary administration introduced. One man would be sent up as the first Superintendent or Political Agent, with a platoon or two of riflemen from some little-known and semi-irregular corps; he would stay ten, fifteen or twenty years and set his mark on the country, as John Shakespear did among the Lushais. Head-hunting was stopped and raids on the plains, but not much else; it was a light and loose administration. The Chiefs kept many powers, local customs which did not involve homicide were left undisturbed. Every officer who came to live among these people came to feel a warm affection for them and for their hills.

There was nothing aloof about camping among the tribes who used to be head-hunters. Lydall has described a tour meant to remind them that this practice was forbidden; he would ask conversationally whether they had taken any heads lately and they would deny the fact reproachfully — for they shared his own view that the question was in poor taste — and then he would give a gramophone recital. Another account speaks of waking in a Lushai village to the crowing of jungle-cocks; the writer is sleeping in a hut vacated by the owners for the night — they would rather do this than build him a new hut. He sees as he wakes the first light between the bamboo of the walls, and then: 'The door of your hut is pushed aside and in comes an old man who greets you shyly, walks to the shelf hanging above the fire, removes a bamboo pipe, and walks out. Or perhaps a young girl, flustered and worried, darts in for the bamboo sieve she has forgotten to remove . . .' The bearer comes with a mug of tea, but he is followed by the Chief and two or three Councillors with bottles of *zu* or rice beer. 'No self-respecting Chief will allow his District Officer to get up without a bottle of zu. . . .'

There is fifteen miles of rough track to be walked, and a boundary dispute to settle on the way. It would be as well to start before the sun is hot. But the Chief has a message from his wife. She has prepared breakfast — rice, vegetables and goat. 'Such an invitation cannot be refused although you had a large dinner at the Chief's house last night . . .' The meal is a merry one; everyone in the village comes to the door and there are roars of laughter at clumsy attempts to eat rice with the fingers. It is no use trying to stop; hospitality demands that a guest should eat much more than his fill. Then a pipe must be smoked and at last it is time to start.

It is a walk of seven miles to the scene of the boundary dispute, 'down, down, down, a rough path full of loose stones; but the villagers lighten the way, shouting jokes to each other and singing the latest village songs'. There is the meeting with the people of the other village, the dispute itself, which concerns the identification of a stream and means of course another long descent; more zu; more hospitality, and at last the long climb to the village of the evening halt, where 'a great crowd of villagers is waiting you. They have put up a bamboo arch across the path, with a bamboo bench and table on which there are bottles of zu, oranges and bananas. A bevy of village maidens advance shyly with Lushai cigarettes . . .' And so the day goes on. There is the inspection of the village records, a little amateur doctoring, of which quinine, aspirin and castor oil are the basis, at last a party, with singing and dancing and of course zu. 'The Lushais are a musical race and sing well; they have a catholic taste in songs and the melancholy melodies of the old Lushais mingle with cowboy choruses and Hawaiian love songs.' The district officer too is expected to join in the dancing — but a time comes when he must get to sleep, leaving his people to dance insatiably all night.

That was a day in camp. It was written in 1946 but it was to that same idyllic world that war came in the summer of 1942. And everywhere the primitive tribes displayed a startling, a deeply moving selflessness and loyalty. In the Lushai Hills, McCall, who had been Superintendent for nine years, called the Chiefs together and asked them to join in a voluntary bond, signing a promise to join in a Total Defence Scheme for resistance to the Japanese. He explained the scheme at length; it involved guerrilla hostilities, abandoning villages, denying food and water to the invaders, laying booby-traps, destroying bridges, and supplying information to the British only. They were to choose whether or not they would join and he gave them till next day to decide, insisting that they should think it over and sleep on it. The chiefs elected enthusiastically to resist and McCall promised that he and his wife would stay with them.

They set about organizing the scheme. The area to be covered was nine thousand square miles — sixty miles by a hundred and fifty; something bigger than Yorkshire. The people of every village arranged a secret hiding-place in thick jungle to which they could withdraw when the enemy came into their area. Secret stores of food

were hidden; every village enlisted a band of young braves who prepared ambushes, blockades and stone-chutes. These parties were
later strengthened by men of the Assam Rifles under British officers
of 'V'-force — among whom was Ian Bowman, he who had escaped
from the I.C.S. in the U.P. Later 109 Indian Brigade moved in and
the district had also to find a labour force to look after the brigade,
arrange a supply service by boat, and build a jeep track over the hills
to Aijal, the district headquarters. The Japanese made several
attempts to enter these hills but met with such difficulties that they
seem to have given up the idea.

It was McCall who organized the district for war and it must be
mainly due to his inspiration that there was no instance of a Lushai
helping the enemy. He was recalled at the end of 1943 and his place
taken by A. R. H. Macdonald, who almost at once had to put the
scheme into force. The Japanese drive towards Kohima and Cachar
began and they advanced through the Chin Hills into the Lushai
country. Macdonald went to that part of the country and saw to it
that Total Defence was a fact; then, with a force of Lushai braves,
crossed into the Chin Hills by night and destroyed the ration dump
which supplied the Japanese advanced patrols. Edgar Hyde, too,
who had escaped from the Central Provinces, helped in the Lushai
country and took over the Southern half when it was found too much
for one man to manage.

That summer of 1944 was a long-drawn Waterloo; not all day, but
for weeks, the Japanese attacked the British squares. At last a
moment came when they could attack no longer; the Old Guard had
been launched and failed. The attackers were exhausted and now
came the moment to counter-attack and to sweep them back. One of
those British squares — but they were Indian as much as British —
was at Kohima and the other at Imphal. In each, a burden fell on the
civil administrator, because these were squares of some size and the
battle lasted a long time. Pawsey at Kohima, Gimson at Imphal,
were men enough to take the strain. Both received from the hill
tribes who surrounded them loyal and moving help.

Pawsey had charge of Kohima from the beginning of the retreat
from Burma till the end of the Japanese thrust. He had Indian
refugees to deal with, labour to find for the airfields and the roads, all
the business of hastily improvising the highly complicated battle-
ground demanded by modern war — and that in a slippery terrain of
landslides, floods and earthquakes; mountainous; covered with
jungle; swept by the heaviest rainfall in the world and inhabited by

primitive tribes who were animists and recently head-hunters. All this was done, but he found time too to go all over his part of the Naga Hills, not once but again and again, going into the villages and talking to the people.

And you cannot hurry with such people. However desperate the need for time, you must explain slowly. To them time has another meaning; it is not something to be saved or wasted. He had to get away from headquarters, where Brigadiers and D.A.A.G.s wanted things, where lawyers, Members of the Legislative Assembly and chairmen of village sanitation committees sat on his doorstep; he must get away from a life where every minute was precious, to eat oranges and drink zu with the Nagas and persuade them to do what he wanted. Intelligence was the first thing; the army found that until they had his direct help their system did not work among the Nagas. Guerrilla patrols, obstacles, raids on food dumps, these came next, and there were rewards for Japanese heads.

Gimson had meant to retire in 1938, but he was asked to come back as Political Agent in Manipur, a State, but rather an odd State in that the Maharaja's powers were limited and he had to act in most things that concerned the Manipur Valley on the advice of a Council with a comparatively young I.C.S. officer as President. In the hills, the Nagas and Kukis and the rest, although the Maharaja's subjects, were administered by the President, who at the beginning of the war was T. A. Sharpe. The advantage of this arrangement was that the Maharaja's tribes were administered in the same kind of way as Pawsey's to the North, and those across the Burmese border to the East. Every year the Political Agent from Manipur met the Deputy Commissioner of the Naga Hills at some convenient spot to talk over their problems; in 1941 their joint camp broke up on December 8th and that evening Gimson heard on his camp wireless the news of Pearl Harbour.

From that moment 'things fairly hummed'. Refugees were the first problem; camps, tracks, sanitation, food for people coming out of Burma, all had to be improvised. Roads going into Burma were the next; military supplies would have to go in through the Manipur Valley to Tamu and a road must be built that would take military traffic. Labour for roads, labour for airfields; conferences of military officers — 'sometimes three or four going on at the same time, all of which I had to attend, and they lasted until midnight'. 'Then in the small hours cipher telegrams which I had to decipher personally. . . .'

Then came the main stream of refugees, a tale which has been told by others; Gimson has a postscript of his own to add. A time came when everyone thought the exodus was finished and the staff provided by the tea-planters was withdrawn. 'But the Japs had other ideas. They did not want useless mouths so they sent Indians and Gurkhas across the river to find their way to India. They had no food ... our nearest camps were three or four days' march away through almost uninhabited and malaria-infested jungle.' It was the monsoon; young children and nursing mothers had to make the journey. When they reached the first camp, most of them had dysentery, malaria or smallpox. The camp held about 10,000; they had to stay there till transport could be begged from the Army — who never had enough for their own needs.

That was one anxiety; Chinese troops coming out of Burma were another; two Chinese generals came to lunch and caught a Chinese soldier stealing vegetables from the garden. 'I heard afterwards that he had been shot; I hope it is not true.' These anxieties, however, paled after Imphal had been bombed; water and electric supplies were cut; the bazar was gutted by fire; 'human and animal corpses lay about for three or four days until we could organize squads to bury them'. Servants and clerks fled; 'I am sure that no Political Agent has ever emptied so many commodes as I did in the next few days.'

'It was seven weeks before the clerks came back. They came in sackcloth and ashes, ashamed and penitent. I cursed them all ... but was so glad to see them ... that I could hardly keep a straight face ... I promised never to taunt them if they behaved well in future and they did not let me down again ... though the days of the invasion must have been a heavy trial.'

Then came the siege, when the Japanese closed in on Imphal and the British and Indian forces kept them out. 'As the defences on the Western side were on the edge of the Residency garden I slept in my clothes for three weeks with a rifle by my side.' Then on June 22nd, 33 Corps joined up with 4 Corps and the siege was over. And at this point Gimson adds: 'All through the War, including the siege, I gave a gramophone concert in the Residency every Sunday evening. The audience consisted of civilians, army officers, nurses ... The war seemed further away.'

It would be easy to fill a book, and a very interesting one, with the effects on this small and secluded valley of these two crowded years. Two points must do. Manipur had been almost self-supporting, money rare and little used. All this was changed and in a few weeks wages rose from less than fivepence a day to seven shillings and six-pence — twenty-fold. There had been virtually no market for vegetables, but now the troops needed them; Gimson and his people supplied seeds to neighbouring villages, showed them what to do, and were able to provide the troops with between 20,000 and 40,000 lb. weight of vegetables daily over a period of nearly two years.

But it was the Nagas and the Kukis and other hill tribes who were the heroes of the story. 'They were magnificent', wrote Gimson. 'Their devoted loyalty stood every strain. Even when the Japs occupied their villages, they co-operated with them as little as possible. Under compulsion, they gave food, shelter and labour, but information was reserved for us . . . A system of ground signals was developed by which Nagas indicated to the R.A.F. where Japs were camping. The people of one village . . . signalled to the R.A.F. to bomb their own village because the Japs were there.'

That might serve as the final verdict on the work for fifty years of Assam district officers.

But before leaving Assam, two more names must be mentioned. Sharpe, who had been President of the Manipur Council in the early days of the war, came back at the beginning of April 1943 to make a reconnaissance in the hills. He was by this time part of 'V'-force, the semi-military formation designed to make the best use of the Nagas and their hills. He went up with an orderly, two riflemen and two or three porters and was never seen again. According to one story, the porters came back, saying that Sharpe was warned there was a Jap patrol in the neighbourhood but that he dismissed this as idle gossip and walked right up to a bungalow where the Japanese were shelter-ing. The commander gave orders for the whole party to be killed; Sharpe pleaded for the others and the commander released the porters — so they said — and sent them back. They saw Sharpe led into the jungle for execution. His body was never found.

The last is Sir Keith Cantlie, a member of the Board of Revenue, at the end of his service and due to retire. But a Labour Corps had been raised from the Khasis, a hill tribe whom he knew well; there were plenty of recruits at first but when they heard that they would have to go where there was bombing and danger of being cut off, the flow of recruits dried up and it seemed very doubtful whether the Corps would move. Cantlie took leave, gave up his post and led them to the front, where he showed them the use of slit trenches and saw that they did their work all through the Japanese attacks on Kohima. They followed him because they knew him and trusted him.

5. LAMBRICK AND THE HURS

At the other side of India in Sind, H. T. Lambrick was offered in March 1942 a task which might just as well have been the lot of Sleeman or Malcolm a hundred years before. He was at the time Secretary to the Governor; he was offered special powers in two districts and the task of restoring public confidence in an area almost abandoned by the well-disposed to a fanatical sect known as the Hurs. It was just when the hot weather was beginning; it was like, as he says himself, exchanging a staff berth in Cairo and Shepheard's Hotel for a Desert Commando.

Sind is full of hereditary saints, each descended from some famous Muslim of the past whose spiritual authority he inherits. One of these was the Pir Pagaro, most of whose disciples owed him no more binding allegiance than the disciples of other Pirs; they would pay their respects once a year and make a present but that would be all. But some of the Pir Pagaro's disciples believed him to be incarnate God on earth to whom obedience was the sole virtue. They were bound by fearful oaths at initiation and were as completely oblivious of any moral standard but their own as the Thugs had been. These were the Hurs.

If the reigning Pir was a good or even a sensible man, the Hurs could be kept in order, but the last Pir was neither good nor sensible. He was tried for murder in 1930, but though no one can doubt that he had connived at many murders, he was acquitted on a capital charge and sentenced on other charges to eight years imprisonment. Like any other prisoner, he was allowed interviews in jail. After an interview, it would quite often happen that someone else known to be out of his favour would be murdered.

When his sentence expired, provincial autonomy was about to be introduced; everyone knew that in the elections of the spring of 1937 his followers would vote as he told them — both those of the inner circle and the ordinary disciples; candidates he did not approve might easily be murdered by his Hurs. He was therefore courted by political leaders and after the election his price had to be paid by the new Government. It involved the return of the more dangerous Hurs who had been exiled from the province and the relaxation of control over the rest.

Since then things had been getting steadily worse; the reports of the two District Magistrates who had Hurs in their jurisdiction 'read like Mr. Churchill's speeches in 1938-39' and achieved no more result. Violent crimes increased and the Pir began to quote an old prophecy which foretold that the seventh of his line should sit on the temporal throne of Sind. Police were murdered, railways cut and finally the Chief of Police of the neighbouring State of Khairpur was attacked at night when encamped with a large force of armed police; he himself and a number of his men were killed.

It was this which led to the passing of a special Hur Act and the appointment of Lambrick as Special Officer. There were by now half a dozen large bands of outlaws operating simultaneously over the area; the police were collectively demoralized, peaceful people had left the area, Hindu villages, if not entirely evacuated, were paying blackmail to the Hurs; postmen, canal officials, keepers of land records, were threatened with death if they went on with their work; cultivation was at a stand-still and the Hurs even demanded that taxes should be paid to them instead of to the Government. 'Not a night passed without murders and dacoities on every side. Virtually no good information could be obtained, though the Hurs barely troubled to conceal their movements; the country people were either their sympathizers or blind, deaf and dumb from the influence of terror.'

The first thing, Lambrick decided, was to restore police morale and end the defeatist attitude of the villagers who were not Hurs; to do this, he must get the police out of their police-stations and lead them to the attack. Night patrols, ambushes, almost anything to attack the Hurs and keep them on the move and to show that there were still Government forces in being — these were the beginning.

Arms and ammunition not securely held were a danger to the holders, inviting attack; these were called in. Next came the rounding up of eight hundred prominent Hurs not yet outlawed or in hiding but known to operate occasionally with the gangs. Detachments from the Frontier Constabulary and the Zhob Militia now came to strengthen Lambrick's forces; the Sind Horse, who had served Jacob so well, were now no longer in Sind, being regulars and armed with tanks. Three flying columns were organized, each with its own Intelligence staff, with its own guides and trackers. Each was to move swiftly here and there, with no prepared programme, striking wherever they believed there was a chance of meeting the Hurs in the field and beating them.

Before this could happen, one band of Hurs derailed and looted the Lahore Mail, killing many of the passengers who survived the accident. Part of this gang was caught by one of the three flying columns; meanwhile Lambrick was marching, with a small force of Frontier Constabulary mounted on camels, towards a point thirty miles into the Desert where he had heard that two gangs were to rendezvous.

'We marched all night and the following day routed one small party, inflicting casualties, but this delayed us and we were compelled to bivouac some miles short of our objective. We had arranged for a supporting force to follow but before it joined us a night attack was made on my party, while a sandstorm was blowing, by a gang which outnumbered us by about three to one. Our police picket was overwhelmed, the majority being killed or wounded . . . but the Frontier Constabulary with admirable coolness repulsed the enemy, inflicting heavy loss . . . This expedition was certainly a rash one, but in my view justified, for the moral effect of penetrating the Hurs' most difficult country to fight them.'

The derailment of the Lahore Mail convinced the Government of India that the Hurs must be taken seriously and that it would be no bad thing to train some young troops in the area. First a brigade was sent; later the strength was increased to that of a division; martial law was proclaimed and Lambrick became Civil Adviser to the military Administrator. Twelve months later, the resistance no longer required military action; Lambrick however remained as Special Commissioner for the Eastern half of Sind, with very extensive powers, for three more years. Among the many problems that remained, one was the education of Hur children. The adult Hurs were beyond hope of reformation.

This, the second Hur Rebellion, was directed against the Government, not because it was British — which indeed the Government of Sind could hardly now be called — but because it was opposed to the Pir Pagaro. 'The movement', wrote Lambrick, 'had a strong antisocial and anarchical tendency and will remain a problem for the Government of Pakistan.' But its place in this book is to complete a series. Lambrick may fall in beside Sleeman and Jacob; he fought under the same colours and in the same war. And he developed just the same affectionate, fascinated personal regard as they had done for the men he was hunting.

6. THE WAR AT THE CENTRE

While Lambrick chased Hurs in Sind and Macdonald blew up an enemy food dump in the Lushai Hills, most men continued their usual work in conditions steadily deteriorating. Many had to learn new tasks, familiar enough to civil servants in England but strange in India, and all added to the normal district work. Air Raid Precautions, Food Rationing, Cloth Rationing — they were all new to India and it was less easy to make such schemes work there than among a people who were used to reading and writing and who listened every morning and evening to the news. But the men who did this work enjoyed it. Lines, who was moved some time after the '42 rebellion to the district which includes Jamshedpur, Tata's great steel city, revelled in the contrast between this modern industrial district and his tours among the Hos. The Hos were cousins of the Sonthals and, if not strictly aboriginal, were earlier dwellers in India than the Hindus. Lines enjoyed 'meeting the friendly carefree aboriginals, visiting their clean attractive villages with their gaily patterned and painted houses, watching the extremely beautiful dances, learning of their songs and folklore, tasting their beer — ' and he found all this derived an additional relish from his ordinary life 'in the great cosmopolitan city of Jamshedpur. Tata's steelworks, covering 11 square miles, employing close on 40,000 men, pouring forth more steel in a year than any other steel works outside the U.S.A., with a metallurgical laboratory claimed to be as good as any in the world; tin-plate works employing 6000 men; the cable factory, Sir Indra Singh's wire and rolling mills; the Indian Copper Corporation's mines and smelter with their thousands of employees; A.R.P. as concentrated as anywhere in India; a constant stream of visitors from all parts of the world, generals, industrialists, religious leaders, Governors, Tibetans, even members of the British Parliament, Indian political leaders, trade union leaders, all to be met by the Deputy Commissioner. And in the intervals, dealing with all the industrial and labour problems and political troubles thrown up for an Administration by a vital cosmopolitan expanding, intelligent and nationalistic community.'

Or hear Lane, now with five years' service, as Regional Food Controller in Meerut. 'It was an entirely new kind of job, without precedent and without a book of the rules. It was therefore of absorbing interest and kept me constantly busy . . . .' That is the authentic voice of the service. 'New methods of control, new laws and regulations naturally led to new forms of graft and corruption and one was kept constantly on the alert to avoid peculation. One tended to become too cynical about this and to consider that graft was a peculiarly Indian vice,' — but when he came to see post-war England

Lane came to feel less sure of this. 'Control was piled on control' he writes, 'and regulation on regulation; all this led to a mass of paper work which in more organized countries is channelled through many different officials but in India had all to go through the district officer It was all they could do to keep the wheels from getting clogged and they had no time for keeping in touch with public opinion, which was in any case veering sharply away from any thought of a return to pre war styles of administration. . . .'

In Delhi more than in a district, and more in war than in peace work covered the same kind of subjects as in Whitehall, but it was dealt with in a different way, because, with all the growing complexity, everyone who mattered still knew everyone else and the Secretaries to Government still had direct access to the Viceroy. He saw them regularly, not in the presence of the Member of Council responsible for the Department. It was an arrangement that a high spirited Member of Council might have been expected to find intolerable, but there was still a distinction, widely recognized though not explicitly stated, between matters of pure administration and those with political implications which must go to Council. Politics in Delhi were still often regarded less as a means of controlling administrative policy than as an excrescence — and a regrettable and slightly dishonest excrescence — on a system of pure administration

There came a stage when it seemed the war was falling into two halves, when communication with England was possible only by wireless and there was a likelihood that even that might be seriously interrupted, when the Eastern Group of territories — India, Australia Africa and New Zealand — had to become self-supporting in supplies. Delhi was the centre of that Eastern Group and Jenkins in the Supply Department held perhaps as important a post for the war's issue as any man could hold. But the whole tale of shells, tents, boots rifles, guns, foodstuffs, will not be told here. It is enough to indicate the scale. The Indian Army expanded from less than 200,000 to 2,500,000, which is I suppose the biggest army ever raised without conscription. In 1943, 113 million garments were made; altogether 50 million pairs of boots were made. And there was much more — delicate things such as surgical equipment and electric apparatus — heavy things such as floating docks, ships and cranes, few of which had been made before in India. It was done; it was a superb achievement, the last effort of the old administration, now fast running down It is enough to say that there were a handful of men — Dow, Jenkins Hydari, Coates, Wood, Hutchings, Trivedi — with the ability to work the system in wartime and to extract from India what was needed. All was concentrated on that.

7. THE BENGAL FAMINE

Something, however, must be said of the Bengal Famine, which looked like a failure of the administration. Under the old system, it will be remembered, famine had been recognized as endemic and schemes had been prepared which could be put into effect as soon as scarcity was recognized. The last famine under the old system had been in the U.P. in 1908; then there had been eleven deaths directly attributable to famine, and special mention was made in the reports on the rare occasions when 'emaciated persons' appeared on the relief works. The death rate was above the ten-year average only in four months out of the twelve, and for the whole year was thirty-six for every thousand against a ten-year average of thirty-two.

But in the last months of 1942 and the first half of 1943 Indian newspapers showed photographs of women and children dying of hunger in the streets of Calcutta. Public health had improved since 1908, and the five-year average of deaths was nineteen in a thousand, but it rose to thirty-one, a much sharper increase than in the U.P. in 1908. The average annual death rate in Bengal for the five years ending in 1942 was 1,184,000, while for 1943 it was 1,873,749, an increase of 689,000. Most of those extra deaths could be put down to dysentery, cholera, pneumonia, malaria and tuberculosis, but some were directly due to hunger and most were indirectly the result of malnutrition. There are 60,000,000 people in Bengal; the extra deaths in that year were more than ten in every thousand.

The famine was not on the same scale as the old famines of 1770 and before, when vast stretches of land had gone out of cultivation for lack of people to till it; in 1943 and 1944 — for two years in succession — there was an increase of several hundred thousand acres under the plough. But statistics carry no weight when you have seen children's bones showing through their skin; daily in the towns of Bengal there were heart-rending sights, a shame and a reproach to men of English blood. And it was much worse than anything under the pure administrative system since 1866.

There had been no serious failure of the monsoon; the crop in 1942 was only a little less than usual. In fact, it was a conclusion of the Famine Inquiry Commission that whereas 1942 had begun with a stock of five weeks' supply for the whole of Bengal, 1943 began with six weeks' supply. But the current supply for 1943 was enough for forty-three weeks only, which with the six weeks carried forward made forty-nine. Supply fell short by three weeks only. There was however no rationing scheme; about half the rice crop was normally kept and eaten by producers, who ate as much as usual. Again, among those who had to buy their grain there were many — in Calcutta about two million out of four — who were 'priority consumers', protected and fed by their employers. The shortage fell on those who were left and for them it was more than a shortage of three weeks' supply in fifty-two.

Normally, Bengal brought in from Burma rather more rice than was sent out of the country, but the gain was so slight that it hardly counted when you came to count up the totals. It was important, all the same, because the threat of cheaper rice from Burma steadied prices; Burma rice was a kind of reserve bank for the whole complex system. In 1943, Burma was cut off. Even so, there would have been enough rice to keep the province in health if it had been properly distributed. A cut of three in fifty is not one that cannot be borne. But, as in Orissa in 1866, the authorities were late in realizing that the trouble had arisen. This was partly because Bengal still suffered from the permanent settlement — because Cornwallis, the amateur, had overruled Shore, the professional, a century and a half before, because there was no system of contact with the village, such as Munro's in Madras or Bird's, which had proved a model for half India. The Government, therefore, were late in learning of the danger. When they did begin to realize what might be coming, they were faced, it must be admitted, with a problem that would not have been easy even if the machinery of government had been as taut, as delicate and as rigid an apparatus as in 1908.

But in fact it was nothing of the kind. Ministries in Bengal since 1937 had been coalitions, contrived in the French manner by elaborate personal intrigue, decently veiled from the public. Ministers had to spend much of their energies keeping their places; in August of 1943, for instance, the High Court gave judgment in two cases to the effect that the Honourable the Premier had interfered in the course of justice by a series of letters, and by the dispatch to a District Magistrate and to one of his subordinates of a personal emissary — an Ex-Mayor of Calcutta — with propositions too delicate for writing. The cases being not very remarkable or important in themselves, this interference with justice was presumably done to preserve friendly relations with some local magnate whose influence might sway votes; the political balance was always precarious and ministers had therefore much less time than their predecessors for administration.

District officers and the Secretariat were overworked — a 'file-flattened bureaucracy' *The Statesman* called them in Bengal — and while the Provincial Government were busy maintaining themselves, the Government of India were thinking of the war. In the old days, when the instrument of government was as sensitive as a well-balanced trout-rod, the first tremor of a rise of prices would have been detected at the centre and if the Provincial Government had not given good reasons they would have been sharply asked why. But now the joints of the rod were loose and ill-fitting, the whole instrument limp, sagging and unresponsive. The Provincial Government were reluctant to admit the seriousness of the situation, to ask for help or to receive advice. The Government of India, even if fully aware of what was happening, could hardly give orders to an autonomous province with an elected ministry. The Viceroy could, in exercise of his special powers, in the last resort override the ministry, and so could the Governor, but obviously only when all else failed. Prices rose steadily. In the ten years before the war, the price of 80 lb. of rice had varied between three and five rupees, usually being nearer three; it was seldom it cost so much as three farthings for a pound's weight. In January 1943, the price for 80 lb. varied between ten rupees and fourteen, in March between eighteen and twenty-five, while in May it was hard to get any for thirty rupees and soon rice even changed hands at fifty rupees — which is about one shilling a pound. *The Statesman* published daily articles on the deaths in the Calcutta streets. But it did not appear to the public that the Viceroy took any action until October 1943 when Lord Wavell succeeded Lord Linlithgow, went at once to Calcutta to see things for himself, and ordered the army's great machine to distribute supplies.

The causes were complex and to put the famine down to one of them entirely would be misleading. It was not that the defence forces had bought up all the grain; they did in fact buy very little in Bengal. It was not that imports from Burma had stopped; they had stopped, of course, but their effect was in any case usually more psychological than directly economic. But, if two causes are to be named, it was a famine due to panic and to divided control.

At a time when the administration was strained by war and weakened by political experiment, a harvest rather below average started a rise in price. In ordinary times, it would have lasted a few weeks perhaps, and then rice from somewhere else would have come in. But now there was nowhere else for rice to come from and the air was full of rumours; the Japanese were coming, the English were going, Calcutta was being bombed, all the ships on the sea were being sunk, Burma and its rice were lost, it would soon be every man for himself To everyone who had money, it seemed that it would be a good thing to buy rice. And a great many people had money. There had been war contracts and, what was more, many carts and boats had been taken up as a precaution against Japanese invasion and compensation had been paid for them. Much of that compensation went into rice.

And of course as prices rose, from twelve shillings a hundred-weight to five pounds a hundredweight, panic increased and more and more rushed eagerly to buy. There was no clear or firm handling from the centre; there were no instructions from the Provincial Government. District officers, jealous for their own charges, forbade the export of grain; neighbouring provinces did the same. In Bengal, there was little grain in the markets and that at a price too high for any but the rich. The rice-growers had enough; the rich had enough. Most of the town middle-classes had seen what was coming in time and bought early. Bell, a young civilian, tells how his bearer — personal servants are middle-class in India — went off to buy fifteen months' supply for himself and his family. The industrial worker had grain supplied him by his factory. But the casual labourers who bought day by day had nothing; the landless labourers from the villages sometimes had nothing and flocked to the towns. It was an urban famine, and that was one thing that made it so shocking; the casualties were concentrated where they could be seen.

The famine schemes, which in the North were reviewed and reconsidered every year, had been forgotten in Bengal, where famine was regarded as obsolete. The Ministry formed a food department in Calcutta in the autumn of 1942, but it began slowly, with no Government drive behind it, its policy being apparently to interfere as little as possible with the normal channels of trade. The Japanese, however, had already interfered, and in any case that policy had been out of date in the time of Sir George Campbell in 1874. Later the department went over to control, reverted sharply to complete free trade and tried control again, but by then there was no rice to buy. Most of the world's rice is grown in the parts of South-East Asia which the Japanese held. And rice-eaters will not eat wheat.

Everyone was over-worked, pre-occupied, slow to see what was happening. The Provincial Government pretended they had no real power; the Central Government said the whole business was the Provincial Government's responsibility. Neither can avoid a share of blame. The moral was clear now, even for those who had not seen it before; dual control, under whatever name, had lasted long enough. Responsibility was blurred; neither Englishman nor Indian felt it was his failure but the other man's when he saw a pregnant woman lying dead of starvation in the streets. It had become high time for power and responsibility to be clearly fixed. And the English for some time had been moving along a road on which there was no going back; they must go forward; that meant they must leave India.

CHAPTER VII

THE END

'**M**OST sensitive Indians', writes Lane, who is always representative of the younger generation, 'looked on victory not as the end of anything but as the beginning of a vast forward movement.'

It was true, and it bred a certain resentment in the English. 'If we had not concentrated on winning the war, you would not be making your plans for freedom', was the feeling in many English minds. And a reciprocal irritation was present on the Indian side, because the English, feeling 'a little vermiform' after seven or eight years without leave, were not eager to share in plans for a new India. It was hardly to be expected, because the old system was clearly at an end, changed values were in the air and plans — if they are to be realistic — must be made by the people who are going to carry them out. Politics anywhere mean compromise, surrender, bargaining; that is more than ever likely to be the case where power is newly won. A man who has been brought up to rule his district as he thinks right will not take kindly to instructions to conciliate a minister's supporter — and in the new India there was bound to be a certain amount of such compromise with individual conscience.

Almost everyone in the Service, then, pictured an independent India and since few believed that it could rightly hold a place for themselves, their old whole-hearted confidence could hardly be maintained. They had known that they would be supported and that they were in the service for life. Now they must think of where to live in England and how to educate the children. Yet, distracted by such thoughts as these, tired by the war years, they must still hold on to their districts in a world in which the old bluff hardly held good any longer. The people of their districts began to wonder whether it might not after all be true that the English really were going; once that was generally believed, once the District Magistrate had nothing to offer either as reward or punishment, then the quicker he made way for someone with real power the better.

Everyone then, English or Indian — and by now the service was almost half Indian — was thinking of what was to come next. Hardly anyone in 1946 was giving his heart and soul to the task of the moment. No one, however, thought the end would come quite so soon as in fact it did. The change of Viceroys was announced in February 1947; in August 1947 came the end of British rule.

It is not easy to write of what took place in those few months. It is still too close and few of the documents have been published; violent emotions were roused and we are in the realm of folklore. What is more, there are several distinct bodies of folklore which do not agree with each other. No judgment, then, can be final. It is impossible to know all that happened and difficult to judge what was significant and to write of it fairly. Nor indeed is it the purpose of this book to give a connected account of the course of political events. But certain broad aspects must be mentioned, because they affected the way the Guardians felt when the time came to go.

The English often claim with a kind of inverted pride to be not very logical and it is perhaps illogical to be so resolute in war as we have shown ourselves for some six or seven centuries and yet so concerned about human life in times of peace. Whether because we have become accustomed over the centuries to being a small people in a small island, or whether because we are at heart more Christian than we usually suppose, we do still think an individual life is important.

There is another way of looking at human life, in terms of numbers, of graphs, of biological evolution. 'We are a nation of ninety million Muslims,' a Muslim, now a Pakistani, said to me in 1946, 'what does it matter if we lose ten million to gain our freedom? There will be eighty million of us left.' That is a way of seeing life that may seem natural to those sprung from the teeming loins of Asia or Germany; it was not the way the Indian Civil Service had been trained to look at things. When in 1931 four hundred lives were lost in the Cawnpore riots, the District Magistrate's career was finished; it was a disaster. As near as could be, in a country with some four hundred million inhabitants, the English had tried to ensure that no one should fall to the ground by violence without an inquiry and a report to Government. For that reason, the first maxim of the English in India, that there should be no interference with religion, was over-ridden where homicide was involved; they had interfered with customs that were sanctioned by religion to save widows from the pyre, travellers from the noose, and infant daughters from suffocation.

In the last resort, however, the English themselves were ready to sacrifice life to preserve all that makes life worth living, all that is understood by the simple and old-fashioned word freedom. Indians

— Hindu or Muslim — had other aims than ours in the war but they were no less serious about freedom and they too had a right to make sacrifices. To many of them it must have seemed hypocritical that the English should insist until 1947 upon the importance of not losing lives. It must have seemed a mere excuse for clinging to power. But there can hardly have been an Englishman left in India in 1946 who did not recognize that it was no longer a matter of whether we went but of how. Some perhaps snatched at any excuse for putting off the evil day, but for many the mood was one of impatience to be off, to brush aside regrets, and to start the arduous construction of a new career. It was not hypocrisy that made the English anxious for a peaceful end. It was long training and a desire to leave a good job well done.

To the Viceroy, then, and to his official advisers it had been a cardinal principle to avoid loss of life. There were other considerations too. No political party in England was prepared to use force on a large scale to enforce a settlement on any considerable section of the people. It was out of the question to fight for the subjugation of India and just as unthinkable to force Muslims to submit to Hindus. That was a pivot on which all thought had to turn. On the other hand, we had given India political unity and we wished to preserve our handiwork. Nor could we lightly abandon interests which had on the whole supported British rule, the Princes, the depressed classes, the aboriginals, the planters — all the minorities who anxiously claimed some special protection. And we wanted to hand over power to someone who could keep the country stable.

These considerations made a complex position from which to bargain. And it was a position weakened by the fact that both the other parties — that is, the Congress and the Muslim League — knew that opinion in England, which in this matter was at one with the rudimentary beginnings of world opinion, was not prepared to coerce by force. In any kind of bargain or settlement, whether you are buying a house or handing over an Empire, it is of immense advantage to be unhampered — to be a principal not an agent, to know just what you want and what you are prepared to pay, and to have no conditions attached to the transaction. In all these respects the Viceroy was hampered until 1947 — and to a much greater extent than the other two parties to the negotiations.

All this is a simplification and to simplify is always to falsify. But it is only by that kind of false simplification that thought is freed from clogging detail and action achieved. For years the problem of handing over power had been clogged by detail; the assumptions of the services — set out with such admirable clarity and perception in the Simon Report — had been that everyone must be protected. The Princes, the untouchables, the Muslims, and a great many more — all must be guarded; unity must be preserved and life must not be lost. It was on these assumptions that the services had been brought up and it was because those assumptions were unquestioned that England had a wolf by the ears. It required great courage to simplify and falsify the problem, to ignore those complications, to disregard the snapping jaws and quietly let go of the ears. It was dangerous and courageous; it was the right thing to do.

It has been necessary to speak of this because of the shock to many of those who had once been Guardians which the end involved. They saw the price paid and not all of them saw that without paying some price the disengagement was impossible. Nor did all of them perceive that the price grew with delay. It is only necessary to count the dead, month by month, from the day of Germany's defeat to see how true this was. It had to be done quickly. Perhaps the urgency was not so great as was believed in England; one can see now that the Congress was not in immediate danger of disintegration, that India was not in immediate danger of falling into the hands of the Communists — but bitterness was growing day by day.

One may agree that a false simplification had to be made and a price had to be paid, and yet wonder — with many of the old Guardians — whether the price need have been so high. Unity, the minorities, the preservation of life — on all three counts the bill was a large one. Unity, say the Pakistanis today, is only an abstract concept; it is the welfare of the people that is important and we are better off in two states than in one. And in any case, they go on, unity was lost as far back as 1919, when the Hindus decided not to co-operate in the reforms and instead to give their movement universal force by appealing to the religious emotions of the peasantry. To this India would answer that loss of unity is loss of wealth and wasted effort. And much of that wasted effort, one must at once admit, is due to another item on the bill, the failure to make a clean settlement with that important minority, the Princes.

Men of the Political Service had for years encouraged, guided and sustained the Princes, on lines — it is true — which to many people seemed shortsighted because too considerate. Still, it had been done and the name of England committed. You might deplore the lack of a democratic constitution in Hyderabad State, but His Exalted

Highness the Nizam had for nearly two centuries proudly styled himself Faithful Ally of the British Government and until the spring of 1947 his powers had been limited and his affairs partly controlled by his faithful allies. The same applied in some degree to every Prince; now all were told, surely with either cynicism or pedantic blindness, that they were free to come or go, to stay out or come in, to make such terms as they chose with whom they liked. 'Paramountcy is not transferable', — that was the cry raised. But paramountcy was a concept invented to describe the relationship between the English Crown and the Princes and, just as it had been invented to fit circumstances, it could, surely, be modified to fit new circumstances. The phrase was in fact a piece of meaningless jargon. Paramountcy — whether transferable or not — was transferred. No State except Kashmir had any choice; the rest had to elect quickly for their nearer or more powerful neighbour and take what terms they were given. It would surely have been more realistic, more just and more honest to direct and control that transfer of paramountcy. The result of that meaningless phrase is a Southern Asia split by hostility. It is not surprising that some of the Political Service felt that their friends had not been fairly treated and that their work had been wasted.

Nor is it surprising that there should have been sadness and shock among men who had worked the best part of their lives in the Punjab. In that province, taken as a whole, there was just — but only just — a Muslim majority over Sikhs and Hindus together. It had therefore been the not unreasonable ideal of the Unionist party to maintain a united Punjab under a Government in which a Muslim should lead, but Sikhs and Hindus should be represented by ministers. It was inevitable that British officials should sympathize with such aims and hope to avoid at all costs a situation in which all the Muslims should be in one party and everyone else in the other. This was avoided — sometimes, it is true, by turning a blind eye to electoral practices that in England would have seemed old-fashioned — until very early in March of 1947, when events forced zealotry on one moderate Muslim after another and the last remnant of the Unionist Muslims resigned from office. The Muslim League could not quite command a majority in the Assembly and did not wish to take office; the Governor, Sir Evan Jenkins, had to assume personal charge. He was faced with that division of the Punjab on clean-cut communal lines — Muslim against Hindu and Sikh — that had always been regarded as the most dangerous possible contingency.

The history of the previous eight months was not encouraging.

No one knew how many had been killed in the rioting of August 1946 in Calcutta; an estimate had been four thousand but there were perhaps many more. There had followed the killings of Hindus in East Bengal and of Muslims in Behar; in the United Provinces again there had broken out a pointless, senseless slaughter. There was fear of the unknown on both sides; it would suddenly flare up when one side had the other at a disadvantage. It was something against which all the old known precautions were useless. In the 1942 rebellion, communications and police-stations had been attacked; there were points to guard. In ordinary communal trouble there was usually some point of focus, a mosque or a temple or a pipal tree. In a city, main thoroughfares could be patrolled. But this was unaccountable; no one could foretell where it would come next. In a village where Hindus and Muslims had lived peacefully side by side for centuries, sudden fear would blaze up and the weaker would be slaughtered with every kind of barbarity, babies being killed before their mother's eyes, women and children burnt in their huts. No district officer could prevent it by force unless he could station a platoon in every village.

The tale of deaths had been mounting steadily; wave followed wave, the whole continent pulsating with every turn of the negotiations. Now, in March 1947, it spread to the Punjab and here it was worse; here the numbers were more evenly matched and here there was real ground for fighting. The British were going and no one knew who would succeed them; if, for instance, it was possible to wipe out the Sikhs and Hindus in Lahore, then the Muslims would be unquestioned masters of the city.

The first outbreaks in March were brought under control; there followed a lull and then a communal war of succession which lasted until the British had gone. In June it was announced that the date on which power would be handed over was August 15th, 1947, that there would be two successor states and that the Punjab would be divided. It was a province of thirty million virile and warlike people; the long discussion had whipped them into a state of religious frenzy. They had been told that the authority which had held the ring for a century was going almost immediately, that their province would be divided into two parts by a boundary driven through an area homogeneous in everything but religion, a boundary which would probably convert its two principal cities into frontier towns. It was not surprising that there should be disorder.

By early August, it was reckoned that five thousand people in the

Punjab had been killed and three thousand seriously injured since the beginning of March; the number of people homeless as a result of arson no one tried to estimate. These figures were shocking but there was evidence that many people in the Punjab were preparing for August 15th as a day of reckoning that would far surpass anything that had so far occurred. That was in fact the case. On that day of anger, slaughter began. It went on and on. No one knows how many were killed; one estimate, by a cautious authority, is half a million dead and twelve million homeless.

It was a time when, to villagers of the Punjab, and to those soldiers and policemen who never ceased to be villagers, it must have seemed that heaven and earth were moving. Every party of refugees had to face the risk at every moment of attack by armed men who, when they did attack, slew without mercy; when there was anyone to protect them, their protectors were as a rule men of the Indian Army who did not know what was happening in their own villages. They had seen blackened ruins around them, desolate mud walls standing in the ashes of their own thatch with the corpses heaped in the yard. They could only guess what things were like at home. In that hour, when all they knew was failing, one thing stood firm, the faith and discipline of the Indian Army.

That slaughter was one reason why some men left with a feeling that their life's work had been wasted. It is not easy to look at things with cool detachment when you have spent your life trying to prevent bloodshed and leave the scene of your work with corpses piled indiscriminately shoulder-high at your garden gate. Nor is it easy to accept with equanimity such imputations as were cast on the service in its last months. The Congress suggested, before the day of anger, that British officers in the Punjab were stirring up trouble themselves in their own districts — a thing which surely in his own interest any ordinarily balanced person would avoid — and that they were doing this in the interest of the other side. The Muslims were not behindhand with the same kind of allegation. Since both sides brought the same charges, one may suppose that impartiality was maintained till the end.

A charge was brought too that in those last months British officers were indifferent to what became of their districts. They shrugged their shoulders, the accusation runs, and left things to the politicians. To consider such a charge in detail would require an inquiry in half the districts of the Punjab; enough has already been said of the technique of dealing with riots to show that every hour of every day will present a choice of action and it is never possible to say with certainty which is right. No final judgment is possible but two comments may be made. First, it had long been the practice to post British officers to the storm-centres where riot was likely; this was done for the simple reason that it was much easier for a British officer than for an Indian to maintain a middle course between Sikh and Muslim. When riots came, they came where they were expected, that is to say, where there were British officers. Secondly, to deal with a riot takes courage, not only physical courage but that moral courage which comes of confidence. And it would not be surprising if in those last two or three months, confidence was impaired. Officers had been used to carrying out the partition of a peasant's holding between his sons. The quality of the soil in every field, the flavour of the fruit on every tree, would be discussed and weighed and, at last after many hearings, a balance struck in which all these things, as well as area, were meticulously taken into account. Now they saw a mighty empire divided much more swiftly and with far less attention to the interests of the parties. All their assumptions, all their experience, seemed to be ignored. In such circumstances, a man might well hesitate before taking that robust action which might avert calamity but might also be pilloried as brutality.

Wherever blame lies, trains rolled into Delhi and into Lahore loaded with the dead. No wonder that there were heavy hearts. Men left the Punjab with pistol cocked, ready if need be to fight during their last train journey in India, and probably not for themselves but for some carriage-load of defenceless folk who might otherwise be slaughtered on the way. It was not so in most of India and for most men feelings were far from simple. One young man wrote: 'I will not dilate upon the personal distress of this uprooting, since it was only a distress of my own mind and I suppose selfish, not to be compared with the trials of our colleagues in the Punjab and Bengal, still less with the ghastly experiences of the minorities in those Provinces. Enough that though I felt it my duty to leave India, I shall never cease to yearn for another glimpse of a land that gave me so much happiness.' There were older men who found their thoughts turning to the past, to the blood that had been shed so liberally to win what was now given away. In such a mood, the mind might dwell on the bullet-pitted walls of the Residency, on the moment of decision at Assaye, on

The dead from Chillianwallah, the watchers of Mardan;

on the countless days and nights of toil and danger, the sweat and anxiety that had gone to bridge a river, to break a dacoit, to bring home the mean murder of some defenceless woman, or to the more prosaic task of simply ensuring that each man's field was properly entered in the papers.

There was a mood of lonely wakefulness in which the two million English graves that marked that immense effort seemed wasted. But in the daytime, it would be clear again that the effort was neither ended nor wasted, that what had been done was its own reward even if there had not been Indians in the services who, in their own new way, not as mere imitators, would continue what had been begun and fulfil the thought of Hastings, Elphinstone and Metcalfe. There were few who at one time or another did not feel as Philip Nash felt when he gazed down on the House of Representatives in Burma and heard the Burmese Prime Minister declare for independence rather than partnership in the Commonwealth. Looking down from the gallery on 'all the dignity of our Parliamentary procedure in that different, gaily coloured setting, I felt not only regret — who wouldn't have? — but pride. That setting, that speech may have meant the end of an epoch but they represented in themselves an achievement . . .' How much stronger was that feeling in India.

For most men, perhaps, the prevailing thought was simply that we had done our part and that the time had come to go. To stay could only blur responsibility and it was a sense that they were now responsible for all that would happen that India's leaders were going to need at once. The cord must be cut. A few stayed on in Pakistan, to become as a rule as ardent as any Pakistani; in India most Englishmen felt that it would be in no one's interest to remain. There were practical things to think of, passports and visas, packing and passages, where to live and how to earn enough to educate the children. These were surface thoughts, useful to keep the mind from things better kept hidden; beneath were regrets for chances missed and things not done, friendships not pursued and letters left unanswered, all the sadness of leaving, and the sadness double when opportunity has been so great and the little done so little. The faces that came to the window of the railway carriage and that came back in dreams to most were the faces of simple people, servants and orderlies, people who had worked cheerfully and not always very efficiently for very little, who had perhaps brought a cup of tea every morning, had stood gravely by the bedside in sickness, had perhaps told of a child's death with choked utterance. For others the memory was of bewildered voices asking for help that could not be given.

But all that was sentimentality to be firmly repressed. And if, as he bent once more to the luggage labels with eyes a little blurred, his thoughts could not be controlled and he must look back, hardly one man would have chosen his life differently. As to whether the job had been well done, that was a question time alone could settle. An answer came when the two dominions decided that after all they did not want to leave that odd association of peoples that had once been called the British Empire.

It had been a long journey since Hawkins had landed and the subjects of the Great Mogul had made him welcome 'after their barbarous fashion'. It is as well to bring an affair of the heart to a formal end; let it end then where it began, by the sea, on February 28th, 1948. The farewell parade to the last British troops in India was commanded by Lieutenant-Colonel Prithi Pal Singh of The Sikh Regiment. The 1st Battalion of the Somerset Light Infantry, the last British troops in India, bear on their cap badges the word *Jellalabad*, in memory of the illustrious garrison of which they had been a part in the least just of British wars, a hundred years before. On this last parade, they were presented with a silver model of the Gateway of India, with an inscription 'to commemorate the comradeship of the soldiers of the British and Indian Armies', and the dates — 1754-1947. The date looked back to the arrival of that battalion that was to become the 1st Battalion of the Dorsetshire Regiment, — *Primus in Indis*. Indian Guards of Honour from The Indian Grenadiers, The Maratha Light Infantry, The 2nd Royal Battalion The Sikh Regiment and The 5th Royal Gurkha Rifles, presented arms in a Royal Salute; the bands played *God Save the King*; The Somerset Light Infantry presented arms in a Royal Salute and the bands played *Bande Mataram*, which six years before had been the rallying song of insurrection; the King's Colour and the Regimental Colour were trooped through the Gateway of India, the bands playing *Auld Lang Syne*.

It was over. The long years of partnership and strife were ended and divorce pronounced.

EPILOGUE

THE curtain has fallen but it is a civilized custom to drink a glass of wine with a friend and discuss the play before going home. Was it tragedy or triumph, bitter and meaningless or insipid and flat? Would other actors have played it better?

Look back to Akbar's three aims, a united people, a stable treasury and a stable peasantry. All three seemed at one time in sight, but now one has certainly not been realized, the second and the third are for the moment precariously achieved but are in the balance. Look to another aim, glimpsed by Munro and Elphinstone, by Macaulay and the Act of 1833, explicitly proclaimed in 1917 — and it is clear that the change from government *for* Indians to government *by* Indians has been carried through successfully. As to the ultimate value of the whole incursion, not perhaps for two centuries will it be possible to judge whether English ideas have bred with Indian as Roman did with Gaulish.

On the surface, much remains. In Delhi, Karachi and Lahore, bugles call you from sleep as they did in Kitchener's time. In the Shalimar Gardens or the Red Fort, you will see the Pipe-Major swagger before his men in Campbell tartan or Royal Stuart and toss his baton with the old assured arrogance; you will see pipe banners gay with the arms of officers long dead, *pagris* as stiffly starched and spats as immaculately pipe-clayed as before. The precise movements of ceremonial drill, the wording of a legal document, a judge's assumption that his word will bind a government to whom it is unwelcome, a parliamentarian's deference to the Speaker—all these are still there and may last. They may even survive a formal abandonment of all links with the Commonwealth, as things English and Spanish have survived in the Americas. Less substantial is the deep goodwill with which, seven years after partition and in spite of the Kashmir wound left unhealed, a former Guardian is welcomed, both in India and in Pakistan. But that goodwill depends on circumstance; it is a historical phenomenon which may disappear and change, as such feelings have changed in the past. It throws light on the essentially family nature of the old quarrel and is as necessary to a proper understanding as are the generalized bitterness that followed Jallianwala Bagh, the strong personal affections on both sides, the shifting play of light and shade falling on many thousands of individuals over three centuries.

'Conquest is very rarely an evil,' said Ram Mohun Roy, a century and a quarter ago, in words more confident than English lips today would venture to use, 'when the conquering people are more civilized than the conquered ... India requires many more years of English dominion so that she may not have many things to lose while she is reclaiming her political independence.' It is in this light that the nineteenth century should be considered, the light in which events appeared at the time; but the very virtues that were the strength of the Guardians in the nineteenth century made it inevitable that their rule should end in the twentieth and that they should be regarded with impatience by their wards. The twentieth century must be looked at with different eyes. In this context the quotation to remember is Guy Wint's: 'Every conquest and rule of one country by another has in it a stain of evil.'

Soon after the Kaiser's War, a brigand made himself famous throughout the United Provinces and far into Behar and the Punjab. His name was Sultana Daku; it was so much feared that at one time men in a lonely police-station would turn out and present arms when he went by. He left few women unviolated and no man alive to give evidence against him in the villages he raided. He was feared and hated; in the end, he was hunted down and caught by a policeman whom everyone knew as Freddy Young. There was a play called *Sultana Daku*, a favourite at fairs all through Northern India, in which at first Freddy Young was the avenging hero and the crowd cheered when the villainous Sultana was brought to book. But as the play was repeated — it was probably never printed — and as the memory of the real Sultana grew fainter, gradually year by year the parts were reversed, until Sultana was the hero, a gallant Robin Hood who befriended the poor and robbed the English, while Freddy Young became the comic villain, fat and cowardly, continually calling for whisky.

The same kind of change took place everywhere in the way Indians came to think of Englishmen, earlier here and later there, at different times with different individuals, the whole process being spread over about a century. For Tod and Sleeman, for Malcolm and Munro, in the 'twenties of the nineteenth century, Indians of all classes felt respect and even affection. They had been saved from anarchy and chaos and were aware of the benefit. That first affection settled down into a more complex feeling; Nirad C. Chaudhuri has described, in his *Autobiography of an Unknown Indian*, his impression, while he was growing up, that there was a protecting Government who would always look after the people. 'Overhead there appeared to be, coinciding with the sky, an immutable sphere of justice and order, brooding sleeplessly over what was happening below . . . ' But during the South African War he was conscious, in himself and among his friends, of a barely acknowledged delight when English arms suffered a reverse. He did not go so far as to wish for their defeat, but he was glad to see them taken down a peg. It was, in fact, a feeling very similar to that many boys have felt for their fathers and schoolmasters, a feeling which may develop into sharp antagonism and may last until liberty is obtained.

'The feeling of there being a watching and protecting Government above us vanished at one stroke with the coming of the nationalist agitation in 1905', Chaudhuri wrote. Many other Indians felt that a change had taken place, but not all gave it the same date. It was not however Young the policeman who changed, but the popular idea of him; it was not the Government which had altered, any more than those scenes of childhood, once so impressive, which look so small and shabby when revisited. India had changed; India had outgrown the system.

India had outgrown the system and it was right that she should. The wards had advanced far enough to need something more flexible — and not the wards only. The times had changed and in the twentieth century the time had already gone for a rule that was just, impartial, benevolent and considerate. India was passing through three revolutions at the same time, social, industrial and political. And in revolutions there is no room for impartial leaders. India — by the 'thirties if not earlier — needed a leader of her own people, a partisan with strong, indeed violent, views on such questions as child marriage, industrial slums and manhood suffrage. But to believe that impartiality was not the virtue most needed in the twentieth century is not to question its value in the nineteenth. It is unreasonable to criticize the Guardians for not having done more, in the 'eighties and 'nineties, to develop the country by active measures on the part of the Government. India was always more socialist than England but it is absurd to expect that she should have been governed on principles absolutely opposed to those in force in the controlling country.

It has not been the purpose of this book to analyse the methods of the administration in India nor even to attempt a final appraisement of the system. I have tried to show the kind of men who were Guardians and the kind of situation they had to face. The appraisement may be left to someone else, many years from now. But on one aspect of the story the verdict may be awaited with some confidence.

All through, from Peter Mundy to Lambrick, one is aware of men with a sense of duty who did their best to finish the thing that was there to be done, whether it was the work of the Company or the Viceroy, of the Sikh Maharaja or the Congress Government; they did it as well as they could without asking many questions about the ultimate object. They were content, as Lord Radcliffe has said, to be themselves; they usually did what seemed to them just without waiting for orders or looking up rules and they found that most of the inhabitants of India were content to accept their decisions. And it is clear that the kind of men England sent to India were throughout successful, indeed movingly successful, with Hos and Sonthals, Nagas and Lushais, and indeed, to a lesser extent, with people everywhere until they were politically awakened. The feeling was mutual; the English liked soldiers, servants, orderlies, tribesmen, the simple people, the people who liked them. Or to put it another way, they liked those who still accepted the old paternal relationship.

There is much more doubt about the far more difficult transition to self-government and about relations with educated Indians. It can however be claimed that a system devised when *laisser-faire* was the ruling doctrine in England, and when colonial rule was taken for granted, did somehow — with many errors no doubt — make the transition to independence and was in fact continued with no revolutionary changes after independence. This happened partly because the Guardian system was never quite what it seemed to be, a rigid Platonic rule by all-powerful Guardians.

It was fashionable, in the 'twenties and 'thirties, for those who wished to prolong the fatherly power to talk about a steel frame. It is a chill and repellent metaphor and surely quite as inexact as most. It would be inexact again to take another architectural metaphor and say the system was more like a weaverbird's nest than a steel frame, but there would be some truth in that too. All kinds of odd fragments were woven into the fabric, things found on the spot and made use of because they worked. In Garhwal, for instance, at least as late as 1939, four of the six main police and administrative posts were still hereditary.

But a catholic readiness to accept anything that worked was only one of the reasons why the system was neither a steel frame nor exactly what Plato had dreamed of. Another was the strong character of individual men, on which already enough stress has been laid.

And there was a third. Plato's castes were rigid; the gold in a man's soul was there for life and it was inheritable. Plato would have been on the side of the Orientalists in the controversy about education in the time of Macaulay; he would have had the people taught a charming myth which would keep them in their place. But the English could not bring themselves to take, openly and explicitly, so illiberal a decision; they decided that the state system of education should be Western. And if that decision contained an element of arrogance it was ultimately altruistic. They knew what it meant; already in Jacquemont's day they were saying that it meant revolt and in the end liberty. It was the official doctrine that the English were trustees until the time when Indians should have the political experience needed to work a democracy.

Rule by the Guardians then deliberately decreed its own end because it would not accept as a conscious philosophy the Platonic caste system. But having taken that decision on the conscious level, nearly everyone, in India and England, for another century went on denying it in practice. There would be time later for opening the ranks of the Guardians to Indians; meanwhile, there was something to be done and the man on the spot did it. As Edye said of his own early days, it had simply never occurred to him that he ought to be standing aside and training the municipal secretary. For the man on the spot, those practical tasks often obscured the end; to analyse and assess the rival sets of values must be left to that far off future historian. But standing back, closing the eyes to detail, musing on what might have been, one can hardly help thinking of some other cases where men found themselves faced with the problem of ruling vast territories. There is room for only a glance at these. But even a glance will be enough to bring out the difference. Let us take first another English example, more or less contemporary.

The Cape Colony had been administered by the Dutch East India Company until the Napoleonic wars, when the English Crown took it in charge. But the Cape was not entrusted to the Honourable East India Company and for fifty years its history was in sad contrast with that of the Company's territories. Whitehall was not very interested in colonies and was certainly not prepared to pay for them; it was the fashionable theory that they would drop off when they grew ripe and in the meantime they were a drain on the parent's strength. The Governors sent out were as a rule soldiers, usually without experience of civil administration. They came with vaguely liberal intentions and vaguely liberal instructions, usually given under some pressure from the missionary societies and Exeter Hall. They arrived to find no framework, steel or otherwise, but administrative officers recruited locally; it was an administration of amateurs, like the English justices of the peace; with one or two noble exceptions, some of Dutch ancestry, these amateurs were not noticeably more thoughtful for Bushmen and Bantu than their English counterparts for poachers. It was seldom that the new Governor's intentions or instructions were definite enough to survive very long against the advice of people who inevitably looked on the tribes on the one hand as a danger and on the other as a source of labour. As a rule, the first raid on a frontier farmer's cattle was enough to scatter liberalism to the winds.

The Cape then had an amateur administrative service with — as a rule — an outlook much the same as the indigo-planters in the district where Beames had intervened on behalf of the cultivator in the 'sixties and Mr. Gandhi in the 'twenties. Of course South Africa was an utterly different country from India, but it does seem fair to suppose that the Hottentot, the Bushman and the Bantu might have received more consideration than they did if the Colony had been administered by a Company who sent out such servants as Metcalfe, Elphinstone and Munro.

Nor was picking men the sole virtue of the Company. In the time of Cornwallis, pay had been fixed at levels which varied very little — in nominal value — over a century and a half. The real value of course declined steadily as the work increased, but there was always in real value a remuneration which very few people in England today would despise. What was more, it was decided that there should be an annuity on retirement of £1000 a year, a level which did not change for over a century, and which was unaffected by the officer's career. Everyone had the same when he retired, the dullest clodhopping Collector, the most brilliant twice-installed Governor; everyone knew that whatever he said or did, it would be very difficult to get rid of him. That bred an immense, an unrivalled, confidence and independence. The idea of an impartial and irremovable civil service is now a commonplace, but it was the Company who showed the Government in Whitehall the way and presented them with a service and a system for which there was no parallel in the Crown's directly ruled colonies.

Another Empire, founded not much earlier and also maintained across wide seas, might have been expected to develop on similar lines. But nothing could have been more different. The Spanish possessions in America were regarded as the property of the Crown of

353

Castile, and this in an even more intimate degree than the home territories in Spain. Queen Isabella had provided the capital for the voyages of discovery and she and her heirs in the kingdom of Castile were not only sovereigns but sole proprietors in a gigantic joint stock company. The whole vast continent was an estate, and one of the main pre-occupations of the Crown was to make sure the royal stewards in America did not cheat their master. The Crown, though advised by the Council of the Indies, was absolute; the Council was no more than a means of getting the King's business done. It met daily and dealt with an immense amount of detail that had much better have never come to Spain.

In Spain, centralization; in America, jealous suspicion of the stewards — these were the keynotes. There were two Viceroys, in Mexico and Peru, and many Governors and Chief Commissioners under varying names. The Governors were at first paid very little and left to reimburse themselves from the Indians, but about the time when Cornwallis perceived that the Honourable Company's servants must be properly paid, there was a reform of the Governors in America; they were reduced in number, given a more reasonable pay and larger provinces. Spaniards of a much better class were for a short time found. Both the old Governors and the new, however, were generally appointed on the advice of the Council of the Indies, not of the Viceroy. And — staggering though it seems — they were permitted to correspond direct with the Council without the knowledge of their Viceroy.

This of course was intended as a check on the Viceroy and to an Englishman would seem an effective insurance against harmony or efficiency. But it was not enough for the Crown of Spain. Every Viceroy, every Governor, before he began his term of office conducted an inquiry, known as a *residencia*, into the shortcomings of his predecessor; he would announce the dates as soon as he arrived at his capital and sit in open court, perhaps for a month or more, to hear complaints, each of which would be judicially considered. The Spanish are not an unpractical people and a Viceroy would usually maintain an agent in Spain who would wait upon the new Viceroy as soon as he was appointed; the two would discuss the question of the residencia and come to an understanding; it would usually turn out that the new man was not severe. But even with a working arrangement of this kind, it is hard to imagine a system better adapted to kill initiative.

Even this was not enough. There was also the *visita*, when the Crown or the Council would appoint a special inspector who would arrive at the capital and inquire into every circumstance of the administration, corresponding direct with Spain and having power to suspend his victim if need be. The visitas were occasional; it was possible to escape without undergoing one. But it was a frequent practice.

In short, Spain's administration of America was deeply suspicious of the administrator, while in India the reverse was the case. Except in the latter part of the period of stress and transition, the district officer was trusted and that was his strength. In America there was never the least sign of anything like a Guardian system developing; even if it had, it would have been killed by suspicion.

Two thousand years earlier, Roman rule had spread over the civilized world, but this was no more maintained by a service of guardians than the Spanish. There was in Republican times a net of alliances with states who acknowledged the paramountcy of Rome in treaties not unlike those which bound the Indian States, but that was an early stage. In the greater part of the Empire, local mayors and magistrates were appointed to operate municipal institutions similar to Rome's own and the Governor brought with him from Rome a personal staff. Under the Republic, the Roman element was mainly amateur; later, the staff from the centre became nearer what we should call professional administrators, but they still came with the Governor, they did not belong to the territory; they were superimposed on a previously existing framework of municipal institutions. The first civil servants of the Empire in the Augustan period were freedmen of the Imperial household; gradually, these were replaced by men drawn from the equestrian order, an essentially middle-class rank, based partly on a property qualification and partly on promotion for services rendered. The sons of senators passed through the equestrian rank and at first it was necessary to carry out a qualifying period of military service. But that condition was forgotten and it was one cause of the downfall of the Empire that the civil servants were divorced from control of military power. They could never be thought of as Platonic guardians; silver, not gold, was the best metal to which they could lay claim, the Senate being always the grade above them. One may detect a tenderness for indirect rule, and in its aloofness and its impartiality Roman rule resembled British. But the form was utterly different and there was the essential difference that Rome did not operate across seven thousand miles of sea. In people, in culture, in religion, her empire spread in concentric rings over continuous material.

Another empire of vast size was superficially much more like the Indian. The Chinese too were governed by guardians selected by competitive examination. The candidates having assembled, and having been searched as a precaution against cheating, the subjects were announced and the candidates required to write a number of essays and a poem. Each candidate wrote his name on a corner of the paper and gummed it down. Each was inclosed in a cell from which he might not emerge till he had finished; he was allowed three days. The style must be ornamented with elaborate antithesis and simile, heavily loaded with quotations from the classics; the most polished essayists were the winners. There were examinations at three levels, local, provincial and imperial; those who ultimately triumphed required both staying-power and perseverance. There were no marks for interview and record and one might have guessed that the system would not produce either balanced or forceful administrators, that they might, in Plato's language, be philosophical but not spirited. There seems, however, good reason to suppose that, at any rate in recent centuries when European observers were able to report on the system, it was modified in practice; many pure scholars did get in but others were somehow or other included who qualified perhaps more by determination and knowledge of the world.

Once they were in, the service was surprisingly like the Indian. There were, at various times, between eighteen and twenty-three provinces, each divided into something very like commissioner's divisions, districts and sub-divisions. In each area, the presiding mandarin was collector of revenue and dispenser of justice, and in general 'the residuary legatee' for any other functions of government. He was not supposed to serve in the province of his birth. At each headquarters, from a commissioner's upwards, there was a council, boards of revenue, commissioners of salt and opium. At the centre were six boards, dealing with civil office, revenue, rites, war, punishments and works. It is all most familiar, so long as you look only at the machinery; perhaps the surprising thing really is that such an obvious way of running a country was hit on only by the Chinese and by the English in India.

It would be fascinating to compare in detail the Chinese system at the beginning of the Manchu dynasty, say in the K'ang Hsi period, with the Indian in the period of reform; the comparison, it will be remembered, had occurred to Elphinstone in the early part of the nineteenth century. There was a foreign dynasty and Manchus — Elphinstone's Tartars — were to hold half the posts in the civil service, native Chinese the other half; the final examination was held both in Peking and Nanking and in both sections there was far more competition for the Chinese than for the Manchu vacancies. Again, there was a larger field in the South than in the North, so that it was very difficult to get a Chinese vacancy in Nanking, with the double result that the Southerners were the most intelligent members of the service while there was a large class of unemployed failed candidates.

But there is no room here for such a comparison. It is enough to say that the similarities lie in form and machinery, the differences in spirit. The mandarin had no security of office and had to support his staff from his pay, which, even with an anti-extortion allowance thirty times his salary, was quite insufficient to provide for the future. The system certainly did not provide a service free from corruption, while the judicial procedure included torture in open court as a means of extracting evidence. In Manchu times, conquest by a people who recognized the justice of the Chinese view that they were barbarians with no culture of their own had led to a slavish reverence for the past and for traditional forms. 'The type of mind that entered the civil service', wrote C. P. Fitzgerald, 'was a mind closed to all idea of progress, almost incapable of grasping the possibility, still less the need for change.' There have, of course, been people who thought the I.C.S. was like that; such a view does not fit the evidence that has been led in this book.

There is one more system which in bare outline and in all but one respect resembled Plato's even more closely than India's did. The Ottoman Empire was ruled by an imperial service who were all members of the Emperor's slave family. From time to time a recruiting party would go out and, where likely boys were found, would take them in lieu of tribute, or in Indian terms land revenue. These boys must be Christian, or at least not Muslim, a rule which no doubt arose because it was not lawful to enslave a fellow Muslim. They were chosen from simple and hardy families, often in mountain country; on arrival in the capital they were graded according to physique and ability. All had open to them a career that might be envied; for those judged best the prospect was brilliant. After some years of education, during which it was usual to be converted to Islam, the fortunate youth, proficient by now in languages, law, riding and military exercises, would receive a responsible appointment in the imperial household; if he was still successful at twenty-five or thirty years of age he might leave the palace to command an army or govern a province. He would own a slave household of his own but he was still a slave, even if he became Grand Vizier of the Empire. Slavery, however, was not regarded as dishonourable; the whole household was recruited from peoples who were not Muslim and the Emperor's mother and the mother of his son were slaves who had been Christian. The Emperor himself was the son of a slave and a former Christian and in ancestry much closer to his slaves than to his free Muslim subjects; he alone, of the whole governing institution which he headed, could expect his son to follow him. The slaves who were his viziers and generals founded families, but their sons, being Muslims born, were debarred from slavery and the Imperial Service.

It was a system with features that would have appealed both to Plato and to Akbar. At its best, under Suleiman the Magnificent, it seems to have achieved its two main objects, which were clearly that the members of the service should be aloof and disinterested — as Plato's and India's were — but also entirely dependent on the Emperor — as it was the Guardians' strength that they were not. This dependence was maintained throughout, members of the ruling system being liable to execution or degradation at the Emperor's will, a fate that sometimes befell a man even at the end of the most brilliant career and even for the most trivial fault. The Turkish training was longer and more thorough than the English, but its object was the same, the Platonic ideal of music and gymnastic, mind and body tuned in the perfect man. But while the English Parliament decided that the executive officer in charge of a district should also have some judicial authority — though less than Plato would have allowed him — the Ottomans, whose State in theory at least was theocratic, separated their judicial system sharply from their governmental institution. The law was sacred and based on the Koran; it was administered by Muslims born, usually of old family. It was perhaps this provision alone which reconciled the Turks to a system which reserved all high executive office in the Empire for infidel peasants.

Looking then at these four forms of imperial government, Spanish, Roman, Chinese and Ottoman, one may feel confident that the Spanish system of jealous royal ownership by an absolute monarch can in no way be regarded as preferable to the rule of the Guardians. The Chinese system was in form almost identical with the English but in practice — at the stage regarding which we have independent evidence — had failed to provide uncorrupt and impartial civil servants. Their training and selection had perhaps become too formal, they had not been given the security to enable them to act with confidence; the benefit of their subjects was not the main object they considered. The Ottoman system was based on absolute power; it aimed at efficient administration, certainly not at the development of autonomous institutions; for its own purpose it was admirable provided there was a Suleiman at the head of it. But in fact Suleiman was succeeded by Selim the Sot, of whom no more than his nickname need be mentioned; unless the head of the institution was just, wise, and energetic, the complete dependence of every member on the Sultan was a disastrous weakness. The Roman system however does give pause for reflexion.

No greater Englishman than Warren Hastings ever ruled in India; it had been his ideal to influence without direct rule. A Roman administration would have been less indirect than Hastings would have wished, but it is pleasant, if not very likely to be fruitful, to consider what India's development might have been if from a very early stage it had been the object to develop municipal boards and district boards on Roman lines. There would have been Indian chairmen, the district officer, or perhaps the commissioner, with a small staff from metropolitan Britain, holding a watching brief, guiding and directing, but not imposing English law. Local government was perhaps hardly developed enough in England by Cornwallis's day to provide a model, but there is a more fundamental objection. Such a system may be well suited to a primitive people, who, once they have passed beneath the yoke, are ready to accept the ways of their conquerors; but it is surely hardly enough to awaken to new life a people possessing an ancient and complex civilization which has ceased to develop, who are highly contemptuous of foreigners and foreign ways. Gaul and Britain could be Romanized by indirect rule but not Judea, Hellas or Egypt. Indirect rule may suit Africa but it would have been likely to leave Bengal stagnant.

It is by the new spirit which it awakens that a foreign conquest is justified. Voltaire atones for the wrongs of Vercingetorix and it is by the new vigour of India and Pakistan that the old system must be judged. Any rule less direct than that which in fact developed would probably have failed to give encouragement to new growth in the earlier periods. And perhaps in the last years it would have failed too to provide the second essential for vigorous growth, which is hard pruning. Indian nationalism throve on a repression which it would hardly have received from an indirect system. That it throve in unexpected ways is surely a sign of health. There is, one must acknowledge, a certain smugness in any endeavour to guide another people in the way they should order their affairs. But the English were not permitted to play the part for which they had cast themselves. Instead of becoming the kindly and paternal guides of a people meekly content to imitate, they were directed to perform the more stimulating and creative — if less pleasant — function of a counter-irritant, a moral mustard-plaster, which restored the circulation and began a brisk reaction.

There is the part actually played, assigned by providence; there is the part consciously intended. And the more one looks again at other Empires and their ways, the more they seem to differ not so much in form as in spirit from the rule of the Guardians. All tried to ensure some aloofness in their public servants. This aloofness, often charged against the English as a fault, was in fact, in the special circumstances of their Empire in India, doubly a virtue. It provided not only impartiality but the ability to disengage; the English could complete their task and go home. This had never been the aim of the others, and indeed their aims were wholly different. The Ottomans came nearest to Plato in their disregard of the family and the home, the ties of common men. But their intention was not Plato's. The Ottoman and the Chinese were afraid that the Pasha or the Manderin might conspire with his subjects and snatch supreme power. But Plato wrote:

'All who are in any place of command, in so far as they are indeed rulers, neither consider nor enjoin their own interest but that of the subjects on behalf of whom they exercise their craft. . . .'

That was why he wished to prevent his guardians from owning land and houses, gold or silver, or mingling with their fellow men; they might in that case become: 'householders and cultivators instead of guardians; and hostile masters of their fellow-citizens rather than their allies.'

That was the Platonic ideal and — suitably reduced to practical terms — it was the English ideal. It was secondary with the Ottomans. It was primary with the English. This Empire consciously professed to provide rulers who would be sheep-dogs not wolves. That was the difference; on the success of the ideal, the future must pronounce.

When all has been said, one simple point remains. It was put clearly by Lord Wavell in an informal speech made after he left India. The English would be remembered, he believed, not by this institution or that, but by the ideal they left behind of what a district officer should be. At the other end of the long line, Warren Hastings had expressed a similar thought. 'It is on the virtue', he had said, 'not the ability, of their servants that the Company must rely.' And if today the Indian peasant looks to the new district officer of his own race with the expectation of receiving justice and sympathy, that is our memorial.

In the *Spectator* for August 11th, 1950, there appeared a poem by Lord Dunsany which seemed to me to express the feelings of many members of the service when the end came. With Lord Dunsany's permission, I quoted the whole of it in the first draft of the chapter called 'The End'. But on re-reading this chapter, I felt that to quote the whole poem involved too great a change of style and mood at a most important point, while to quote only a part would not do the poem justice. I have in the end quoted only one line, but there remains a debt to be acknowledged and the whole poem does express a mood so exactly that I feel it ought to be repeated. Here it is:

A SONG IN THE RUINS

Troubled with influenza, a politician said
The men that died for India came floating round my bed,
The dead from Chillianwallah, the watchers of Mardan,
The ones who held the Khyber against Afghanistan,
The victors of Sobraon, the dead from frontier fights,
With those that guarded Lucknow for eighty-seven nights.
They were side by side and touching, though born so far apart,
And with reproaches in their eyes that cut one to the heart.
The men that put down thuggee, the men that bridged the streams
And built the roads of India were worrying my dreams.
It was only influenza. I feel all right by day.
But by night I'm always dreaming of an empire thrown away.
I call and call to Kipling, 'What other course had we?'
But he only sees the soldiers and he will not look at me.
Last night I questioned one of them, and 'Tell me, then,' I said,
'What could we do but what we did?' He turned away his head.
Only a dream, I know, and yet it means I must be ill.
One thing a soldier said at last that I remember still.
He said, 'We went to carry on the work begun by Clive;
If you did not want an empire we might have been alive.'

DUNSANY

The following figures and facts are taken from official records. They do not claim absolute accuracy, nor are they complete; but they may serve to give a general idea of

    (a) the strength, composition and distribution of the service, and

    (b) the education and social standing of its members at different periods.

In 1842 the total strength of the East India Company's Service was 836 — all British. Of these 776 were employed in India and the remainder either in the Court of Directors in London (24), or as Agents in various places (including Margate, Deal, Dartmouth and Limerick) in the British Isles (14) or abroad (22) (including Canada, the Cape, St. Helena and Vienna).

Those serving in India were distributed as follows:

	Secretaries to Government	Judicial posts	Executive posts	Total
Bengal (60 Districts and Delhi 39 Residencies and Agencies)	5	59	377	441
Madras (23 Districts, 6 Residencies)	2	37	166	205
Bombay (12 Districts, 16 Residencies)	3	19	108	130
Totals	10	115	651	776

NOTE: Until 1842 the Company's servants were called Senior Merchants, Factors or Writers according to seniority. In 1842 the titles were changed to Civil Servants 1st, 2nd and 3rd Class.

The strength and composition of the I.C.S. from 1859 to 1939 are given in the following table:

Year	Europeans	Indians	Total
1859	846	—	846
1869	882	1	883
1879	907	7	914
1889	884	12	896
1899	988	33	1021
1909	1082	60	1142
1919	1177	78	1255
1929	881	241	1122
1939	759	540	1299

NOTE: These figures do not include the 'Listed Posts', i.e. posts filled by Indians or Anglo-Indians who did not start their careers in the I.C.S. but were selected after approved service in the Provincial Services and then taken into the I.C.S. There were 85 posts so filled in 1939, of which 49 were Executive, 35 Judicial and 1 Secretarial.

The distribution of the service in 1929 and 1939 is shown in the following tables:

APPENDICES

DISTRIBUTION – 1929

	Secretariat			Judicial			Executive & Miscellaneous			Totals		
	European	Indian	Total	European	Indian	Total	European	Indian	Total	European	Indian	Total
Government of India	56	8	64	—	—	—	32	0	32	88	8	96
Bengal	7	1	8	19	4	23	61	37	98	87	42	129
Madras	14	2	16	19	2	21	79	32	111	112	36	148
Bombay	12	4	16	19	1	20	65	25	90	96	30	126
United Provinces	9	2	11	24	4	28	91	33	124	124	39	163
Punjab	18	0	18	14	1	15	52	22	74	84	23	107
Bihar and Orissa	9	1	10	13	1	14	52	19	71	74	21	95
Central Provinces	6	1	7	14	1	15	42	23	65	62	25	87
Assam	6	1	7	2	1	3	26	5	31	34	7	41
North-West Frontier	3	0	3	1	0	1	6	0	6	10	0	10
Burma	14	2	16	21	3	24	75	5	80	110	10	120
Totals	154	22	176	146	18	164	581	201	782	881	241	1122

NOTES:
1. The Executive Officers shown against the Government of India were nearly all employed in the Indian Political Department (which also employed officers from other Services).
2. Listed posts are omitted. There were 35 Judicial and 39 Executive in 1929; 1 Secretariat, 35 Judicial and 49 Executive in 1939.
3. I.C.S. Officers serving in Chief Commissioners' Provinces (Delhi, Ajmer-

	Secretariat			Judicial			Executive & Miscellaneous			Totals		
	European	Indian	Total	European	Indian	Total	European	Indian	Total	European	Indian	Total
Government of India	49	21	70	—	—	—	59	5	64	108	26	134
Bengal	18	2	20	21	13	34	63	74	137	102	89	191
Madras	13	6	19	12	11	23	51	58	109	76	76	152
Bombay	5	6	11	7	10	17	46	36	82	58	52	110
Sind	4	1	5	2	3	5	5	9	14	11	13	24
United Provinces	5	9	14	17	12	29	75	64	139	97	85	182
Punjab	13	2	15	11	18	29	51	39	90	75	59	134
Bihar	5	5	10	{12	7	19}	40	28	68	57	40	97
Orissa	4	2	6				6	7	13	10	9	19
Central Provinces	5	6	11	8	2	10	24	27	51	37	35	72
Assam	6	1	7	2	1	3	20	10	30	28	12	40
North-West Frontier	4	0	4	0	2	2	4	0	4	8	2	10
Burma	16	6	22	17	5	22	59	27	86	92	38	130
High Commission	0	4	4	—	—	—	—	—	—	0	4	4
Totals	147	71	218	109	85	194	503	384	887	759	540	1299

Merwara, Baluchistan, Coorg and the Andamans) are included in the figures of the provinces from which they were drawn.

4. During the 1939-45 War the number of I.C.S. officers employed under the Government of India rose to 240. This large expansion, combined with the cessation of recruitment to the I.C.S. after 1939, necessitated a considerable reduction in the number of I.C.S. officers serving in Executive posts in the provinces.

APPENDICES

Official lists give the number of entrants to the service in each year, together with

  (a) the Professions of their fathers,
  (b) the Universities (if any), and
  (c) the Schools (if any) at which they were educated.

Examination of a number of these lists suggests a few general conclusions.

1. Most members of the I.C.S. came from the professional (as opposed to the labouring, trading or leisured) classes. In the earlier years the sons of clergymen and army officers seemed to predominate; a fair number were the sons of merchants; but the I.C.S. itself never produced any large number of candidates. As time went on, the field of recruitment widened; but even in the early years there was striking variety. In four lists between 1859 and 1879 'Fathers' included an upholsterer, a miller, a butcher, a draper, a druggist, an undertaker, and several tailors, ironmongers and clerks.

2. In four consecutive years from 1855 there were 73 entrants. Of these 26 had been at Oxford, 17 at Cambridge, 8 at other English Universities, 5 at Scottish and 17 at Irish Universities. Over 50 years later, out of 44 successful candidates 18 came from Oxford, 15 from Cambridge, 1 from London, 5 from Scottish and 4 from Irish Universities, while one eschewed all Universities and apparently spent 3 years at a 'Crammer's'. There were always strong Scottish and Irish elements in the service, though of course many individuals from both these countries were educated in England.

3. The large number of schools represented was remarkable throughout. Indeed it was exceptional for any school to provide more than one or two successful candidates in any one year. In the earlier years the larger Public Schools produced a high proportion, but even in the 'seventies a fair number of the smaller Grammar Schools and High Schools were represented. In 1929, by which time competitive examinations were held both in London and India, supplemented by a limited number of nominations, the 52 successful candidates came from 48 different schools, including 16 in India and at least as many small Grammar Schools, High Schools or Secondary Schools in England, Scotland or Ireland.

[This Appendix is based on research carried out by Messrs. R. V. Vernède and Hugh Lane at the suggestion of Sir Richard Tottenham, who has combined the figures into tables and analysed the results.]

NOTES ON THE AUTHORITIES

This does not profess to be a work of research and for the student there are bibliographies in the *Cambridge History of India*, which will lead him on to others. The list that follows is meant only to indicate the books I have used most and to acknowledge the original manuscripts and notes lent to me:

PART I

Sir Bartle Frere, John Martineau: for Frere, see also *The Exploitation of East Africa* and *Isandhlwana*, both by R. Coupland: *The Memoirs of John Beames*, unpublished, lent me by C. H. Cooke: Bignold's poems are collected with the title *Leviora: Life of Lyall*, Mortimer Durand: *Twenty-one Days in India*, Aberigh-Mackay: Plato's *Republic* (in translation): *Competition for the Civil Service*, Sir Percy Waterfield, which appeared in *Oxford*: Mr. R. A. H. Way's letters to his mother were sent to me by himself and have not been published: The unpublished memoirs of A. R. Bulman: *A Civilian's Wife in India*, Mrs. Moss King: 'Binks of Hezabad' comes from *Departmental Ditties*: *India: Its Administration and Progress*, Sir John Strachey: for famine, see Sir Verney Lovett in the Cambridge History and Sir John Strachey's *India*, also Sir George Campbell's *Memoirs* and the reports of the 1880 and 1908 Commissions: for grain rotting at the stations in Madras in 1877, my authority is *Work and Sport in the Old I.C.S.*, W. O. Horne: the letters of Herman Kisch were kindly lent me by his daughter, Mrs. Waley-Cohen: *History of Upper Assam*, Shakespear: *Travels and Adventures in the Province of Assam*, Captain John Butler: *Forty Years in Burma*, Dr. Marks: *Scott of the Shan Hills*, Mitton: G. E. Harvey's chapters on Burma in the Cambridge History: Professor Hall's *Introduction to the History of Burma* and the *Dalhousie-Phayre Correspondence*, also G. E. Harvey's *History of Burma* and his short *British Rule in Burma*. *The Soul of a People* by H. Fielding is useful background on Buddhism and the Burmese but to be taken with handfuls of salt: Phayre's obituary by Yule in the Proceedings of the Royal Geographical Society: *Burma Past and Present*, Fytche: *Burmah*, F. Mason: *The North-West Frontier, 1890-1908*, Collin Davies: *Life of Sir R. Sandeman*, Thornton: *Eighteen Years in the Khyber*, Warburton: *The Forward Policy and its Results*, Bruce: *The Indian Borderland*, Holdich: *Allan Octavian Hume*, William Wedderburn: *William Wedderburn*, S. K. Ratcliffe: *Romesh Chandra Dutt*, S. N. Gupta: *A Nation in the Making*, Surendranath Banerjea: *New India*, Sir Henry Cotton: *Musulmans and Moneylenders in the Punjab*, Thorburn: *The Punjab Peasant in Prosperity and Debt*, Malcolm Darling: *The Land of the Five Rivers*, Trevaskis: and *Ancient Law*, Maine. Romesh Chandra Dutt's *Famines in India* is answered by Lord Curzon's Resolution of January 16th, 1902: *India Called Them*, Beveridge: Sir Auckland Colvin's correspondence with Hume, entitled *Audi Alteram Partem*: *Speeches on various Occasions*, Rash Behari Ghose. Annie Besant's *How India Wrought for Freedom* contains the resolutions of all the early Congress meetings; there is also a good deal about how the rosy fingers of the Dawn Maidens touched the Indian sky and the Sun of Freedom rose to irradiate the Motherland: *The Little World of an Indian District Officer*, R. Carstairs: *Life in the Indian Civil Service*, Sir Evan Maconachie: *Twelve Indian Statesmen*, George Smith: *Life of Lord Curzon*, Ronaldshay. The Census Reports of the Punjab, 1881, and of India, 1901; Ibbetson's Settlement Report of the Karnal District.

CHAP. IV. There is a detailed account in L. S. S. O'Malley's book *The Indian Civil Service* of the many changes in the age limits for the examination. Changes were made in 1855, 1860, 1865, 1866, 1879, 1892, 1906 and 1921. No two Royal Commissions held exactly similar views but I do not feel the detail is of much interest except to students of education and to other Royal Commissions. Roughly speaking, up to 1892, boys were taken at the school-leaving age and given two or three years in England on probation; after 1892 the examination was meant for university graduates who had a shorter period of probation. Educated Indians such as Surendranath Banerjea felt the earlier age a great handicap to Indian candidates and pressed strongly for the later age.

I have long thought that the artistry with which he presents his arguments conceals for many people the horror of Plato's conclusions. He is, I believe, the father of Hegel and Nietzsche and of the Prussian and the Fascist state and I do not see how he can be absolved of some responsibility for Marxism, and indeed for all theories of the state that equate us with ants and bees. I am grateful to Lord Samuel for lending me K. S. Popper: *The Open Society and its Enemies*, in which these views are worked out in detail.

CHAP. V. I have had full notes on canal colonies in the Punjab from Sir Geoffrey de Montmorency, who was Governor of the province from 1928 to 1933, and from Sir James Penny, Mr. C. V. Salusbury, and Mr. H. S. Williamson. I have, as so often, far more detailed information on this subject than I can use without upsetting the balance of the book and feel grateful to these officers for the trouble they have taken and apologetic that I have not been able to give it more space.

CHAP. VI. On Burma, I am indebted to writers so different as Maurice Collis, J. K. Stanford, and G. E. Harvey, all originally Indian Civilians, and to Professor D. G. E. Hall, not only for their various writings but for what they have told me in conversation.

Thompson and Garrett allege a competition in atrocities between English and Burmese in the war of 1824. I am assured by Mr. Harvey that there is no evidence for this and much to the contrary. The English could not afford men to watch prisoners; when their surgeons had patched a man up, they let him go, often with a rupee in his pocket. The Burmese general, Bandula, was so much impressed by this that he revolutionized Burmese military practice by orders as follows: 'should any of the foreigners fall into our hands, take care that they are not killed or maltreated in any way . . .' The truth is more creditable to humanity than Edward Thompson would have us believe.

CHAP. VII. The literature on the Frontier is immense; Mr. Davies prints a bibliography described as 'Select' which covers twelve pages. I am indebted to a note by Sir James Penny on Dera Ghazi Khan and to conversations with many Frontier officers, both civil and military, and particularly with Sir Francis Wylie, Sir Arthur Parsons, Sir George Cunningham and Charles Duke. Needless to say, they have not seen what I have written and would hardly agree with it.

CHAP. VIII. There is a full account of the Cowan episode in Sir Douglas Forsyth's *Autobiography and Reminiscences:* see also Khushwant Singh: *The Sikhs.*

CHAP. IX. On pigsticking I have used notes sent me by Sir Percy Marsh, General Wardrop and others, for which I am most grateful. I have referred to an unpublished book by E. H. H Edye and another by S. T. Hollins of the Indian Police, and used a good deal of personal hearsay. For Pennell, I have to thank Messrs. Ife and Reid for information.

CHAP. X. I am very grateful for Mrs. Macphersons' Journal of the Durbar, a simple and to me moving account of something that will not happen again, and also to R. A. H. Way for notes on Whish and other subjects and to Sir R. H. Macnair, Sir Benjamin Robertson and several others for notes on Tawney.

PART II

See the Cambridge History: *Indian Unrest*, Valentine Chirol: *My Experiments with Truth*, M. K. Gandhi: *Mahatma Gandhi*, Louis Fischer (but this is not reliable for facts): *Life of Minto*, Buchan: *Dyarchy*, Lionel Curtis: *An Indian Diary*, Montagu: *India as I knew it*, O'Dwyer: *The Lost Dominion*, Al Carthill: *A Nation in the Making*, Surendranath Banerjea: *India Insistent*, Harcourt Butler: *The Simon Report*: The Government of India Act, 1935: *Mission with Mountbatten*, Alan Campbell-Johnson: *The British Impact on India*, Griffiths: *Constitutional History of India*, Keith: *Kingdoms of Yesterday*, Sir Arthur Lothian: *The India We Served*, Sir Walter Lawrence: *Pomp of Yesterday*, Sir Kenneth Fitze (unpublished) and other memoirs by political officers: *Madras Occasional Verses: Autobiography of an Unknown Indian*, Nirad C. Chaudhuri.

CHAPS. I and II. Conversation with Lionel Curtis and Lord Hailey has been a great help and I have quoted from the report on the 1919 disturbances which Lord Hailey wrote for the Punjab Government. E. H. H. Edye's unpublished papers were lent me by Mrs. Edye; for the letters of Loftus Tottenham and a note on his life and character I am indebted to Sir Richard Tottenham, his distant cousin.

CHAP. III. The letter about Lucknow is my own, edited. I could find nothing else that illustrated my point so directly. I have quoted from *Enough of Action*, Edward Lydall, only part of which is about India, and from *The Role of the Administrator*, A. D. Gorwala (The Gokhale Institute of Politics and Economics). I have also used a note by Hugh Lane, *The Young Man in the last Ten Years* and notes by H. Macdonald-Tyler of Madras on the non-co-operation movement. Much of this chapter is based on personal experience and conversation. My debt to R. V. Vernède is acknowledged in the text and I have also used a note by D. S. Barron.

CHAP. IV. I have used some privately printed poems of J. A. Thorne; a note on Soil Erosion in the Punjab by Sir James Penny; Sir Harcourt Butler's speech was lent me by J. K. Stanford; other speeches of his were lent me by L. M. Jopling.

CHAP. V. For the Frontier, see *Mizh, A Monograph on the Mahsuds* by Evelyn Howell. Everything else about the Frontier comes from conversation. As before, I owe much to Sir Francis Wylie, Sir George Cunningham, Sir Arthur Parsons and others.

CHAP. VI. I am very grateful for material received from R. N. Lines, Hugh Lane, Sir Robin Hutchings, Messrs. Wallace, Gledhill, Gimson, Bowman, McCall, Lambrick, Bell and Sir Henry Knight.

CHAP. VII. Most of the information contained in the last chapter comes from conversation. It has been one of my difficulties that many of those most intimately concerned in the last days do not wish to be quoted or do not feel themselves at liberty to allow their papers to be made use of. I am very grateful for permission to quote part of Lord Dunsany's poem and for the loan by the Somerset Light Infantry of a copy of their Regimental Journal. I am grateful to Brigadier Humphrey Bullock for information as to the number of British graves in India and to Lt.-Gen. Peter Rees for the history of 4 Indian Division, which is admirable on the last days. I have also used a note by Philip Nash.

EPILOGUE. *Briton, Boer, and Bantu*, Macmillan: *The Cape Coloured People*, J. S. Marais: *The Spanish Empire in America*, C. H. Haring: *The Rise of the Spanish Empire in America, The Fall of the Spanish Empire in America*, Madariaga: *The Cambridge Ancient History*, vols. x, xi, xii: *Roman Colonial Administration*, Stevenson: *A History of the Later Roman Empire*,

NOTES ON THE AUTHORITIES

Bury: *China, a short cultural history*, C. P. Fitzgerald: *Society in China*, R. K. Douglas: *The Ottoman Empire under Suleiman the Magnificent*, Libyer.

I thank F. N. Crofts for preparing the index and Sir Richard Tottenham, R. V. Vernède and Hugh Lane for Appendix B.

I must also express my thanks to Mr. H. L. Greenaway of the old India Office Library for his unfailing helpfulness.

INDEX

INDEX

de Montmorency, Sir Geoffrey, 112
Depressed classes, 340-1
Deputy Collectors, 108, 148, 173
Deputy Commissioner, 240; in non-regulation provinces, 88; on the Frontier, 141, 153; in Andamans, 321; in Naga Hills, 325 (*see* District Officer)
Dera Ghazi Khan, 142-4, 148
Dera Ismail Khan, 148
de Tocqueville (quoted), 66
Dharam Vir (quoted), 257
Dinapore, 200
Dinkar Rao, Raja, 66
Disraeli, Benjamin (Lord Beaconsfield), 13
District, life in, 15, 70 (*see* Touring); Reforms and, 254, 303, 308
District Boards, 20, 61, 70-2, 218, 246, 252-3, 276-9, 302, 303, 359
District Judges, 88-90, 251, 309
District Officer (Magistrate), independence, 15, 56-7, 70, 216, 297; work, 19, 20, 44, 48, 91-3, 194, 291, 303, 321, 331; Reforms and, 19, 20, 212, 218-21, 246-7, 274, 302, 328, 334; and Joint Magistrate, 47, 214, 256, 278; visitors, 48, 93, 172, 222, 321; and Police, 53; type of, 56; District Boards and, 70-2, 218, 252, 277-9; Judges and, 89, 251; houses, 93; famine and, 104, 109, 336; powers, 168, 184, 338, 358; qualities, 180, 214-17; ideals, 182, 189, 360; use of force, 244-6; non-cooperation and, 248-51; loss of influence, 249; riots and, 257-66, 339, 343; and Political Officers, 270; responsibility, 274; life of, 281; and forests, 287; Indians as, 301, 360; in World War II, 314-16, 335; trust in, 355
D'Oyly, Mr., 128
Duke, Charles Beresford, 294
Dufferin, Lord, Viceroy, 165, 166, 208
Dunsany, Lord (quoted), 345, 361
Durand, Sir Henry, 128
Durand, Sir Mortimer, 74, 150; Durand Line, 150-1
Durga Singh, 32-3
Dutch, 225, 352, 353
Dutt, Romesh Chandar, 156-9, 169, 175, 176
Dyarchy, 211, 218, 233-5, 238, 246, 268
Dyer, Brig.-Gen., 240-2
Dysentery, 119, 298, 326, 333

EAST INDIA COMPANY, 78, 196, 352, 360, 363; supersession, 27-8
Eden, Sir Ashley, 61, 175

Education, 16, 66, 330, 352; effect of, 16-17, 95, 155-6, 169, 173, 198; unrealistic, 20; Muslims and, 19, 209
Edwardes, Sir Herbert, 28, 36, 88, 139, 215, 311
Edye, E. H. H., 21, 179, 212-14, 215-19, 220, 225, 249, 253, 352
Egypt, 187-8, 359
Elections, 19, 71, 198, 342; separate electorates, 209, 234, 267
Elgin, Lord, Gov.-Gen., 39
Elizabeth I, Queen, 202
Elliott, Sir Charles Alfred, 62, 176
Elphinstone, Mountstuart, 16, 28, 29, 37, 39, 162, 346, 348, 353, 356
English in I.C.S., 193 (*see* British)
Etawah, 163
Europeans, jurisdiction over, 72-3, 174
Executive branch, and judiciary, 38; separated from judicial, 89, 167-8, 178
Executive Council, Viceroy's, 210; Provincial, 210
Exeter Hall, 353
Ezechiel, David, 185

FALKLAND, LORD, 32
Famine, 60, 68, 86, 88, 98-114, 157, 158, 236, 304, 333-7; causes, 98-100; remedies, 101-8, 336; relief works, 102, 103; circle officers and, 104-5; Famine Commissions, 102, 103, 109, 333; Code, 103
Faqir of Ipi, 293
Federal Assembly, 268
Federation, 268-9, 272
Ferozepur, 307
Finance Member, 62, 70, 77, 188
Finlay, William Waters, 310, 311
Fire Services, 259, 262, 319, 320
Fitzgerald, C. P. (quoted), 357
Foreign Secretary, 62, 68, 77, 187
Forest Department (Service), 286-7, 300; Inspector-General, 91, 286; officers, 287
Forests, 286-7; development of, 128, 286-7, 318; *panchayats* for, 287
Forsyth, Douglas, 172
Fort William, College of, 45, 46, 80
Francis, Sir Philip, 196
French, 123, 133, 135, 168, 214, 225, 244
Frere, Sir Bartle, on Elphinstone, 28; and Indians, 28, 173; in Satara, 29; in Sind, 29-35, 140, 143; in Mutiny, 35-6, 37; on religion, 36-7; and British rule, 37, 208, 216, 287; and Council of India, 38, 210; character, 39, 42-3, 151, 291; Gov. of Bombay, 39; reforms, 39, 41; and Lord Lawrence, 40-1; later career, 41-2

376

INDEX

378

INDEX

INDEX

Punjab (*cont.*)
Census Report, 189; Land Alienation Act, 237; outbreaks in, 238-43, 343-5; Ministry, 247, 302, 305, 342; Governors, 290, 342; East Punjab, Governor, 301; partition of, 342-4
Punjabis, 25; language, 48
Purdah, 117, 173, 198
Pushtu, 152

Qanungo, 108

RACIAL INTOLERANCE, 173-5, 241
Radcliffe, Lord (quoted), 351
Radice, Peter Wolf, 321
Railways, 30, 112; in famine, 101, 104, 107, 109, 110; British capital for, 110; India and China compared, 110-11
Rainfall and famine, 98, 158
Rajputana, 68, 98, 100
Rajputs, 223
Ram Mohun Roy (quoted), 176, 349
Rangoon, 119, 120, 126, 130, 131, 315, 316, 321
Ranjit Singh, 48
Rasra, 312
Rationing, 331, 334
Rebellion in 1942..., 307-13, 331
'Red Tape', 14-15, 40, 59-60, 195, 216-17
Reforms—Lord Curzon's, 193, 194, 197-8; Morley-Minto, 207-10; Montagu-Chelmsford, 210-11, 242, 267-8; of 1935..., 211-12, 267; of 1947... 212; Edye on, 217-18; and district officers, 218; pace of, 18, 19, 75, 220, 228, 270, 272; and I.C.S., 220-1, 224-5; and World War II, 300
Regulation III of 1918..., 167
Reily, Mr., 185-6
Religion, 16, 18, 339; religious disputes, 244-5 (*see* Communal troubles)
Rent, record of, 81; remission of, 103; Rent Acts, 72
Reserved departments, 20, 211
Residents, 41, 62, 120, 122, 270
Revenue, remission of, 103; records, 81-3, 86-7, 116, 282; Commission, 29; system in Burma, 125
Riots, 243, 244-5, 258-66, 271, 274, 284, 290, 343-5
Ripon, Lord, Viceroy, 70-3, 75, 172, 187, 234
Risley, H. H., 189
Rivett-Carnac, Miss, 61
Rivett-Carnac, Sir James, 61; family of, 61
Roads, building of, 30, 70-1, 109, 126, 191, 325, 361; state of, 46; in famines, 101, 104, 107, 109, 110; in Garhwal, 275-9

Roberdeau, Henry, 21
Roberts, Lord, 25, 60, 64
Romans, 225, 273, 348, 355, 358, 359
Roorkee, 85
Roos-Keppel, Sir George, 294-5, 296
Rowlett Acts, 227-8, 238-9
Roy, Ram Mohun (quoted), 176, 349
Rudd, Mr., 55
Rural Development Department, 261, 303-4
Russia, 69, 73, 149, 152, 198, 244

SADI (quoted), 238, 239
Sadiya, 132
Saharanpur, 282
Salisbury, A. J., 309
Salt, 303, 315, 356; taxed, 56; Department, 91; agitation over, 248
Salween, River, 133
Samastipur, 309
Samil (tribal division), 153
Sandeman, Sir Robert, 142-7, 150, 151, 291, 294
Sanskrit, 78, 157
Satara, 29; Raja of, 29
Sawbwa, 133-5
Sayyad Ahmad, Sir, 177
Scots, 164, 193, 202
Scott, Sir George, 131-6
Scouts, the, 294-5
Scurvy, 119
Secretariat, 15, 90-1, 116, 130, 165, 195-7, 216-18, 221-2, 300, 303, 310, 335
Secretary of State, 91, 148, 162, 164, 170, 171, 186, 196, 246, 254
Secretary to Government, 164, 165, 193, 197, 212, 216, 217, 332
Selim the Sot, 359
Separate electorates, 209, 234, 267
Servants, 17, 94, 293, 336, 346, 351
Settlement, Permanent, *q.v.*; officers, 28-9, 61, 183, 189, 236, 289
Shah Alam, Emperor, 200
Shah Jehan, Emperor, 200
Shahpur, 289
Shakespear, John, 322
Shan peoples, 117, 119, 132, 135; States, 132-6, 202
Sharpe, T. A., 325, 327
Sherani tribes, 142, 147, 148
Shias, 146, 244
Shore, Sir John (Lord Teignmouth), 99, 334
Shooting, 59, 87, 153, 154, 181, 183, 213, 281, 285, 300
Siam, 123, 128, 133, 314-15
Sikandar Mirza (Major-Gen. Iskandar Mirza), 295
Sikhs, 113, 133, 139, 140, 159, 171, 236, 238, 262-3, 268, 302, 342, 343, 345, 351; wars with, 115, 126, 307

383

INDEX

INDEX

JONATHAN CAPE PAPERBACKS